# Chinua Achebe
## *Tributes and Reflections*



Edited by
Nana Ayebia Clarke
and James Currey

ayebia

An Adinkra symbol meaning
Ntesie matemasie
A symbol of knowledge and wisdom

First published in 2014 by the Ayebia Clarke Publishing Limited
7 Syringa Walk
Banbury OX16 1FR
Oxfordshire
UK
www.ayebia.co.uk
**ISBN 978-0-9569307-6-7**
Distributed outside Africa, Europe and the United Kingdom
and exclusively in the USA by
Lynne Rienner Publishers Inc
1800 30th Street, Suite 314
Boulder, CO 80301
USA
www.rienner.com

Distributed in the UK and Europe by TURNAROUND Publisher Services
at www.turnaround-uk.com



British Library Cataloguing-in-Publication Data

Chinua Achebe photo, front cover image © Lotte Weitner-Graf, London (1967)
Cover Design by Steve Fleming at Workhaus

Typeset by FiSH Books, Enfield, Middlesex, UK.
Printed and bound by CPI Group (UK) Ltd, Croydon, CR0 4YY

Available from www.ayebia.co.uk or email info@ayebia.co.uk
Distributed in Africa, Europe, UK by TURNAROUND at www.turnaround-uk.com
Distributed in Southern Africa by Book Promotions a subsidiary of Jonathan Ball Publishers in South Africa. For orders contact: orders@bookpro.co.za

# About the Editors

**Nana Ayebia Clarke MBE** – founder of Ayebia Clarke Publishing Limited is a Ghanaian-born publisher. She was Submissions Editor of the Heinemann African Writers Series (AWS) for 12 years until 2002 when Heinemann discontinued publishing new titles in the Series. She started her own publishing imprint Ayebia with her husband David in 2003 as a way of looking to new directions. She was awarded an Honorary MBE by Her Majesty Queen Elizabeth II for services to the British publishing industry in 2011.

**James Currey** worked from 1967 with Chinua Achebe on the first 100 titles in the Heinemann African Writers Series (AWS). The last title he added to the Series was No 270 *African Short Stories* edited by Chinua Achebe and Lyn Innes in 1985, the year in which he and Clare Currey founded James Currey Publishers.

Between them they worked on the Heinemann African Writers Series for a total of 30 years.

# Contents

# Acknowledgements

The editors are thankful to all the contributors for giving generously of their time in responding to our call for contributions in honour of Chinua Achebe.

I would also like to acknowledge those who were instrumental in championing my career and development at Heinemann; these include the late John Watson, Vicky Unwin and Robert Sulley, and Paul Richardson for his support of Ayebia. During my time editorial advice was given in particular by F. Abiola Irele, Adewale Maja-Pearce, Abdulrazak Gurnah and Irene Staunton.

The following essays and images are reproduced with kind permission from:

Wole Soyinka – 'An Elegy for a Nation (For Chinua Achebe, at Seventy)' Reprinted from *Samarkand and Other Markets I Have Known*: Methuen, UK: (2002), with permission from the author.

Lyn Innes – *Chinua Achebe (1930-2013): Obituary, Founding Father of African fiction whose novels chronicled Nigeria's Troubled History.* (First published 22.3.2013 in *The Guardian*, UK).

Maya Jaggi – Profile: *Chinua Achebe – Storyteller of the Savannah* (First published 18.11.2000 in *The Guardian*, UK).

Ngũgĩ wa Thiong'o's – *Chinua Achebe: The Spirit Lives* (first published in the University of Leeds African Studies Bulletin No. 75: October, 2013).

*Biodun Jeyifo – Chinua Achebe: His Wondrous Passages: (A revised version of a tribute published in Transition Magazine, US, 2013).*

Binyavanga Wainaina – *How To Write About Africa*, (originally published in *Granta* 92: 2005) and reprinted with permission from The Wylie Agency, UK.

Helon Habila – *An Interview with Chinua Achebe* (first published in *Sable* and in the print edition of *The Africa Report in 2007).*

Ali A. Mazrui – *Things Fall Apart Revisited: The Prose and the Poetry*; (Originally presented at the 50th Anniversary of Chinua Achebe's *Things Fall Apart* (1958) at the Library Congress, Washington, DC, US, 2008).

Véronique Tadjo: 'Chinua Achebe's Legacy', first delivered at the "Fall for the Book," George Mason University, Fairfax (US), 21 September 2008 and published in Recherche Littéraire/Literary Research, Vol. 25 – Summer 2009.

Chimamanda Ngozi Adichie: *Chinua Achebe at 82: We Remember Differently.* (Originally first published in the *Premium Times, Nigeria*: 23 November 2012 with the author's permission.)

Anne V. Adams: *I Haven't Seen You In 400 Years!*: Chinua Achebe and African American Writing; Given as keynote address at the Festival of African & African-Diasporic Literatures, Bayreuth University, June 20, 2013.

Chinua Achebe photo, front cover image © Lotte Weitner-Graf, London (1967); courtesy of James Currey.

Chapter One

# A Tribute

## Once More for Chinua Achebe!

*Nana Ayebia Clarke*

The news of Chinua Achebe's death in the US on the morning of 22nd March 2013, in the middle of the 39th Annual African Literature Association (ALA) Conference in Charleston, South Carolina sent shock waves not only through the African literary community that was present at the conference but also through the global literary world. The Convener of the Conference, Simon Lewis arranged 'A Tribute to Chinua Achebe' at 7pm that evening. By 6.30pm, the ballroom was filled to capacity with standing room only. Contributors to this event included; Ernest Emenyonu from the University of Michigan-Flint, Anthonia Kalu from The Ohio State University (the then ALA President), Eustace Palmer from Georgia College and State University, Bernth Lindfors from University of Texas, Austin, Maureen Ngozi Eke from Central Michigan University, Helen Chukwuma from Jackson State University and Abena Busia from Rutgers University. Some of the contributors to the Achebe Tribute at Charleston have also contributed to this volume.

I had the privilege and sadness of contributing to the African Literature Association tribute on behalf of my colleagues at the Heinemann African Writers Series. It was suggested afterwards that Ayebia Clarke Publishing follow up with a book of tributes on the achievements of Chinua Achebe in the establishment of African literature over the last fifty years both by his own writing and by his work as Founding Editor of the African Writers Series.

James Currey and I worked on the Series for a total of thirty years between us and I asked him to join me.

The publication of this book is my own tribute to Chinua Achebe. As a woman, an African and as a publisher and champion of African writing, I am extremely proud and grateful for his enduring contributions to raising the profile of African writing and publishing on the international stage.

Chapter Two

# Preface

*Nana Ayebia Clarke and James Currey*

Much of the work has been especially written for this volume. But the book also serves a purpose as a record of some of the pieces which were written for journals and newspapers all over the world soon after Chinua Achebe's death. It was Nadine Gordimer who expressed so well her pleasure that her obituary, published in Johannesburg and London, would appear 'in the more permanent form of a book along with the contribution of my comrade writers in the world.'

The book starts with the authoritative obituary by Lyn Innes from *The Guardian* London. It is followed from the same newspaper by the influential interview made by Maya Jaggi at the Bard College celebration at the time of Chinua Achebe's seventieth birthday in 2000 when his importance as a key writer in world literature of the twentieth century was becoming recognised beyond Africa.

Nobel Laureates Wole Soyinka, Toni Morrison and Nadine Gordimer lead the international chorus of tributes to Chinua Achebe's writing and legacy. The volume features 49 contributors and includes a host of other distinguished writers, critics, scholars and publishers who in paying tribute to his literary life, also anchor it within his activism and mediatory role as a great spokesman and defender of Africa.

It is not often remembered how much of a publisher Chinua Achebe was himself. The editors have therefore clustered together the articles by contributors who have with him made it possible for writers from Africa to assume that it is possible for them to get published.

And to the great Igbo poet there are tributes in verse in African languages.

Chapter Three

# Chinua Achebe (1930–2013) Obituary

## Founding father of African fiction whose novels chronicled Nigeria's troubled history

*Lyn Innes*

(First published in *The Guardian*, 22.03.2013)

Chinua Achebe, who has died aged 82, was Africa's best-known novelist and the founding father of African fiction. The publication of his first novel, *Things Fall Apart*, in 1958 not only contested European narratives about Africans but also challenged traditional assumptions about the form and function of the novel. His creation of a hybrid that combined oral and literary modes and his refashioning of the English language to convey Igbo voices and concepts, established a model and an inspiration for other novelists throughout the African continent.

The five novels and the short stories he published between 1958 and 1987 provide a chronicle of Nigeria's troubled history since the beginning of British colonial rule. They also create a host of vivid characters who seek in varying ways to take control of their history. As founding editor of the influential Heinemann African Writers Series, he oversaw the publication of more than 100 texts that made good writing by Africans available worldwide in affordable editions.

Born in the traditional Igbo village of Ogidi, eastern Nigeria, some 40 years after missionaries first arrived in the region, Achebe was christened Albert Chinualumogu by his Christian convert parents. Later, in an autobiographical essay entitled Named for Victoria, Queen of England, he told how, like Queen Victoria, he "lost his Albert."

Growing up as a Christian allowed him to observe his world more clearly, he wrote. The slight distance from each culture became "not a separation but a bringing together like the necessary backward step which a judicious viewer might take in order to see a canvas steadily and fully."

At the local missionary school, however, the children were forbidden to speak Igbo and were encouraged to disown all traditions that might be associated with a "pagan" way of life. Nevertheless, Achebe absorbed the folk tales told to him by his mother and older sister, stories he described as having "the immemorial quality of the sky, and the forests and the rivers."

When he was 14, Achebe was sent to the prestigious colonial Government College at Umuahia, where his schoolmates included the poet Christopher Okigbo, his close friend. In 1948, he won a scholarship to study medicine at what became the University of Ibadan. After his first year, however, he realised it was writing that most appealed to him and he switched to a degree in English Literature, Religious Studies and History.

Although the English curriculum closely followed Britain's, teachers also introduced works they considered relevant to their Nigerian students, such as Joyce Cary's African novels and Joseph Conrad's *Heart of Darkness.* But such works were at odds with the changing mentality brought about by the anti-colonial movements in West Africa following the Second World War.

Achebe was among several future literary stars, including Wole Soyinka, who, between 1948 and 1952, contributed stories and essays to student magazines with a nationalist orientation. Even in these early pieces, one can discern Achebe's characteristic qualities: a coolly amused view of the educated elite, a carefully balanced structure of contrasts, a pleasure in mimicking or parodying various modes of discourse, an interest in rural Nigeria and the uneasy interaction between western and Igbo cultures, and an insistence on what he saw as the crucial Igbo value of tolerance. It is in one of these stories that a favourite proverb of his makes its first appearance: "Let the hawk perch and let the eagle perch."

By the time he graduated in 1952, Achebe had decided to be a writer telling the story of Africans and the colonial encounter from an African point of view. One of his motivations was Cary's Nigeria-set novel *Mister Johnson,* which, though much praised by English critics, seemed to him "a most superficial picture of Nigeria and the Nigerian character". He thought: "If this was famous, then someone ought to try and look at this from the inside."

What had originally been planned as one long novel, beginning with the colonisation of eastern Nigeria and ending just before independence, turned into two shorter novels, *Things Fall Apart* (set in the late 19th century) and *No Longer at Ease* (set in the decade before Nigeria gained its independence). While the second novel takes up and retells the plot of *Mister Johnson* – the story of a young Nigerian clerk who takes a bribe and is tried and sentenced by the colonial administration – the first seeks, with consummate success, to evoke the culture and society *Mister Johnson* and his ancestors might have come from.

*Things Fall Apart* recreates an oral culture and a consciousness imbued with an agrarian way of life and demonstrates, as Achebe put it, "that African peoples did not hear of civilisation for the first time from Europeans." At the same time, he sought to avoid depicting precolonial Africa as a pastoral idyll, rejecting the nostalgic evocations of Léopold Senghor and the francophone Négritude School of writing.

The protagonist, Okonkwo, emerges as a heroic but rigid character, whose fear of appearing weak leads him to act harshly towards his wives and children and to participate in the sacrifice of a young hostage from another village. Its characterisation and enclosed rural world have been compared to *The Mayor of Casterbridge* by Thomas Hardy, a novelist Achebe admired. *Things Fall Apart* has sold millions of copies and has been translated into more than 50 languages.

*No Longer at Ease*, set in 1950s Nigeria and published in 1960, takes up the story of Okonkwo's grandson, an idealistic young Nigerian civil servant who returns home after studying in England, finds his salary inadequate for his expected lifestyle, and takes a bribe.

By this time, Achebe himself had been on the first of many trips abroad. As Head of the Talks Department at the Nigerian Broadcasting Service (NBS), he was sent in 1956 on a short training course with the BBC in London. Back in Nigeria, he edited and produced discussion programmes and short stories for the NBS in Enugu, eastern Nigeria and learned much about how good dialogue works. There, he met Christie Chinwe Okoli, a beautiful and brilliant student from Ibadan University. They married in 1961 and had four children.

While preparing a feature on the response of Nigerians to early colonial rule, Achebe investigated the story of an Igbo priest imprisoned for refusing to collaborate with the British. Fascinated by the tale and the priest's proud character, he made it the focus of his third novel, *Arrow of God* (1964). Some critics regard this as Achebe's greatest achievement, with its complex structure and characterisation, and its interrogation of the interstices between subjective desire and external forces in the making of history.

The concerns with responsible leadership that inform *Arrow of God* are taken up more explicitly in his satirical fourth novel, *A Man of the People* (1966). It exposes the corruption and irresponsibility of politicians and their constituents, ending with a military coup – as indeed happened in post-independence Nigeria in 1966, a coup that led to the attempted secession of Biafra and a civil war in which more than a million people died.

When the massacre of Igbos began in the north following the coup, Achebe was working for the Nigerian Broadcasting Commission in Lagos. Warned that he might be in danger (a cousin was one of the military leaders assassinated), Achebe took his family to eastern Nigeria. He became a strong advocate of Biafra's independence, travelling the world to seek support. In his view, Biafra was not only a territory that could ensure the survival of Igbo peoples, but also an ideal. Speaking in 1968, he declared: "Biafra stands for true independence in Africa, for an end to the 400 years of shame and humiliation which we have suffered in our association with Europe … I believe our cause is right and just. And this is what literature should be about today – right and just causes."

Although the war ended in defeat for the Biafran cause, Achebe was determined the Igbo presence and perspectives should continue within the Nigerian nation. His collection of poems *Beware Soul Brother* (1971) and the volume of short stories *Girls at War and Other Stories* (1972) drew on the experiences of the war. He became a Senior Research Fellow at the University of Nigeria, Nsukka, and in 1971 he and a group of Nigerian academics founded *Okike*, an important journal for African creative writing and critical debate. He also wrote several books for children.

In 1972, Achebe accepted a Visiting Professorship at the University of Massachusetts Amherst, where he taught African literature and continued to edit *Okike*. It was there that I first met him and worked as an assistant editor for *Okike*. I also attended and occasionally co-taught his course on African writing, and admired his patience with students who sometimes made all too evident their ignorance and prejudice with regard to African culture.

That tolerance, and indeed friendship, extended to colleagues such as a professor who jokingly promised to provide native girls for all the members of his department when he became head. I looked across at Achebe and saw him raise an eyebrow. Despite his passionate condemnation of racism and imperial arrogance, it is Achebe's gentle irony, ready laughter and his delight in anecdotes about our children's antics that I most vividly remember.

He did not retreat from controversy. In essays, lectures and interviews, he declared the need for committed writing in the African context and derided writers and critics whose attitudes to Africans he found condescending or racist. At the University of Massachusetts, he denounced *Heart of Darkness* in a lecture that caused many in the audience to walk out in protest and still arouses debate.

Achebe returned to Nigeria in 1976 to be Professor of Literature at the University of Nigeria, where he continued to teach, became Chairman of the Association of Nigerian Writers and edited *Uwa ndi Igbo: the Journal of Igbo Life and Culture*. He was also elected Deputy National President of the People's Redemption Party and published a political pamphlet, *The Trouble With Nigeria*, in 1983.

Achebe not only created a new kind of novel, but was also unwilling to repeat the same formula. Each novel set up a dialogue with its predecessor, technically and formally as well as with regard to character and social milieu. This process culminated in his fifth novel, *Anthills of the Savannah* (1987), which commented on the forms and themes of his own works and those of other African writers. The novel insists there is no one story of the nation, but a multiplicity of narratives, weaving continuities between past and present, Igbo and English cultural forms and traditions. The philosophy, structure and aesthetic of *Anthills of the Savannah* and indeed of all of Achebe's fiction, is summarised in the final sentences of his essay "The Truth of Fiction": "Imaginative literature … does not enslave; it liberates the mind of man. Its truth is not like the canons of orthodoxy or the irrationality of prejudice and superstition. It begins as an adventure in self-discovery and ends in wisdom and humane conscience."

In 1990, a car accident left Achebe paralysed. Bard College, New York, offered him and Christie the possibility of teaching there and provided the facilities he needed. Now using a wheelchair, he continued to travel and lecture in the US and occasionally abroad. His talks at Harvard in 1998 were published under the title *Home and Exile.*

His more recent lectures and autobiographical essays were published in *The Education of a British-Protected Child* (2009). He moved to Providence, Rhode Island, in 2009 after being appointed Professor of Africana Studies at Brown University. In 2012 he published *There Was a Country: A Personal History of Biafra*, which reiterated his belief in the ideals that had inspired the nationalism of his younger days. His account of the events that led to the civil war, its conduct and aftermath have stirred strong reactions from supporters as well as opponents of the Biafran cause.

Achebe received numerous awards and more than 30 honorary doctorates, but among the tributes he may have valued most was Nelson Mandela's. "There was a writer named Chinua Achebe," Mandela wrote, "in whose company the prison walls fell down."

He is survived by Christie, their daughters, Chinelo and Nwando and their sons, Ikechukwu and Chidi.

Chinua Achebe, writer, born 16 November 1930; died 21 March 2013.

Chapter Four

# Profile: Chinua Achebe

## Storyteller of the Savannah

*Maya Jaggi*

(First published in *The Guardian*, 18.11.2000)

The founding father of African writing in English, he challenged the perspective of colonialist white writers and fell foul of successive regimes in Nigeria. Just turned 70 and living in the US, his latest novel is a return to his troubled homeland.

While Nelson Mandela was serving 27 years in jail, he drew consolation and strength, he says, from a writer "in whose company the prison walls fell down." For Mandela, the greatness of Chinua Achebe, founding father of the modern African novel in English, lies in his having "brought Africa to the world" while remaining rooted as an African. As the Nigerian Achebe used his pen to free the continent from its past, said the former South African president, "both of us, in our differing circumstances within the context of white domination of our continent, became freedom fighters."

Mandela's tribute was videoed in honour of Achebe's 70th birthday on Thursday, and sent to leafy Bard College in upstate New York, where Achebe is Professor of Languages and Literature. The Professor, born into the Igbo nation of eastern Nigeria, sat through a two-day celebration in the red fez-like hat of the Igbo elder. He was sent greetings from the UN secretary-general, Kofi Annan, and Nigeria's first civilian leader in 16 years, President Olusegun Obasanjo, and homage was paid by fellow writers, including three Nobel laureates: Toni Morrison, Wole Soyinka and, in absentia, Nadine Gordimer. It is rare, Achebe remarked later with gentle irony, to hear such concerted singing of your praises "unless you're a Third World dictator."

Achebe has suffered for challenging just such strongmen in Nigeria. But his present exile has a different cause. In March 1990, only weeks after attending a gathering that anticipated his 60th birthday in the eastern Nigerian town of Nsukka, a car crash on the country's lethal roads left him paralyzed from the waist down, and in a wheelchair. He was airlifted to Britain for surgery ("the damage was so severe they didn't think I'd survive"), told he would never walk again and advised to move for therapy to the US, where he took up a Professorship at Bard, in Annandale-on-Hudson.

"I thought I'd go home after a year," he recalls in his clapboard bungalow on campus. "But home has simply got from bad to worse in terms of hospital facilities. I've had severe infections and you need proper antibiotics, not fakes. When you say a country has broken down, that's what it means." The annulment of Nigeria's elections in 1993 by President Ibrahim Babangida militated against his return. A subsequent coup by General Sani Abacha brought even harsher dictatorship – marked by the hanging of the writer Ken Saro-Wiwa in 1995. Last year's return to democracy has scarcely begun to reverse the country's decline.

This summer in the US, Achebe brought out a volume of essays, *Home and Exile*, to be published in Britain in January. In it, he hankers for the homeland where his fiction is rooted – "where I could see my work cut out for me." He places his oeuvre within Salman Rushdie's notion of "the empire writes back": postcolonial writers countering Europe's fictions by seizing the right to tell their own story.

Achebe is known across continents for his landmark first novel, *Things Fall Apart* (1958), a tale told "from the inside" about the destructive impact of European Christianity on precolonial Igbo culture amid the scramble for Africa in the 1890s. Published on the eve of Nigerian independence in 1960 when its author was 28, it helped reshape literature in the English-speaking world, but it was not the first novel by an African: precursors included fellow Nigerians Amos Tutuola and Cyprian Ekwensi, South Africa's Peter Abrahams and, in French, Senegal's Ousmane Sembène and Camara Laye from Guinea. It has sold more than 10m copies internationally and been translated into 45 languages, making it one of the most widely read novels of the 20th century. A biography by Ezenwa-Ohaeto was published in 1997 (published by James Currey).

For Soyinka, *Things Fall Apart* was "the first novel in English which spoke from the interior of an African character, rather than portraying the African as exotic, as the white man would see him." Nigeria's two literary giants are friends, though rivalry is often assumed: the critic Chinweizu deems Achebe superior in "decolonizing the mind," while others judge Soyinka's politics more "radical." When Soyinka won Africa's first Nobel for literature in 1986, Achebe warmly congratulated him, but put the Swedish accolade in perspective as a "European prize." Last year they were billed with Derek Walcott at the Word festival in London's Hackney Empire as "two Nobel laureates and a legend."

Another Nobel laureate, Toni Morrison, says Achebe sparked her "love affair with African literature" and was a major influence on her beginnings as a writer. "He inhabited his world in a way that I didn't inhabit mine – the things he could take for granted – insisting on writing outside the white gaze, not against it," she says. "His courage and generosity were made manifest in the work; and that's difficult to do: to talk about devastation and evil in such a way that the text itself isn't evil or devastating."

Achebe's arguments are delivered with force but in a deceptively soft voice. Though he can seem melancholic, his talk is punctuated by laughter and shafts of dry humour. As his birthday showed, he can bring together people who agree on nothing but their affection for him. Chinweizu, of a Nigerian school of critics known as the Bolekaja Boys (street slang for "jump up and fight"), sat in the same hall as Soyinka, whom they once pilloried as a "Euro-assimilationist." They were in turn put down as "neo-tarzanist primitivists." Soyinka shared a platform with his intellectual sparring partner, the historian Ali Mazrui, as they declared themselves on their "best behaviour."

In *Home and Exile*, Achebe has stepped further into autobiography. "Maybe that's what turning 70 does, though I don't feel any different; you tend to move in the direction of memoir. The ideas I wanted to pursue took an autobiographical turn because the final authority I could bring was that of my own experience."

He was born in 1930 in Ogidi, an Igbo village near the Niger, 400 miles east of Lagos. The fifth of six children, he was baptized Albert Chinualumogu, but "dropped the tribute to Victorian England." His father, Isaiah, was a Christian convert and evangelist, with "gallows humour." He and Achebe's mother, Janet, were "ardent followers, but not fanatical"; while the family sang hymns, Isaiah's relatives offered food to what he considered idols." An accommodation with the church developed after initial struggle," says Achebe. "Common sense and the strength of Igbo culture slowly reasserted themselves."

His parents were "extremely profound people, of few words but strong convictions; great believers in education;" with few resources, they sent their children to school. Chike Momah, a classmate, recalls Albert Achebe as a brilliant conversationalist – a trait shared with his father – and says his headmaster predicted, "he would make the rain that would drench us all."

"We lived at the crossroads of cultures," wrote Achebe, who learned English at eight and whose passport declared him a British Protected Person ("an arrogant lie because I never did ask anyone to protect me"). He contrasts the slow, quiet education of his home village with the louder, formal education of mission school. "I knew I wanted to understand the life of the society, the stories and masquerades," he says. "It's curious how brainwashed we were; quite a bit of my growing up was discovering that fact."

In a 1973 essay, "Named For Victoria, Queen Of England," he describes *Things Fall Apart* as "an act of atonement with my past, the ritual return and homage of a prodigal son." He says: "It's that fascination with the scraps and pieces of information I could gather about my ancestors that developed into a desire to write my story. Colonial education was saying there was nothing worth much in my society and I was beginning to question that, to see there were things that were beautiful even in the 'heathen'."

Enrolled at Ibadan University to study medicine ("a false step"), Achebe switched to the arts. In the new essay "My Home Under Imperial Fire," he describes how he was spurred to write partly by being made to read Joyce Cary's 1939 novel *Mister Johnson*, with its "bumbling idiot" of a Nigerian character: "It began to dawn on me that although fiction was undoubtedly fictitious, it could also be true or false." He explains: "I'd read so-called 'African novels' in school, by Rider Haggard and John Buchan, in which white people were surrounded by savages but managed to come out on top. But I didn't recognize them as relating to me until I read Mister Johnson: this book was not talking about a vague place called Africa but about southern Nigeria. I said, 'wait, that means here; this is our story.' It brought the whole thing home to me: this story is not true, so is it possible the others are not either? It opened up a new way of looking at literature."

That "landmark rebellion" caught a wider moment. "The 50s were also the time when the ferment for freedom was at its highest. India was independent, so it was only a matter of time for West Africa. The Second World War was fought for freedom; when they told us to collect pine kernels for the war effort, they said each one would put a nail in Hitler's coffin. Nigerians returning home from the war asked, 'where's the freedom we were told about?' So the two things were together: the political ferment and the revolution in the classroom." Achebe credits Amos Tutuola's *The Palm-Wine Drinkard* (1952) with opening "the floodgates to modern west African writing" in the 50s. "It's as if this thing was waiting to be told; the time was ripe," he says.

The precolonial society of *Things Fall Apart*, whose tragic hero Okonkwo mounts doomed resistance to encroaching European power, was far from idyllic. Achebe insists on "an unflinching consciousness of the flaws that blemished our inheritance." He says: "Of all the things I remember, that was the clearest: I must not make this story look nicer than it was. I went out of my way to gather all the negative things, to describe them as I think they were – good and bad – and ordinary human beings as neither demons nor angels. I dare anybody to say, 'these people are not human.'"

He wrote in English, as arguments against using the language of the coloniser were gathering steam. "It was part of the logic of my situation – like the inevitability of my writing at all – of countering stories about us in the same language in which they were written. Writing in English is a painful choice. But you don't take up a language in order to punish it; that language becomes part of you. And you can't use language at a distance; you introduce English and Igbo into a conversation, as they are in my daily life – that's fascinating." The Igbo art of storytelling became central to the tale, since "proverbs are the palm oil with which words are eaten." Achebe, who writes poetry in both Igbo and English, says, "I insist on both."

For the critic Simon Gikandi, Achebe showed that "the future of African writing did not lie in simple imitation of European forms but in the fusion of such forms with oral traditions." Kwame Anthony Appiah, Professor of Afro American Studies and Philosophy at Harvard, says Achebe "solved with deceptive ease difficult technical questions, such as how you represent the language of one society in the language of a very different one. His use of a variety of registers of English came to be seen as obvious; it set modern African literature in English on a certain path." The Kenyan writer Ngũgĩ wa Thiong'o, who in the 80s renounced writing fiction in English in favour of Gikuyu, believes "Achebe created a third position out of the tension between Igbo and English, which becomes the base of his creativity; you feel there's an African voice in his work being rendered in English."

After working as a radio producer, Achebe had come to London in 1957 to train at the BBC staff school. "It was the first time I saw the great British empire at close quarters and it brought England a couple of pegs down: to find a white man in dirty overalls filling holes in the road was unbelievable." He sent the longhand manuscript of *Things Fall Apart* to William Heinemann, where a reader pronounced it "the best first novel since the war." But at a time when many in the metropolis believed, according to the publisher James Currey, that "an African could not reach the standards of an English publishing house," a modest 2,000 hardbacks were printed.

Then in 1962 Heinemann Educational Books launched the African Writers Series with four novels, including *Things Fall Apart* and its sequel, *No Longer At Ease* – set on the cusp of independence, in the era of Okonkwo's grandson. It was an inexpensive paperback imprint that emulated the Penguin revolution down to its orange covers, while selling 80% of copies in Africa and keeping titles in print. It proved that a readership existed and was a signal for Africa's writers, says Achebe, who selected the first 100 titles.

He was able to do what was an unpaid job as series editor for 10 years because he had jobs in broadcasting and then academia. (The late Heinemann director Alan Hill recalled him as "the very image of a modern Nigerian yuppie," with sharp suit, dark glasses and a Jaguar.) "I thought it was of the utmost importance," Achebe explains. "People in England were sceptical, so I knew I was a conspirator. I was naive enough to think that if you do good work, you'll get your reward in heaven."

For Ngũgĩ wa Thiong'o, Achebe "made a whole generation of African people believe in themselves and in the possibility of their being writers." The Somali novelist Nuruddin Farah says he learned his craft from him: "He taught us a way of integrating what we know from being African with what we've become – hybrids of a kind."

After travelling through southern Africa on a Rockefeller scholarship in 1960, "the winds of change in my sails," (vexing the Northern Rhodesian authorities by sitting in the front of a segregated bus near Victoria Falls), Achebe became the first Director of Voice of Nigeria, the state-run radio's external arm, where he remained till the eve of the Biafran war in 1966. He met his wife to be, Christie Chinwe, then a student, in Broadcasting House in Lagos, where she had a holiday job. She later became a Professor.

The couple have two sons and two daughters (one of whom, Chinelo, is a writer), and two grandchildren. "Christie saves my life every other day," says Achebe. "And she suffers my pain more than I do. When I had the accident, she left her classroom and never really got back." Though she is now a Psychology Professor at Bard, she was forced to leave her field of education, a sacrifice Achebe feels keenly. "When I was drifting in and out of consciousness I remember saying I wanted her to go with me – to England. That's been her life ever since."

After his third novel, *Arrow of God* (1964), set in Igboland in the 1920s – which won the Jock Campbell New Statesman award – Achebe wrote a satire on corruption in a fictitious African country following the "collusive swindle that was independence." *A Man Of The People* (1966) proved prescient about Nigeria's first attempted coup, which happened two days before its publication. Some, absurdly, thought the author complicit in the Igbo-instigated coup. As massacres spread against Igbos in northern and western Nigeria, Achebe and his family went into hiding. They fled Lagos for Igboland, where Achebe took up a post at the university in Nsukka.

On the eve of the Biafran war of 1967-70, Achebe went on a peace-seeking mission to President Leopold Senghor of Senegal, founder-poet of the francophone Negritude movement. "I was sent by the government of Biafra because I was also a writer, in the hope of stopping the war," Achebe recalls. "We talked about Biafra for 10 minutes and literature for two hours." But as war broke out, Achebe served on more diplomatic missions for the breakaway Biafran republic. "I was deeply disappointed with what was happening in Nigeria," he says." I was ready just to go to my village, but I did whatever I was asked."

The war was shattering for Achebe; his house was bombed and his best friend, the poet Christopher Okigbo, was killed. On the "wrong side" when the secessionists were crushed, Achebe was refused a passport, but finally left in 1972, for professorships in the US before returning to Nsukka as Professor of English in 1976. He had first visited the US in the early 60s, when he met writers including Ralph Ellison and Langston Hughes. His unsentimental recovery of the dignity of Africa's past chimed with the notion of "black is beautiful" among African Americans brought up to see Africa as an embarrassment. John Edgar Wideman recalls the shock of finding "language being refashioned from another centre I didn't know existed."

Achebe embraced writers of the Diaspora, calling Africa a "spiritual phenomenon born of a painful history... which binds every Black person." He launched the journal *Okike* and later a bilingual Igbo journal. *Beware Soul Brother* (1971), which won the Commonwealth Poetry Prize, and *Girls At War and Other Stories* (1972) both reflected the trauma of the civil war. He also published children's books, essays and a heartfelt polemic, *The Trouble With Nigeria* (1983), when he became involved in party politics. But there was a gap of 21 years before his fifth novel.

Lyn Innes, Professor of Postcolonial Literatures at the University of Kent, co-edited two Heinemann African anthologies with Achebe. In her view, "his fiction was concerned with portraying a society, and Nigerian society was so totally destabilized he found it difficult to write a sustained work – only fragments." Achebe says: "I don't think it damaged my work; it gave it a new direction for a while into poetry and short stories. I regard all of them equally."

Achebe's friend James Baldwin savoured the elegance of Achebe's essays as "not a mere pleasure but a benefaction." The dissection in the essays of Europe's self-serving myths of Africa and how they shored up slavery and empire, are a prelude to Edward Said's *Orientalism* (1978) and Toni Morrison's scrutiny of the black presence in American literature in *Playing In The Dark: Whiteness and the Literary Imagination* (1992). In a famous lecture on *Heart Of Darkness* in Massachusetts in 1975 (included in *Hopes and Impediments*, 1988) he described Joseph Conrad as a "thoroughgoing racist," disputing that a novel which dehumanizes a portion of the human race could be called a great work of art (one American professor stalked off, saying, "How dare you?").

Achebe attacked the "perverse arrogance" of reducing Africa to a "setting and backdrop which eliminates the African as human factor." In his view: "Conrad saw and condemned the evil of imperial exploitation but was strangely unaware of the racism on which it sharpened its tooth."

"I'm surprised it's gone on being controversial, but it has," he says. Some still argue that to accuse Conrad of racism is anachronistic. Achebe responds: "Long before Conrad, there were people who refused to be racist. Time does contribute something to what we think, but good people are never prisoners of their era." As for Conrad's prose: "It would have been better if the beautiful prose were used to unite the human race, rather than separate it. The best works, whether written or oral, seem to me to have an intrinsic morality; it's not Sunday school morality, but I've not encountered any good art that promotes genocide."

Achebe's stance is sometimes misunderstood as censorship. "I'm not Ayatollah Khomeini," he objects. "I don't believe in banning books, but they should be read carefully. Far from wanting the novel banned, I teach it." By the same token, he advocates closer reading of V.S. Naipaul ("a new Conrad... purveyor of the old comforting myths of race") and Elspeth Huxley ("the griot [story-telling caste] for white settlers").

In his introduction, with poems, to *Another Africa* (1998, Lund Humphries), photographs by Robert Lyons, Achebe writes: "The vast arsenal of derogatory images of Africa amassed to defend the Slave Trade and, later, colonization, gave the world not only a literary tradition that is now, happily defunct, but also a particular way of looking (or rather not looking) at Africa and Africans." He warns against the enduring tendency to act for, or upon, Africa while failing to listen to its inhabitants.

In a 1998 lecture to the World Bank, he urged the cancellation of Third World debt, having told western bankers in Paris a decade before: "You talk about 'structural adjustment' as if Africa was some kind of laboratory... But Africa is people!" Achebe has called himself a "missionary in reverse". Lyn Innes, who sat in on his classes in the US in the 1970s, says, "ill-informed students would ask outrageous questions about cannibalism, or from reading his work as anthropology not literature. But he was always patient and tolerant, trying to turn them around."

Achebe's fifth novel, *Anthills of the Savannah* (1987), revived his reputation in Britain when it was shortlisted for the Booker. Set in a military regime in present-day West Africa, it introduced a female intellectual, the journalist Beatrice, some say in response to criticism of his earlier work. "Feminists would like to take credit; I've no objection, but I don't need anyone to scare me into realizing the paradoxical position of women," says Achebe, who is working on a new novel with women at its heart.

"The female presence is there in all my novels. It seems as if it's not important – which is the reality of how it looks in Igbo society – till you get to a crisis which threatens survival. When the British came, that was a critical moment; the men fought and lost. But there were events in Igboland where women stopped the British in their tracks. That's been happening in my fiction; the incremental involvement of women in political matters. It's not straightforward; it's a struggle for power."

Morrison believes Achebe's early work leaves a lot of space for women, which was like a revelation to her: "the notion here in America is that slavery was about the imprisonment and emasculation of black men. But with Achebe

I never felt the male claw grabbing up the entire canvas; there was feminine space where women existed without permission from the man."

Others could step into that space. Farah, whose novel *From a Crooked Rib* (1970) was written from the point of view of a circumcised Somali woman, points out that the central consciousness, even of *Anthills of the Savannah*, is still male, but says his own writing was partly in response to the absences he felt in Achebe's oeuvre. He says it was important for someone to deal with the bigger quarrels of Africa and colonialism – "but it left me free to cover quarrels within the community – between men and women."

Last year Achebe visited Nigeria for the first time since his accident. His initial impressions of Lagos were "confusing and very depressing; the place looked deserted, not well looked after, with potholes in the landing strip." Only after a bitter quarrel was a wheelchair found to take him off the plane. "I went incognito; I didn't want a red carpet. That's normally my style because I want to see the country as it is." Pained, he murmurs the unthinkable: "Maybe somebody wanted me to bribe them."

In *The Trouble With Nigeria*, Achebe insisted: "Nigerians are what they are only because their leaders are not what they should be." He swiped at General Obasanjo for his "flamboyant, imaginary" idea of a great Nigeria. On his recent trip, however, Achebe met the general, now civilian President, "to encourage him." Although Nigeria is "sicker than we feared" (he identifies the Muslim sharia law as the greatest threat to the federation), Achebe clings to hope: "Even Nigerians are not entirely immune from learning from their history."

He had to steel himself for the 400-mile car journey to Ogidi: "you might suddenly find a ditch in the middle of the road. Life is so unsafe," he says. "Things had got much worse in nine years; for the first time you saw beggars camped out by the roadside. But I always return to the good things: the whole village had turned out and waited all day." His arrival was hailed with an artillery salute. "It was a tremendous experience. I almost found myself in tears; there are good things going on. My people deserve better than they've had by a long chalk."



## Life at a glance

**Albert Chinualumogu Achebe**

**Born:** November 16 1930, Ogidi, Nigeria.

**Education:** Church Missionary Society primary school, Ogidi; University College, Ibadan. **Married:** 1961 Christie Chinwe Okoli (two daughters Chinelo,

Nwando; two sons Ikechukwu, Chidi). **Career:** Editor, Heinemann African Writers Series; 1971- founding editor *Okike*; 1985- Emeritus Professor of English, University of Nigeria, Nsukka; 1990- Charles P. Stevenson Professor, Bard College, New York. **Some books:** Fiction: *Things Fall Apart* (1958), *No Longer At Ease* (1960), *Arrow of God* (1964), *A Man of the People* (1966), *Girls at War* (stories, 1972); *Anthills of the Savannah* (1987). ***Poetry:*** *Beware Soul Brother* (1971) *Another Africa* (1998). **Essays:** *The Trouble with Nigeria* (1983), *Hopes And Impediments* (1988), *Home And Exile* (2000).

**Awards:** Commonwealth Poetry Prize, 1979.

Chapter Five

# Elegy for a Nation

## (For Chinua Achebe, at Seventy)

*Wole Soyinka*

**1**

Ah, Chinua, are you grapevine wired?
It sings: our nation is not dead, not clinically
Yet. Now this may come as a surprise to you,
It was to me. I thought the form I spied
Beneath the frosted glass of a fifty-carat catafalque
Was the face of our own dear land – 'own', 'dear',
Voluntary patriotese, you'll note – we try to please.
An anthem's sentiment upholds the myth.

Doctors IMF, World Bank and UNO refuse, it seems,
To issue a certificate of death – if debtors die
May creditors collect? We shall turn Parsees yet,
Lay this hulk in state upon the Tower of Silence,
Let vultures prove what we have seen, but fear to say –
For if Leviathan is dead, we are the maggots
Probing still her monstrous womb – one certainty

That mimics life after death. Is the world fooled?
Is this the price of hubris – to have dared
Sound Renaissance bugles for a continent?
Time was, our gazes roamed the land, godlike,
Pronounced it good, from Lagos to Lake Chad.
The ghosts of interlopers would be exorcised,
Not throwing the baby out with the bathwater, but –
Enthroning ours as ours, bearing names

Lodged in marrow of the dead, attesting lineage.
Consecrated brooms would sweep our earth
Clean of usurpers' footprints. We marched

To drums of ancient skins, homoeopathic
But against the boom of pale-knuckled guns.
We vied with regal rectitude of Overamwen –
*No stranger breath* – he swore – *shall desecrate*
*This hour of communion with our gods!* We
Died with the women of Aba, they who held
A bridgehead against white levy, armed with pestle,
Sash and spindle, and a potent nudity – eloquent
Abomination in the timeless rites of wrongs.

Grim cycle of embattled years. Again we died
With miners of Iva valley who undermined
More than mere seams of anthracite. All too soon,
Alas, we would augment, in mimic claims,
In our own right, the register of martyrs. Oh,
How we've exercised the right of righteous folly
In defence of alien rhetoric … *what God has joined*, etcetera.
For God, read white, read slaver surrogates.

We scaled the oranges of Obudu, prospected
Jos Plateau, pilgrims on rock-hills of Idanre.
Floated on pontoons from Bussa to silt beds
Of eternal Niger, reclaimed the mangrove swamps,
Startling mudskipper, manatee, and mermaids.
Did others claim the mantle of discoveries?
Let them lay patterns on ancestral lands, lay claim
To paternity of night and day – ours
Were hands that always were, hands that pleat
The warp and sunbeam and the weft of dew,
Ours to create the seamless out of paradox.

In the mind's compost, meagre scrub yielded
Silos of grain. Walled cities to the north were
Sheaths of gold turbans, tuneful as minarets.
The dust of Durbars, pyrotechnic horsemen
And sparkling lances, all one with the ring of anvils
From Ogun's land to Ikenga's. Rainbow beads, *jigida*

*Iyun* glow and Ife bronzes, luscent on ivory arches
Of Benin. Legend lured Queen Amina to Moremi,
Old scars of strife redeemed in tapestries
Of myth, recreating birthpang, and rebirth. And, yes –

We would steal secrets from the gods. Let Sango's axe
Spark thunderstones on rooftops, we would swing
In hawser hammocks on electric pylons, pulse through cities
In radiant energies, surge from battery racks to bathe
Town and hamlet in alchemical light. Orisa-oko
Would heal with herbs and scalpel. Ogun's drill
Was poised to plumb the earth anew, spraying aloft
Reams of rare alloys. Futurists, were we not
Annunciators of the Millennium long before its advent?
In our now autumn days, behold our leaden feet
Fast welded to the starting block.

Vain griots! Still, we sang the hennaed lips and fingers
Of our gazelle womenfolk, fecund Muses tuned
To Senghorian cadences. We grew filament eyes
As heads of millet, as flakes of cotton responsive
To brittle breezes, wraith-like in the haze of Harmattan.
Green of the cornfields of Oyo, ochre of groundnut pyramids
Of Kano, indigo in the ancient dye-pots of Abeokuta
Bronzed in earth's tonalities as children of one deity –
We were the cattle nomads, silent threads through
Forestries and cities, coastland and savannah,
Wafting Maiduguri to the sea, ocean mist to sand dunes.

Alas for lost idylls. Like Levi jeans on youth and age,
The dreams are faded, potholed and joints and even
Milder points of stress. Ghosts are sole inheritors.
Silos fake rotundity – these are *kwashi-okor* blights
Upon the landscape, depleted at source. Even
The harvest seeds were long devoured. Empty hands
Scrape the millennial soil at planting.

But Chinua, are you grapevine wired? Do you
Tune in, listen? There is old music in the air.
The word is out again, out from the closet.
Renaissance beats are thumbed in government lairs,

In lobbies, caucuses, on promotion posters,
In parliaments. Academe's close behind. Renaissance
Haunts beer and *suya* bar, street and rostrum,
Inhaled as tobacco smoke, chewed as kola,
Clerics beautify the word, lawyers invoke it.
Never word more protean, poised to incarnate
In these, conferences, investments. A historic lure
Romances the Diaspora. Gang-raped, the continent
Turns pregnant with the word – it's sworn, we shall be
Born again, though we die in the attempt.

But then, our offsprings, Chinua, have they leisure
To play at love? To commune with Source, shaded
By coarse-grain village walls at noon? Crush wild mint
Between their fingers, let the *agbayun* coat
Their tongues, at war with the bitterness of kola?
Raid the hoards of gods and ancients,
Recite their lineage praise-names, clan histories?
Or have the rigours of survival bread a race
Of naked predators? Is sharing out of fashion?
Community a dirty word, service an obscenity?
Are ours the emerging children of Molucca
Born to burn at six, slaughter at seven,
Rinse their hand in the throat's death gurgle,
Secure in the arch-priest's absolution? Attuned
At noon to dissolution of the bond of dawn, deaf
To neighbour cries? Easy reddened are the wafers
Of Communion – have we been here before?

Still, here you sit before the travelled world, gathered
To pay homage. Survived the *kwashi-okor* days.
You've fed on roots, barks and leaves
Your world contracted, ringed with iron
Fenced with the wringing hands of the world
As unctuous in neutrality as Pontius Pilate
But you made flesh what is so often said –
*Sweet are the uses of adversity* – as even now
Your silent eloquence attests. The ancient pot-stills
Turned refineries. Neglected herbs, mystery silica
Powered transistors to accuse the world, screaming
*We are not dead, but dying.* And iron monsters

Rose furtively from forest bays, hammered
From the forges of Awka. Who can forget the errant
*Ogbunikwe* that rose skywards, plunged to blast
A fiery tunnel through encircling steel?

Absences surround your presence – he
The great town crier, Okigbo, and other griots
Silenced in infancy. The xylophones of justice
Chime much louder than the flutes of poets,
Their sirens lure the bravest to their doom.
But some survive, and survival breeds, it seems
Unending debts. Time is our usurer, but earth remains
Sole signatory to life's covenant – and thus I ask:
Whose feet are these upon the storehouse loft?
Shod in studded boots or jewelled sandals,
Khaki crisp or silk embroidered – who are these?

Did time appoint these bailiffs? Behold
Enforcers out of time, shorn of memory but –
Crowned are the hollow skulls, signets on talons.
Their advent is the hour of locusts – behold
Cheeks in cornucopia from the silos' depletion
While the eyes of youth sink deeper in despair
Death bestrides the streets, rage rides the sun
And hope is a sometime word that generations
Never learnt to spell.

Chinua, I think with you I dare
Be indelicate – we scrape our feet upon
The threshold of moral proof, denying
The ancestors yet awhile our companionship –
May that day learn patience from afar! –
On the stage at Bard, behind the lectern,
Gazing across time to your staunch spirit
Wedded to a contraption we neither make nor mend
My irreverent thoughts were – There sits the nation,
All faculties intact, but wheelchair bound.
Your lesson of the will, alas, a creative valour
Marks the gulf between you and that land
We claim our own.

## II

There are wonders in that land, Chinua
Are you wired? Tuned to images of cyber age?
Severed wrists will soon adorn our walls
And Conrad's *Heart of Darkness* be fulfilled.
The cairn of stones is building for the first
Butchery in a public square, a female scapegoat
Tethered for primordial rites that men devise
To keep their womenfolk obedient to the laws of man.

An encampment is on the move, biped
Amorphous tents, a sorcerer invasion choreographed
In castration shrouds, visors no less secretive
Than face-masks, twin to ancestral masquerades
Proclaimed infidel. They slink through streets
And markets – yes, it is our women on the move
Our mothers, wives and sisters, comrades-in-arms
Bereft of limbs and faces, *haute couture* decreed
By encyclicals of eunuch priests. Features
Mummified by laws of terror. Oh my compatriots,
Shaved bare-skull at initiation, convertites,
Dipped body and soul in the waters of salvation
Are yours these zombies of the age, are these
The paracletes of the new millennium?

They'll murder heritage in its timeless crib,
Decree our heroes, heroines out of memory
Obliterate the narratives of clans, names
That bind to roots, reach to heavens, our
Links to ancestral presences. The Born-Agains
Are on rampage, born against all that spells
Life and mystery, legend and innovation.
Imprecations rend the air, song is taboo,
The stride of sun-toned limbs racing wind a sin,
Flesh is vile, wine, the gift of earth, execrated.
These tyrants have usurped the will of God.
How did we fail to learn, that guns and boots
Are not essential to a coup d'état?

Shall *Ala* die? *Ahiajoku* be anathematized? Does
*Oya* defile her streams, *Ifa* obstruct the paths
Of learning and councils of the wise? *Praise the Lord*
And launch the bulldozer – they've razed
The statues of *mbari* to the ground, these
Christian *Talibans*. Their brothers in Offa
Murder Moremi in her shrine, shrieking *Allah akbar*.
Rivals else, behold their bonded zeal that sanctifies
Alien rape of our quiescent Muses, extolling theirs.

We who neither curse their gods nor desecrate
Their texts, their prayer mats or altars –
What shall we do, Chinua, with these hate clerics?
While we sleep, their fingers spread as brambles,
Deface our Book of Life. How teach them:

Some are born pagan, wedded to life's seamlessness
Tuned to the breath of things, magma and animus.
The waters of the Holy Gospel bounced against
This splinter of Olumo Rock, retreated
In despair, seeking more porous earth. How reveal
The sublimity of godhead that abhors
The murdering tyranny of Creed? Has gore
Proved godlove on Kaduna streets – ten thousand
Mutilations and three thousand dead of faith?
But the sun rose still the following dawn, indifferent.

Let all creeds be recast, if the gates of Paradise
Are locked behind the Pope's demise,
We wish him blessed occupancy of yonder realms
With all the Heavenly Host. Has the last Imam
Been here and gone? Then, *Bon Voyage*
Seek me out among the questers, creed-divorced,
In covenant only to that solvent that is earth.

How shall they be taught, Chinua, that Ajapa
Lives, but no longer borrows feathers from the birds
To survey earth? Myths are our wise cohabitants. Icarus
Transcended wax, new trajectories lace the spheres.
The galaxy is boundless host to a new race
Of voyagers, seeking the once forbidden. Cinders

From Promethean dares, shards of Ajapa's shell,
Are constellations by which ships of space are steered.

The jealous gods are no more. Age by age
We inched towards the sun, then raced beyond
To drink the heady draught of space, returned to earth
Emboldened. The voices of new prophets are not voided
In the wilderness but fulfilled. Applause
Is the new music of the spheres – it's heard
In other lands, I am told. I have not heard it here.

But we survived, Chinua. And though survival reads
Unending debt – for time, alas decrees us
Witnesses, thus debtors – earth alone remains
Our creditor. Yet I fear the communion pots
Lie broken at the crossroads, kola nuts and cowries
Scattered by scavengers. Couriers turn coat,
Turned by profit, priest, predator and politician.

The Masquerade's falsetto may reveal, not
Artifice but loss of voice, its gutturals camouflage
Death throes, not echoes of our spirit realms.
The strongest eagle, wing-span clipped, talons
Manicured in gilded thumbscrews may not hold
Nor bear the weight of sacrifice. Our caryatids
Are weary of cycles of endless debts. Incense
Of burnt offering, heavy with abominations
Hung close to alter, dissipates between Earth
And Sky. Shorn of new alibis, our intercessors
Falter at the door of judgement. What shall we say
To the years that drift past, accusing?
What shall we chant to their dew-bright notes –
Our new tuned buglers of the Renaissance?

Chapter Six

# Chinua Achebe

## African American Institute Award: (9.22.00)

*Toni Morrison*

Good Evening.

I take great pleasure in having this opportunity to say some things in public which I have never said to the person who is the subject of these comments – Chinua Achebe. My debt to Mr Achebe is the best kind. Large, minus repayment schedule and interest free. Let me describe it to you.

In 1965, I began reading African literature, devouring it actually. It was a literature previously unavailable to me, but by then I discovered a New York bookstore called African House which offered among other things, back issues of *Transition, Black Orpheus* and works by a host of African writers from all over the continent. Amos Tutuola, Ayi Kwei Armah, Ezekiel Mphahlele, James Ngũgĩ, Bessie Head, Christina Ama Ata Aidoo, Mongo Beti, Leopold Senghor, Camara Laye, Ousmane Sembène, Wole Soyinka, John Pepper Clark: the jolt these writers gave me was explosive. The confirmations that African literature was not limited to Doris Lessing and Joseph Conrad was so stunning it led me to secure the aid of two academics who could help me anthologize this literature. At that time African literature was not a subject to be taught in American schools. Even in so-called "World Literature" courses it had no reputation and no presence. But I was determined to funnel the delight, the significance and the power of that literature into my work as an editor. The publication of *Contemporary African Literature* in 1972 was the beginning of my love affair.

But the more profound and more personal consequence was the impact Chinua Achebe's novels had on my own beginnings as a writer. I had read his essay in *Transition*, on the struggle with definitions of African literature and knew its ramifications for African American writers. In that essay, Achebe quoted James Baldwin's comments on the subject of language choice and manipulation in defining national and cultural literatures and its resonance with marginalized writers. "My quarrel," said Baldwin, "with the English language has been that the language reflects none of my experience... Perhaps I had never attempted to use it, had only learned to imitate it. If this were so, then it might be made to bear the burden of my experience if I could find the stamina to challenge it, and me, to such a test." But theorizing a definition is one thing. Executing a theory is another. Achebe's "answer," so to speak was in his work. He (along with Camara Laye, Bessie Head and others) constituted a complete education for me. Learning how to disassemble the gaze that I was wrestling with – the habitual but self -conscious writing toward a non- black reader that threatened and coated much African American literature; discovering how to eliminate, to manipulate the Eurocentric eye in order to stretch and plumb my own imagination, I attribute these learned lessons to Chinua Achebe. In the pages of *Things Fall Apart* lay not the argument but the example; in the pages of *No Longer at Ease, Anthills of the Savannah* the assumption of the authenticity, the force, the valleys of beauty were abundant. Achebe's work liberated my artistic intelligence as nothing else had ever done. I became fit to re-enter and re-inhabit my own milieu without the services of a native guide.

So in fact that was not a debt in 1965. It was a gift. And I hope my presentation of this award to you Chinua will represent not only the African American Institute's regard and respect for you but also my personal gratitude as well.

Chapter Seven

# Chinua Achebe

*Nadine Gordimer*

*Things Fall Apart*, Chinua Achebe's first novel, is also the founding creation of modern African imaginative literature, the opening act of exploration of African consciousness in terms that took full right to use traditional modes of expression along with those appropriated from colonial culture, particularly the English language.

The Irish poet W. B. Yates's despairing statement of destruction – things fall apart – is for Achebe's novel a presentiment of what was to come, in Nigeria, on the continent of Africa, during the end of the colonial occupations and their aftermath.

But the novel begins by creating what was complete before the situation in the title is to come about, because only with this can the revelation of disintegration be understood.

And only when this is understood, revealed by Achebe with subtle mastery of every literary mode as the story progresses, can things be put together, made whole in a new way that it is imperative for social and political survival in an ever-changing world. That first work was prescient – not only of the creative powers to develop, in subsequent works of a nascent writer, but of the political upheavals, the embattled end of colonialism, the fight for freedom in which and by which the personal lives of the people of Africa have been shaped.

As we all know, Achebe himself lived through these times. A tragic civil war in his country, as an activist in extreme personal danger, finally exile, fulfilling Albert Camus' statement of what it means in terms of human existence to be a writer; "The day when I am no more than a writer I shall cease to be a writer."

During those years, Achebe kept faith with this commitment. Yet during those years, he wrote novels, stories, essays and poems that were a bold revelation to his countrymen and women and the world, of what really happens to people within themselves; of what suppression and oppression really mean. And trust Chinua Achebe to give anew, a definition of colonialism. His collection of essays, recently reissued as a Penguin modern classic, is *The Education of a British-Protected Child* (first published by Alfred A. Knopf: NY, 2009).

Chinua Achebe has not feared to challenge the ideals and practice of justice and humanity, those postcolonial independent regimes in Africa who abuse personal power in every possible way, from banning political opposition, to corruption. His novel *A Man of the People*, a biting satire on corruption in freed African regimes, uses the blade of humour to alert us, his readers, to official greed and the cant which legitimize it.

*Chike and the River* was first published for children in 1966 and was reprinted in 2011. I read it in the sense of extraordinary entry into a brilliant mind (I do not use that word fashionably or lightly) a writer's achievement of penetrating the variety, possibilities, mystery of being a human being in the presence not alone of one's own people and country, but in the presences of the world.

He does not shirk writing of what "I have chosen to call my Middle Passage, my colonial inheritance. To call my experience colonial heritage may surprise some people. But everything is grist to the mill of the artist. True, one grain may differ from another in its powers of nourishment; still we must... accord appropriate recognition to every grain that comes our way."

Writers are always asked for interviews: for whom do you write? What audience, what readers do you have in mind, who is it you are addressing yourself to? Whose eyes do you imagine meeting, who are the people gathered there round you, the storyteller?

The somewhat testy answer is: we write for whoever will read our work.

Because we're not talking of propaganda here, but imaginative literature that does not dictate or persuade, but seeks to discover and illuminate the labyrinths of human existence.

Yes, I think one must admit there are some very special exceptions to our quite proper refusal to discriminate between those our writings may reach.

It surely must mean a great deal to a writer to know that his or her work has reached through prison walls, having been longingly requested and received with difficulty by way of lawyers or rare visitors allowed a political prisoner.

Chinua Achebe had that rather special recognition when someone who was certainly one of the greatest political prisoners of the 20th century, Nelson Mandela, 27 years behind prison walls, told Achebe what his novels brought to him: "There was a writer named Chinua Achebe in whose company the prison wall fell."

## Chapter Eight

# Chinua Achebe as Publisher

*James Currey*

In 1954 Chinua Achebe became a talks producer for the Nigerian Broadcasting Corporation in Enugu. In 1961 he was appointed Director of External Broadcasting in Lagos, which enabled him to disseminate news of the growth of the arts in post-independent Nigeria. He was able to make effective use of the skills he first learned in broadcasting to get African writers published. In December 1962 he agreed to become the first Editorial Adviser to the African Writer Series. His informed and calm efficiency was a factor in getting the Series off to such an extraordinarily fast start. Ideas, links and international contacts were just what was needed to develop a series which set out to represent a whole continent. It is not often remembered how much of a publisher he was himself.

The name of the *Mbari* movement of artists and writers was suggested by Chinua Achebe. As he later explained, the concept was that "Mbari was a celebration, through art, of the world and of the life lived in it (Nwakanma 179)." *Mbari's* publication in paperback of 17 books grew out of work sent in by contributors to *Black Orpheus.* Wole Soyinka, J. P. Clark, Kofi Awoonor, Lenrie Peters, Alex la Guma, Dennis Brutus were all to have their early work published. These elegantly decorated and designed *Mbari* paperbacks were available in Nigeria.

Chinua Achebe was not on that list. William Heinemann in London had published *Things Fall Apart* in 1958. Alan Hill, founding chairman of Heinemann Educational Books, was shocked to find in 1959 that there were hardly any copies of the hardback in Nigeria. He decided that what was needed was the equivalent of the Penguin paperback series for Africa. *Things Fall Apart* was to be No 1 and published about the time of the famous Makerere Conference of June 1962.

Zeke (later Es'kia) Mphahlele, the founding chairman of *Mbari* in Ibadan, joined with the journal *Transition* edited by Rajit Neogy in Kampala to sponsor a conference of African writers. Chinua Achebe was to say at a conference at Guelph in 1989 organised by Douglas Killam (see p. 175): "In 1962 we saw the gathering of a remarkable generation of young African men and women who were to create within the next decade a corpus of writing which is today seriously read and critically evaluated in many parts of the world. It was an enormously important moment, and year, in the history of modern African literature. The gathering took place at Makerere University, Kampala, Uganda."

One evening Chinua Achebe heard a knock at the door of his guesthouse and found a Makerere student who asked him whether he would read the manuscripts of his two novels. At breakfast Achebe recommended them strongly to the Heinemann editor Van Milne who rang Alan Hill in Britain to get permission to take them on. The name of the student was the then James Ngũgĩ and the manuscripts were *The River Between* and *Weep Not, Child.*

Ngũgĩ has only recently published his reflections on this encounter in "In The Name of the Mother" which was first given as a speech arranged by Becky Nana Ayebia Clarke, then Submissions Editor of the AWS to mark the fortieth anniversary of the African Writers Series in 2002 at the African Literature Association (ALA) Conference in San Diego: Ngũgĩ writes:

> ...at the end of May 1962, under the firelight in a village in Kangemi, Kenya, some friends are trying to help type the half- finished manuscript [of *Weep Not, Child* ] for me. I am writing by hand, desperately trying to complete the novel and they desperately trying to finish typing whatever I am giving them. Why by the fireside? There is no electricity in the area and we cannot afford paraffin oil but we are committed to the task at hand. But why this desperation? Because I had been invited to a conference of Writers of English Expression to be held in June at Makerere University College, Kampala, Uganda. Among the prospective attenders was Chinua Achebe. I had to show him the manuscript. It never occurred to me that he might not want, or even have the time, to read it. I had to show it to him, the author of *Things Fall Apart* which had come out in 1958. He did not disappoint me and it was he who introduced my work to Heinemann. I have always appreciated the generosity of his spirit and more so when later I realized that he was then in the midst of writing *Arrow of God*... (2)

At the Guelph conference Chinua Achebe went on to say: "As for the African Writers Series in that same eventful year of 1962, I was invited to be its Founding Editor and I was to spend a considerable part of my literary energy in the following ten years wading through a torrent of good, bad and indifferent writing that seemed in some miraculous way to have been waiting behind the sluice gates for the trap to be released.' Alan Hill had realized that Chinua Achebe would be "a magnet for young writers."

Keith Sambrook found the final revised manuscript of Ngũgĩ's *Weep Not, Child* on his desk when he took over the development and marketing of the Series on 1 January 1963. He and Alan Hill were confident that there were many other writers of similar calibre to be found in Africa. They also decided that *Weep Not, Child* was to be first published in hardback before it went into the paperback African Writers Series. Only hardbacks were then reviewed in London and librarians relied on those reviews. This was the moment of take-off. Heinemann Educational Books took on a role, at that time performed in London by general literary publishers. As Dennis Brutus was to say in 1970, he wanted to be considered just as "someone writing poetry in English."

Aig Higo, a poet who like Ngũgĩ had taken a postgraduate degree in literature at Leeds, took over Heinemann Educational Books in Ibadan in January 1965. Nigerian writers like Cyprian Ekwensi, T. M. Aluko, Elechi Amadi, Flora Nwapa and John Munonye were published. Other writers were taken on from West Africa such as Kofi Awoonor from Ghana and Lenrie Peters from Gambia. Chinua Achebe and Aig Higo captured against several well-established rivals many of the most outstanding writers. It became the Series of first choice. Before Christopher Okigbo rushed east in 1966 he handed over to Aig Higo for the AWS the manuscript of *Labyrinths* which brought together his new poetry with his three books already published by *Mbari.*

Alan Hill has noted that: "By 1967 we were on to something big and I invited James Currey of the Oxford University Press to run the African Writers Series as his specialism." In February 1967, while still working out my notice at Oxford University Press, Keith Sambrook asked me to come round to meet Chinua Achebe who was visiting London on diplomatic business for the eastern part of Nigeria, which later that year declared itself Biafra. During the meeting I produced with some diffidence, because I had failed to get the book accepted at the Oxford University Press, the translations from Arabic of short stories by the Sudanese writer Tayeb Salih under the title *The Wedding of Zein.* The two men looked carefully at the work and within a few minutes had decided that it ought to go into the Series. It was transforming for me to find such self-confident acceptance of worth. Tayeb Salih's work now appears in the Penguin Modern Classics.

The inhibitions that concerned an educational publisher about sex, religion and politics did not concern Chinua Achebe. He wanted the Series to reflect all the richness and variety of an emerging Africa. All these books had to be approved at Heinemann by a formal committee of directors and editors every Wednesday.

After the discussion had gone on for some time about whether the subject would cut it out from schools, Alan Hill in the chair would say, "Well, James, what did the old Chinua say?" He knew, everyone knew, that if I had brought the proposal to the meeting young Chinua, still under forty, would have said "yes." So Alan Hill would say "Right James! You want to do it? Go ahead and do it!"

Chinua Achebe managed to keep in touch with us. Several of the most lengthy meetings I had with him were on the phone when he was passing through Heathrow. I always kept an agenda ready for manuscripts to be discussed, decisions to be made. Trenchant notes would reach us by mysterious means through the Biafran network, often with French stamps. Alan Hill told in his autobiography of the complexity of Achebe's journeys to England: "He used to get into a clapped out Super Constellation aircraft at the Uli-Ihiala airstrip… 'which had been constructed out of a straight bit of road through the rain-forest.' He would fly to the island of Sao Tomé and then on to Lisbon and Heathrow. Then he would come strolling into the office as cool and humorous as if he'd come in from Chelsea or Kensington."

With the imaginative support of Chinua Achebe for the first 100 titles in the Series, Heinemann established that there was a general as well as an educational market in Africa. The big sales of the adopted titles prescribed for exams allowed us to experiment with all sorts of writers. Alan Hill pointed out that in 1984 approximately one-third of the total revenue for 250 titles in the Series came from the sales of Chinua Achebe's books. Their success gave us the freedom to recycle our surplus into investment in new writing until new owners stopped us. We were determined with Chinua Achebe to get people outside Africa, as well as in Africa, to take writing by Africans seriously.

I have given an account in *Africa Writes Back: The African Writers Series and the Launch of African Literature* about the publishing history of Heinemann companies with Chinua Achebe's five novels and other books. He tells the story in a *Paris Review* interview of how in 1957 the sole handwritten manuscript of *Things Fall Apart* seemed to have been lost at a typing agency. Alan Hill later asked Chinua Achebe whether he would have ever rewritten the manuscript. His reply was: "I would have been so discouraged that I would have probably given up writing altogether… and if I had rewritten it, it would have been a different book."

Just after the end of the war on 21 June 1970, Chinua Achebe wrote to Alan Hill accepting an invitation from Heinemann Nigeria to become a Director. "Each of your letters was a real tonic. Christie and I are most grateful for your real friendship which you have always shown us but especially for your kind thoughts during our recent troubles… Aig has just visited us again bringing as usual much material – and spiritual – comfort. I am sure that the children think of him as a kind of fabulous godfather" (21 June 1970).

I visited Chinua and Christie Achebe at the University of Nsukka in 1971 after the end of the civil war. The house was a shell. The walls were black. There was no power. Chinua Achebe gave me a manuscript of his short stories called *Girls at War* which was to become AWS 100 when it was published on the tenth anniversary of the Series in 1972. He told me that it was writing poetry, especially in Igbo, which suited his mood. It was portable and could be worked on in an unsettled life. His first book of poetry after the war was *Beware Soul Brother.* He said that the time had come to hand over his role as Editorial Adviser; it was then that we awarded him the hard-earned title of Founding Editor.

Chinua Achebe had become a publisher himself just before the war. Soon after reaching Enugu in August 1966, the poet Christopher Okigbo persuaded him and the novelist V.C. Ike to establish Citadel Press. In 2012 Chinua Achebe said in *There Was a Country*: "By the time we all arrived back in Eastern Nigeria, after escaping the massacres in the rest of the country, it became clear to me that it would be beneficial to the cause of Biafra if intellectuals worked together to support the war effort. Christopher came to me and requested that we establish a publishing house. It immediately seemed to me to be a very good idea, for we believed it was necessary at this time to publish books, especially children's books, that would have relevance to our society (176)." It is significant to find that Henry Chakava, who in the seventies became Managing Director of Heinemann in East Africa, records the priority that Chinua Achebe and Ngũgĩ both gave to publishing childrens' books (see p. 36).

Chinua Achebe said in an interview with Obi Nwakanma in his biography of Christopher Okigbo that the motivating force for Citadel was: 'To really help build a body of African and black literature. It got to the point when we could not leave the fate of such a venture to other foreign interests" (p. 237). He saw the establishment of Biafra as the time for taking new initiatives. Immediately Chinua Achebe put together for Citadel an international list with poetry by Gabriel Okara, Keorapetse Kgositsile from South Africa and Kofi Awoonor from Ghana. Sooner rather than later new poetry by Christopher Okigbo would have been added to that list. Chris Okigbo did not tell Achebe, his friend and business partner that he was going to head for the battlefront. Okigbo "cut his own pips" and promoted himself Major of his group of freebooters. He died in September 1966 fighting the federal soldiers, whom he considered to be barbarians – they had just torn his library apart on the Nsukka campus. Most of his new poetry disappeared in the battlefield.

I found it surprising that, in these desperate times Chinua Achebe and John Iroaganachi wrote and published *How the Leopard Got his Claws.* Okigbo had persuaded Cambridge University Press to publish Chinua Achebe's *Chike and the River* in 1966 which has recently so impressed Nadine Gordimer (see p. 29). He dedicated it to his first daughter Chinelo and to his nephews and nieces.

Soon after the war Chinua Achebe on a visit to London made me realise as a young father how I took for granted the wealth of books for my children in my own culture. He described to me one afternoon, after he had just been in the children's department of a West End London bookshop to find books for Chinelo, how the shelves were full of beautiful books with coloured illustrations but without a brown child in sight. Where were the books he could give his own children with stories and pictures of African children? Ngũgĩ in the early eighties was to get the support of Henry Chakava at Heinemann in Nairobi in publishing his childrens' books in Gikuyu with full colour illustrations. Chinua Achebe in a reflective piece in 2009 in *The Education of a British-Protected Child* called "My Daughters," says: "I learned that if I wanted a safe book for my child I should at least read it through and at best write it myself." He starts the article with "All my life I have had to take account of the million differences – some little, others quite big – between the Nigerian culture into which I was born and the domineering Western style that infiltrated and then invaded it"(p. 68).

Achebe's experience with *Mbari* and with Citadel made him realize the importance for Nigerian writers of the originating publishers being in Nigeria and thus controlling and selling the sub-lease and subsidiary rights to international publishers. After the war Chinua Achebe used his energy and prestige to support new publishers in eastern Nigeria. He gave his collection of poetry *Beware Soul Brother* to Arthur Nwankwo at Nwamife in Enugu as originating publishers in 1971 and they sub-contracted it to Heinemann in Britain and Doubleday in the United States (AWS, UK: 1972; Doubleday, US: 1973). In a lecture in the American edition of *Morning Yet on Creation Day* titled "Publishing in Africa" given at the University of Ife in 1973, Achebe commented that "we have got to a point where our literature must grow out of the social dynamics of Africa [...] What we need is an organic interaction of all three elements –writer, publisher, reader." He went on to warn with severity of publishers getting reputations of being "shoddy businessmen." Abiola Irele, the distinguished academic and publisher, also came to appreciate the importance of being the originating publisher and controlling the rights from within Nigeria (see p. 58).

On the occasion of Chinua Achebe's seventieth birthday in 2000 in a conference at Bard College in New York State College, there were contributions by the three Nobel prize-winners who are quoted on the back of this book. Ngũgĩ said on that occasion in 2000 in an interview with Maya Jaggi (see p. 8) that Chinua Achebe "made a whole generation of African people believe in themselves and in the possibility of their being writers."

Chapter Nine

# Remembering Chinua Achebe

*Henry Chakava*

Chinua Achebe who died in Boston, US, on 21st March 2013 at the age of 82 will be remembered variously as a teacher, novelist, storyteller, literary critic, poet and essayist. His literary life spanned over fifty years, from the publication of his first novel, *Things Fall Apart* (1958) to *There Was a Country* (2012), a memoir of the Nigeria Biafra war in the 1960s.

I first met Achebe in London in late 1973, in the office of Mr Alan Hill, then Chairman of the Heinemann Group of Publishers. Achebe's first novel, *Things Fall Apart* had been published in hardback by a sister company, William Heinemann, in 1958. In spite of good reviews, sales were modest and the book was virtually unavailable in Africa. It was Alan Hill who re-branded, re-packaged and re-published it in paperback in 1962, as the first title in the newly launched African Writers Series by Heinemann Educational Books, another sister company within the Group. The paperback became an instant success and found its way onto many school lists across Anglophone Africa. Indeed Hill was able to successfully use it as a flagship in establishing Heinemann branches in Africa.

On that day in October 1973, the three of us went out for lunch. Although I was a young editor of 27 on attachment to the Head Office, I did not fail to notice his simplicity and ease of communication and the fact that he gave equal attention to both of us. A few weeks later, we were to share a guest room in the home of the Managing Director of Heinemann Nigeria in Ibadan and we drove in the same car to the first conference on Indigenous African Publishing at Ile-Ife, where he was a key speaker. Not long afterwards, in early 1974, we met again this time at a Commonwealth Writers' Conference in Kampala, Uganda. We had become good friends, judging by the familiarity with which we now regarded each other.

1972 is the same year Achebe resigned as General Editor of the African Writers Series, offering consultancy services only if and when needed. An internal policy decision was made that future titles to be published in the Series would be done through mutual agreement between the Heinemann offices in London, Ibadan and Nairobi. As the Publishing Manager of the Nairobi office from 1974, I had access to Achebe, the two other offices and any other advisors I wished to consult, such as Ngũgĩ wa Thiong'o.

I was invited in 1986 by the Zimbabwe International Book Fair Committee to chair the opening address at a conference on publishing for children where Achebe and Ngũgĩ were the principal guests. Speaker after speaker emphasized the need to write in African Languages, especially children's books. Achebe was not moved, he said; "I think everyone should be allowed to write in a language they are most at home in."

Back at the hotel that evening, Achebe told me of an Igbo proverb which says, roughly put, "Where one thing stands, another stands beside it." He said that was his guiding principle. For him, it was never a question of either/or. Colonialism was bad but Western Civilization had its benefits; "it does not make sense to totally embrace Capitalism and condemn Communism. Publishing African languages need not mean deserting the English language, etc., etc.," he explained.

At the end of the Harare conference above, I felt the need to start publishing Children's books and asked Achebe if he would be willing to come to Nairobi to launch my project. Not only did he agree but he signed over four of his own children's books; *How the Leopard Got its Claws*, *Chike and the River*, *The Drum* and *The Flute*. When he arrived in Nairobi in November 1988, we had around 20 new children's books, including his own. In a highly publicized event, he toured most parts of the country giving public lectures and addressing university, college and school audiences. During that fortnight, because of high demand, we reprinted most of his novels, the rights of which we had acquired from Heinemann UK in the mid-1980s and even 2 of his new children's books! We concluded the visit in my village in Vokoli, Maragoli, where Achebe enjoyed *ugali* and smoked fish with my mother. When he heard that my elder brother had recently died, he suggested that we go and stand at his graveside, covering the half a mile distance to his compound on foot. The following day, the day we flew back to Nairobi, Achebe said he wanted to take some fish home to his wife Christie. So we went together to the fish market in Kisumu and selected smoked fish and had it properly packed for air travel.

It was not long after that visit in 1990, that Achebe had the car accident that was to change the rest of his life. His son was driving him to the airport in Lagos when they hit a tree. Quick action by those present and later, his publishers, saved his life. He was flown to a private spinal injury hospital in the

UK where he spent several months. I visited him twice over this period and it is his courage, positive attitude and the constant care and presence of his wife Christie that kept him going. He was finally discharged from hospital paralyzed from the waist down and would forever be confined to a wheel chair. Only American universities were able to employ him and provide him with the special care he needed, hence his decision to work there to his last days.

In 1996, I decided to put together some of my essays and conference papers into book form under the title *Publishing in Africa: One Man's Perspective.* In his brief introduction to my book, Achebe likened me to Alan Hill, the founder of Heinemann Educational Books and the African Writers Series mentioned earlier and made some very flattering remarks about me. God rest his soul in peace.

I remember in 2003 after *A Man of the People* had been prescribed as a set book again for Kenya Certificate of Secondary Education (KCSE), and had already done two and a half years, a section of the Catholic Church lodged a complaint about parts of this novel which they found sexually explicit and wanted it either revised or withdrawn. A visibly agitated Achebe called me from New York and in his almost shrill voice swore he would not change a single word in that novel.

"I have a medal from the Catholic Church for my writings, I don't understand this fuss over a book that has been around for so many years," he exclaimed. The book was eventually prematurely removed from the set books list.

The last time I met Chinua was at the University of London some two years ago at a celebration to mark 50 years of the African Writers Series. He looked frail in his wheelchair but happy to see me again. There was much to talk about. He told me how he would have liked to come back to Nairobi but said that he nowadays allows himself only one trip per year out of the US and that his travel arrangements were too cumbersome, anyway. He asked to see my wife and I presented her later. Little did we know that we were seeing him for the last time.

I have lost a friend, teacher, mentor and a father figure. Our 40-year-old relationship will remain etched in my memory forever. Achebe was a simple man, instantly likeable, patient, easy to communicate with and a good listener. He was a man not trapped in any ideology, who used simple words with rich meaning and whose world vision was not easily swayed. He was not an avid Christian, but he believed in strong family and social values. His philosophy of life, espoused in the Igbo proverb (where one thing stands, another stands beside it), explained above, enabled him to avoid extremes and look at things as they were, in a balanced and non- partisan manner. He was slow to anger but could react sharply when provoked. I have never forgotten the incident at the 1974 Kampala conference when he rebuked a pestering Western critic who was trying to pillory him over one of his books. "Go and write your own book if that is how you want it," he snapped.

Although Achebe is gone, he has left us *Things Fall Apart*, the book that tells us where the rain started beating us and others which are equally prophetic of our time. Indeed and without any doubt, he is the father of modern African Literature by not only having been at the forefront of it, but also trailing the blaze and helping so many of our early writers get published. He is immortalized in his works which will remain beacons of hope and inspiration for many generations to come.

MAY GOD REST HIS SOUL IN PEACE. AMEN.

Chapter Ten

# Chinua Achebe

## The Spirit Lives

*Ngũgĩ wa Thiong'o*

I first met Chinua Achebe in 1961 at Makerere University in Kampala. His novel, *Things Fall Apart,* had come out, two years before. I was then a second year student, the author of just one story, "Mugumo" published in *Penpoint,* the literary magazine of the English Department. At my request, he looked at the story and made some encouraging remarks. What I did not tell him was that I was in the middle of my first novel for a writing competition, organized by the East African Literature Bureau; what would later be published as *The River Between.*

My next encounter was more dramatic, for my part, at least and would impact my life and literary career, profoundly. It was at the now famous 1962 conference of writers of English expression. Chinua Achebe was among a long line of other literary luminaries that included Wole Soyinka, J. P. Clark, the late Eski'a Mphahlele, Lewis Nkosi and Bloke Modisane. The East African contingent consisted of Grace Ogot, Jonathan Kariara, John Nagenda and me. My invitation was on the strength of my short stories published in *Penpoint* and in *Transition.* The novel most discussed at the Conference as a model of literary restraint and excellence was *Things Fall Apart.*

But what most attracted me was not my being invited there as a 'writer' but the fact that I would be able to show Achebe the manuscript of my second novel, what would later become *Weep Not Child.* It was very generous of him to agree to look at it because, as I would learn later, he was working on his novel, *Arrow of God.* Because of that and his involvement in the conference, he could not read the whole manuscript, but he read enough to give some useful suggestions.

More importantly, he talked about the manuscript to his publishers, William Heinemann, represented at the conference by June Milne, who expressed an interest in the work. *Weep Not Child,* would later be published by William Heinemann and the paperback by Heinemann Educational Publishers, the fourth in the now famous African Writers Series, of which Achebe was the Editorial Adviser.

I was working with the *Nation* newspapers when *Weep Not Child* came out. It was April 1964 and Kenya was proud to have its first modern novel in English by a Kenyan African. Or so I thought, for the novel was well publicized in the Kenyan Newspapers, the *Sunday Nation* even carrying my interview by de Villiers, one of its senior feature writers. I assumed that every educated Kenyan would have heard about the novel. I was woken to reality when I entered a club, the most frequented by the new African elite at the time, who all greeted me as their Kenyan author of *Things Fall Apart.*

Years later at Achebe's 70th birthday celebrations at Bard College attended by Toni Morrison and Wole Soyinka, among others, I told this story of how Achebe's name had haunted my life. When Soyinka's turn to speak came, he said that I had taken the story from his mouth: he had been similarly mistaken for Chinua Achebe.

The fact is that Achebe became synonymous with the Heinemann African Writers Series and African writing as a whole. There's hardly any African writer of my generation who has not been mistaken for Chinua Achebe. I have had a few such encounters. Every African novel became *Things Fall Apart* and every writer some sort of Chinua Achebe. Even a protestation to the contrary was not always successful.

The last such encounter was in 2010 at Jomo Kenyatta Airport. Mukoma, the author of *Nairobi Heat* and I had been invited for the *Kwani?* Festival whose theme was inter-generational dialogue. Mukoma, my fourth son and I fitted the bill perfectly. As he and I walked towards immigration, a man came towards me. His hands were literally trembling as he identified himself as a Professor of Literature from Zambia. "Excuse me Mr Achebe, somebody pointed you out to me. I have long wanted to meet you."

"No, I am not the one," I said, "but here is Mr Achebe," I added, pointing at my son. I thought the obvious youth of my son would tell him that I was being facetious. But no, our Professor grabbed Mukoma's hands, before Mukoma could protest, grateful that he had at last shaken hands with his hero. The case of mistaken identity as late as 2010 shows how Achebe had become a mythical figure and rightly so.

He was the single most important figure in the development of modern African literature as writer, editor and quite simply a human being. His novel, *Things Fall Apart,* the most widely read novel in the history of African literature, since its publication in 1958, became an inspiring model. As the general editor of the Heinemann African Writers Series, he had a hand in the emergence of many other writers and their publication. As a human being, he embodied wisdom that comes from a commitment to the middle way between extremes. And of course courage in the face of personal tragedy!

The last time I met him face to face was at his 70th birthday celebrations held at Bard College. With me was Njeeri, my wife and our five year old son Thiong'o and six year old daughter, Mumbi. When I introduced James Currey and mentioned that he had been Achebe's publisher, Thiong'o decided to write his own novel on the spot. On a piece of paper, he made many marks, folded the piece and handed the one page manuscript to James Currey. James politely accepted it. Within the next one hour Thiong'o wrote several other one-page novels and began rushing them to the publisher. James Currey resorted to avoiding his new writer for the rest of the party. Mumbi reacted differently, drawing a portrait of Chinua Achebe and gave it to him when my wife took them to be photographed with Uncle Chinua. Mumbi, now a second year college student, recalled that encounter and the line drawing, when I told her about Achebe's passing on.

Achebe bestrides generations and geographies. Every country in the continent claims him as their author. Some sayings in his novels are quoted frequently as proverbs that contain a universal wisdom. When my book, *Dreams in a Time of War*, was launched in Nairobi a year or so ago, the guest speaker P.O. Lumumba interspersed his speech with proverbs. They were all taken from Achebe's *Things Fall Apart.* His passing marks the beginning of the end of an epoch. But his spirit lives on to continue inspiring yet more African writers and scholars of African literature the world over.

(First published in Leeds African Studies Bulletin No. 75, October 2013).

## Chinua Achebe: Mwandĩki wa Andũ

Ngũgĩ wa Thiong'o

Chinua Achebe aarĩ mũndũ wa andũ
No ti ta Cibũ Nanga wa ibuku rĩake

Ndamenyire ũguo rĩrĩa rĩmwe okire Kenya
Na tũgĩthiĩ nake Kamĩrĩthũ
Atumia athuuri makĩmũmbĩrĩra
Nĩ twagũtũma ũtuĩke kanua gaitũ
Wĩre thĩ yothe cia hinya witũ ithuĩ mũingĩ
Wĩre Thirikari ĩtige gũtuoha kanua
Kaania thirikari gũtũrutũrũra gĩthimainĩ gĩa gĩkeno gwitũ

O nake aacokire kũrutũrũrwo gĩthimainĩ kwao Naijĩria
Aatũire kũraya Amerika
Acoka Naijĩria akĩona mũtino njĩrainĩ
Iria aatũire oigaga irũngĩrwo andũ
Aratũire gĩtĩinĩ kĩa ngaari atindĩkagwo
No ndaatigire kũgana rũgano
Rwa gwĩkĩra ngoro mbarĩ ya Okonkwo a Abirika

Igai aratũtigĩire mabukuinĩ make
Achebe ta Aggrey nĩ mũndũ wa Andũ
Gũtirĩ handũ ha kana ha Abirika kana Thĩ
Ũtegũkora ciana ikumĩrĩire mbuku
Mũreka atĩa?
Tũrathoma Chinua Achebe
Tũrenda kũigua rũrĩa aratũganĩra

Achebe arĩ o muoyo mĩoyoinĩ ya mamirioni
Amaaragĩria na ciugo thuranĩre
Amathimagĩra thimo cia ũthamaki
Mũndũ wa andũ
Mwandĩki wa andũ ũmũ†hĩ na rũciũ

## Chinua Achebe: A Writer of the People

(Author's translation)

Achebe was a man of the people
But not like Nanga of his book

I knew this when he once came to Kenya
I took him to Kamĩrĩthũ
Village women and men mobbed him
We send you out there to be our tongue
Tell the world of the power within us
Tell the State to cease tying up our tongues
Ask them not to drive us from where our joy springs

He himself was driven from where his joy sprung
He dwelt far away from home in America
He returned to Nigeria and fell victim to crooked ways

He had always urged the powers to mend
He lived on a wheelchair
He never stopped telling story
That empowers Okonkwo's people of Africa

He left us books for a legacy
Achebe like Aggrey is a man of the people
Wherever you go in Africa and the world
You will find children bent over a book

What are you doing?
We are reading Chinua Achebe
We want hear the story he is telling us

Achebe is still alive in millions of lives
He talks to them in beautiful prose
He tells them proverbs of wisdom
He is a man of the people
A writer of the people now and tomorrow

Chapter Eleven

# Far From Ogidi

## Diary of a Belated Encounter

*Simon Gikandi*

### 1. April 2005: Meeting the Legend

It will take many years for me to meet him and when I finally do, the moment seems awkward and belated. The encounter takes place at Princeton University, where he has come to give a lecture on Afro-pessimism and I am one of the respondents. Up to this point I have prided myself on two things: First, as the perpetrator of what the author himself considers to be blasphemy – the idea that he invented African literature – and second, the undisputable factor that I, one of his major critics, have never met the author and can hence cling on to the fiction of total objectivity that once reigned in literary criticism. On the verge of my first encounter with the author, my fear is that the near anonymity that enabled me to make grandiose claims on his behalf will be tested, if not compromised. On this day, the evening of April 15, 2005 to be precise, I will try to find the longest route to the lecture hall, my nerves coming between me and the long-postponed encounter; I need to buy time to find the right language for our introduction. My task is made more daunting by the awkwardness of our relationship: I think I know him intimately through his works, but I don't know him as a person. What will I call him? Over the years I have heard my mentors Abiola Irele and Henry Chakava refer to him as "Chinua:" but I, of course, cannot assume the familiarity adopted by my elders. And yet, I can't call him Mr Achebe because that would be too familiar; nor can I call him Professor Achebe because that would be too formal, especially in a situation where everyone assumes I know him well simply because I have spent years writing about him. Trivial issues, no doubt, but this is what happens when one goes to meet a legend. I will eventually summon the courage to make it to the lecture hall and walk up the stage where he sits calmly in his wheel chair wearing a black beret; I will make my way right next to him and extend my hand; but the words of introduction will not come easily:

– Mr Achebe, I presume.

He will respond with a big smile and flatter me with the comment that he considers me the best critic of his works, but those words will be repeated to me by others because, in front of the legend I, who revels in language, is lost for words.

– Mr Achebe, I presume.

Did I say that? Later, I will realize that my choice of words was perhaps misplaced, that the cliché I have chosen to break the ice was first played out by two famous (and some might say ruthless agents of empire) in the heart of Africa. I will cringe at the idea that my first meeting with Chinua Achebe, the person who made me a writer and critic, will be rehearsed in the language of imperial encounter, the meeting between John Morton Stanley and David Livingstone at Ujiji, Tanganyika sometime in the dark days of empire. How could I reproduce an imperial cliché in front of the foremost anticolonial writer of his generation? Struggling to account for the return of the colonial repressed that once occupied the centre of my history books – in 1871 Stanley met Livingstone at Ujiji, we used to chant in fourth grade – I will be comforted by the fact that no one knows better than this author how difficult it is to exorcise the ghosts of colonialism. His big smile was perhaps recognition of the irony of the historical situation that has created Africans as subjects.

My anxieties about this first encounter with the famous writer will also be generated by a sense of belatedness, the realization although I'm just about to meet the person, I have had an intimate relationship with the author for years, that I have actually been living with him, or the idea of him, since I first read *Things Fall Apart* in my early teens. At this first encounter, I quickly discover that there is clear tension between my idea of him and the reality of his person. Having assumed that the booming and commanding voice I think I hear in his novels and the imperative nature of his writing, reflect the person who writes, the first thing that throws me off guard is the softness of his voice and the modesty of his demeanour. As I discover in the course of the evening, the source of his authority is not the preacherly, loud, voice, but the quiet tone. I will come to know this quiet authority well in future encounters, including several events commemorating the 50th anniversary of *Things Fall Apart.* Still, the problem of separating the person from the author will continue.

Having gone to university in the age of theory, I should know that there is a radical distinction between the person who writes and the institution of authorship and that the field of modern literature had been driven by an overriding imperative to topple what Roland Barthes aptly called the "empire of the author." Achebe has not expressed strong feelings about the moment of structuralism – the one that wanted the author to die so that the signs of language would triumph; at the same time, he is not overtly invested in the institution of authorship as such. Indeed, compared to his countryman, the Nobel Laureate, who has riled against structuralist mythologies, Achebe rarely includes authors as subjects in his works. And yet, now that he is gone, one cannot escape his presence in his own books, both as the centre that holds things together and as their informing mythology. In death, he emerges to loom large over his texts. Previously read as events in the emergence of a canon of African letters, these works now need to be reread against the shadow of the figure who produced them.

For me, this is not a simple task. When I didn't know him as a person, before that encounter in April 2005, I could ignore his presence and delve deep into the empire of signs, tracking down signs and signifiers, ideologies and psychologies, oblivious that there was a person writing. In a sense, I assumed that the best way of thinking about his works was to assume his absence, wish him dead as it were. And so long as he was living and thriving, I didn't feel bad wishing him dead because it was only through the imagined death of the author that his works would be liberated from the mythology of the writer. Moreover, given his foundational and dominant role in the institution of African literature, the only way one could read his works was to assume that he had no corporeal presence, that there was no body or voice behind the texts. In short, I wanted to think about his works without him and it was easy to do so when I knew he was alive somewhere – in Nssuka, in Amherst, Annadale, or Providence – going about the business of living, which was separate from the task of writing. However, imagining Achebe dead was different from thinking about his actual death.

## 2. March 2012: Intimations of Mortality

It is in March early 2012, seven years after that initial encounter in Princeton. I'm working at home when I get a call from the Nigerian correspondent of a major US newspaper; he wants to interview me about Chinua Achebe and to reflect on his literary legacy:

– What would you say was Achebe's major contribution to African literature?

– Was?

The posthumous nature of the question hits me like a brick.

– Yes, what was his major contribution…?

– Was? You mean he is dead?

There is a pause on the line.

– Is Achebe dead?

The journalist laughs and apologizes for any misunderstanding. He is just writing an obituary.

– How can you write an obituary if he is not dead?

Then I remember that obituaries – which are one of my favourite genres – are written in advance and apologize for my snappiness.

– We wish him a long life, but the time has come for us to prepare for the inevitable.

It is a polite explanation, but it doesn't resolve the crisis the intimations of the author's mortality had triggered. Confronted with the possibility, one may even say inevitability, of the author's death, my system of understanding texts by separating them from authors is thrown into crisis. Asked to think about the works in the absence of their author, I feel unhappy, thrown off track; suddenly, I have this compulsion to think about Achebe as a person and insert his presence into his texts. If my ability to write about his works was achieved at the expense of the person, now I feel the urge to rescue the personality behind the works before it disappears. But, of course, as I will learn over time, rescuing the repressed author is complicated by many factors: Firstly, the works have colonized the author so that the person who writes is only available to us through his books; there is no author outside his texts. Secondly, unlike some of his old friends from Government College, Umuahia, or University College Ibadan, those who have memories of him before he became the author, the institution of interpretation imprisons my notions of Achebe. For me, he did not exist before he was an author. Achebe the author and Achebe the person are inseparable in my mind. How then can I speak of him and my loss of him, outside the professional mandate?

## 3. April 2013: Letter to My Mother

As often happens when there are important transitions in my life and when I am struggling to put things in the context of ordinary life, I write to my mother to inform her that the month of March 2013 has been a difficult one:

– We have lost a person who was very important to us, mother

– We have lost an important African

– We have lost the conscience of Africa.

And as I often do when I have to communicate serious matters to my mother, I go to the only text she reads – the *King James Bible*, or "Gods Book" as it is called in her church – and chose the verses that will convey my loss – the opening verses of Lamentations:

> How doth the city sit solitary, that was full of people! how is she become as a widow! she that was great among the nations and princess among the provinces, how is she become tributary!
>
> She weepeth sore in the night and her tears are on her cheeks: among all her lovers she hath none to comfort her: all her friends have dealt treacherously with her, they have become her enemies.

In reply, my mother will send me a message asking for more information about this person that I have lost:

– Who was he?

– Who were his people?

She has never heard of *Things Fall Apart*, so literary genealogies will not help. I struggle to find a nomenclature that might capture the author's significance, but I find myself locked again in the vocabulary of authorship and the necessity of its translation so that my mother, for whom things literary are alien, can appreciate my loss:

– Mother, I have lost an important person.

– I have lost the person who made me an author and critic.

That is what I start writing in an email, but I don't complete or send this message because if I continue on these lines, my mother will want me to explain my relationship with this person in terms that are familiar to her. The questions that she will ask me will be predictable:

– Was this person your teacher?

– Was he your sponsor?

– How did he help you?

– What do you owe him?

How do I explain that what he was and meant to my generation and me cannot be explained in the grammar of debt and obligations?

Maybe I can translate authorship in terms that will enable it to carry the aura of writing and the scriptural economy that my mother and her generation of colonized Africans were so familiar with. I could tell her that this man, from a place called Ogidi, Nigeria (the land of Bishop Samuel Ajayi Crowther whom she read about in the *Brave Christians of Africa*) was a *Muthomi*, a reader. I could even call attention to his representation of this culture of reading in *No Longer at Ease*, especially Isaac Okonkwo's utter and complete belief in the written word as a sign of power, especially white power:

> The result of Okonkwo's mystic regard for the written word was that his room was full of old books and papers – from Blackie's Arithmetic, which he used in 1908, to Obi's Durrell, from obsolete cockroach-eaten translations of the Bible into the Onitsha dialect to yellowed Scripture

> Union Cards of 1920 and earlier. Okonkwo never destroyed a piece of paper. He had two boxes full of them. The rest were pre-served on top of his enormous cupboard, on tables, on boxes and on one corner of the floor.

With a proper translation, my mother would understand this kind of household because she and I grew up in Isaac Okonkwo's household, or one that resembled it. My mother grew up surrounded by catechists; she spent most of her life as the dutiful wife of a schoolmaster; she is certainly familiar with the people of the book. Maybe I could give my mother a sense of the magic of writing itself. I could send her a translation of that famous scene in *Arrow of God* where Ezeulu equates one's ability to write with the left hand with white power:

> When I was in Okperi I saw a young white man who was able to write his book with the left hand. From his actions I could see that he had very little sense. But he had power; he could shout in my face; he could do what he liked. Why? Because he could write with his left hand. That is why I have called you. I want you to learn and master this man's knowledge so much that if you are suddenly woken up from sleep and asked what it is you will reply. You must learn it until you can write it with your left hand. That is all I want to tell you.

This might just work. Once when I was a child, I remember my mother and her associates in the women's guild of the local church marvelling at the intelligence of the new Scottish doctor at the Tumutumu Mission Hospital. By all accounts, Dr Greene was an outstanding surgeon, but what impressed my mother and her friends was not his magic with the scalpel, but the fact that he wrote with his left hand.

However, representing Achebe as a reader is not enough; what I urgently need to convey is the significance of Achebe as a writer, a producer of texts, not its mere consumer. Above all, I need to capture the aura of writing without falling into mysticism. If I am to convey the true nature of Achebe and his meaning to me, I need to find a way of describing the author who has departed as a figure of authority without adding to my prior blasphemies. Etymologies might help in this task. In Latin, author (auctor) connotes invention, influence and command. According to the OED, the author uses invented words and is authorized by the mastery of the imagination, "to make to grow, originate, promote, increase." The modern usages of the word correlate creativity and authority in unmistakable ways, so I could safely tell my mother that Achebe was an inventor or creator (the first two definitions in the OED); I could even go further and define him as a master of written statements presented with authority (definitions three and four); I would then crown it all with the claim that he was one "who had authority over others; a director, ruler, commander." These definitions might work, especially for a generation like my mothers, which grew under colonial command. However, given his strong views on colonial and postcolonial governmentality, Achebe would be uneasy with a portrait that associates his work with command, or one that gives his voice an ecumenical status. The last thing I would like to convey to my mother is the idea that the person I have lost was as powerful as a colonial administrator or the postcolonial commandant, that he had the power of a God (to create) or Christ (to generate miracles).

I find it difficult, then, to find words that might convey the significance of Achebe in absentia. When he was still around, I could fall back on an inherited scholarly language to make large claims about the author within the institution of literature. My previous commemorations of him were conducted through his works. The Singularity of *Things Fall Apart*, I argued in an article published in *Research in African Literatures* was the mark of his presence and influence:

> For my generation of Africans born at the cusp between colonialism and decolonization, the most important event after the independence of Ghana (1957) was the publication of Chinua Achebe's *Things Fall Apart* (1958). This may appear to be an exaggerated claim especially now that we live in an age where books have lost their aura, but as a novel and event, the influence of *Things Fall Apart* in shaping the literary sensibilities of African readers was unprecedented. But the influence of Achebe's novel went beyond questions of sensibility. *Things Fall Apart* transformed the African social imaginary, the stories Africans tell about themselves, their relation to the world and their place in the narrative of modern times. It also transformed the institution of modern literature and the English language, heralding the emergence of what has come to be known as the postcolonial canon. The publication of *Things Fall Apart* changed our understanding of English and its institutions of criticism. Finally, the novel had, and continues to have, an affective, almost magical quality. In Robben Island, where he had been imprisoned for opposing the Apartheid State in South Africa, Nelson Mandela turned to *Things Fall Apart* for solace – the novel provided him with the narrative anchor that would mitigate what was supposed to be a life sentence.

Why is it easier for me to commemorate the author and his book than the person who writes? Perhaps I fail to make a distinction between commemoration and remembrance.

## 4. June 2013: Far from Ogidi

How can one mourn an institution? This is the question I will be asking myself as I take the train to Washington, DC to attend an event organized by Achebe's family to celebrate his life. The event takes place on the evening of June 2, 2013 in the hallowed halls of Andrew W. Mellon Auditorium, a federal government building. The commemoration is a memorable affair, with many distinguished scholars joining the family to celebrate the life, not work, of Achebe. In the course of the evening I will come to appreciate why that distinction – between life and work – is important. I will listen to the touching words of those who knew Achebe well – his former classmates, his family and close acquaintances. They will speak of him not as the author of *Things Fall Apart*, but as a schoolmate, a friend and a father. A close family friend will praise Achebe for having raised a great family; his Umuahia classmates, dressed in red blazers, will sing their school song together and remember him as a bad singer and poor athlete; his grandchildren will speak of his love and their loss. The most touching words and songs will be in Igbo, the mother tongue that captures the essence of family and kinship. In the midst of it all, I, an outsider to this inner circle, will struggle to see him other than the author, wondering whether the words that bring tears to the eyes of others can bring me closer to the absent one.

But why so many tears where we should be having nothing but praise songs, I wonder as the evening wears on? It is hard to tell whether we are gathered here to mourn or to celebrate.

The anthropologist Mircea Eliade called death "the paradigmatic model of all significant changes in human life." Where there is death there is meaning and understanding. But as Catherine Cole has reminded us in this paradigmatic rite of passage, "the central figure is absent." Watching footage of Achebe's funeral at Ogidi and attending his memorial in Washington DC, I will be struck by the paradox underlying the mourning rituals that surround the man of letters. By all the measures that my mother would understand Achebe has lived a full and satisfactory life:

> The days of our years are threescore years and ten; and if by reason of strength they be fourscore years, yet is their strength labour and sorrow; for it is soon cut off and we fly away. (Psalms 90: 10)

The family that leads the celebration of his life is an African success story, his professional accomplishments are obvious, the powerful take his words seriously; where then, does the heavy grief come from? It is as if the cornerstone of the African house has been smashed and everything hangs over our heads precariously. I had assumed that the powerful trooping to the funeral at Ogidi would bring nothing but crocodile tears, but on the faces of Presidents Jonathan and Mahama I see sincerity, a rare quality among the postcolonial ruling class. In Africa, where politicians have not hesitated to send authors to prison or the gallows, the powerful mourn Achebe at public forums and their grief, too, appears genuine. If Sani Abacha was alive, jokes a friend, he would have been attending the funeral at Ogidi and the hangman's grief might well be genuine. Daniel Arap Moi, the former president of Kenya, spent most of the 1980s and 1990s hunting down authors and intellectuals, banning books and controlling the curriculum to expunge it of imaginary subversives, but it is said that he had a soft spot for Achebe and his message of condolences seems to bear this out:

> Former President Daniel arap Moi sent his message of condolence describing him as a literary icon in Africa.
>
> "Chinua had, in his readable and witty literature, awakened the African peoples to the gradual disintegration of their cultures and moral values under the impact of western influences," he said in a statement released by his Press Secretary Lee Njiru.
>
> He said when he met Chinua about 25 years ago, he found him humble and self-effacing despite his immense fame worldwide.
>
> "I join his family, countrymen and his fans in mourning this great and yet humble son of Africa", said Moi.

There is one final paradox at the site of mourning: We celebrate Achebe's life universally, we grief for our loss, but our lamentations don't console. It is as if our build-up of sorrow only serves to magnify the loss. Why this deep feeling of loss when the absent one has completed his work here and proudly danced on to meet his ancestors?

## 5. September 2013: The Final Word

I have been reading *There Was a Country*, which we can now definitely take as his last word (others will be published posthumously). As I make my way through the book, ignoring the controversies that his death has now silenced,

I realize that although his death was sudden, his work was coming to a close, that this controversial book was the writer's last will and testament. Indeed, this book will put the unspeakable event at the centre of Achebe's life and that of his nation – the Biafran war – in the public sphere, so that this painful moment can be spoken of as the genocidal event that it really was rather than be hidden behind the mask of euphemism. *There Was a Country.* The startling title calls attention to the interplay of mourning and melancholy. The prose of the book has the power and authority of a rule of judgment:

> 1970 and the Fall in Biafra, the Harmattan Season leading into 1970 was particularly harsh. I remember vividly the suffering of the people; everything seemed particularly bleak. The dry, sandy air seemed to be an additional torment, delighting in covering the body with layers of this Sahara Desert's fine dust, blown in from hundreds of miles away. This made it impossible for bare, weeping, vulnerable skin lesions to heal. It was particularly hard on the children. Looking around one could see a proud, devastated people.

What is mourned is the nation that could have been. The melancholy is a reminder of repressed desires, the desire of that nation that remains repressed. But the voice that speaks, especially now that it is freed from its body, ensures that the truth witnessed cannot be denied.

Chapter Twelve

# 'A' is for Achebe

*Margaret Busby*

Two decades ago, in an interview printed in the Winter 1994 issue of the *Paris Review*, Chinua Achebe described something of his early education and being among the first graduates of the illustrious University of Ibadan, which began as an appendage of London University. "We were the University College of Ibadan of London. So I took a degree from London University. That was the way it was organized in those days. One of the signs of independence, when it came, was for Ibadan to become a full-fledged university." A particular professor he encountered there, an Englishman, told him: "We may not be able to teach you what you want or even what you need. We can only teach you what we know."

It was an admission that clearly stayed with Achebe all his life, featuring again in his essay collection *The Education of a British-Protected Child*; and it resonated powerfully with me too, Britain-educated African native that I am, who graduated from London University in the mid-sixties having been taught a literature course totally devoid of African content or component. Of course, I was not alone. In his essay "African Literature as restoration of Celebration," Chinua Achebe wrote:

> I went to a good school modelled on British public schools. I read lots of English books there. I read *Treasure Island* and *Gulliver's Travels* and *Prisoner of Zenda*, and *Oliver Twist* and *Tom Brown's School Days* and such books in their dozens. But I also encountered Ryder Haggard and John Buchan and the rest, and their "African Books."[1]

I realise now that it was, indeed, Chinua Achebe who rescued me, in a manner of speaking. When *Things Fall Apart* was first published, with its message "that African people did not hear of culture for the first time from Europeans" (as the author himself put it in his often-quoted essay "The Role of the Writer in a New Nation") I was still at an English boarding school, from which I effected an escape at the age of 15 by way of precocity at passing GCE examinations, then headed back to Ghana for what might now be called a gap year.

Soon enough, university claimed me for further education, by which time Heinemann's African Writers Series (AWS) had been launched under Achebe's editorship; and 1962 was also a milestone year for the African Writers' Conference at Makerere University in Uganda, the first major gathering of writers and critics of African literature on the African continent.

Thus it was that Achebe and the writers he chose for the list came to mentor me, privately, from afar, unbeknownst to them. In parallel to my official curriculum, during the three years in which I read for my English degree, I indulged in an unofficial curriculum that I found more relevant, which featured a dozen or so of the most inspirational writers I could have encountered during that self-alienating drought, when soul music and Black American poetry helped slake my thirst.

Achebe, of course, was number 1 in the AWS and although, then as now, statistics favoured Nigerian authors, from Equiano to Ekwensi, there were representatives from every part of Africa, including from the east of the continent James Ngũgĩ, from the south Peter Abrahams and more centrally, Cameroon's Mongo Beti. Over the ten years during which Achebe steered the list, I was introduced on the page to a diverse selection of the African continent's finest literary talents, including Ayi Kwei Armah and Flora Nwapa and Dennis Brutus and Kofi Awoonor and Wole Soyinka and Christopher Okigbo and Ousmane Sembène and Bessie Head (my AWS diet occasionally supplemented with an offering from OUP's Three Crowns series, such as by Lewis Nkosi).

In later life I would not only publish writers who would share that august company – including Buchi Emecheta and Nuruddin Farah – but there were several of that pioneering generation of internationally recognised African writers whom I would be privileged to encounter in person: Armah and Awoonor and Nwapa and Head, Brutus and Ngũgĩ and Soyinka; and of course Achebe, even meeting him on his home ground in the village of Ogidi in 1983 when I holidayed with mutual friends, Mike and Yinka Ikenzes. A special edition of the *Guardian* magazine devoted to Africa that I co-edited in 1989 would not have been complete without the favour of an Achebe contribution.

"There was a writer named Chinua Achebe in whose company the prison walls fell," was Nelson Mandela's heartfelt tribute. Achebe's words similarly continue to liberate the imagination of many – including, of course, writers of a younger generation in Nigeria such as Chimamanda Ngozi Adichie, A. Igoni Barrett, Lola Shoneyin; but the enduring legacy of his work is that it traverses borders, languages and categories. What better reminder that, given humanity's origins, we are indeed all African.

The last time I saw Chinua Achebe was at a conference celebrating the 50th anniversary of the publication of *Things Fall Apart* in London in 2008. I was left with remembrance of his perspicacity and humility, of what made him so fundamentally "pan-human". Ama Ata Aidoo in her poem "Questions"[2] once asked:

> Who would have us
> be human in a world
> of cruel beasts
> and even more cruel men?

Yet, time and again, Achebe responds in his writing with the Bantu wisdom that, "a human is a human because of other humans." To be in his purlieu enhances us all as African readers and writers. Our best choice is to start at the beginning; and in the African literary alphabet, as much as in world ranking, 'A' is always for Achebe.

Chapter Thirteen

# Chinua Achebe (1930–2013) A Summing-Up

*F. Abiola Irele*

## I

For twenty years and more before his death last March, Chinua Achebe experienced in his very person – literally, in his own flesh and blood – the kind of tragic irony that could well have been a product of his imagination. The circumstances that led to this experience have been well established. Returning from a landmark celebration of his life and work at the University of Nsukka in February1990, Achebe was involved in one of the commonest of the dramas that mark daily life in Nigeria – a road accident. The car in which he was travelling was reported to have overturned, pinning him helpless to the ground. And although he was extricated from the wreckage and flown rapidly to Britain for medical attention, he emerged from the ordeal paralyzed from the waist down and obliged to spend most of his life thereafter confined to a wheelchair. This condition seems to have had a drastic effect on his habitual contemplative mien, driving him further into the depths of the individual self. Fortunately, this development did not manifest itself as a total withdrawal from the world, as testified by the series of annual seminars on the African situation that he inaugurated when he moved to Brown University in the autumn of 2009, and most notably, the recent appearance of *There Was a Country*, the last of his works to be published in his lifetime.

What makes the irony of Achebe's experience even more striking is the fact that he was never so much celebrated as in these last years of physical incapacitation and distress, with tributes from around the world rising to a crescendo in 2008, on the fiftieth anniversary of the publication of *Things Fall Apart.* It was in this context that Achebe began to be hailed as the "father of African literature," and even credited with having "invented" the phenomenon. Claims such as this oblige us to take account of the entire field of literary expression on the continent, in order to take a proper measure of Achebe's achievements, considerable as these have been. The problem is that, in these claims, which are no doubt well meant, the term "African literature" tends to be employed in a restrictive sense, one in which the continent's literary history has been abbreviated. The term thus becomes inappropriate, if by using it, we seek to encompass the full scope of the African imagination. We hardly need to be reminded that before any of the written literatures in Africa came into being, there existed a vibrant oral tradition, as Achebe himself was well aware – a tradition that not only served as the expressive mode for the representation of life and consciousness in our indigenous cultures, but also as a foundation and an enduring background for the written literatures in the African languages as well as those inherited from Europe. This observation draws attention to the considerable range of works written in the various languages native to Africa produced throughout the history of the continent since ancient times, as in Ethiopia, for example, not to mention the literature in Arabic – works that constitute an essential part of our literary heritage. Unfortunately, the term "African literature" as currently employed tends to exclude these other areas of our expressive culture.

It can of course be argued that it was the literatures in the colonial languages that have marked the advent of what we now designate as "African literature" – the corpus that serves as reference for a new literary tradition in the making on our continent and has come to be recognized as a durable testimony of African literary achievement. In the development of this corpus that I have referred to elsewhere as "modern African literature," Achebe's work has undoubtedly played a determining role. But it is important to situate this work in the broader perspective that gives it significance. The point is that, in the process that may be termed the advent of African literature as we now understand the term, Achebe's work was preceded by earlier developments; what is indisputable, however, is that his genius came to give to this new literature a definitive consecration.

We are obliged to locate the beginnings in South Africa, in the work of early writers such as Tiyo Soga, Benedict Vilakazi and especially Sol Plaatje, whose novel *Mhudi*, published in 1913, builds on an ancestral myth to recount the fortunes of a primordial couple as symbolic of the very genesis of African self awareness – a narrative strategy that was has been reprised by Zakes Mda in his historical novel, *The Heart of Redness*, published in 2000. The force of statement in Plaatje's work and much of this early literature in South Africa determined the character of an African awakening in what may be considered the first Renaissance, anticipating developments that were to follow on a broader front in later times. Here, we are obliged to acknowledge the accomplishment of the Francophones, in their movement of cultural reclamation heralded by René Maran's forceful novel, *Batouala*. For all its ambiguity, Maran's work bears a special historic significance, anticipating Achebe by nearly a quarter of a century in the major areas of fictional reference and expressive modes that we have come to consider as distinctive of the African novel: specifically, the repudiation of colonial ideology, carried on the stream of a reinvented narrative idiom and grounded in a celebration of the African environment.

Maran's work calls attention to the special importance of the French-speaking writers in the development of modern African literature as a dimension of our new literary and cultural estate. In any account of this development, Senghor's historic 1948 anthology must be considered a significant landmark. Appearing a decade before the publication of *Things Fall Apart*, it established around the concept of "Negritude" an area of literary and ideological activity that has been productive of images and ideas from which the African affirmation derived a powerful impulse. It is significant that Olumbe Bassir's pioneering anthology, *West African Poetry*, was composed largely around the work of these Francophone writers and it is not without interest to observe that it was in this anthology that many English-speaking African readers became acquainted with Francophone African literature. It must be stressed however that, in addition to poetry, the genre privileged by the Negritude movement, the novel assumed an arresting African presence in the work of the remarkable constellation of writers represented by such figures as Paul Hazoumé, Mongo Beti, Ferdinand Oyono, Ousmane Sembène, Camara Laye and Cheikh Hamidou Kane. The impact of Oyono's *Houseboy*, which has been translated into some 14 languages, bears witness to the vitality of the Francophone novel as it came to acquire a distinctive profile, before the signs of a literary ferment became clearly recognizable in Anglophone West Africa. This ferment was signalled by the work of Kobina Sekyi in the Gold Coast, now Ghana, and the so-called pioneer poets in all the former British colonies, with Mabel Segun and Michael Dei-Anang as arguably the outstanding voices. And it was no mere chance that it was during this period that, in Nigeria, the work of Amos Tutuola, Cyprian Ekwensi and Gabriel Okara began to invite informed attention. There is a direct connection between their work and the emergence of a new idiom of African literary expression in English not only in Nigeria but also in other parts of Anglophone Africa, including East Africa

There is obviously a fuller account to be had of the development of modern African literature, but even the bare evocation of the emergence of a new literature in Africa serves to generate our understanding of this literature as testimony of our responses to the pressures of the African experience as it was defined by a new and distinctive phase of evolution. In this sense, the summary account above provides an important perspective on the work of Chinua

Achebe, for it brings into view the considerable expanse of literary creation within which this work was to find its special place – in other words, the broad stage upon which Achebe stepped out with the publication in 1958 of *Things Fall Apart.* As we are well aware, the novel rapidly assumed an innovative significance, one which it has never lost, going on to lend to modern African literature as a whole the world-wide resonance that derived from its status as a modern classic.

## II

It is instructive of the uncertain destiny of the literary work that, despite its eminent status, *Things Fall Apart* continues even now to encounter reservations, of the kind voiced by Adewale Maja-Pearce, who seems to have assumed the role of resident cynic among us. It is of critical interest in this regard to quote his summary of Achebe's novel:

> I have always considered *Things Fall Apart* a bad book, although its suffocating sentimentality about a vanished kingdom where men were virile and women virtuous – the past is always a better place, in Nigeria no less than elsewhere – presumably accounts for its 10 million readers in 50 languages who evidently like their literature to be uplifting, in this case that Africans once had cultures of great depth and beauty.

This seems an indictment which we are invited to take seriously, especially as it has been echoed by other readers, in terms that may be less gross but which lend credence to the view expressed by Maja-Pearce. It must be said, however, that the summary of the novel that he offers reflects a superficial reading of Achebe's novel. What it misses is not only the narrative power evident in the work but also the artistic integrity that informs Achebe's fashioning of his fictional world. For, contrary to the dismissive view expressed in the summary, the novel does not offer a romantic and unilateral image of the African past of the kind presumed by Maja-Pearce but presents itself rather as a reconstruction that is both complex and challenging.

It must of course be recognized that the revaluation of the African past certainly represents a major element of the ideological project that underlies the novel and Achebe has all along been quite explicit about this point in his essays, right up to his last work, in which he returns again and again to a statement of his purpose as a writer – the vindication of Africa as source and bearer of human values. In the circumstances, the novel's restatement of an African coherence before the colonial intrusion cannot but be considered legitimate, given the negative image that was presented to us of our own world in the discourse of empire, as it came through especially in colonial literature. There is perhaps no aspect of Achebe's novel that undermines this discourse more effectively than its creative recasting of the African experience in terms that resonate with our own indigenous sense of location within a specific universe of being and expression.

But it must be stressed that ideology inheres in the novel essentially as a theme that grounds the narrative structure rather than as a defining mode of imaginative thought. It functions as an element of its formulation that also entails a comprehensive re-appraisal of African historical and cultural antecedents, a task compelled by the encounter with Europe and its unsettling consequences for African existence. Thus, while the polemical intent that the fiction subserves arises clearly from the colonial context of its elaboration, this aspect of the work emerges ultimately as secondary to the effort of meditation on the African experience in which the past and its ambiguities are central to the organizing vision that informs the novel. This element runs through the work as a tension between the system of obligations and solidarities that constitute the bedrock of social experience in the precolonial, traditional society, on one hand, and on the other, the stresses exerted by the severe imperatives of material existence in an environment entirely dependent on a rudimentary technology. As one reads his first novel, one senses the contrary pulls of this tension within Achebe himself, who is writing as a westernized, educated African, caught between an identification with the social and moral values that animate and regulate collective life in Igbo society – considered here as a paradigm of precolonial Africa – and responding to the appeal of the aesthetic and symbolic order that serves to establish and to consolidate the affective bonds that make for its solidity, while he is obliged at the same time to assume an ironic and discriminating attitude towards certain defining traits of the human world that is the object of his immediate attention. We come to understand that this is an attitude inspired by the realization of the disabilities that the traditional community displays to a modern consciousness, evident in its harsh impositions on individuals and groups alike, a cultural orientation inherent in its limited understanding of the world, as judged in the light of an alternative intelligence, an expended vision, already available to Africans of Achebe's generation and education.

Thus, when Maja-Pearce speaks of the novel's re-creation of a "vanished kingdom where men were virile and women virtuous," we sense a hasty reading based on a misrepresentation of Achebe 's intention, for this is a novel that in fact projects a critical stance, amounting to a disavowal in the specific context of the novel, towards the ideal of virility. Indeed, a fundamental aspect of its narrative progression is its deliberate "deconstruction" of the masculine ethos enacted within the very dynamics of the novel. It is not without interest in this regard to observe that *Things Fall Apart* is an account of the tragic undoing of its hero, Okonkwo, the very embodiment of this ethos – a fate that derives as much from the inflexible cast of his character as from the unfolding of an implacable destiny. Moreover, far from manifesting an excessive valuation of virility as has so often been asserted, the novel reflects in its tone and movement the balance of gender values that obtains in the sphere of lived experience upon which it is focused. This aspect of the work is registered as a subtle but insistent emphasis on the feminine sensibility as a mode of social intercourse in traditional Igbo culture, and this, not so much in opposition to the masculine ethos as rather its essential complement. Thus, while the immediate functional significance of masculinity is avowed, given expression in the physical exertion required to ensure survival in the natural setting depicted by the novel – the paean to yam being the most eloquent testimony to this burden of nature – the centrality of femininity to the affective life and to the conceptual horizons of the society as registered by the novel are no less given their due. This is a theme that comes to the fore in the evocation which occupies Part Two of the novel where we are afforded a clear and endearing image of the womenfolk – the *umu-ada* – in Okonkwo's maternal village. We must add that throughout the novel's charting of the specificities of communal life in Umuofia, the figure of Chielo is accorded a prominence that reflects her distinctive status as the priestess of Agbala – in other words, as the spiritual voice of the community. Thus, in Achebe's novel, the feminine principle represents not only the province of domesticity and sensibility, but also an inviolable realm of the sacred.

## III

When we turn to *Arrow of God*, undoubtedly Chinua Achebe's masterpiece, we encounter a broader and more functional conception of the interactions between the various spheres of the communal life reconstructed in *Things Fall Apart*. It is notable in this respect that, in the later novel, the category of the sacred has come to assume a sharper sociological character, the politics of which are made manifest in the contest of wills between Ezeulu and Nwaka, the two protagonists who dominate the novel's action, each one invoking the authority of his titular deity in his claim to power and social preferment. Here, the role of the sacred has to do specifically with the internal order of the traditional system that the novel explores. For while the colonial encounter serves as the historical reference in this novel, it remains for the most part in the background, external to the daily routine of life of the native population. In other words, the colonial event is hardly deployed to sustain the narrative tenor, but serves merely as a frame that shapes Ezeulu's responses to events and points us in the direction of his fall. It is only with this tragic resolution that the colonial factor emerges as the underlying key of the novel's expressive purpose: to register the momentous shift in the African mode of relation to the world occasioned by the incursion of Europe.

*Arrow of God* is thus concerned with a fundamental moment of transition in the collective existence. Achebe's deliberate focus on the internal tensions of the native condition needs to be appreciated in this perspective, for this is a novel that goes to the very heart of the institutional and ideological fabric by which the communal compact was sustained in the demanding circumstances of traditional society and experience. The rhetoric of public discourse that occupies so much of the novel appears in this light as a mode of address designed to ensure civility in the most literal and profound sense of the term – that is, as a code that serves to impose a constraint upon individual impulses and narrow interests, while accommodating divergent but deeply held principles of social participation and religious function. Even at its moments of greatest tension, *Arrow of God* proposes a positive image of this ideological system as a stabilizing force and its expressive possibilities. At the same time, in a kind of ironic counter thrust to its valuation in moral and aesthetic terms, the narrative as it unfolds turns upon the progressive breakdown of this system, along with the entire social framework within which it functions.

The point is that this progression is inherent in the logic of history as embodied in the colonial encounter, a logic that assumes an implacable character registered early in the novel, in Ezeulu's consciousness. It can be said indeed to constitute a major point of reference for the pronounced reflective disposition of the character, emphasized by the fact that so much of the narrative is focused on Ezeulu's family ties and preoccupations, a feature that endows the narrative with a peculiar density and symbolic meaning. Ezeulu's patriarchal stature is thus conveyed not only in his superior intelligence and moral demeanour, but also in the depth of feeling that he demonstrates for his offspring, a concern that is charged with the sense of a foreboding about the implications of the white man's making his abode in their midst. We may note in this regard the special attention that is devoted to the relationship between Ezeulu and his son, Obika, whom he expects to succeed him in his priestly functions and who occupies the foreground of the novel at crucial moments. Indeed, what appears as Ezeulu's positive response to the white man is conditioned by this relationship, so that the tolling of the church bells is immediately associated with Obika's conversion to Christianity, despite what we recognize as its ambiguity and is read perceptively by Ezeulu as the sign of the passing of the traditional ways. The sense of an impending disruption of the order of things that hovers upon the course of events in the novel is fully transmitted in the powerful narration of Obika's death while running with the masquerade. The shattering effect of this incident on Ezeulu may be interpreted as a premonition of the catastrophe that overwhelms him and comes to portend the dissolution of the spiritual ground upon which the integrity of the community he represents has rested through the span of time.

The depiction of Ezeulu's personality and its bearing on the crisis of his society illuminate Achebe's conception of the character, brought out in its full dramatic significance in the scene in which Ezeulu is seen returning to his village after his release from the colonial prison, accompanied by a lone member of his household, a scene that recalls King Lear's final moments in Shakespeare's tragedy. The pathos of this scene and his descent into madness lend grandeur to the character of Ezeulu, for in his confrontation with events, he emerges as a "world historical" figure, in the same company as the victims of conquest in universal history – figures such as Turnus, Hector and Vercingentorix in western literature and more to the point, Samory and Overranwe Nogbaisi in the African context – heroes who are vanquished and yet remain significant figures of historical and moral reflection. In other words, beyond its local reference, Ezeulu's very destruction bears the sign of the paradox of history, the inscrutable principle – the "hidden god" as it were – of human experience. *Arrow of God* plumbs the depths of this experience as inscribed in our own circumstances. It is from its engagement with this theme, from the quality of enunciation of this theme, that the novel derives its effect and power.

In any appraisal of Chinua Achebe's achievement, the two novels examined here must take pride of place. They are important not only for the effort of historical and cultural reformulation to which they testify, but also for the insight they provide into the workings of Achebe's creative mind. For these are reflective novels, in a self-conscious kind of way and the responses they bring to light proceed from a double perspective, arising from the two frames of reference of Achebe's cultural location and inspiration. The primary impulse has to do with what may be termed his traditionalism, an affective embrace of what seem to him the sustaining values of the precolonial dispensation in Africa.

But it must be observed that Achebe's traditionalism was not a naïve promotion of a way of life in decline, but a principled rejection of the terms of the colonial disparagement of Africa. Over and against this ideological position must be placed a clear-sighted intellectual perception of the inadequacies of the traditional culture in the context of an emergent modernity associated with the West, an understanding that recognizes the inevitable displacement of the structure of thought that predominates in precolonial society and the life choices it determines in the objective world. That is to say, Achebe's intuition of the supercession of tradition in vital areas of thought and action upon the world haunts the extended meditation in his novels upon the African experience. The observation of this awareness points to an ideal of

African renewal as the primary reference of a commitment to modernity that Achebe has indicated as a determining element of his thought – a commitment that may not be unconditional, but one that moves decidedly beyond a passive acceptance. In short, a profound ambivalence is at the heart of Achebe's work – an ambivalence that he was never able to overcome in his long and fruitful writing career.

Chapter Fourteen

# Remembering Chinua

*Ama Ata Aidoo*

Over the last twenty odd years, there are a couple of stories Chinua Achebe seemed to like telling his audiences about me, whenever and wherever he and I found ourselves on the same panel or in any kind of a meeting. Meanwhile, and invariably, his wife Christie would be around too, nodding her head and openly cheering him on. One had to do with me as a 'small girl' who, way back in the mid-1960s showed up in his Lagos office when he was the Director of External Broadcasting at the Nigeria Broadcasting Corporation.

Corroborating any of the stories was never a problem, except that my versions start from two or so years prior to the Lagos visit. Like a few other lucky young African writers –then! – I had the privilege of fleetingly meeting Chinua Achebe in 1962. We had been invited by Ulli Beier of Mbari Club and later *Black Orpheus* fame, to a *workshop for young writers* at the University of Ibadan, Nigeria. The list of invited participants in the workshop had been made out of those of us who had sent in entries for their just-ended short story competition. They were on their way back to their various final destinations after the more 'executive' first Makerere African Writers' Conference. Obviously, Achebe and the other greats of African Literature had been asked to come by our workshop to inspire the budding lot of us.

If my memory serves me correctly at all, the more established writers we had with us at the workshop included Wole Soyinka, Kofi Awoonor, Ezekiel Mphahlele, Christopher Okigbo. John Pepper Clark, aka [Clark-Bekederemo] Cyprian Ekwensi and Lewis Nkosi. Actually, I can't remember whether Lewis was there as a young writer, or a 'veteran.' Of course, and in fairness to myself, that also goes to show how ageless Lewis was until he actually passed on. And then, can you believe this? Also visiting us were Langston Hughes [!], and

Sammy Allen, another icon of African American literature. Although we are both from Ghana and I had known of her, it was also at that time that I properly met Frances Ademola, the writer, editor, and pioneer art gallery owner. Of course, I am dropping names.

Of us the young writers, that was when I met Omolara Ogundipe and others like Lenrie Peters for the first time, However, I hope I can be forgiven either way, for including the names of people who may not have been at the workshop and more importantly, for omitting to mention many of those who had been there. Looking back, what I tell myself these days is that it was just as well that at the time I had no idea of what an incredible opportunity it all was and for symbolism, how auspicious.

A couple of years later, Ulli Beier and his second wife, the British artist Georgina Betts invited me again to Nigeria, this time to their home in Oshogbo. It is now clear to me that the purpose of the invitation was to get me to read my one story [entered for the competition] and to get me to consider myself as a writer, even at that early stage. It became obvious in the days after I got to Oshogbo that I was there to also meet his first wife Suzanne Wenger, as well as a group of young artists the trio was nurturing, including Taiwo Olaniyi, aka Twins Seven-Seven. That was when, on my way back to Ghana and at the grand age of 25, I decided to stop in Lagos and go in search of Chinua Achebe, properly.

As told by Achebe, I had emerged from somewhere in Lagos, entered the Nigeria Broadcasting complex, found my way to his office, walked to his secretary and asked her if I could see the Director. I remember that after recovering from whatever minor shock she had suffered from my gumption, the secretary had asked me whether I had an appointment. 'No', I had replied rather truthfully. Another nasty little shock to the poor secretary's system. Then sensing that the hapless secretary was going to ask me to leave, I had pleaded with her to at least, let the Chief know that I was around. The secretary obliged and Achebe had asked her to let 'the visitor' in. Given the nod, I rushed into the office of the Director of External Broadcasting at the Nigeria Broadcasting Corporation and without so much as 'good afternoon Sir,' I had raised up my hands, audibly exhaled and declared that that afternoon I had 'indeed arrived at the shrine'. By the time he got to that point, Achebe himself would be so enthralled by this story, he would double up laughing so infectiously that the audience would start laughing with him. I cannot recall how the rest of the visit to 'the shrine' progressed, or ended. What I know is that Achebe went on being Achebe. He became a bigger chief and stayed as an icon for me, even though I continued to write and in time gathered enough courage to see myself as a writer in my own right. And definitely long after I had stopped being a 'small girl.'

What I also remember is that after one of those events, some colleagues and other well-wishers who had found the story objectionable on my behalf came to commiserate with me. Their point exactly? Their point was that by insisting on telling the story over 40 years after the event and from very public platforms, Chinua Achebe was trying to assert his big male African writer self at the expense of the woman writer who had been 'the small girl. They had a point there. Or did they? The fact is that try as I did, I could not bring myself to be angry with Achebe. Why? Because he *was* Achebe. The last time I heard Achebe tell the story was in 2010 when he was giving his inaugural public lecture as the Marianna Fisher University Professor and Professor of Africana Studies at Brown University.

Now looking back, it took *Things Fall Apart* an amazingly short time between when it was published in 1958, to when, as a student, it made a difference to my perception of Literature. I was in the English Department at the University of Ghana, Legon, [1961-1964], and until I encountered this novel, I had honestly assumed that Literature, definitely with the big L, was only produced in England and by a group of writers who belonged to some sacred society called The Great Tradition. Then I encountered *Things Fall Apart* as a recommended text and it promptly took care of all that. Now, like countless African teachers on all levels of education and other millions of individuals around the world, I am intensely aware that it is *Things Fall Apart* that has chalked all those very well-documented and amazingly stellar statistics for its author. Having said all that however, I must confess that *Arrow of God* is the Achebe novel that I taught to university students all over the place and over a longer period. It will also be one of the 10 books I would take with me when I get marooned on that proverbial island.

On September 24, 2010, Achebe was awarded the lavish Dorothy and Lilian Gish Prize. The previous year, he had come to join the faculty of the Africana Studies Department at Brown University, as the Marianna Fisher University Professor and Professor of Africana Studies. It was all in order that members of the faculty were given invitations to attend the award ceremony on October 27, 2010.

So there we were, Karen Allen Baxter, Managing Director of the Department of Africana Studies Rites and Reason Theatre, Kathy Moyer, then Assistant to Professor Achebe and I, on the highway from Providence, Rhode Island to New York. Even though it was almost rained out, our trip was absolute fun, with quite a few diversions on the way. We did get to Broadway if only in the nick of time. Since it was Broadway, finding a room to change in was not a major challenge. We entered the Hudson Theatre, nice and dry, to join a beaming Chinua Achebe. It turned out to be a great evening that was made more glorious because of course Christie was present and so were a great number of his family, close and extended. Other friends and colleagues who had joined him for that evening included Sonja Sanchez, the late Jayne Cortez and Ekwueme Michael Thelwell, the renowned Jamaican writer and activist. In fact, it was Thelwell, along with Lisa Philips, who presented Achebe with the prize.

Talking of rain-sodden journeys to see Chinua and Christie and arriving just on time, the trip from Brown University to Bard College in the fall of 2004 was another. I had contacted Jesse Weaver Shipley about me visiting the Achebes. Jesse was also teaching at Bard then, and very busy campaigning and raising funds to set up The Chinua Achebe Centre for African Writers and Artists. Within the shortest possible time Jesse came back to me. The couple's response was not only that they would be delighted, but they all thought it would also be a good idea if I could read, speak, or do a little of both to the Bard community. It was raining when I got into the rented car in Providence and after about 5 hours on the road, it was still raining when I stepped out of it in Annandale-on-Hudson, New York and Bard campus. But the hall was packed and Achebe could not prevent himself from opening his remarks with you-know-which-tales!

So my confession is that I had not found it easy to mind the fact that Achebe would share reminiscences about me, especially if their telling made him feel good and hurt me none: including my pride. The other story Achebe liked telling on such occasions was the one about me making the trip in 1990 to visit him at the Paddocks Hospital in Buckinghamshire, England. He would insist on sharing that too with his audience and unwittingly, reduce Christie to tears. That had been a train journey. Had it rained that day too? Quite frankly, I had felt too anxious on that journey to even notice the weather outside. But it was fall, or autumn in England and most likely a rainy day. In any case, being African, I would still have considered it a good omen: of the wonderful news when I got there. That he would live. The rest? We do not want to go there. 'Nuff said. We miss Chinua Achebe already and always will.

Chapter Fifteen

# The Assault on Culture

## Achebe on the Crisis of Identity in Colonial Africa

*Emmanuel Akyeampong*

### Introduction: What Crisis of Identity?

As a professor of African history, I have used Achebe's novels, particularly *Things Fall Apart* (1958) and also *Arrow of God* (1964), for years to provide undergraduate students with an understanding of a West African society in the later 19th and early 20th centuries encountering Christian missionaries and the imposition of European colonial rule. Achebe paints his native Igbo society in vivid colours that brings the face-to-face communities of Umuofia (*Things Fall Apart*) and Umuaro (*Arrow of God*) alive in their quest to subsist and prosper in their natural environments, the reverence for ancestors and deities who are an integral part of daily life, the values and norms that structure social relations in the communities, and the interesting mix of meritocracy and hierarchy that characterized non-centralized Igbo society.[1] The reader empathizes with Okonkwo in *Things Fall Apart*, regrets the corrosive effect of missionaries, and potentially loses sight of the fact that the crises that ground the novel were reflections of tensions within Igbo society itself.[2] Whereas in *Things Fall Apart*, tradition in the person of Okonkwo appeared resistant at the turn of the twentieth century to change in its persistence of practices like the exposure to death of twins, seen as a abomination in a society where everything out of the ordinary had the potential to bring disequilibrium, in *Arrow of God*, shrine priests had pioneered innovations such as the abolition of facial scarification in the face of community resistance. Now in the early 20th century, tradition seemed to be actively renewing itself to stay relevant. Whereas in *Things Fall Apart*, Okonkwo's son, Nwoye, had joined the Christians to the disappointment of his father, in *Arrow of God* the chief priest of Ulu, Ezeulu, sends his son Oduche to the Christian mission school and church to became his eyes and ears in this new religion the now politically dominant white man had brought. Both novels end with indigenous religion in seeming disarray, traditional values questioned and Christianity on the ascendancy. Both novels sharply portray the crisis of identity that Christianity and colonial rule presented.

For West Africans who were born after independence and grew up in independent West Africa, with economies that were non-settler but African peasant-based, it might be difficult to comprehend the colonial period as a crisis of identity. Whether one should regard the "colonial moment" as just an episode in Africa's long history or acknowledge it as short but hugely transformative for African societies and economies continues to be debated. One may look at Ngũgĩ wa Thiong'o's *Decolonising the Mind* (1986) on the psychological and discursive impact of colonialism on the African mind and language and conclude that this might have been the reality of a settler colony like Kenya, but not Nigeria or Ghana.[3] In the early years of Ghana's independence, Kwame Nkrumah, its first head of state, creatively explored what it meant to forge an independent African state. A philosopher himself, he dialogued with philosophers like Arthur Abraham in the Philosophy Department at the then recently established University of Ghana in the 1950s and early 1960s about the philosophy and material culture of the Ghanaian nation-state. Abraham and his protégés, such as Kwasi Wiredu and Kwame Gyekye, would produce tomes that would outline Ghanaian – and Akan – thought and philosophy. For a young Ghanaian growing up in Ghana in the post-1970s, reading the prognosis of Ghanaian philosophers that Ghana has a crisis of identity at the national and personal levels would be startling. To begin with, many would not even discern that there was a crisis of identity. Wiredu locates this crisis in colonialism.

> But why is there a problem of identity in the first place? Individuals, let alone nations and whole continents, do not start wondering whether they are what they ought to be if everything seems to be going well. It is when things go wrong that critical self-analysis tends to begin. However, not everything that goes wrong with a people precipitates a crisis of self-identity; it is only the kind of reverse that injures human dignity and saps self-confidence that causes that type of soul-searching. In Africa colonialism has been such an adversity.[4]

Wiredu points to the missionary factor as instrumental in the transformation of the African worldview and as a source of this identity crisis. He comments on the missionary conflation of religious and cultural conversion, capitalizing on the superiority of European science and technology.

It was, of course, no mistake on the part of our ancestors to recognize this superiority. I mean the superiority in science and technology as manifested in the techniques and products of the colonialists. But the question is not so clear-cut when it comes to the religion, law, statecraft, mores, language, etc. which came as part of the colonial package. Having accepted one part, our people were led to transfer their approval to other parts of the package. How were they 'led' to this? It was principally through the teachings of the missionaries who came along with the colonialists to 'civilize' us and save our souls. Their campaign was only too successful. The result? A formidable distortion of the African identity.[5]

The result has been the wholesale rejection of African culture and values. For the second or third generation Christian growing up in Ghana, this might sound strange, unable to reconstruct or connect to the world that has been lost. Achebe's novels have been central in the reimagining of precolonial West Africa.

## Christian Missionaries and the Assault on African Culture

In my modern West African class, I have students read *Things Fall Apart* and an article I wrote on tradition, modernity and Christianity in the life of the Asantehene (king of Asante) Agyeman Prempeh I, who reigned from c.1888 to 1931. Prempeh was deposed and exiled to Sierra Leone in 1896, and at the beginning of the twentieth century to the Seychelles Islands, where the British held political exiles from the empire. In his desire to return home, Prempeh sought to prove his changed character by becoming Christian, adopted the name Edward on baptism, took up lessons to become literate in English, and assumed a European style of dressing. In a letter written home from the Seychelles, he encouraged the Asante to take up Christianity and literacy as their gateway to their changing world.[6] Together with *Things Fall Apart*, students are treated to a historical reconstruction and a novel, and are struck by how the themes in one source reinforced by the other. By the end of *Arrow of God*, set in the 1920s Igboland, Achebe recounts how the Christian god had literally supplanted the principal deity of Umuaro, Ulu and yams were being harvested in the name of the Christian god as protection for those who chose to defy Ulu and harvest their yams against the sanction of Ulu's priest Ezeulu. Fast forward to the 1960s, and we find that the Igbos had come to consider Christianity a central component of Igbo identity, and Igbo spokespersons would represent the Nigerian civil war between 1967 and 1970 as the assault of a Muslim Nigeria on an Igbo Christian nation.[7] Indeed, by the mid-twentieth century, an Igbo Muslim had become a contradiction in terms, and Igbo who converted to Islam from the 1930s onwards were compelled to assume Hausa names and dress. It is only recently in the 1990s with the emergence of Igbo Muslim scholars and clerics that the Igbo have managed to disentangle religion from ethnicity.[8]

How did this happen? I would rather respond to this question from the more familiar Ghanaian historical and cultural setting that I grew up in, and reflect on the missionary impact on the Akan through the instrumentality of the mission boarding school. This institution was central in the remaking of young psyches and a major contributor to the identity crisis discussed above. Missionary control of education for much of the colonial period in Ghana allowed this system to reproduce itself. Boarding schools have become central to the Ghanaian educational experience, but not many know their origins and rationale. The first generation of independent African leaders tackled the colonial and missionary legacies and Nkrumah was significant in this endeavour. While Ghana has become a predominantly Christian nation, there remains an urgent need to engage the past and to resolve the identity crises generated under colonial rule, and normalized in our lives today.

The Portuguese introduced Christianity and Roman Catholicism, to the Gold Coast settlement of Elmina in the 1480s. Dislodged by the Dutch in the 1630s, Catholicism disappeared from the Gold Coast until its return in the 1880s with the Society of African Missions. Protestant missionary history in Ghana began with the Moravians in the 1730s, followed in the mid-18th century by the Anglicans (Society for the Propagation of the Gospel or SPG). The first Anglican missionary to Ghana was the Rev. Thomas Thompson, who had been a fellow and Senior Dean of Christ's College in Cambridge. He resigned his position to take up vocation as a missionary, and he requested that the SPG post him to Ghana in 1751. He took up residence in Cape Coast, headquarters of British trading during the era of the Atlantic Slave Trade. Thompson opened a school for Africans at his own expense but closed it down due to poor attendance. Ill health forced Thompson to return to England in 1756, but he took with him three Ghanaians to be educated and trained as missionaries. Of the three only Philip Quaque survived and received Anglican orders, and returned to his native Cape Coast in 1766 as missionary, catechist and schoolmaster. Quaque run a school in Cape Coast Castle for mulatto and African children. He died in 1816, having made few converts to Christianity.[9]

Between 1828 and 1904, six major missionary societies began work in Ghana, led by the Basel Evangelical Missionary Society. By 1843 the Basel Mission had set up schools in the coastal town of Osu and the hilltop town of Akropong. Methodism gained firm roots with the arrival of the Rev. Thomas Birch Freeman, son of a West Indian father of African descent and an English mother. Freeman did not suffer the fate of earlier European missionaries who had succumbed to fevers (malaria and yellow fever), and he spent more than 52 years in Ghana as a Methodist missionary. Freeman would encourage a local ministry, aware of the heavy toll West Africa took on European lives, and appreciative that real conversion would commence once Africans had fellow

African Christians as their role models. The 19th century witnessed phenomenal expansion in missionary schools, and David Kimble has noted how Western education "was brought to the Gold Coast not in response to any pre-existing demand, but as an essential part of missionary programmes."[10] As missionary education provided employment opportunities as teachers in mission schools, in the lower echelons of the colonial bureaucracy, and as clerks in expatriate commercial companies, African demand for education grew stronger as it became associated with social mobility and the material advantages of the European.[11]

Missionaries had initial difficulty converting adult Ghanaians to Christianity despite good relations. They turned to children and to boarding schools, and Asimpi explains the rationale.

> In spite of their intimate relationship with the Ghanaians among whom they prosecuted their mission, the missionaries had little success, it is noted converting adults. For this reason, they turned to children for whom they opened schools and began to raise and nurture them in the Christian faith. To ensure their complete conversion, the missionaries felt that their converts must not live in their own communities but must instead be segregated. Behind this approach was the missionaries' conviction that the Ghanaian indigenous social and religious institutions were 'depraved' and filled with 'heathenism'. They therefore decided to create segregated communities that would physically and socially isolate the missionized.[12]

Asimpi observes that within months of his arrival in Ghana in 1838, Rev. Freeman wrote to the Wesleyan Mission Committee in London recommending the establishment of a boarding school, which would be set apart from the community.[13] Schools were built on mission stations, usually located outside the town, and students were allowed little or no contact with the local community. Seeing African culture and lifeways as the impediment to Christian conversion, buoyed by feelings of racial superiority, missionaries in addition to academic subjects instructed African children in the mission boarding schools in European ways of life – dress, food, music, etc. Missionaries forbade school children from participating in indigenous religious and traditional ceremonies. Segregated communities for the missionized were a strong feature of the Basel, Bremen, and Methodist Missions.

The relationship between education and proselytization lay at the heart of mission schools. Missionaries saw their aim as the conversion of Ghanaians to Christianity. Education was a primary avenue for achieving this goal; in short, "schools became the tools of evangelization."[14] Initial experimentation with day schools was unsatisfactory for the missionaries, as they viewed pupils as still being in touch with "pagan" environments. Missionaries took Ghanaian children into their homes as students to insulate them from their local communities, and the success of this endeavour encouraged the setting up of boarding schools. The Basel Mission set up the first boarding schools in 1853: two in Abokobi and Aburi for girls offering instruction in the local languages of Ga and Twi; and two in Christiansborg and Akropong for boys also offering instruction in Ga and Twi. The Basel Mission would reform its school system between 1858 and 1861, setting up six-year primary and four-year middle schools. Together they provided the equivalent of the English elementary school, and they emphasized religious instruction and character training. The middle boarding schools were usually headed by a missionary and offered instruction in Theology, Exegesis, Mathematics, Geography, World History and Science. The vernaculars were the medium of instruction and English and Greek were offered in the final year of the middle school to prepare those going to seminary. The Basel Mission's education structure was adopted by the colonial government and made the model for all other mission societies.[15] The Basel Mission established a seminary at Akropong in 1848, which also doubled as a teacher training college. Vernacular was again the medium of instruction at the seminary.

For the Basel Mission, the priority was to convert Ghanaians to Christianity with enough education for them to read the Bible, use the hymnal, and to be in a position to proselytize in their local communities. Their concern was not to provide an academic education, and hence the mission did not establish secondary schools along the model of the English Grammar School or the German Gymnasium. As late as in 1933 the Basel Mission and its associated Scottish Mission denied its membership the need to establish a secondary school in Ghana. Though the leadership of the Basel Mission was highly educated and was drawn from elite families in Switzerland, the missionaries who were sent to Ghana were from humble social backgrounds with average education. It was difficult for these men in the field to appreciate the need for a higher education for Africans.[16] With this foundation, there is a sense in which the system reproduced itself over the colonial period, as missions sought to attract their talented students as teachers and catechists, who then taught the next generation of students. There were novel experiments, such as Mfantsipim in Cape Coast, founded on the initiative of educated Fante in partnership with the Methodist Mission in 1876, in pursuit of a new type of secondary education for Gold Coasters. These educated Fante provided part of the funding for Mfantsipim. The first government secondary school was Achimota College, established in 1927. So for much of the colonial period the provision of education in Ghana was under the direction of Christian missionaries.

## An African Renaissance: Independence and the Rebirth of African Culture

On independence, Ghana's first head of State, Kwame Nkrumah, wrestled with this colonial legacy, and identified the twining of political and cultural nationalism as an urgent necessity. There was the challenge of building an "African nation-state" due to the desire of nationalists not to replicate the colonial state or the metropolitan government of the colonizer. This required an excavation of the African past, a plumbing of both history and culture. A philosopher, theologian, historian and sociologist, Nkrumah explored the construction of a requisite African philosophy to guide his attempt at forging a political economy ideally suited to the African condition and reflective of Africa's past. He named his philosophy *Consciencism.* This philosophy would take cognizance of what Nkrumah termed Africa's triple heritage, yet transcend the limitations inherent in these.

> African society has one segment which comprises our traditional way of life; it has a second segment which is filled by the presence of the Islamic tradition in Africa; it has a final segment which represents the infiltration of the Christian tradition and culture of Western Europe into Africa, using colonialism and neo-colonialism as its primary vehicles. These different segments are animated by competing ideologies. But since society implies a certain dynamic unity, there needs to emerge an ideology which, genuinely catering for the needs of all, will take the place of the competing ideologies, and so reflect the dynamic unity of society, and be guide to the society's continual progress.[17]

Nkrumah thus appreciated the importance of the past, and how a viable society and it's ideology needed to be based on its past. But the institution that best represented the past in Ghana, chieftaincy, was also what framed tribalism, seen as an impediment to nation building. Nkrumah thus faced an important paradox: chieftaincy, the one historical and cultural institution that promised an indigenous political culture on which to found an African nation-state, was also the institution with deep local loyalties that buttressed ethnic identities. Nkrumah's solution was to tap into the material culture of chieftaincy from the several ethnic groups in Ghana, creating, as it were, a composite national political culture, reflective of the whole, but not the mirror any particular chieftaincy tradition.

Nkrumah commissioned research, created state paraphernalia that included a state stool, sword used for swearing in ceremonies, ceremonial horns and even a state linguist or spokesperson. In a spirit of religious pluralism, state ceremonies were inaugurated by prayers by an Imam, Christian priest or minister, and an indigenous priest (libation). He tapped the chief priestess of Akonedi Shrine in Larteh, Nana Akua Oparebea, to found the Ghana Psychic and Traditional Healing Association.[18] This was the cultural nationalism that was an essential part of African political nationalism. Nkrumah was a patron of a philosophy circle and the first and second generations of philosophers at the University of Ghana, prominently William Emmanuel Abraham, Kwasi Wiredu and Kwame Gyekye, wrote nuanced works about Akan and Ghanaian cultures and communities, examining morality, values and ethics and the relationship between community and the individual.[19] The timing of the publication of Achebe's two novels referenced in this work, *Things Fall Apart* (1958) and *Arrow of God* (1964) is instructive, as they form part of this larger quest to recreate the lived experiences, the thought patterns and the spirituality of a past era for a newly independent Africa. They were published shortly after the independence of Ghana and Nigeria respectively. What happened to this vibrant era of cultural, literary and intellectual creativity? The overthrow of Nkrumah in 1966 encouraged a turn against all things Nkrumah, including his cultural experimentation.

The advent of the born-again movement in Africa from the 1970s, marked by the new Pentecostal or "Charismatic" movement reinforced this turn against indigenous religion and culture. Concerned with "ancestral curses," born-again Christians advocate the complete rejection of the past, unwilling to distinguish between indigenous religion and culture, afraid that opening the door to one would lead to the other. Birgit Meyer observes, how "by emphasizing continuously that being *born again* entails a 'complete break with the past,' Pentecostals even celebrate the notion of rupture much more than the nineteenth and early twentieth-century Protestant missionaries."[20] For reconstructions of the Ghanaian past, we can turn to the work of historians and philosophers and Ghanaian philosophers trained under the aegis of Abraham have produced some of the most illuminating studies of the Akan and other peoples.[21] But how many Ghanaians, Africans or non-Africans turn naturally to works of philosophy or history for information on the African past or to acquire a flavour of past times? This is where works of fiction have been instrumental and novelists like Achebe through a creativity that is historically informed write novels like *Things Fall Apart* and *Arrow of God* that keep us turning the pages.

## Conclusion

In 1949, barely a decade before Ghana's independence in 1957, Christians comprised 30% of the Ghanaian population with indigenous religionists accounting for 66% and Muslims for 4%. Christians had become the largest religious denomination in 1960, representing 42.8% of Ghanaians, indigenous religionists 38.2%, and Muslims 12%. By 2000, Christians constituted a large majority with 68.8% of the total population, Muslims had grown to 15.9%, and indigenous religionists had declined to 8.5%. Lived spirituality is, however, more complex and the inter-penetration of different religious influences in the lives of individual Ghanaians are common. Ogbu Kalu notes how indigenous worldviews penetrate the context of urbanity and urban culture and how even Pentecostal practices originate in rural contexts.[22] Signboards of shrines by the major roads in Ghana, especially in the countryside, provide a point of entry into the collage that informs Ghanaian religiosity and on a recent road trip (August 2013) from Accra on the coast to Bole in Northern Ghana, I had opportunity to take several photographs.

In labelling Africa's crisis of identity a normative one, Wiredu also raised a set of dilemmas that come through change, voluntary or imposed, that Ghanaians have to deal with today. Ghanaians under colonial rule may have had Christianity foisted on them. Today we have third and fourth generation Ghanaian Christians born into Christian families. Whereas the first generation of independent African leaders felt the need to recuperate an African past or political tradition as the basis of an African nation-state, Ghanaians and Africans today might be content with the western democratic institutions that they seek to work with. Wiredu frames the conundrum succinctly.

> 'Why should we be other than we currently are?' The answer of anti-colonial nationalism is: 'Because we became what we are now, not of our own free will, but rather through a colonial imposition.' But suppose what we are now happens to be better than what we used to be? Or suppose that even though what we are now is no good, still what we were in the past was either no good or, if good in its time, ill-suited to the present time. Then what?[23]

I argue not for a return to a past culture, but to be informed of our history and culture. As a third-generation Christian, I cannot envision living my life by any other faith. At the same time, signboards like the two above and Ghanaian and Nigerian video films with their preoccupation with witchcraft, are reminders of cultural and historical legacies that are ill understood. The result is a schizophrenic Christianity, with Ghanaians, Nigerians and other Africans reluctant to interrogate the sensibilities that inform their spirituality and largely unaware of the impact the colonial assault on our cultural identities have had on the lives we live today. Crises become the moment of truth, revealing where African religious loyalties lie in their search for spiritual intervention or aid. Novels like Achebe's *Things Fall Apart* and *Arrow of God* are immensely important in leading Africans and non-Africans back into African community life on the eve of colonialism and under colonial rule and they kindle a broader interest in African history, philosophy, art, music and other disciplines.

Chapter Sixteen

# "I Haven't Seen You In 400 Years!" Chinua Achebe and African American Writing

*Anne V. Adams*

The first visit to the US in 1963, by the young Nigerian journalist, by then the author of two novels, was animated by his desire to "find out how the Africans in the Diaspora were faring" (1987: 554) and particularly to meet the African American novelist James Baldwin, whose work he had become acquainted with at home in Nigeria. (Ironically, in his British colonial education, where American literature, considered unworthy, was absolutely not taught, the sole text by an American that was available to Achebe – or to African pupils in any of the British colonial schools around the continent – was Booker T. Washington's autobiography, *Up From Slavery*.) Hence, having encountered Baldwin's *Go Tell It on the Mountain*, the young writer Achebe was "instantly captivated. …It combined the strange and familiar in a way that was entirely new" (Terry 554). In fact Achebe was so taken by the novel that he successfully prevailed upon the American Embassy's library in Lagos to stock more of this American writer's works. So, in accepting a UNESCO fellowship to visit the US he "wanted very much to meet this man with the fearless utterance of Old Testament prophets, and the clarity, eloquence and intelligence of ancient African griots" (2002: 502).

However, as Baldwin was sojourning in France when Achebe arrived in the US, he had to wait nearly two decades, until 1980, to meet his admired writer. By this time, as both men's works were being read all over the world on literature courses, the meeting happened at a public event, the annual conference of the then young African Literature Association, in Gainesville, Florida. The meeting was climactic for both of them and momentous for the community of African and Diaspora literature. After his decades-long "trek," finally brought the two writers face-to-face in "the jungles of Florida" (Terry 554), Achebe's greeting amounted to a *signifying* version of Henry Stanley's salutation to David Livingston, in the jungles of Africa: "Mr Baldwin, I presume." Baldwin, visibly delighted and equally ready with a *signifying* riposte, replied, "You're the brother I haven't seen in 400 years! … It was never intended that we should meet." (Achebe 2002: 503)

As though affirming the long-lost-brotherhood, Baldwin said of Achebe's *Things Fall Apart*, which he had read while in France (when Achebe was in the US looking for him) – that although the book was about people and customs unfamiliar to him, nevertheless, "'reading it I recognized everybody. … That man Okonkwo was my father. How he got over I don't know, but he did.'" (qtd. in Achebe 2002: 503). In another version of that meeting, recounted in an interview, Achebe said that Baldwin put it this way: "That book is about my father!" Baldwin's father who, in the son's opinion, could not bend but only be broken. Certainly, a stark "family resemblance" can be found between the rigid, tyrannical, self-righteous Okonkwo of Umuofia, who despises his sensitive son Nwoye for his deviation from the path of righteous Igbo manhood and the equally rigid, equally self-righteous Gabriel of Harlem, a figure based largely on Baldwin's own father, who similarly despises his sensitive son John for his childhood resistance to the path toward righteous African American manhood. About their meeting Baldwin said, further:

> I want to suggest an enormous proposition which I want you to think of very seriously. It is not an accident that we are here tonight. It is not an accident that my brother crossed so much water, and so many miles, and so many years to be here. It is not an accident that we both arrived here 400 years ago chained to each other because he spoke one tribal language and I spoke another. And had we been allowed to speak to each other, the institution of chattel slavery would have been doomed (Tsuruta 75–76).

However, when Achebe did take the opportunity to articulate Baldwin's qualities as a writer that resonated with him, he referred to Baldwin's non-fiction. Achebe's evaluation centred around Baldwin's insistence on the notion that black people simply wanted to be acknowledged and treated as human beings. Achebe cites the Uncle James's advice to his namesake nephew in Baldwin's *The Fire Next Time*, warning the youngster that "[I]t was intended that you should perish in the ghetto. Perish by never being allowed to go behind the white man's definitions, by being never allowed to spell your name, your proper name" (Baldwin 336; qtd. in Achebe 1989: 6). Or, as in Baldwin's essay, "Fifth Avenue, Uptown," which Achebe quotes: "*Negroes want to be treated like men*: a perfectly straightforward statement containing seven words. People who have mastered Kant, Hegel, Shakespeare, Marx,

Freud and the Bible find this statement impenetrable" (Baldwin 211; qtd. in Achebe 1987: 555, emphasis in original). Such "a wilful, obdurate refusal," as Achebe paraphrases Baldwin, resonates particularly with Achebe's now-famous criticism of Joseph Conrad's *Heart of Darkness*, about which more will be said below.

Achebe would take one final opportunity to inscribe James Baldwin's significance for him into his own oeuvre, when Baldwin's death, in 1987, impelled his Nigerian admirer to have his publishers stop the presses in the production of *Hopes and Impediments* in order to add a "Postscript" in remembrance of this historical and intellectual 'brother.' So, in his "Preface" Achebe tells of the "curious coincidence" of being able to conclude his essay collection that opens with the criticism of Joseph Conrad's racism, with a tribute to Baldwin, "one of the most intrepid fighters against racism":

> Conrad and Baldwin; two very different writers separated by almost every barrier we cherish – *time* (Baldwin was born the very year Conrad died); a Polish exile in England and an American exile in France and greatest of all perhaps, *race* (one white and the other black).
>
> This last turns out to be the most crucial in its consequences, for while Conrad casually wrote words that continue to give morale to the barricades of racism, Baldwin spent his talents subverting them. Impediments and Hopes! (1988: xiii-xiv)

Of the invaluable oeuvre that Achebe has bequeathed to the world of letters, to the pursuit of morality, especially, through art, it is the little piece, the now canonical essay, "that was heard all over the world," "Image of Africa," his analysis of racism in Joseph Conrad's *Heart of Darkness*, re-printed as the opening essay in the collection *Hopes and Impediments*, that I want to set in dialogue here with a critical study by another African American writer, Toni Morrison's essay series *Playing in the Dark: Whiteness and the Literary Imagination.*

We recall that Achebe's text was presented originally in 1975 as the second Chancellor's Lecture at the University of Massachusetts, Amherst, and was published subsequently in *The Massachusetts Review* and re-published in 1989 in *Hopes and Impediments.* Acknowledging Conrad as a major writer deserving of the status, Achebe nevertheless branded him, in the lecture, a "bloody racist," revising it in the published version to "*thoroughgoing* racist." Regardless of the nuanced choice of descriptor, "racist" was the operative noun. We know also of the sensation caused by the essay, prompting rounds of published defences of Conrad and of the sanctity of this novella, by scholars from around the world, including Africa; attacks on Achebe, even accusing him, in giving the talk, of "relish[ing] the prospect of stirring things up, perhaps shocking his hosts and taking a cultural revenge" (Watts 197). While most of the rebuttals are not such attacks, they essentially defend Conrad through Marlowe as a liberal but a product of his time: Bruce Fleming, who titled his article "Brothers under the Skin" writes, in a conciliatory tone: "We may place Achebe and Conrad side by side, ...even teach them together – but at the same time we must acknowledge that neither can hope to win such a confrontation. They are caught in history, like us all and hence related for that reason: related in their very divergences" (Fleming 98).

In fact, the proposition to "place Achebe and Conrad side by side," as Fleming rhetorically suggests, is exactly what eventually came to pass: Thirteen years after the "lecture that was heard around the world" was given, the 1988 Norton Critical edition of *Heart of Darkness* included Achebe's essay. So that, as Padmini Mongia, in her essay abstracting the major arguments in the critics' campaign to "rescue" *Heart of Darkness* and its author, sums up the state of the debate: "Achebe's perspective has become virtually as canonized as Conrad's novella, so that Conrad and Achebe are often taught in the Euro-American academy alongside each other" (Mongia 308).

Let us review what Achebe said and did in that lecture that became a literary-historic event. As Mongia, in contrast to the other critics, points out, Achebe's subject was *not* a critique of *Heart of Darkness.* Rather, she emphasizes, it was Achebe's exposition of what he perceived as "the desire – one might say the need – in Western psychology to set Africa up as a foil to Europe, as a place of negations at once remote and vaguely familiar, in comparison with which Europe's own state of spiritual grace will be manifest" (Achebe 1989: 2–3). Acknowledging that, since he doesn't possess the "tools of the social and biological sciences," Achebe announces that he approaches the matter, rather, as a novelist reading a novel. His choice of Conrad's *Heart of Darkness* not only "displays that Western desire and need...better than any work I know," but because of that work's canonical status, as a work of "permanent literature – read and taught and constantly revaluated by serious academics," (1989: 3), it was numbered "among the half-dozen greatest short novels in the English language" (qtd in 1989: 3).

The specific aspects of Conrad's work that inspire in Achebe the epithet "bloody/thoroughgoing racist," are the dehumanization of the Africans, through depriving them of language and the representation of them as "rudimentary souls" in comparison with the Europeans.

> Africa as setting and backdrop which eliminates the African as human factor. Africa as a metaphysical battlefield devoid of all recognizable

> humanity, into which the wandering European enters at his peril. Can nobody see the preposterous and perverse arrogance in thus reducing Africa to the role of props for the break-up of one petty European mind? But that is not even the point. The real question is the dehumanization of Africa and Africans which this age-long attitude has fostered and continues to foster in the world. And the question is whether a novel which celebrates this dehumanization, which depersonalizes a portion of the human race, can be called a great work of art. My answer is: No, it cannot. I do not doubt Conrad's great talents. Even *Heart of Darkness* has its memorably good passages and moments. Its exploration of the minds of the European characters is often penetrating and full of insight. But all that has been more than fully discussed in the last fifty years. His obvious racism has, however, not been addressed. And it is high time it was! (1989: 12-13).

In spite of the supposed indefensibility of Achebe's arguments, scholars nevertheless continued to "write back" to him on the issue for years to come. And, in 2000, while contending that it was not his intention then or now to spend the rest of his life in Conrad controversy, Achebe did restate his point in an essay accompanying a book of photographs on Africa, *Another Africa.*

In the final analysis, a major part of Achebe's legacy is having impacted the course of Western literary criticism, through initiating this exploration of the issue of racism in *Heart of Darkness.* Whether the accusation of "deliberately provoking the critical establishment" (Mongia 309) is justified or not, through this iconoclastic act, Achebe brought the engagement with both Western and African literatures to a new level. Its significance is only heightened through the context in which it was given, that is, the prestigious Chancellor's lecture of one of the most liberal of American education institutions.

That was, ironically, precisely the same provocative situation of Toni Morrison's William E. Massey Sr. Lectures in the History of American Civilization, at Princeton University, in 1990, which became published as *Playing in the Dark: Whiteness and the Literary Imagination.* As with Achebe, Morrison is speaking from her position as a *reader* and *writer*, not as a critic. In fact, in emphasizing that position Morrison even makes use of the same working term as had Achebe, who described himself as "a novelist responding to one famous book" (1989: 3), lacking the "*tools* of the social or biological sciences"; Morrison, describing herself as first a reader-who-became-a-writer, would not be "bring[ing] to these matters … the *tools* of a literary critic" (Morrison 3).

Acknowledging, however, the intention to sketch what was to unfold as a critical project that would be "attractive, fruitful, and *provocative*" (3),

Morrison declares as her project the "extending [of] the study of American literature into...a wider landscape" (3) with the specific objective of "avert[ing] the critical gaze from the racial object to the racial subject; from the described and imagined to the describers and imaginers; from the serving to the served" (90). In effect, this is what Achebe had initiated: he extended the study of a work of European literature into a wider landscape, averting the gaze from the Africans to Marlow and Kurtz. Now, whereas Achebe, in his 1975 lecture, took on only one writer, Morrison, lecturing a quarter-century later, takes on a gang of them, heavyweights: Ernest Hemingway, Edgar Allan Poe, Willa Cather and Mark Twain.

To convey the effects of a black presence in mainstream American literature Morrison adapts the term "Africanism" to her purpose: "for the denotative and connotative blackness that African peoples have come to signify as well as the entire range of views, assumptions, readings and misreadings that accompany Eurocentric learning about these people" (6-7). For Achebe it was a "willful tenacity with which the West holds" ... to its heart...distortions and cheap mystifications" (18) a stereotype image of Africans.

Both writers, again using the same language, point out the passive presentation of blacks as inconsequential "props": Morrison, describing her early readings of some American classics: "I assumed that since the author was not black, the appearance of Africanist characters or narrative or idiom in a work could never be *about* anything other than the 'normal,' unracialized, illusory white world that provided the fictional backdrop" (16). Achebe, in the contextualizing remarks of his lecture, tells of a comment from a Scottish student who said of *Heart of Darkness*: "Africa is merely a setting for the disintegration of the mind of Mr Kurtz," which stirs Achebe's reaction: "[This is] partly the point. Africa as setting and backdrop which eliminates the African as human factor. Africa as a metaphysical battlefield devoid of all recognizable humanity, into which the wandering European enters at his peril" (1988: 12).

However, beyond the appearance of being mere backdrop, the two writers recognize a critical function of the Africanist presence in contributing to the construction of the white subjects themselves. The continuation of Achebe's reaction to the Scottish student's point expresses his full vitriol at such ego-centricism on the part of Europeans: "Can nobody see the preposterous and perverse arrogance in thus reducing Africa to the role of props for the break-up of one petty European mind?" (1988: 12). For Achebe, such racial ego-centrism was the product of what he had identified as the Westerner's desire, if not need, of the African as a foil to establish Europe's own "state of spiritual grace" (1988: 2–3).

We recall that, for Achebe, the crucial human feature that Conrad denies the Africans is language. Underscored by Marlow's labelling of the Africans as "rudimentary" souls, it is on the factor of the human feature of language that Achebe's labelling of "racism" ultimately rests:

> [T]he most significant difference [between the white woman and the African Amazon] is the one implied in the author's bestowal of human expression to the one and the withholding of it from the other. It is clearly not part of Conrad's purpose to confer language on the "rudimentary souls" of Africa. In place of speech they made "a violent babble of uncouth sounds." They "exchanged short grunting phrases" even among themselves (1988: 8).

The denial of the human-defining attribute of speech to the Africanist presence is the object of Morrison's detailed scrutiny of Ernest Hemingway's novel *To Have and Have Not* (1937). Discussing the "nigger" that Hemingway has created, hired by the protagonist, a white man named Harry, Morrison says: "This black character either does not speak (as a 'nigger' he is silent) or speaks in very legislated and manipulated ways. Enforcing the silence of the 'nigger' proves problematic in this action-narrative and requires of Hemingway some strenuous measures" (71). After all, hadn't Morrison asserted, in her Nobel lecture, her idea of the power of language "partly as a system, partly as a living thing over which one has control, but *mostly as agency – as an act with consequences*"? (Nobel Lecture, Dec. 8, 1993, emphasis added).

Morrison locates the source of her project with American literature as arising from what she knows "about the ways writers transform aspects of their social grounding into aspects of language" (4). As such, she finds that national literatures "end up describing and inscribing what is really on the national mind" and that "[for] the most part, the literature of the United States has taken as its concern the architecture of a *new white man*" (14-15). Citing Ralph Waldo Emerson as an articulator of this idea, Morrison calls attention to the "deliberateness of the construction, the conscious necessity for establishing difference" (39), particularly in 19th-century American literary works.

Transferring this theory to Conrad's Britain, Morrison's notion of the contribution of national texts to the construction of the European national male persona inspired a historian's re-examination of Britain's canonical national history text, Thomas Macaulay's *History of England*, focusing on the late 17th century, but published in the mid-nineteenth century, about half-a-century before Conrad's *Heart of Darkness.* Catherine Hall, the British historian who has written the article "*Playing in the Dark* ... and racing Englishness," credits Morrison's book as both inspiring and speaking to her directly about her discipline, history, "and the ways that it might be possible to rethink how British historians have encoded and evaded the issue of race" (Hall

88). Extending Morrison's theory to her own discipline, Hall says: "[N]ational histories, like national literatures, both describe and inscribe what is on 'the national mind'" (89). Similar to Morrison's idea of the crucial presence of the American Africanist Other in the construction of the American self-image, Hall reached the conclusion that "Empire...was central to definitions of Englishness" (88). And, even though Morrison was writing about a white American whose Africanist Other was physically a part of his landscape, Hall found, of Britain, that race "was lived *outside*, through empire, and that outside was constitutive of the inside" (Hall 88). She cites attributes of Englishness as being essentially the same as those mentioned by Morrison for America: "freedom, liberty, the rights of the individual, the antithesis of which was slavery" (Hall 88–89). Yet Macaulay's *History* mentions nothing about the slave trade:

> the Royal African Company, the expansion of London and its docks, the slave ships in Bristol, the merchants who made their fortunes in that trade and became key players in the new global financial markets. Nor about the sugar which gradually became part of the consumer revolution, bringing sweetness to those teas, coffees and chocolates which were arriving from the empire. ...The history of England as Macaulay imagined it could be told outside of empire (Hall 89).

Achebe and Morrison, in entering what each felt was uncharted territory, by scrutinizing classic texts of Western literature for the function of the presence of blacks, express an urgency for this previously unattended-to task to be taken up. Indeed, in calling Conrad a "thoroughgoing racist," Achebe justifies his point by saying that "white racism against Africa is such a normal way of thinking that its manifestations go completely unremarked" (1988:12). Therefore, Achebe says later, "Although the work of redressing which needs to be done may appear too daunting, I believe it is not one day too soon to begin. Conrad saw and condemned the evil of imperial exploitation but was strangely unaware of the racism on which it sharpened its iron tooth" (1988: 19).

There is one point that I have identified as a divergence between the positions of Achebe and Morrison: that is the matter of the accusation of racism on the part of the writer himself. But I think it is less a divergence than a refinement in the focus of attention, resulting partly from the evolution of the debate over time. While Achebe declared Conrad, the author, to be the "bloody racist," Morrison wanted to make it clear that her project was not concerned with the author's own racial attitudes. Nor did she take a position on the quality of a work based on the "attitudes of an author or whatever representations are made of some group" (90). (Was she thinking of Achebe's essay here?) But she did go on to say that such evaluations of works of some other canonical European writers are indeed taking place and that such studies do "fall within the reach" of her project (90).

Morrison, in her lectures, was indeed taking on the task urged by Achebe, of "redressing," and with the same emphasis as Achebe's, for the *correcting of the historical record.* She says: "Reading and charting the emergence of an Africanist persona in the development of a national literature is both a fascinating project and an urgent one, if the history and criticism of our literature is to become accurate. … A major item to be added … must be an Africanist presence – decidedly not American, decidedly other" (48).

I am convinced that Morrison's work is a beneficiary of Achebe's: her *Playing (…)* could be *heard* because of the *noise* that Achebe's essay had made a quarter-century earlier. Symbolically, James Baldwin's greeting to Achebe about not having seen his 'brother' since four centuries earlier was an acknowledgment of Pan African literary connections that were already in formation and that buttressed other Pan African intellectual connections since the colonial era. Hence, through such specific connections as exemplified between the writers Achebe and Baldwin and through theoretical connections as exemplified here between the work of Achebe and Morrison, Achebe's legacy substantiates the "African" of "African American" in literature. Of equal importance, his legacy leads the way to a re-setting of the racial gaze in the criticism of European/American literature.

Chapter Seventeen

# Chinua Achebe at 82

## We Remember Differently

*Chimamanda Ngozi Adichie*

I have met Chinua Achebe only three times. The first, at the National Arts Club in Manhattan, I joined the admiring circle around him. A gentle-faced man in a wheelchair.

"Good evening, sir. I'm Chimamanda Adichie," I said, and he replied, mildly, "I thought you were running away from me."

I mumbled, nervous, grateful for the crush of people around us. I had been running away from him. After my first novel was published, I received an email from his son. *My dad has just read your novel and liked it very much. He wants you to call him at this number.* I read it over and over, breathless with excitement. But I never called. A few years later, my editor sent Achebe a manuscript of my second novel. She did not tell me, because she wanted to shield me from the possibility of disappointment. One afternoon, she called. "Chimamanda, are you sitting down? I have wonderful news." She read me the blurb Achebe had just sent her. *We do not usually associate wisdom with beginners, but here is a new writer endowed with the gift of ancient storytellers. Adichie knows what is at stake, and what to do about it. She is fearless or she would not have taken on the intimidating horror of Nigeria's civil war.* Adichie came almost fully made. Afterwards, I held on to the phone and wept. I have memorized those words. In my mind, they glimmer still, the validation of a writer whose work had validated me.

I grew up writing imitative stories. Of characters eating food I had never seen and having conversations I had never heard. They might have been good or bad, those stories, but they were emotionally false, they were not mine. Then came a glorious awakening: Chinua Achebe's fiction. Here were familiar characters who felt true; here was language that captured my two worlds; here was a writer writing not what he felt he should write but what he wanted to write. His work was free of anxiety, wore its own skin effortlessly. It emboldened me, not to find my voice, but to speak in the voice I already had. And so, when that e-mail came from his son, I knew, overly-thrilled as I was, that I would not call. His work had done more than enough. In an odd way, I was so awed, so grateful, that I did not want to meet him. I wanted some distance between my literary hero and me.

Chinua Achebe and I have never had a proper conversation. The second time I saw him, at a luncheon in his honour hosted by the British House of Lords, I sat across from him and avoided his eye. ("Chinua Achebe is the only person I have seen you shy with," a friend said). The third, at a New York event celebrating fifty years of *Things Fall Apart*, we crowded around him backstage, Edwidge Danticat and I, Ha Jin and Toni Morrison, Colum McCann and Chris Abani. We seemed, magically, bound together in a warm web, all of us affected by his work. Achebe looked pleased, but also vaguely puzzled by all the attention. He spoke softly, the volume of his entire being turned to 'low.' I wanted to tell him how much I admired his integrity, his speaking out about the disastrous leadership in my home state of Anambra, but I did not. Before I went on stage, he told me, "Jisie ike." I wondered if he fully grasped, if indeed it was possible to, how much his work meant to so many.

History and Civics, as school subjects, function not merely to teach facts but to transmit more subtle things, like pride and dignity. My Nigerian education taught me much, but left gaping holes. I had not been taught to imagine my precolonial past with any accuracy, or pride, or complexity. And so Achebe's work, for me, transcended literature. It became personal. *Arrow of God*, my favourite, was not just about the British government's creation of warrant chiefs and the linked destinies of two men, it became the life my grandfather might have lived. *Things Fall Apart* is the African novel most read – and arguably most loved – by Africans, a novel published when 'African novel' meant European accounts of 'native' life. Achebe was an unapologetic member of the generation of African writers who were 'writing back,' challenging the stock of Western images of their homeland, but his work was not burdened by its intent. It is much-loved not because Achebe wrote back, but because he wrote back well. His work was wise, humorous and humane. For many Africans, *Things Fall Apart* remains a gesture of returned dignity, a literary and an emotional experience; Mandela called Achebe the writer in whose presence the prison walls came down.

Achebe's most recent book, his long-awaited memoir of the Nigerian-Biafra war, is both sad and angry, a book by a writer looking back and mourning Nigeria's failures. I wish *There Was a Country* had been better edited and more rigorously detailed in its account of the war. But these flaws do not make it any less seminal: an account of the most important event in Nigeria's history by Nigeria's most important storyteller.

An excerpt from the book has ignited great controversy among Nigerians. In it, Achebe, indignant about the millions of people who starved to death in Biafra, holds Obafemi Awolowo, Nigerian Finance Minister during the war, responsible for the policy of blockading Biafra. He quotes Awolowo's own words on the blockade – 'all is fair in war and starvation is one of the weapons of war. I don't see why we should feed our enemies fat in order for them to fight harder' and then argues that Awolowo's support of the blockade was 'driven by an overriding ambition for power for himself in particular and for the advancement of his Yoruba people in general.'

I have been startled and saddened by the responses to this excerpt. Many are blindingly ethnic, lacking in empathy and, most disturbing of all, lacking in knowledge. We can argue about how we interpret the facts of our shared history, but we cannot, surely, argue about the facts themselves. Awolowo, as *de facto* 'number two man' on the Nigerian side, was a central architect of the blockade on Biafra. During and after the war, Awolowo publicly defended the blockade. Without the blockade, the massive starvation in Biafra would not have occurred. These are the facts.

Some Nigerians, in responding to Achebe, have argued that the blockade was fair, as all is fair in war. The blockade was, in my opinion, inhumane and immoral. And it was unnecessary – Nigeria would have won anyway, it was the much-better-armed side in a war that Wole Soyinka called a shabby unequal conflict. The policy of starving a civilian population into surrender does not merely go against the Geneva conventions, but in this case, a war between siblings, people who were formerly fellow country men and women now suddenly on opposite sides, it seems more chilling. All is not fair in war especially not in a fratricidal war. But I do not believe the blockade was a calculated power grab by Awolowo for himself and his ethnic group; I think of it, instead, as one of the many dehumanizing acts that war, by its nature, brings about.

Awolowo was undoubtedly a great political leader. He was also – rare for Nigerian leaders – a great intellectual. No Nigerian leader has, arguably, articulated a political vision as people-centered as Awolowo's. For Nigerians from the west, he was the architect of free primary education, of progressive ideas. But for Nigerians from the east, he was a different man. I grew up hearing, from adults, versions of Achebe's words about Awolowo. He was the man who prevented an Igbo man from leading the Western House of Assembly in the famous 'carpet crossing' incident of 1952. He was the man who betrayed Igbo people when he failed on his alleged promise to follow Biafra's lead and pull the Western region out of Nigeria. He was the man who, in the words of my uncle, "made Igbo people poor because he never liked us."

At the end of the war, every Igbo person who had a bank account in Nigeria was given twenty pounds, no matter how much they had in their accounts before the war. I have always thought this a livid injustice. I know a man who worked in a multinational company in 1965. He was, like Achebe, one of the many Igbo who just could not believe that their lives were in danger in Lagos and so he fled in a hurry, at the last minute, leaving thousands of pounds in his account. After the war, his account had twenty pounds. To many Igbo, this policy was uncommonly punitive and went against the idea of 'no victor, no vanquished.' Then came the indigenization decree, which moved industrial and corporate power from foreign to Nigerian hands. It made many Nigerians wealthy; much of the great wealth in Nigeria today has its roots in this decree. But the Igbo could not participate; they were broke.

I do not agree, as Achebe writes, that one of the main reasons for Nigeria's present backwardness is the failure to fully reintegrate the Igbo. I think Nigeria would be just as backward even if the Igbo had been fully integrated – institutional and leadership failures run across all ethnic lines. But the larger point Achebe makes is true, which is that the Igbo presence in Nigerian positions of power has been much reduced since the war. Before the war, many of Nigeria's positions of power were occupied by Igbo people, in the military, politics, academia and business, perhaps because the Igbo were very receptive to Western education, often at the expense of their own traditions and had both a striving individualism and a communal ethic. This led to what, in history books, is often called a 'fear of Igbo domination' in the rest of Nigeria. The Igbo themselves were insensitive to this resentment, the bombast and brashness that is part of Igbo culture only exacerbated it. And so leading Igbo families entered the war as Nigeria's privileged elite but emerged from it penniless, stripped and bitter.

Today, 'marginalization' is a popular word in Igboland. Many Igbo feel marginalized in Nigeria, a feeling based partly on experience and partly on the psychology of a defeated people. (Another consequence of this psychology, perhaps, is the loss of the communal ethic of the Igbo, much resented sixty years ago. It is almost non-existent today, or as my cousin eloquently put it: Igbo people don't even send each other).

Some responses to Achebe have had a 'blame the victim' undertone, suggesting that Biafrians started the war and therefore deserved what they got. But Biafrians did not 'start the war.' Nobody with a basic knowledge of the facts can make that case.

Biafrian secession was inevitable, after the federal government's failure to implement the agreements reached at Aburi, itself prompted by the massacre of Igbos in the North. The cause of the massacres was arguably the first coup of 1966. Many believed it to be an 'Igbo' coup, which was not an unreasonable belief, Nigeria was already mired in ethnic resentments, the premiers of the West and North were murdered while the Eastern premier was not, and the coup plotters were Igbo. Except for Adewale Ademoyega, a Yoruba, who has argued that it was not an ethnic coup. I don't believe it was. It seems, from most accounts, to have been an idealistic and poorly-planned nationalist exercise aimed at ridding Nigeria of a corrupt government. It was, also, horrendously, inexcusably violent. I wish the coup had never happened. I wish the premiers and other casualties had been arrested and imprisoned, rather than murdered. But the truth that glares above all else is that the thousands of Igbo people murdered in their homes and in the streets had nothing to do with the coup.

Some have blamed the Biafrian starvation on Ojukwu, Biafra's leader, because he rejected an offer from the Nigerian government to bring in food through a land corridor. It was an ungenerous offer, one easy to refuse. A land corridor could also mean advancement of Nigerian troops. Ojukwu preferred airlifts, they were tactically safer, more strategic and he could bring in much-needed arms as well. Ojukwu should have accepted the land offer, shabby as it was. Innocent lives would have been saved. I wish he had not insisted on a ceasefire, a condition which the Nigerian side would never have agreed to. But it is disingenuous to claim that Ojukwu's rejection of this offer caused the starvation. Many Biafrians had already starved to death. And, more crucially, the Nigerian government had shown little regard for Biafra's civilian population; it had, for a while, banned international relief agencies from importing food. Nigerian planes bombed markets and targeted hospitals in Biafra and had even shot down an International Red Cross plane.

Ordinary Biafrians were steeped in distrust of the Nigerian side. They felt safe eating food flown in from Sao Tome, but many believed that food brought from Nigeria would be poisoned, just as they believed that, if the war ended in defeat, there would be mass killings of Igbo people. The Biafrian propaganda machine further drummed this in. But, before the propaganda, something else had sown the seed of hateful fear: the 1966 mass murders of Igbo in the North. The scars left were deep and abiding. Had the federal government not been unwilling or incapable of protecting their lives and property, Igbo people would not have so massively supported secession and intellectuals, like Achebe, would not have joined in the war effort.

I have always admired Ojukwu, especially for his early idealism, the choices he made as a young man to escape the shadow of his father's great wealth, to serve his country. In Biafra, he was a flawed leader, his paranoia and inability to trust those close to him clouded his judgments about the execution of the war, but he was also a man of principle who spoke up forcefully about the preservation of the lives of Igbo people when the federal government seemed indifferent. He was, for many Igbo, a Churchillian figure, a hero who inspired them, whose oratory moved them to action and made them feel valued, especially in the early months of the war.

Other responses to Achebe have dismissed the war as something that happened 'long ago.' But some of the people who played major roles are alive today. We must confront our history, if only to begin to understand how we came to be where we are today. The Americans are still hashing out details of their civil war that ended in 1865; the Spanish have only just started, seventy years after theirs ended. Of course, discussing a history as contested and contentious as the Nigeria-Biafra war will not always be pleasant. But it is necessary. An Igbo saying goes: If a child does not ask what killed his father, that same thing will kill him.

What many of the responses to Achebe make clear, above all else, is that we remember differently. For some, Biafra is history, a series of events in a book, fodder for argument and analysis. For others, it is a loved one killed in a market bombing, it is hunger as a near-constant companion, it is the death of certainty. The war was fought on Biafrian soil. There are buildings in my hometown with bullet holes; as a child, playing outside, I would sometimes come across bits of rusty ammunition left behind from the war. My generation was born after 1970, but we know of property lost, of relatives who never 'returned' from the North, of shadows that hung heavily over family stories. We inherited memory. And we have the privilege of distance that Achebe does not have.

Achebe is a war survivor. He was a member of the generation of Nigerians who were supposed to lead a new nation, inchoate but full of optimism. It shocked him, how quickly Nigerian fell apart. In *There Was a Country* he sounds unbelieving, still, about the federal government's indifference while Igbo people were being massacred in Northern Nigeria in 1966. But shock-worthy events did not only happen in the North. Achebe himself was forced to leave Lagos, a place he had called home for many years, because his life was no longer safe. His crime was being Igbo. A Yoruba acquaintance once told me a story of how he was nearly lynched in Lagos at the height of the tensions before the war; he was light-skinned and a small mob in a market assumed him to be 'Igbo Yellow' and attacked him. The Vice-Chancellor of the University of Lagos was forced to leave. So was the Vice-Chancellor of the University of Ibadan. Because they were Igbo. For Achebe, all this was deeply personal, deeply painful. His house was bombed, his office was destroyed. He escaped death a few times. His best friend died in battle. To expect a dispassionate account from him is a remarkable failure of empathy. I wish more of the responses had acknowledged, a real acknowledgement and not merely a dismissive preface, the deep scars that experiences like Achebe's must have left behind.

Ethnicity has become, in Nigeria, more political than cultural, less about philosophy and customs and values and more about which bank is a Yoruba or Hausa or Igbo bank, which political office is held by which ethnicity, which revered leader must be turned into a flawless saint. We cannot deny ethnicity. It matters. But our ethnic and national identities should not be spoken of as though they were mutually exclusive; I am as much Igbo as I am Nigerian. I have hope in the future of Nigeria, mostly because we have not yet made a real, conscious effort to begin creating a nation (We could start, for example, by not merely teaching Maths and English in primary schools, but also teaching Idealism and Citizenship).

For some non-Igbo, confronting facts of the war is uncomfortable, even inconvenient. But we must hear one another's stories. It is even more imperative for a subject like Biafra which, because of our different experiences, we remember differently. Biafrian minorities were distrusted by the Igbo majority, and some were unfairly attacked, blamed for being saboteurs. Nigerian minorities, particularly in the mid-west, suffered at the hands of both Biafrian and Nigerian soldiers. 'Abandoned property' cases remain unresolved today in Port Harcourt, a city whose Igbo names were changed after the war, creating "Rumu" from "Umu." Nigerian soldiers carried out a horrendous massacre in Asaba, murdering the males in a town that is today still alive with painful memories. Some Igbo families are still waiting, half-hoping, that a lost son, a lost daughter, will come home. All of these stories can sit alongside one another. The Nigerian stage is big enough. Chinua Achebe has told his story. This week, he turns 82. Long may he live.

## An Igbo Eulogy on the Passing of Chinua Achebe

Chimamanda Ngozi Adichie

Ife mee.
Nnukwu ife mee.
Chinua Achebe anabago.

Onye edemede nke di egwu,
onye nnukwu uche,
onye obi oma.

Keduzi onye anyi ga-eji eme onu?
Keduzi onye anyi ga-eji jee mba?
Keduzi onye ga-akwado anyi?

Ebenebe egbu o!
Anya mmili julu m anya.
Chinua Achebe, naba no ndokwa.
O ga-adili gi mma.
Naba na ndokwa.

**(English Translation by Ike Anya)**

Something has happened, something dreadful has happened
Chinua Achebe has departed
The famed writer, the great thinker, the good hearted man
Of whose accomplishments will we now boast?
Who will stand for us abroad?
Who will be our bulwark now?
A devastating tragedy has occurred!
My eyes are filled with tears
Chinua Achebe, go in peace, it will be well with you
Go in peace.

Chapter Eighteen

# Chinua Achebe

## A Writer and a Half and More

*Akin Adesokan*

He sits there in the front row, looking baffled by the effusion of encomiums falling all around him like snow, a little overshadowed in the serene placidity of the wise old man that he is. Once in a while, as the person reading on stage hits on a funny note and the audience comes to life with muffled guffaws, he too shakes a bit from the effort of laughing. Chinua Achebe, Africa's most famous novelist and author of *Things Fall Apart*, a classic of 20th century fiction, will be 70 in two weeks, but there is an early start to the celebration, this weekend of November 3–4.

That was in 2000, more than twelve years ago, when Bard College, the school in upstate New York that Achebe had made his home following his tragic accident in 1990, decides to honour this path-breaking man of letters, bringing an unprecedented number of writers and scholars together in Annandale, a tiny university town on the bank of the Hudson River. For me, it is the largest gathering of writers of African descent and intellectuals and scholars and business people with a stake in African arts and letters around a single moment, that is, since May 1988 when an international symposium took place in Lagos to celebrate Wole Soyinka's Nobel Prize for Literature, earned two years before. Speaker after speaker, from Nelson Mandela (who sends a message from South Africa) through Toni Morrison to Ali Mazrui and John Edgar Wideman tells the house what encountering Achebe's masterpiece means to them.

The F.W. Olin Language Centre is packed on every occasion. It doesn't make sense to start listing names, so I won't even try. It should suffice to say that everyone who is aware, or is invited, or is able to make it, is present. This gathering of the merchants of African literary culture is an autograph-hunter's dream. All the hotel rooms in Kingston, the closest midscale town to Annandale-Upon-Hudson, Bard's location, are sold out. Reporters come from as far afield as Lagos and Frankfurt. There are functionaries of the United Nations in the audience. In one single row sit Nuruddin Farah, Ngũgĩ wa Thiong'o, Tsitsi Dangarembga and Kwame Anthony Appiah, listening to a speech by the political scientist Richard Sklar, who has taken the floor after Ekwueme Michael Thelwell. The ongoing performance on stage is also a tribute, although an oblique one, as it turns out.

It is also my first close encounter with Achebe, a writer that I had met in print since upper elementary school when I read but half-understood the story of a man named Obi who has a girlfriend named Clara whom he really cannot marry, but he has to go to jail for taking a bribe. And there was also the encounter from a distance, in 1989 or so, when he stepped out of a Jeep in front of Trenchard Hall at the University of Ibadan, waving a feathered fan at a band of dancers and drummers serenading this guest arriving to receive an honorary degree from his *alma mater.* I would read the other books later, out of duty (*A Man of the People*; *Girls at War*) or curiosity (*Arrow of God*; *Things Fall Apart; Anthills of the Savannah*), and for someone trying to read his way towards an idea of how to make his own books, those novels became part of my growing imaginative world.

Not so their author, or not at first. Achebe the man came to me first through controversy – his startling statement in 1987 that the national burial accorded to the recently deceased Chief Obafemi Awolowo was a "national swindle." Unlike Soyinka who first came into my consciousness in Civics quizzes as "the person who suggested Swahili," there was no comparable context for identifying Achebe. "Who wrote *Things Fall Apart*?" is a joke trusting in the sophistication of Wit, elder sister of Humour. But although I took notice of the statement regarding Awolowo, it did not at the time play any role in my growing appreciation of Achebe's work or person.

That – forming an opinion of the writers' work or person through events happening outside the books – would come later, when my reading matured enough to nudge itself in the direction of the essays. In the stories, it was one thing to indulge in the proverbs and the idioms of the so-called "tribal life," but quite another to be confronted by the phrase "Okonkwo almost choked on his anger," or the incredible imagery of a finger of sweat crawling down Captain Winterbottom's back, like an insect. These were gems to make one want to write, but I also realized, quite intuitively, that his limpid prose was not to my temperament. It was not so much that I disliked it as that it taught me that he was not my kind of writer. For me, *Arrow of God* is the best-achieved of Achebe's novels, the one I am likely to be caught re-reading, as the author himself once revealed.

It was in the essays, in these works of cultural and political analysis that I began to form an opinion that was specific, complex and yet incomplete. In the essays – *Morning Yet on Creation Day, Hopes and Impediments, Home and Exile, The Trouble with Nigeria, The Education of a British Protected Child* – Achebe brings to life a particular literary and political attitude which could be appreciated apart from the novel, in a way that one cannot say for a writer like Gabriel García Márquez or Jorge Amado, two contemporaries with whom he was sometimes compared. I might say that the essays help in clarifying for me what the deeper aims of his fictional works are. And if there is one essay that encapsulates these aims – assuming that there could be such a thing as a representative essay in Achebe's prose work – it will have to be "The Novelist as Teacher." It is here that he declares, in his evergreen and inimitable voice that "I would be quite satisfied if my novels (especially the ones I set in the past) did no more than teach their readers that their past – with all its imperfections – was not one long night of savagery from which the first Europeans acting on God's behalf delivered them."

The person reading on the stage has stopped and applause is ceasing. He offers his reason for reading that particular excerpt about a small-town mock-warrior who wanted to take on Adolf Hitler: "This is just to show that we have our own fighters, our people of courage. It's a tribute to Achebe, to the courage that Achebe's life has given us. He has shown the beauty and importance of Christian life and family. We hope some of us will be around to attend your 80th birthday." With those words Wole Soyinka, the performer, walks across the stage, hugs Ike Achebe along the way and goes on to embrace the pensive figure sitting in a wheelchair, recording a truly emotional moment in those two days of many emotional moments.

There are three other such instances. The first occurs soon after this fraternal act. Sonia Sanchez, the African American poet and performer, reads a long poem that links Okonkwo's act of resistance to the spirit of rebellion, the sense of historical duty which informs the creative choices of the Black Arts Movement of the 1960s. Sanchez is a prominent figure of this movement and her poetry, like the poetry of Amiri Baraka and Haki Madhubuti, is marked by formal experimentation and spiritual rousing. When she is done with the first poem, such is the depth of emotion she has whipped up by intense chants and daring stage acts and so complete her own exhaustion, that the audience simply rises at once and goes on clapping and calling for more.

Later in the day, Achebe and Toni Morrison hold a Conversation. Leon Botstein, president of Bard College, moderates this session. The responses from the two authors are very uneven. Morrison tends to see the questions as linked to the dialectics of the creative process and her role as a user of language and metaphor in a "race-inflected milieu," while Achebe gives straight and pungent answers with a simple sophistication that readers of his essays will find familiar. Then Botstein asks a fan question, something like, What's your favourite novel?

Achebe answers: "Mine will be Toni Morrison's *Beloved.* This is because Morrison is the only writer who is probing what James Baldwin calls 'the African conundrum.' What happens when someone does the kind of thing that that woman does, by killing her own child? What happens when this happens, when you try to avoid abomination by committing another abomination? Because that child will come back to haunt you." In this fascinating, deceptively simple way, Achebe links the problem of guilt and powerlessness that haunts Africans and African Americans over the historical fact of the Atlantic Slave Trade.

A therapeutic sigh rises from the audience. Toni Morrison seems to be crying. Her voice quavers when Botstein turns to her. Achebe quips: "Well, it doesn't have to be a novel of mine" and everyone laughs. She gives an honest but ambiguous answer that I've heard her give before: that her favourite novel is the one she likes to read and because it does not exist, she has to write it.

Achebe's great theme was anti-colonialism and in this he was not alone. The late Senegalese filmmaker Ousmane Sembène was like that, to some degree. Achebe was an Nkrumahist, a cultural figure who views the ideas and maybe the methods of the great Ghanaian leader as indispensable to forming a sense of self-awareness and dignity by Africans. But in his works, and especially in the early novels, he expressed this theme from the perspective of Igbo culture. The crisis faced by that culture, best exemplified by the civil war fought between the Nigerian government and the secessionist southeastern Republic of Biafra, affected Achebe's literary productivity. He did not produce another novel until 1987 when he published the middling *Anthills of the Savannah*, twenty-one years after *A Man of the People.* He filled the hiatus with the essays, collection of stories and poetry, the pamphlet *The Trouble with Nigeria* and his tenure as a professor in Nigeria and American universities.

The theme of anti-colonialism is a complex and necessary one for writers and artists speaking for and about previously misrepresented communities to embrace. It is one to appreciate in this manner: to Soyinka's famous quip about the tiger not needing to proclaim his "tigritude", we have Léopold Sedar Sénghor's rejoinder that the tiger had to proclaim his being because it had been conclusively called into question in the past. One of the satisfying things about this kind of position-taking, to my way of looking at things, is that I don't have to worry about them or choose between them as I try to make my way in the world. Why choose between Karl Marx's "Thesis on Feuerbach" and Walter Benjamin's "Theses on the Philosophy of History"? Does one not complement the other? Colonialism has left its indelible scars on the lives of the people it dominated (Achebe calls this "the wound in the soul") and it has been the definitive experience for most modern African intellectuals. But there were colonialisms on the continent before the European one and there remain varieties of that phenomenon, in other guises. Every writer has to tell stories that suit his or her taste and temperament – that is the point of Morrison's response to the question by the fan.

However, the civil war quickly gave Achebe another theme and a cause – the championing of the Igbo in the uneasy contraption called Nigeria. This is why he had to write the divisive *There Was a Country* and why it took him so long to do so.

A phone call from Lagos woke me to the rumour of Achebe's death early in the morning of March 22. The caller, journalist and author Kunle Ajibade, was not sure and he wanted me to call Nigerian friends to confirm or dismiss the news. I left several voice messages and the one person who picked my call said something very significant, moments after we had come to terms with the news. Chika Okeke-Agulu, an artist and art historian said, after listening to my view of the writer's personal account of the war, that Biafra, not literature, was the defining ideal for Achebe. That is a point of supreme importance. With it as a point of reference, it would not be difficult to understand why a writer of Achebe's status continued to use the expression, "my people the Igbo", and why he would describe Awolowo as a politician fighting for "his Yoruba people." It stands to reason.

Now but for his international stature as the author of *Things Fall Apart* it would have been difficult or impossible to argue forcefully for these two themes at once. He lost faith in Nigeria, the country with great but repeatedly undermined potential, but he kept faith with Biafra, the country that is no more. While the controversy around *There Was a Country* raged, I opted to read Salman Rushdie's *Joseph Anton*, published in the same month as Achebe's work. Rushdie's memoir is another account of a writer's encounter with his deeply held values, one for which he was close to paying the supreme price. It is true that Rushdie has no dream of being the martyr of any cause – he is too ironical and sensuous for that. But he gives an unvarnished, remarkably honest and frequently funny account of his experience in those nine difficult years. He does not spare himself. How many writers would confess that one of his best friends slept with his wife and that he turned to this same friend later to publish his next book? How many will reveal directly that his son briefly engaged in pilfering? His account of his brief embrace of Islam during the ordeal is an admirable piece of self-criticism. On the contrary, reviewers of Achebe's book have pointed to the author's refusal to present a detailed account of his own involvement at the highest level of decision-making in Biafra as one of the unforgivable flaws of the book.

This also stands to reason: during the *fatwa* episode, a Nigerian academic, Theo Vincent, met Rushdie at a PEN event in Europe and during small-talk, Vincent asked Rushdie how he managed to write a novel as monumental as

*The Moor's Last Sigh* under those conditions. The writer's response was that writing was his business, the one thing he had to do no matter what. Achebe was confronted with a similar question, but in reverse: how come he had not produced another novel in years? His response was that under the circumstances of and following the war, novel writing would be a frivolous exercise.

Yet Achebe invested in writing in other areas, especially during that long spell of drought. While he lectured and taught and wrote essays, he also initiated the founding of the Association of Nigerian Authors, co-founded Nwamife Publishers, a literature imprint and *Okike: A Journal of New Writing*. During the Second Republic, he joined the left-leaning People's Redemption Party and served as its Vice-President.

The third emotional moment occurs differently; it is perceptible throughout the two days. The gathering of virtually everyone interested in African literature, within and outside academia, from the US, Nigeria, South Africa, England, Australia, to celebrate the birthday of one of Africa's illustrious sons is itself a matter to sigh and ponder, or dance and laugh over. In Soyinka's excerpt from *Aké* and embrace of Achebe, in Sanchez's evocative poem, in Achebe's profound reading of *Beloved*, the community to which every self-aware writer caters and which is located inside a room, in a country or in the entire universe, that community is enacted with memorable camaraderie. This is what I find at Bard College.

On the way to the birthday celebration, I read Achebe's new book of essays, *Home and Exile*, texts of three lectures he gave at Harvard University in December 1998. It was forty years after the publication of *Things Fall Apart*. The book chronicles the mental conditioning that gave rise to the novel – more of the same indignation at colonial novels of Africa by Joyce Cary and Joseph Conrad that one will find in Achebe's previous essays. It also assesses the novel's fortune for literatures from Africa and other previously colonized societies and calls for a balance of stories in the world. There's a straight-faced critique of trends in contemporary fiction and the threat of cultural homogenization posed by the usual suspect – "Western culture." The blurb says: "Achebe contends that to redress the inequities of global oppression, writers must focus on where they come from, insisting that their value systems are as legitimate as any other."

I take just two issues with the fine book. The first is a minor error of fact that puts Tai Solarin's period of sojourn in England at the 1950s (the late headmaster returned to Nigeria in 1951, after ten years abroad). The second is more substantial. Achebe misunderstands the dynamics of power between the hunter and the lion, as contained in a Masai proverb which goes thus: Until the lions produce their own historian, the story of the hunt will glorify only the hunter. He rejects the lion as a messenger of truth because it is also a powerful animal. The lion is truly powerful, but there is no balance in the exercise of power between this animal and the hunter. Unlike the lion, the hunter has a gun. I insist on this because dismissing the lion amounts to discounting the humanity of the weaker counterpart and placing the burden of history on only the hunter. What is missing in the contest is the balance, not the potential of power. That is why Achebe could contest Cary's story.

Chapter Nineteen

# Reflections On Chinua Achebe

## A Priceless Encounter with A Gentle Voice

*Zaynab Alkali*

Chinua Achebe's contributions to the rise, evolution and expansion of Anglophone African Literature with the publications of his epic novels, *Things Fall Apart* (1958) and *Arrow of God*, (1965) among many others, offer compelling representation of African life-styles, debunking the denigrating image of Africa one finds in some Western narratives such as that of Joyce Cary's *Mister Johnson.*

Apart from such an achievement, putting modern postcolonial African Literature on the literary map has set the stage for succeeding generations of African writers on the continent to tell their own stories in new and different ways. Although the pioneer novels are products of the unique socio-cultural, historic and geo-political conditions of the author, succeeding non-Igbo generations of Achebe realize that the Igbo fictional world is hardly different from their own worlds. Ezeulu the chief priest of Ulu in *Arrow Of God* and Okonkwo of *Things Fall Apart*, are familiar faces and voices I grew up with in my village. The old man, Joro, who still kept his clay gods under his bed and would not touch the Christian God with a ten-foot pole, but would send his children to the missionary schools to read 'boko', can be found on the pages of Achebe's novels. What about Jamji, the stubborn mule, my grandfather's next -door neighbour, a hard working groundnut farmer whose favourite pass-time was to thwart all Christian evangelistic activities by challenging their activities and questioning their creed.

Achebe's fictional world, his characters, the social and cultural activities of the people have set a landscape and provided a road map for young writers to follow. Not only that, his creative use of English language has greatly influenced a younger generation of writers who are now confident enough to manipulate the English language in such fresh and creative ways as to invest the language with the peculiar idioms of native African languages. According to Achebe, the imposition of Prospero's language had given Caliban a unifying mode of communication: "If English failed to give the colonized a song, it at least gave them a tongue for singing."

His literary output, from his first publication in 1958, to his novels of 1961-1966, has produced a series of narrative descriptions of African life which introduced the modern literary reader to a veritable African imagined community in transition that is rife with intractable contradictions, painful self-becoming, all in an attempt to explore the wider order of things in the African context.

His involvement with the Heinemann African Writers Series between 1962-1972, as an influential editor, had produced an iconic collection of African writings from notable names like Alex La Guma, Doris Lessing, Cheik Hamidou Kane and Okot p'Bitek among many others. The publications of nationalist intellectuals such as Nelson Mandela, Kwame Nkrumah, Kenneth Kaunda, Jomo Kenyatta under his editorship, not only popularized modern African Writing within the wider literary world, but also provided openings for succeeding distinguished writers. Opportunities under his watch opened up for younger writers the securing of lucrative contracts from international publishing houses. This favourable development owes much to Achebe's pioneering efforts and vanguard role, as well as the struggles and sacrifices of the first post-independent group of writers that he nurtured under the Heinemann imprint.

Achebe's collection of essays on literature, cultural politics and colonial history, from the early *Morning Yet On Creation Day* (1975) to the later *Hopes and Impediments* (1989) and *Home and Exile* (2000), helped raise the question of the African voice in critical and theoretical circles. These critical interventions have continued to frame much of the critical discourse surrounding postcolonial studies in general and African literature in particular, an example is Achebe's essay on Joseph Conrad's *Heart of Darkness*: "An Image of Africa: Racism in Conrad's Heart of Darkness." *Hopes and Impediments, Selected Essays 1965- 1987*, New York: Doubleday 1989, 1-13. For many literary critics, Achebe's essay changed traditional literary criticism of Conrad and *Heart of Darkness.*

Achebe's penchant for speaking the truth to power and conscience, mark of great a man, can be seen in his essay, *The Trouble with Nigeria*, (1983), in which he argues that, "the trouble with Nigeria is simply and squarely a failure of leadership . . . the unwillingness and inability of leaders to rise to the responsibility, to the challenge of personal example" (p.1). In this book and the last one before his exit, *There Was a Country*, he leaves behind a legacy of the critical, intellectual opposition. The impact of his interventions as a literary critic/agent "provocateur" will remain for a long time to come. His last book, *There Was a Country: A Personal History of Biafra* (2012), generated pained, divisive and intense critical debate especially within Nigeria. The controversy the book generated equates with the discordant, argumentative, critical and interrogative life that Achebe himself had led and the legacy he has left behind.

Not many in the literary world can boast of the quality of awards Achebe had garnered between 1982 -2010. He is believed to have received over 30 honorary degrees from universities across the world; England, Scotland, Canada, South Africa, the United States and his home country, Nigeria. He was awarded the Commonwealth Poetry Prize, an Honorary Fellowship of the American Academy of Arts and Sciences, the Nigerian National Order of Merit, the Peace Prize of the German Book Trade, The Man Booker International Prize and the 2010 Dorothy and Lillian Gish Prize. In 1992, his novel *Things Fall Apart* became the first African novel to be published in the Everyman's Library collection published by Alfred A. Knopf.

Achebe was fortunate enough to witness the fiftieth anniversary of this historic first novel, which also witnessed a phenomenal increase in readership. In a tribute to Achebe, Leon Botstein, President of Bard College, where Achebe taught for some time, observed that, "Chinua Achebe is one of the great intellectual and ethical figures of our time." Not only is this a fitting description of Achebe's legacy, it is also a tribute to the author of *Things Fall Apart*, a novel that is not only the most widely read African fictional work, but also one of the great African narratives of the 20th Century.

Yet, perhaps, another enduring legacy he has left behind is the spirit of cultural edification and an exemplary commitment to the principles of critical thinking and the vindication of creative innovation in all its forms.

The handsome tribute paid to Professor Chinua Achebe by President Barack Obama and his wife Lady Michelle, sums up the power of the Professor's impact, not only on the literary world, but on humanity. Says the couple on the Professor:

> A revolutionary author, educator and cultural ambassador, Chinua shattered the conventions of literature and shaped the collective identity of Nigerians throughout the world. With a dream of taking on misperceptions of his homeland, he gave voice to perspectives that cultivated understanding and drew our world closer together. His legacy will endure in the hearts of all whose lives he touched with the everlasting power of his art.

Achebe: A Priceless Encounter With a Gentle Voice.1986 – Association of Nigerian Authors (ANA) Convention: National Theatre Igamu, Lagos.

As an emerging writer, making fresh entrance into the literary world, I was overwhelmed by the company I found myself in. Famous Nigerian writers I have heard about, but had not yet met, converged in Lagos for the ANA yearly convention. I had travelled from Maiduguri to Lagos, having the previous year won the ANA award with my debut novel, *The Stillborn.* After a year I was still euphoric, everything seemed surreal. I had to be in such a terrific mood to have travelled across the country, from Maiduguri to Lagos, for the first time, carrying a baby barely six months old.

I moved in the circle of writers, learning their names and peering into their faces. The name that kept on reverberating was that of the great Achebe. Everybody seemed to be looking out for him, but there he was, surrounded by older, established and famous writers. I knew the face from the blurbs of his books. I slowly inched my way towards where he was standing, but now the convention was about to start. Organizers were urging the participants to take their seats. There was a mass movement towards seats.

Suddenly some men barged in on us, hastily introduced themselves and made a request. In the hall next door, they explained, an important function was about to start. A very important person, (in the Nigerian vocabulary), was expected as a special Guest of Honour. Could we writers be kind enough as to attend their opening ceremony? We should, in fact I believe we were expected to grace this special invitation with our August presence and of course, shift our own opening ceremony for an hour, or so. Just as they had come, they disappeared.

I could never work out to date, how such a seemingly innocuous, albeit arrogant request could cause such a furore that soon degenerated into angry exchanges among honourable writers. I believed a yes, or no answer would have sufficed. My eyes sought for the honourable Professor. Where did he stand in all of this? Yes, just as I had thought, he had quietly slipped away from the chaos and was sitting by himself, his back to the crowd. “Good, this is my chance,” I beamed. Summoning courage, I walked silently, so I thought, rehearsing all the time my opening speech. I was actually sneaking up on him, but of course he heard footsteps and turned. I moved quickly and sat by his side. He looked at me kindly and said nothing. My throat went dry. I had forgotten my opening statement and was panicking in his presence. I just looked back awestruck at this great man. I did not know what to expect, but not this deep serene silence from this master artist, the king storyteller. He must have understood my dilemma.

“Zaynab, how are you?” he simply asked and I freaked out. He knew me and had called my name in that incredible gentle voice! I must have grinned from ear to ear, for now the kindness on his face and his remarkable humility loosened my tongue. I found my voice and prattled on about the brouhaha going on in the hall, as if he did not know. Told him about how some writers wanted to accept this impromptu invitation to grace another opening ceremony, putting our own on hold. How others had objected to what they considered the exploitation of famous writers to swell the group's number and to boast of our presence among them. I took a deep breath. He had not uttered a word, but was still listening, so I continued. When I had finished, the Professor sighed and took a long look at me. I was beginning to feel nervous. It dawned on me that I had been presumptuous with this great man. He had kindly smiled at me and I had intruded on his privacy. He, surely, had wished for privacy that was why he moved away, but I had followed him with the noise. Just as I was about to apologize for taking such liberties, he asked in a quiet gentle voice that further unnerved me, what I wanted to do? I was momentarily taken aback. I did not think for a moment that it had anything to do with me. I had not thought about myself in the scheme of things. I may have just wanted to see him close up, make a conversation, an art I could ill afford, but if I gained nothing from that convention itself, meeting Chinua Achebe was enough reward. "I really do not know," I answered truthfully.

"Zaynab," he called again, "Listen. Don't you, ever, allow anyone to tell you what to do?" We both fell silent. I was thinking, with some seriousness, of what he had just said. In other words, he was telling me not to allow anybody to influence my decisions. I thought, Oh God! And all my life I had allowed just that to happen. A while ago I had not known what to do, to follow the crowd to the hall next door, or to sit tight and wait for our own convention to start? Now I searched my heart. What had I really wanted to do? I realized that I did not really want to go anywhere, but if I had not chosen to search out the great Achebe, I would have followed them anyway. Those simple words uttered by the gentle voice of the great storyteller became one of my cardinal rules.

"Yes, Sir,' I finally responded. "Thank you."

We sat there for a while in profound silence on the steps of the theatre hall. When I saw the smile and the serenity on his face, as he looked into space, I understood that it was this profound silence that the gentle Professor wanted. Together, we sat in the much-needed silence, a silence that was, 'a little more than silence' and waited for ANA to convene the meeting.

It was the first time I had met and talked with the Professor. I was never privileged to see him again. After almost twenty-seven years, I still remember, clearly his advice and will continue to cherish this priceless encounter with the gentle voice of wisdom until the end of my days.

## Chapter Twenty

# "Odupon Kesee Atutu."

## (A Great Tree Has Fallen. Asante-Twi)

*Kwame Anthony Appiah*

For many people all around the world, Chinua Achebe was their first African writer. *Things Fall Apart* has been read and loved (and studied) by millions. And among its many readers were a generation of other African writers for whom he blazed the trail. Of course, that wonderful book wasn't literally the first novel published by an African writer in a European language. But in *Things Fall Apart* – along with *Arrow of God* and *No Longer at Ease,* the two books that followed in his trilogy about life in Igboland – Achebe established, for those who wanted to write fiction in English about African life, the first great model of how it could be done. He found ways to render in his spare and memorable prose the life and the language of traditional village people in Nigeria, in a way that seemed so utterly natural that it is hard to appreciate how magnificent an achievement it was. Achebe had absorbed a wide range of literature in English, both poetry and prose: the King James Bible and the English hymnal, realist and modernist novels; Shakespeare, Wordsworth, Dickens, Conrad and, of course, Yeats who gave him the title of his first book. And from this great treasury he drew a variety of forms of diction: one, for example, to represent the voices of people speaking Igbo; another, for the language in which he described their world. But he also took from the traditions of oral literature that he heard from his family growing up … the proverbs with which the novel is peppered (like a good Igbo soup), the tales of gods and heroes and heroines that hover behind his narrative. The result was a way of talking about Africa in the colonial language that allowed his characters to live for us as richly specific human beings, located in a particular place, but belonging, as all great literature does, to people everywhere.

Chinua Achebe's life was divided, so it seems to me, by two great historical events. The first was Nigerian independence. Though *Things Fall Apart* appeared in 1958, two years earlier than the beginning of the modern history of his country, the trilogy it began was itself a great declaration of literary independence, not just for Nigerian fiction but, for all of us in black Africa. In that period of enormous creativity, Achebe not only wrote these three great explorations, which run from the beginning of European colonization through to independence (along with the post-independence novel, *A Man of the People,* set in an imaginary African country) but he also acted as midwife to scores of other writers through his editing of the Heinemann African Writers Series.

Then came the second great event, Nigeria's Civil War (from 1967 to 1970) in which he played a prominent role in the public life of Biafra, the short-lived state in the east of his country, which included the Igbo societies from among which his own family came. The loss of Biafra – and the monumental suffering and death that went with it – marked him deeply for the rest of his life. He published poetry and essays afterwards and, much later, in 1986, another fine novel, *Anthills of the Savannah.* Last year, he published his last book, *There Was a Country: A Personal History of Biafra,* which displayed the persistence of that trauma into the present. But the Achebe who will live long in the world's letters was the man who wrote those four novels in the incredible decade of creativity that began with *Things Fall Apart.*

Chapter Twenty-One

# Chinua Achebe

## A Dissenting Opinion

*Ibrahim Bello-Kano*

There is no doubt that Chinua Achebe, who died on March 22, 2013 in the United States after a long residence there probably because it was better for him to live there than in Nigeria, was, by many accounts, an acclaimed writer. His first novel, *Things Fall Apart* (1958), received wide critical acclaim soon after its publication, which came in the wake of the great wave of decolonization. A year before the publication of the novel, Ghana became the first independent black African country, in 1957. *Things Fall Apart* was published at a time when non-Western but Western educated intellectuals and cultural nationalists were looking around for indigenous cultural documents that could vindicate precolonial African cultures, in what the British Indian writer, Salman Rushdie once called, in a memorable phrase, "writing back to the Centre" (the West).

It was arguably in that context, the urgent need, by the African literati, to produce an African narrative that would vindicate indigenous African cultures which were heavily denigrated by centuries of Western writers, priests and colonial administrators, rather than the novel's intrinsic literary merits, that brought *Things Fall Apart* to prominence, at least within the post-nationalistic African intelligentsia. The same may be said of Achebe's other novels: their timing, 1960–1966, was fortunate because there was, then, a large literate international English-speaking reading public eager to get access to the new African writing, not to speak of publishers such as Heinemann who were looking to cash in on it all. Again, it was in that context that Achebe's works were appropriated for all kinds of culture wars, especially within the ranks of militant postcolonial intellectuals.

Achebe's collection of essays on literature, cultural politics and colonial history, from the early *Morning Yet on Creation Day* (1975) to the later *Hopes and Impediments* (1989) and *Home and Exile* (2000) sealed his reputation as an African or Black cultural critic, activist and nationalist. His other novels, *No Longer at Ease* (1960), *Arrow of God* (1964), *Man of the People* (1966), not to mention short stories and poems such as *Girls at War and Other Stories* (1972) and *Beware, Soul Brother and Other Poems* (1971) were widely admired by critics and literary historians for their "realistic" and, some would say, vivid, subtle, and complex portrait of the African, or, at least, "the Nigerian condition," which, to this day, has persisted in more complicated forms.

Achebe was also the influential editor of the Heinemann African Writers Series, between 1962 and 1972. Under his direction, the series published some of the most canonical of African writers such as Alex La Guma, Taha Hussein, Ngũgĩ wa Thiong'o, Doris Lessing, Ayi Kwei Armah, Tayeb Salih, Bessie Head, Cheik Hamidou Kane, Okot p'Bitek, and nationalist intellectuals such as Amilcar Cabral, Nelson Mandela, Kenneth Kaunda, Jomo Kenyatta, and Kwame Nkrumah.

Chiefly because of his first novel and his pioneering role as the editor of the African Writers Series, many have considered Achebe as the "father of African fiction" (or the founding father, even the grandfather, of modern African literature), a dubious claim that Achebe himself could not accept, since, as he knew in his lifetime, there were many African writers of fiction and non-fiction that wrote compelling accounts of African cultural and social life well before he was born. Claims for Achebe as being the "father of African fiction or literature" are based on a partial and reductive view of Africa's literary history, or a diminution of African writing to a minor position within the Western literary tradition.

Yet there had been indigenous African writing in native languages. Consider, for example, the case of the Basotho (Lesotho) writer and novelist, Thomas Mopoku Mafolo (1876-1948), the celebrated author of *Chaka the Zulu* (1931), which many literary historians have called a masterpiece, an epic tragedy, and in the words of a reviewer, "the earliest major contribution of black Africa to the corpus of modern world literature." One could cite the example of the celebrated Yoruba writer, D. O. Fagunwa, author of *Odo Ninu Igbo Irunmale* (1936), or the works of the Arab writer, Naguib Mahfouz and countless other writers who wrote in Hausa, Yoruba, Tamashek, Amharic, Wolof, Bambara and so on. Indeed, no one author or person could have begun what we call today "African writing." The African literary tradition is much older, more enduring and more complex than the alleged effort of a single author, however gifted. In any case, the idea of Achebe being the "father of African fiction" is not a scholarly argument but a romantic and naïve one because it ignores the major contributions of precolonial African authors and a huge corpus of African writing in Arabic, French, Portuguese and Spanish.

But whatever the artistic merit of Achebe's work, which is fairly considerable to say the least, it is in his novel, *Anthills of the Savannah* (1988), that his literary-storytelling skills began a terminal decline. Indeed the novel marks a notable decline in his liberal vision and creative acumen. The novel is, by any standard, a trivial thriller and is uneven in linguistic and literary quality. Arguably, large parts of *Anthills* read like pulp fiction, or a crudely crafted political thriller. The storyline is fragmented; the attempt at covert plotting is unsuccessful; the narrative exposition is slow and cumbrous; the style of representation is too thin and shallow; the plot is threadbare and thin, perhaps even superficial in many instances. The dialogue is unconvincing, heavy, and tedious and the characterization is one-dimensional. For example, neither Ikem, Beatrice, Abdul on the one hand nor Professor Okon, Sam and Osodi on the other has any emotional and psychological depth. Indeed no character in that novel has convincing uniqueness of character and none is admirably individuated. Moreover, the characterization and dialogue are stagey, as can be seen in the first person account of the First Witness, Christopher Oriko (Chapter 1) and the dialogue in the opening section of Chapter 2. *Anthill* is also marred by obliquities of narration and an undisciplined, un-integrated multiplicity of viewpoints: the novel's attempt at an epic-scale representation of a dystopian land and its failure to offer an intensely imagined, superbly coordinated narrative irony are telling. Yet all this may be accounted for by the novel's melodramatic structure and the poor quality of its speech representation.

Frankly, *Anthills of the Savannah* is a disappointing work; little wonder it failed to win the 1987 Booker McConnell Prize, Britain's most prestigious literary award. For example, the novel combines melodrama with a political *roman á clef*, as can be seen in the closing section of the narrative, the journey on the "Great North Road" (Chapter 17). Indeed, this chapter presents a veiled dystopian narrativization of northern Nigeria, which is variously called "the scrub-land," "the scorched landscape," "another country," "full of dusty fields [and] bottomed baobab tree[s] so strange in appearance," etc. In this novel, the rainforest ("the rain country") of the South is favourably contrasted with the "parkland of grass and stunted trees... of mud walls and reddish earth," the North. One conclusion, which, of course, may be problematic from a strictly literary-critical perspective, is that unlike the Exceptional Southerners, the Northerners don't know how to make the North "prosperous" (the roads are full of pot holes) so that all the talented, intelligent, hardworking, economically gifted and industrially-savvy Southerners could migrate to the North (perhaps in the mode of *mission civilisatrice*), which is, as of now, wallowing in economic and social desperation (see the opening pages of Chapter 17).

The novel has other defects as well: the author's heavily moralized, didactic view of life repeatedly intrudes in the narrative and, in particular, in the facile and tired representation of the Military Ruler, the Head of State. Ikem and Beatrice's romanticism, their romantic view of social relations, is clearly the real author's because the entire drift of the narrative is towards a heavily moralized view of life (Light versus Darkness; Enlightenment versus Ignorance; Diligence versus Parasitism).

Yet it is in Achebe's collection of essays titled, *The Trouble with Nigeria* (1983), that, his pre-critical romanticism comes full circle. In that book, Achebe argues that "the trouble with Nigeria is simply and squarely a failure of leadership... the unwillingness and inability of its leaders to rise to the responsibility, to the challenge of personal example" (p. 1). This postulation of Achebe's ignores the deep structural constraints on human action and psychology. It is pre-critical to ignore the complex ways in which social structures mediate, modify, condition and constrain human choices. Leadership works within institutional, historical, cultural and economic contexts, which place limits on what human agents can and cannot do. This notion of the structural determination of leadership means that a leader has inevitably to work within, and exist in, a system and a political logic whose proper system, laws and operation his or her "leadership" cannot, by definition, dominate absolutely. The leader, despite his having a certain measure of freedom, has inevitably to be governed by the system within which he or she exists. And although men and women make their own history, they clearly do not make it as an act of will, or in their own freely-chosen circumstances, but under the structural constraints of the accumulated past and inherited traditions. This is what *The Trouble with Nigeria* has missed: Nigerian leaders cannot be the miraculous changed men or women of their country but the changed men and women of their country's changed circumstances. This is the truth of the time-honoured liberal credo that the educator herself needs educating and that if leaders are educators, who will educate the educators?

From this perspective, Achebe's conception of leadership may properly be called "voluntarism," even a form of messianic thinking: on Achebe's flawed logic, all a leader needs do is become, by the force of sheer will power, a morally good person, an absolute moral guide, who has only to lead by example rather than by veritable political principles. Achebe's is another way of saying that Nigeria needs a strong leader, one who has miraculously escaped all the cultural and historical pressures of his community or country; in effect, a Messiah (a modern-day philosopher-priest king a convenient way of avoiding the complex problem of institutional, cultural and historical constitution of subjectivity and moral choice in a multi-ethic, multi-religious country, one with a large, primordial, backward-looking civil society. Indeed one reason for the failure of Achebe's little book to capture the scholarly or popular imagination in Nigeria despite its obvious prophetic tones, was its threadbare romanticism and an anti-modern (in effect, a medieval) vision of political leadership.

Perhaps Achebe's most disappointing book, or to phrase matters differently, his most inferior work, is *There Was a Country: A Personal History of Biafra* (Penguin: London, 2012). As a personal testament, the book vindicates the time-honoured dictum that "the personal is political." In this book, Achebe's supposedly "humanist" perspective repeatedly breaks down, or rather fails to live up to the classical humanist idea of universal human solidarity. We may not be critical of Achebe's passionate defence of his ethnic group, or of his romantic vision of short-lived Biafra and his role in its early development. Yet there is something distasteful about Achebe's open myopia of blind ethnic solidarity towards his own ethnic group. What is striking about the book is its complete lack of a keen political insight, its petty romantic vision of Nigeria's political history. For example, consider the book's untenable, perhaps even chauvinistic, claims, namely that the Igbos wholly deserved their entrenched positions in the military, economic and bureaucratic structures of pre-civil war Nigeria ("... the Igbos led the nation in virtually every sector – politics, education, commerce and the arts," pp. 66-67); that all non-Igbo Nigerians are united by their hatred for the Igbo ethnic group; and that British rule in Nigeria and elsewhere was not, as popularly assumed, an unmitigated disaster. According to Achebe in *There Was a Country*, the British government ruled the Nigerian colony "with considerable care... and competently... British colonies were more or less expertly run" (p. 43). In the same book, however, Achebe accuses British colonial officials of rigging the election and the population census in favour of conservative elements such as Sir Ahmadu Bello, the Sardauna of Sokoto from the "Islamic territories" (p. 46; Achebe does not say that the Igbo were from the "Christian territories"), people who "had played no real part in the struggle for independence" (p. 52). Achebe also claims in that book that it was the British colonial administration's allegedly pro-northern Nigeria policies that sowed the seeds of Nigeria's eventual descent into civil war. If indeed Achebe has this rosy view of colonial rule (that the colonial establishment ruled the Nigerian territories with considerable care and expertise, regardless of its well documented divide-and-rule practices), then his entire corpus of anti-colonial polemic and cultural nationalism has been in vain, or, in a way, a hypocritical effort at self-publicity.

Worse, Achebe argues, in an astonishing moment of historical revisionism, that the originators of the very idea of "one-Nigeria" were "leaders and intellectuals from the Eastern Region" (p. 52). This may explain why he credits Nnamdi Azikiwe with the enviable position of being "father of African independence" ("There was no question at all about that," p. 41). For Achebe, all the greatest and most distinguished Nigerians have been Igbos, from the allegedly gifted Okigbo family to Nnamdi Azikiwe, Kenneth Dike and Flora Nwapa, to mention just a few. In sum, then, there are many instances of sloppy argument and poor judgment in the book, as, for example, Achebe's claim that Nigeria failed to develop because the Igbo, despite their "competitive individualism" and a unique "adventurous spirit," were excluded from Nigerian economic, social and political life. Achebe never, for once, supports his claims with any historical reference or factual illustration. Examples of Achebe's unsophisticated political perception of things are, first, his lack of political sensitivity concerning non-Igbo political leaders such as Obafemi Awolowo, Ahmadu Bello, and Abubakar Tafawa Balewa. The first two are seen by Achebe as ruled by inordinate ambition ("resuscitated ethnic pride") and conservative traditionalism respectively. The latter Achebe almost casts into the role of a lackey of the Western world, which, he claims, turned ("built up") Balewa through flattery into a great statesman (p. 51).

It is thus fair to say that, in *There Was a Country* at least, Achebe is an overwhelmingly "ethnic nationalist," an "Igbo-phile" (or a *philo-Igbonis*, to coin a new term), and a Biafra apologist to boot. He is, in this book at least, a *homo duplex*, the Double Man, in effect, both Biafran and Nigerian; Igbophile and Nationalist; Anticolonial Writer and a Postcolonial Apologist of Expert British Rule. This should explain why the book has a schizoid thematic orchestration and its claims pressed within a phlegmatic stylistic mode, which, again and again, has proved incapable of sustained irony. Surely, then, *There Was a Country* is a patchwork of Achebe's deep, even unconscious, prejudices and his desire to vindicate a questionable ethnic identity. In one moment after another, the book fails to offer a finely integrated presentation of a realistic historical, geographical, economic and culturally diverse, though troubled, country. Things have indeed fallen apart for Achebe in his last book, his last testament, if you like. It is an unfortunate book in that Achebe emerges in it neither as a great artist nor a moral guide for those countless Africans who see in art and the artist a vision of a certain programmatic humanism of freedom, human progress and universal human solidarity.

So while I pay a grudging tribute to this important novelist and essayist, I should remark, at the same time, that we should not, in our usual romantic rush to venerate our (cultural) heroes, forget earlier illustrious and master English-speaking storytellers such as Amos Tutuola (1920-1997) and Cyprian Odiatu Ekwensi (1921-2007). Their books, *The Palm-Wine Drinkard and His Dead Palm-Wine Tapster in the Deads' Town* (written 1946 and published in 1952) and *People of the City* (1954), are two outstanding pieces of literature and narrative self-assertion that blazed the trail for modern, English-speaking African fiction writing. In the same manner, while we remember Achebe and his literary legacy, let us not also forget great postcolonial African storytellers such as Tayeb Salih, Ayi Kwei Armah, Ousmane Sambène, Ngũgĩ wa Thiog'o and, not least, the incomparable Kenyan writer, Meja Mwangi, the author, in my opinion, of the finest African novel ever – *Going Down River Road* (1977).

As for Achebe, I say "goodbye"; for there was indeed a distinguished novelist, but who, tragically, wrote the greatest anti-novel of his career – *There Was a Country: A Personal History of Biafra.* Achebe's wheel, let it be said, has come full cycle: from universal human solidarity to sectional, primordial, ethnic identification.

Chapter Twenty-Two

# From Achebe to Adichie

*Carole Boyce Davies*

When Chimamanda Ngozi Adichie presented a TED talk in which she claimed boldly, "We Should all be Feminists" (April 12, 2013),[1] we witnessed, within the same time frame of Achebe's passing (March 21, 2013), another major transition: a fitting representative of a second generation of African writers,[2] would make a major political intervention that writers, like Achebe, had also done at an earlier historical juncture. In thinking through what I see as the move from Achebe to Adichie, we can also be clear that as a young African woman writer, Adichie is also advancing some of the intellectual and creative positions that women writers of that same earlier generation of writers and scholars,[3] like Ama Ata Aidoo and Buchi Emecheta, Nawal El Saadawi, Flora Nwapa and Bessie Head, had consistently articulated. The fact is that much as we celebrate the contributions of an Achebe, with the kind of world renown that he received, he was also locked into some specific representations of the political issues of decolonization, in which African women were represented in a less than favourable light and for sure, in which African masculinity was posed as the response to European colonial dominance. Thus an entire body of writing by African women created a more nuanced examination of African realities, which included the critique of some of the limitations of the postcolonial state and thereby of male leadership. Thereby, the presentation of the other side of the story, the one in which women lived complex lives of "joys" and pains, was made significant.

So while one celebrates the enormous legacy of Chinua Achebe, one can also mark now the limitations of his historical accomplishments at the level of representation. As I mourned his passing, I also saw him entering history precisely for the timeliness of his work. But I also noted that between Achebe and Adichie, there was half a century of literary production in what is defined as modern African literature. In that period we witnessed the writing back to empire coupled with the revision or correction of the ways that Africa had appeared in the Western imagination. Achebe ended up at the forefront of this discourse with his early and representative *Things Fall Apart,* (1958) which rapidly came to be defined as the "archetypal African novel."

But in that time period between Achebe and Adichie, another generation of African writers, some like Tope Folarin who won the 2013 Caine prize for his short story "Miracle"[4] would be born in the US of Nigerian parents, have different concerns, many of these born of migration. Folarin's work for example is centred in a Nigerian community living in the Midwest US and deals with a blind prophet who produces an unlikely miracle in a small church community of Nigerian migrants, on a young boy who actually needs his glasses. Folarin indicates never having travelled to Nigeria largely because his working class family could never afford to purchase tickets for such a journey.[5] Several of this new generation of African writers have lived in Europe and studied in the US, writers like NoViolet Bulawayo who gained an MFA at Cornell University and hailing from Zimbabwe wrote about these two experiences in her book *We Need New Names* (2013). But it is a stark portrayal of the world from the point of view of a child who knows beyond her years, having to confront all the ills of the postcolonial state and then also manage life in the US and all that that entails as an immigrant. So many of these writers have travelled outside of Africa before becoming recognized and are able to navigate home and abroad with ease. Chimamanda Adichie comes across to me at the forefront of this group and it may be interesting to see if her novel *Americanah* (2013) becomes the "archetypal novel" of its generation.

In an earlier essay on Ama Ata Aidoo,[6] I made the claim that in the field of African women writers, Aidoo has to be also identified as setting some of the early themes and arguments for a more gender-balanced modern African literature and definitely can be counted as setting the pace as it were. Writers in Adichie's[7] generation are able to now articulate those and other related issues raised by a writer like Aidoo because writers in that cohort had already done "daily battle" and so claimed a place for African women's writing. Chimamanda is obviously very clear about this history about Achebe's placement in the hierarchy and about African women's location in all of this. During a visit to India, she was quoted as saying:

> Being a Sub Saharan African writer, you're supposed to be like Chinua Achebe, who is called the father of modern African literature. But you're probably compared to him because people don't know any other writers from Africa," she said. "Then I always want to know who the mother of

> African literature is. And also, why does African literature need a father and a mother at all?"[8]

Although she claims to have been raised literally in the house of Achebe on the Nsukka campus and thereby establishes a patriarchal inheritance in African writing, there is clearly a gap between the two writers in terms of age, influence, concerns, gender and time. Chimamanda Adichie's "The Headstrong Historian" in *The Thing Around Your Neck* is clearly a rewriting of the Okonkwo narrative of *Things Fall Apart*, even with the word play on "Thing" in the book's title. Things have already fallen apart we assume from her narrative. In "The Headstrong Historian", though the person affected by colonialism is a woman, the grandmother, the resisting subject but who importantly is able to take the fight forward via the female line – the granddaughter becomes a thinker and a scholar of African history who wants to re-capture her grandmother's innate resistance and unfulfilled quest for justice. Interestingly, Adichie mentions the presence of such a dynamic and resisting grandmother in her own life.

The TED Talk "We should all be Feminists" is loaded with anecdotes about gender inequality in Africa that span class, age and circumstance and that range from her childhood experience of being denied being a monitor solely because she was a girl to adult circumstances like walking into a hotel unaccompanied and being assumed to be a sex worker or being made invisible when in the company of men. Claiming her own feminism and asserting that her grandmother was also a feminist in practice, she highlights the ridiculous conclusions of men and women in her community, some of them educated, that attempt to return her to a place of acceptance of gender inequality. For Adichie, we have evolved but our ideas have not evolved.

There is a slight nod to Achebe's *Things Fall Apart* though not identified directly in this talk in her referencing about the practice of destroying twins which appears in that novel. She identifies her beautiful twin nieces who would have been victims of that tradition had they been born back then. Her conclusion is of course that people make culture and therefore we change and can change those things that remain inappropriate. Thus she provides for her audience a simple definition of feminism, advanced a bit beyond the definition she acquired via a dictionary in her childhood search, is that of a man or a woman who says yes there is a problem with gender and we must fix it. For scholars it is a much more complicated set of definitions with a body of scholarship to match.

But Adichie is clearly aware of the variety of feminist positions for in the same TED talk, she indicates that she was very familiar with the "systems of oppression" approach which is one of the hallmarks of black feminism. Relatedly, the most advanced articulation of African feminist positions carry the class/race/gender articulation of African women's rights. A journal's 1986 editorial titled "Women on the March"[9] of a special issue on women proposed an economic/class based feminist approach to the democratization of African women's rights in the following terms:

> ... Our vision of feminism has at its very core a process of economic and social development geared to human needs through wider access to economic and political power. Equality, peace and development by and for the poor and oppressed are inextricably interlinked with equality, peace and development by and for women (3).

One sees in this formation immediately a "systems of domination" approach, linked to the development of a full humanity in which political and economic power is shared. Adichie is also well aware of this logic of the critique of inequality as she cites Wangari Maathai's claim that women appear infrequently in leadership in Africa. She also spent time asserting that equal pay for equal work is fundamental and that importantly, rape revealed the depravity of men and not the lack of inhibition of women. In other words, she engages the range of feminist issues anecdotally and descriptively.

Paying significant attention to the issue of sexuality in this talk as well, Adichie challenges the assumptions that women are raised to marry, while men have choices. She describes a woman she knows who pretended domesticity in order to get married and critiques the idea that women must silence themselves and not accept their sexuality. In an interview around the time of the publication of her book of short stories, *That Thing Around Your Neck* (2010), Adichie had described among her current preoccupations, the idea that marriage is not set up for the benefit of women and indeed can be dangerous for women but that women are conditioned to behave "as though marriage is a prize."

It becomes clear that her novel *Americanah,* while it deals with the international migration of Africans to the United States and the United Kingdom and the related issues of navigating these systems via education, offers an unabashed engagement with all aspects of sexuality, in and out of Africa for her generation. Her lead character, a young Igbo woman, reveals a range of tentative sexual escapades as a teenager in Nigeria, migration to Lagos then to the US as a student where she experiences a level of poverty that leads to an encounter in which she prostitutes herself. She ends up living in long standing relationships with white and black American men before returning to Nigeria where things have indeed fallen apart. *Americanah* is about sexuality as much as it is about transnational migration and about the full realization of the African woman as a literary subject, but it is also a critique of life in the postcolonial state.

As we have shown, Achebe as the representative voice of his generation documented well the period of the British colonial incursion into Africa and the im/possibility of a concerted and organized response. In contrast, Adichie is aware of the colossal importance of the United States as a world hegemon. The titling of the book while a play on the way Nigerians refer to those who had gone abroad to the US and returned with affectations, is also about the Americanization of the world which renders Africans at times totally dispossessed both at home and abroad and having to make a way in this world of American dominance which touches one everywhere. For this reason, the experience of her boyfriend in England is less than appealing, as he is reduced to cleaning toilets and ends up in a humiliating deportation. Ironically he is able to achieve a measure of financial success through well-known Nigerian patronage systems in which economic structures are negotiated via a series of connections and contracts with behind the scenes officials and the like. He was able to use a friend made during his difficult days in London as a representative English man. So, colonial England is not really significant in the Adichie scheme of things as it should not be for the contemporary African writer. Our protagonist returns home to Nigeria but it is not an idyllic return, but one fraught with myriad cultural adjustments along the lines of the critique of independence genre of novels, but home nonetheless

Taking the recognition of Adichie to another level, popular singing icon Beyonce's recently sampled Adichie's TED talk, "We Should all be Feminists" for her recent album. In my view, it fulfills perhaps a more elaborate marketing and recognition model than has been seen before. Achebe's *Things Fall Apart*, became a bestseller because of its iconic significance in documenting the precolonial and colonial incursion into Africa and accompanied decolonial politics across the world which became necessary reading for all those interested in learning about African culture. It was used in classes from anthropology to political science and of course in literature, on everybody's reading list.

A section of the Adichie's TED talk is sampled on Beyonce's popular self-titled album's 11th track, "Flawless":

> We teach girls to shrink themselves
> To make themselves smaller
> We say to girls
> "You can have ambition
> But not too much
> You should aim to be successful
> But not too successful
> Otherwise you will threaten the man"

> Because I am female
> I am expected to aspire to marriage
> I am expected to make my life choices
> Always keeping in mind that
> Marriage is the most important
> Now marriage can be a source of
> Joy and love and mutual support
> But why do we teach girls to aspire to marriage
> And we don't teach boys the same?
> We raise girls to see each other as competitors
> Not for jobs or for accomplishments
> Which I think can be a good thing
> But for the attention of men
> We teach girls that they cannot be sexual beings
> In the way that boys are
> Feminist: the person who believes in the social
> Political and economic equality of the sexes[10]

According to reports "At 5 p.m. on December 12, 2013 – the day before the album came out – Amazon ranked *Americanah* #No.861 of all hardcover books. Five days later, the book was ranked #No. 632. Today, the book is ranked #No. 179. It's a staggering rise up the rankings."[11]

Incorporating social media directly in the novel *Americanah* in the form of a blogging lead character, the writer uses a form familiar with her generation. A series of blogs are placed directly in the text, indicated by a different font and are actually used to advance the narrative, as would have proverbs or stories for Achebe. This provides the recognition of the character's political ideas on race in America and some of the conflicting issues and misinformation between African Americans and Africans on these issues. The writer's ideological positions are given full range though via another popular media form the TED talk accessed online internationally and then used in a music video by an entertainment icon with an extensive reach and following. I believe that we are witnessing Adichie becoming the representative for her generation of writers as Achebe was for his. Still, the comparable timelessness of both writers is yet to be proven. We are sure about Achebe. Adichie is very much in the process.

Chapter Twenty-Three

# A Poet Daughter's Farewell*

## Still Morning Yet

*Abena P. A. Busia*

Probably like many people in this room: (at the 39th ALA Conference, the Crystal Ballroom, Marriott on Lockwood Drive, Charleston, South Carolina, US), I first encountered Achebe when I first read *Things Fall Apart* though I don't remember when that "encounter" was; I feel like I have known it all my life. I do remember well when I first met Achebe in person. It was quite to my surprise at the very first exhibition of the now distinguished, then recently graduated from Yale, artist, art historian and curator Richard Powell, at a gallery on Catherine Street in New York. I met him in my first year in this country, when teaching at Yale. When he learned that I had landed a job at Rutgers, he encouraged me to attend his opening. It was October 1981. I remember at some point during the evening, returning to a print hanging at the entrance to the gallery. It is s piece that so struck me I now own it. It was one of the first works of contemporary art that I ever bought. I was standing beside Hazel Carby contemplating the piece (a complex piece of three figures at a kitchen table, one of them a self-portrait of the artist turned away from the other two people in the group) when a soft voice at my right shoulders said, "That is one of those pieces that makes you want to talk to the artist and ask them what was going on that made them capture that moment that way," or words to that effect. I'm sure you all have had similar moments: you spend your life wanting to meet someone you admire and suddenly they show up; in my case there quietly at my shoulder was the great man himself, a guest of the late Melvin Dixon, walking like a regular person amongst us, admiring the works and you're completely tongue tied and stupid; at least I was. I felt all intelligent thought freeze.

Fortunately that first impression of me was not to be the last because we "met" next through poetry. Though I don't recall how the conversation came about, Achebe was still at that time editing *Okike* and he invited me to submit my work for consideration, which I did. A long silence followed. Then in 1982, the BBC World Service ran a poetry competition for new poetry from Africa. At that time no one outside my family had yet seen my poems and feeling fearful, I sent them off to that competition. The award winning poems were published in the Heinemann African Writers Series as *Summer Fires: New Poetry from Africa* after the poem that actually won the competition, one of whose judges was the great Malawian Poet Jack Mapanje and my little poems were included in that collection. Thus three years before I was ever published as a critic, or a year before I even formerly received my doctorate from Oxford, I appeared first in print to the world as a poet.

More important at this juncture is that *before* the announcement of the winners of that competition, Achebe had selected my poems for publication in *Okike*, something about which I am very proud. (It is only the vagaries of publishing in Africa that led to the volume of *Okike* in which my poems appeared coming out after the publication of *Summer Fires.*)

I speak here as one of Achebe's literary daughters. He was a father to all of us. And like many in this room, I have my own memories: breaking bread with him at an African Literature Association Conference; accompanying him to the Library at UCLA to see the *egwungwun* masquerade; walking down the street and having coffee after a lecture in New York; meeting his daughter Nwando for the first time; but my proudest moment was that day in 2008, when at the end of the 2-day Conference, celebrating the publication of *Things Fall Apart* at University of London's School of African Oriental Studies (SOAS), I had the opportunity to be the praise poet as he was wheeled on stage for the interview which ended the conference. I have revisited here the poem I read on that occasion, changing the words a little for then we were celebrating the Golden Jubilee of Okonkwo, now we give thanks for the life of his creator.

New Brunswick NJ,
August 2013.

## Still Morning Yet
## (For Chinua Achebe in grateful memory)

*Abena P. A. Busia*

You *are* well known throughout the seven continents
And even beyond.
Your fame rests on solid personal achievements:
More than fifty years ago you brought honour to us, your people,
By conjuring up the man who could throw Amalinze the Cat.
This much we have said, so much else followed:

Through you we realized
Balance is necessary, but difficult.
Your progeny all of us,
No longer at ease in any dispensations
Old or new, for the arrows of old gods
Full of hope, still meet impediments;
Like a man of the people and the girls at war, we all learned
What the trouble is with us.
And your lessons did not fail.

In the ageless cycle of the time of the anthills
You recorded new poems in an ancient language;
In the evening wisdom of encroaching savannahs
You crafted new language for old stories;
As the moon encircles the changing earth
Our stories must map uncharted territories
And though some died in your shadow, many of us thrived
Because you showed us a way:

And now in the measure of transcendence
And the time of all classics
Things have come together:
No longer in exile, it is morning yet
On your new creation day you have crossed the river home,
Where for you, always,
There was a country.

Chapter Twenty-Four

# Chinua Achebe and the Matrix of Womanhood

*Helen Chukwuma*

It does appear really that the last word has not been written on Achebe despite all the literary criticisms, global scholarship and the profuse eulogiums that attended his death and funeral a few months ago. The continuous flow of literature on Achebe bears eloquent testimony to his greatness and the great impact of his work. Thus Chinua Achebe is dead but Chinua Achebe lives in his works.

One striking aspect of Achebe's work is his avowed philosophy of the African writer. He believes in art as commitment to the society of one's being. As Christopher Nwodo writes:

> Achebe does not write "purely literary essays" nor does he write purely literary anything because of his philosophy of art and on account of his commitment as an artist. His philosophy of art is that art belongs to a community, is the product of a community and should serve the needs of that society. (222)

This indeed has been Achebe's primary concern in his creativity but he did not ignore aesthetics in his writing. His writing teaches and delights, thus performing the consummate function of art. Art as commitment has driven Achebe's creativity. His first novel *Things Fall Apart* (1958) therefore is a redemptive story of the typical African patriarchal society as exemplified by the Igbo. Achebe's first novels clearly valorised manhood and the women characters were tucked away in cultural effrontery in the side and back domains of history. Achebe the master artist realized all too soon that there was cultural imbalance in the scheme of the old village life that denied women visibility and individual worth. He then steeped himself in the matrix of his culture to unfurl the matrix of womanhood. This paper addresses just that.

Matrix as a derivative of mater, mother, womb, uterus, an enclosure in itself, reflects womanhood. Woman is an enclosure of humanity from conception to nurture to the tomb. Such a safe enclosure should not suffer laceration or disjuncture or indeed trauma, death and removal. Womanhood suffered trauma and fear in the early novels of Achebe (*Things Fall Apart* and *Arrow of God*) and the society fell apart because the matrix could not hold. It had *suffered* effacement of the natural order. The men-folk had to learn to accommodate women in their rightful position in the natural order. It is this natural order that Achebe sought to rectify in his later novel *Anthills of the Savannah.*

It is important to stress here that Achebe's matrix is his particular Igbo (Ogidi) culture and by extension African culture. Achebe was culture-bound and this drove his storyline and his characters. He believes in and espouses the basic Igbo cultural concept of dualism as expressed in the Igbo proverb, "Ife kwulu, ife akwude be ya," When something stands, something stands beside it. Nothing in the created universe exists alone. The dualistic structure of life in the created universe is seen in the opposites of night and day, earth and sky, wet and dry, man and woman. The dualistic principle is also governed by the relationship between both parties which in itself introduces conflicts of sorts which if not resolved erode harmony. The Igbo recognize such binary relations between the sexes and thus reflect a system of complementariness whereby each gender performs its role in the schemata. If the female principle continues to suffer silence and exclusion, the society writhes in pain.

In his early novels, Achebe situates womanhood in two crucial aspects of her existence namely, her motherhood and spirituality. The latter we see in his characterization of Chielo, the priestess of Agbala, the oracle of the hills and vales, who despite being female, wields tremendous power in the society. Her power nonetheless rests at the end of her spirit possession when she reverts to her normal life as woman. It is however in woman as mother that Achebe fully harnesses his cultural roots. He delves into the Igbo allotted compound space which has a rigid dual division of obi, man's space aptly situated in the front of the compound to show lordship, guardianship and power," usoekwu" or hearth which is the woman' domain. Here I cite Caroline Mbonu:

> In Igbo life the "mgbala"or Usoekwu, is not merely a fireplace: it is the soul of the household. This soul of the house represents the female domain. While the male is the indisputable head of the Igbo household, the female heads the hearth. That is to say, men control the public sphere; women control the private sphere, reinforcing the binary principle: "ihe di abuo abuo, things exist in pairs" (Amadiume, 19), (113–14).

Achebe highlights this hearth culture to effect in *Things Fall Apart* as the comfort zone for mothers and their children. The hearth therefore is where motherhood reigns supreme. Mbonu continues:

> Within the mgbala, the female passion, compassion and imagination coalesce in the very act of birthing, sustaining and preserving life. In other words, in the Mgbala, life is born and hope nurtured and celebrated; dignity protected and secured. Here, the mother and offspring engage in quality time of togetherness that foster intimacy and respect. (113)

The mother is the heart of the home and the one to come back to. The Igbo celebrate this mother status in names given to their children, e.g. Nneka, mother is supreme, Nnebuchi, mother is chi (personal spirit) Nneamaka, mother is too beautiful. Nowhere did Achebe celebrate motherhood than when Okonkwo fleeing in exile had a ready home in the town of his late mother and her kith and kin. Achebe took time to explain this eternal umbilical tie of mother and son in the family address given by Uchendu, Okonkwo's maternal uncle in *Things Fall Apart* (129).

Achebe in his matrix of womanhood shows how the girl child and the woman stay rooted in the home and thus are still under the thumb of their fathers. Girls are still looked upon as in transit to another patriarchal domain of husbands. In all these, Achebe is able to bring to the fore the tyranny of over-bearing husbands and the burden of violence and physical abuse. He nonetheless offers perks of consolation in the sisterhood of co-wives and extended family ties.

The writer in his social commitment as teacher, realized that flaws do exist in a cultural environment that stifles women's growth and expansiveness. As part of his creative genius, he found the opportunity of elevating the female and free her from the shackles of old time customs and beliefs. The old times were changing to the new and Achebe had to change with it and present a brave new world for women. In a post-independent country, Achebe's women burst their enclosure and stepped out into the sun just as the goddess of his region, Idemili, flees her river abode and stepped into the human domain to change it for the better.

Achebe, a child of his culture in his own reflection and understanding tried to set the records straight. He thus re-visited the history of the river goddess Idemili. Idemili is the goddess of the Idemili river whose totem is the python. It has its cult of followers and worshippers and is an engaging principle for people of the area and Achebe comes from Ogidi which is part of the Idemili Local government so called in the new political and administrative division. Amadiume informs us that: " the worship of Idemili as a goddess, a religion and a culture dates back to 3000 B.C., which almost parallels the beginning of dynastic Egypt"(11). Ani or Ala is the prominent Igbo goddess of earth, fertility, nurturance, morality and regulatory behaviour. The Idemili goddess has a regional domain localized as she is to the towns in Anambra state of Nigeria. The myth of origin of Nnobi a town from which the Idemili takes its course and ends at Idemili Obosi, narrates the conjugal union between a hunter Aho and the goddess which produced the sons and progenitors of the neighbouring towns through which the river flows. This established the bond of kinship that is mother-focused and accounts for the matrilineality of Nnobi. Idemili as a deity signifies industry, assertiveness and a rigorous work ethic. Amadiume reinforces this:

> ...the female gender had the more prominent place in myth, indigenous religious and cultural concepts. There was a strong female-orientation. The supernatural, a goddess, is female. The stream Iyi Idemili is the source of divinity. The cultural result of the mediation of the natural (Aho, the hunter from the wild) and the supernatural (the goddess Idemili from the sacred stream) Edo is a hard-working woman. Thus, both Nnewi and Nnobi (Igbo towns on the river axis) inherit industriousness from females. The most praised person in Nnobi is a hard-working woman (41).

Chinua Achebe used the Idemili phenomenon as both myth and history. Such uses cause some ambivalence especially as he traverses gender lines in his Idemili portraiture. Effigy representation of the goddess itself is male-centric. She is shown as tying one piece of cloth as males do, topless and wearing a long or high black hat. The figure is not reclining or sitting, as one would expect of a female but standing assertively.

Achebe introduces Idemili as a god in *Arrow of God* complete with its totem the sacred python. Achebe cast him here in opposition and conflict with its arch-rival Ulu. Idemili claims precedence over Ulu by age and longevity of worship, but Ulu, a latter day divinity is supreme by its relevance and the centrality of the great power it wields through its chief priest. Achebe, a child of his culture cannot claim ignorance of the femaleness of Idemili. Achebe's reversal of Idemili's gender must be viewed from the patriarchal perspective of his work. The main personae in *Arrow of God* are male both in the realms of man and the supernatural. The various conflicts that dot the storyline are the fight of titans. Ulu won a pyrrhic victory and the society collapsed into anomie.

Achebe in bringing his matrix of womanhood to the fore, had recourse to the myth of Idemili. In his novel *Anthills of the Savannah,* he presents to his readers his ideal female character, cast in the image of the times. She had at last emerged from her cocoon. Any avid reader of Achebe could have seen Achebe's womanly woman emerging. Achebe had done the same in the character of Obi in *No Longer at Ease* who is the grandson of Okonkwo from *Things Fall Apart.* He had to give body to Okonkwo's wish of greater visibility of his daughter Ezinnma who in his (Okonkwo's) limited horizon can only achieve this if he had been a boy. Achebe had to present a woman with remarkable intellect and physical beauty to aspire to and succeed in a male-dominated field of play. Ezinma had to metamorphise into Beatrice, his prototype of the modern woman. In *Anthills of the Savannah*, the enclosed women characters of the earlier novels, the Matefis and the Ugoyes had to make way for the Beatrices and Elewas. Domesticity gave way to professionalism and enclosure gave way to exposure. The character is Beatrice Nwanyibuife cast in the mould of the river goddess Idemili. Beatrice came into the world with the stigma of an unwanted child because she was a "daughter too many," fifth in the line of daughters in a society with heavy premium on sons to satisfy the dictates of patriarchy. Achebe by placing his character in handicap, builds an environment of cultural rebuttal and replacement.

He builds her up as a woman of character and strength, who side-placed by her parents especially her mother decided early in life to be independent of help and accolades. Beatrice informs us that: "Throughout my life, I never sought attention, not even as a child. I can see, looking back at my earliest memories, a little girl completely wrapped up in her own little world"...(77). The author had kept her in hiddenness during her period of development and training. When we encounter her, she was introduced by no other than the President of her country Kangan:

> ...one of the most brilliant daughters of the country, Beatrice Okoh. She is a Senior Assistant Secretary in the Ministry of Finance. The only person in the Service, male or female with a first-class honours in English. We are very proud of her (68).

Beatrice's character build-up signifies the role she will play later. She finds herself in the midst of men with power and influence playing a moderating role. She mediates in the excesses of the President himself and Ikem and Chris. She advises and loses herself completely to the struggle of democracy and the welfare of the less-privileged in society. She as woman is indeed Achebe's court of last resort, the survivor who lives to not only tell the story but charts a new course for the community to follow. The women are really the anthills of the savannah grassland who survive the scorching heat and the debilitating brush fires. Her name Nwanyibuife is challenging enough and the author makes her live out the challenge.

Beatrice's prototype, the Idemili goddess, sought the company of humans and entered into marriage with the hunter Aho. This is to give her status and legitimacy. She could only function within the realm of matrimony which bestowed on her wifehood and motherhood. The goddess is known for her industry and resourcefulness, an example she showed to women from that axis. Beatrice is accomplished and resourceful but she is not married though she was in a relationship. Achebe is making a statement with her singlehood. A new dawn has broken, Beatrice is her own person, whole and entire, sufficient unto herself. She does not need marriage to complete her. She says this herself though here we can sense the authorial voice.

"I was determined from the very beginning to put my career first and if need be, last. That every woman wants a man to complete her is a piece of male chauvinist bullshit I had completely rejected before I knew there was anything like Women's Lib...There was enough male chauvinism in my father's house to last me seven reincarnations!" (80–81)

It thus becomes obvious that Beatrice is Achebe's creation and answer to the marginalization of women. Beatrice is redemptive and Achebe shows the way this can be achieved by his advocacy of education, self-fulfilment and financial independence. Further, the import of Achebe's female ascendancy is not for self–aggrandizement but for the purpose of public good. Beatrice as a character herself did not strive for political appointment as she could have; but she positioned herself as an adviser and an enabler. She gave of herself completely as seen in her relationship with the men and Elewa and Agatha. Through the character of Beatrice, Achebe moved his women to the public sphere in a masterstroke of reconstruction and revision.

Beatrice is thus a hybrid of sorts; a child of her culture and an educated elite. She therefore has been equipped for her role in the novel to take over from the ruins and vacuum created by men. Chinua Achebe himself as a committed writer and social critic has through his writings been searching for the Appian Way to his country's good leadership. From his novel *A Man of the People* (1966) where in utter contempt and dissatisfaction of governance, he cleaned out the Augean stables in a military coup. Eighteen years later, he wrote *Anthills of the Savannah*, to show that the polity had learnt very little from the past and that the greed, corruption and power struggle from the past still persists. He presents to us Woman, the hitherto weak and inconsequential and reversed her name to Nwamyibuife which is that indeed a woman is something.

At the end of the novel, Achebe shows the position of women in the future of the community. They have emerged from the backhouse to the centre and demonstrates their capacity as driving the engine of growth and progress. The hopelessness generated by the deaths of the key male characters was replaced by the new era ushered in by Elewa's new–born baby. Achebe's master revisionist stroke was the functional role of naming the new-born. It fell naturally into the hands of Beatrice in the absence of the men.

The name itself is significant, Amaechina, may the path not close. This assures not only the continuity of life as we know it, but the acceptance of the new order of women's role. Woman has emerged as the true goddess that she is. Of note is the acceptance of the elders of this new role of women based on the answer Beatrice gave to the question, "Who gave her the name?" "All of us here" said Beatrice. "All of you here," repeated the old man. "All of you are her father?" "Yes and mother." This last phrase clinches it all. A mother too as a father both have a stake in the naming of the child. As novel as it sounded, the elders accepted it, blessed it with kolanut and libation.

Chinua Achebe's work with the issue of women is done. He has extricated them from the shackles of patriarchal subordination and pointed the route to follow. His matrix of womanhood has gone the full circle and only now, begs for followership. Achebe's modern woman is the hope of the future. All else has failed. Now is the time envisaged by the river goddess for women to lead the way to a better humanity, a better world.

Chapter Twenty-Five

# The Casualties

*John Pepper Clark-Bekederemo*

The casualties are not only those who are dead;
They are well out of it.
The casualties are not only those who are wounded,
Though they await burial by instalment
The casualties are not only those who have lost
Person or property, hard as it is
To grape for a touch that some
May not know is not there
The casualties are not those led away by night;
The cell is a cruel place, sometimes a heaven,
No where as absolute as the grave
The casualties are not those who started
A fire and now cannot put it out. Thousands
Are burning that had no say in the matter.
The casualties are not only those who escaping
The shattered shell become prisoners in
A fortress of falling walls.

The casualties are many, and a good number well
Outside the scene of ravage and wreck;
They are the emissaries of rift,
So smug in smoke-room they haunt abroad,
They are wandering minstrels who, beating on
The drum of human heart, draw the world
Into a dance with rites it does not know

The drum overwhelm the guns...
Caught in the clash of counter claims and charges
When not in the niche others have left,
We fall.
All casualties of war,
Because we cannot hear other speak,
Because eyes have ceased to see the face from the crowd,
Because whether we know or
Do not know the extent of wrong on all sides,
We are characters now other than before
The war began, the stay- at- home unsettled
By taxes and rumour, the looters for office
And wares, fearful everyday the owners may return
We are all casualties,
All sagging as are
The case celebrated for kwashiorkor,
The unforeseen camp-follower of not just our war.

Chapter Twenty-Six

# Chinua Achebe

## Some Reflections

*Anani Dzidzienyo*

It is not easy writing about Professor Chinua Achebe. This has nothing to do with any complexities about his being or the collective body of his oeuvre.

Quite the contrary. It is much more a matter of doing full justice to him and his place in the world of writing and writers. And for those of us who are neither literary scholars nor specialists in African literature, the challenge is even more daunting. Therein, precisely, lies the rub. I thus embark on this discussion as a matter of situating Professor Achebe within a broader framework which seeks to underscore the import of his work and presence for the world at large.

If *Things Fall Apart* and *Anthills of the Savannah* can be considered as bookends of a sort, with *A Man of the People* lodged in between them, a decidedly idiosyncratic choice, admittedly, and if these two texts convey the journey from changes at home as home headed for changes brought on by the advent of the European colonial contact and its consequences, culminating in the further changes in the wake of Independence and the emergence of the new hybrid classes of political, cultural and economic figures, the temptation to read past the literary into the political can be overwhelming. But, then again, we cannot hold Professor Achebe responsible for the way we each read and interpret his works.

Chief Nanga was not a literary invention. He was a figure who was readily recognizable in early independent West Africa and one who simultaneously embodied envy, contempt and some pity. His sheer wallowing in corruption and his public display of both his corruptibility and his ruthlessness were credible because his ilk could be found all over the place. That Professor Achebe was able to literally photograph this "product" and present him to the world of readers at that time was an important contribution to conceptualization and comprehension of the underbelly of the new nation. [1]

It is this ability to offer portraiture which far transcended caricature which made the issue of corruption and its corrosive impact so palpable. In a certain sense, there is a direct line connecting Chief Nanga and Officer Sam, the leader of the junta in *Anthills.* Not that at the onset, Sam would have vaguely considered himself to be in the same corruption boat as the Chief if only because of the huge differences in their educational and class backgrounds.[2] But, within the context of the nation and considering the consequences of their actions for nation and people, they were in the same place. This is not exactly a comfortable idea for evaluating the uses of formal educational achievement and the obligations and privileges in its train. But, then again, Professor Achebe could not have been said to have been in the business of dishing out comfortable ideas or suggestions for change where the health of the nation, writ large, was concerned. Otherwise, *The Trouble With Nigeria* would not have come to us. Not just Nigeria but the rest of the Continent and the sheer indiscipline and arrogance on the part of power-holders and their minions as concerns in his brief could not be mistaken or underestimated.[3]

What, after all was to be the real test of the meaning of independence for the nation and freedom for the nationals? Were the two ideas twins? Did the first necessarily prefigure the second? Professor Achebe would probably aver that while the first condition was paramount, the equivalent, perhaps, of Kwame Nkrumah's "Seek Ye First the Political Kingdom," with all other things being added, national leaders demanding trust because they considered themselves as custodians of national independence without the slightest attention to the freedom and wellbeing of nationals, would inevitably result in the direct or indirect withdrawing of support, the negation of legitimacy.[4] The road would lead back to history, community, legitimacy, censorship for acts of sacrilege, disrespect, undermining of what was considered acceptable.

The intersection of personal life, changes in national life, transplantation to other habitats, while all the time pursuing the ideal of freedom and justice for all, contradictions notwithstanding, reappear in *Anthills of the Savannah.*

What is the meaning of friendship in historical context? How does a sudden change in fortune affect the nature of solidarities among friends as their inter-personal relations are now catapulted into a larger and more consequential national framework or projected onto a bigger stage? Perhaps Beatrice in *Anthills* best captures this when she avers that the three "friends" acted as if the whole national problem was just about themselves. Having staged a coup, the coup-maker looked to his old friends for support, hoping that their different backgrounds would redound to the benefit of the new regime. It was not to be.[5]

Here again, Professor Achebe's text brings to life developments which would not have been unfamiliar to many West Africans. The question is, and Beatrice implies this: Can a nation be viewed as a family writ large? This is certainly a question that could have been put to Professor Achebe. But, then again, what constitutes family? That his writing could point to such fundamental questions which are applicable to the whole continent is a measure of his value to all of us.

Growing up in a seaport in colonial Gold Coast, yams were a popular foodstuff which periodically made their way into town from elsewhere. There was an awareness of certain ritual symbolic value to them. They were the requisite dish for honouring certain occasions when they were mashed with palm oil and crowned with a boiled egg. Kolanuts were "there," to be chewed for pleasure by some but they were not universally seen as an opening ritual item for visits or confraternisation. And "taking titles" were nowhere near the realities of the hometown. Hence, *Things Fall Apart* opened up a whole new world of life and times in other places. But, other places not just in faraway Nigeria, but even other places in the Gold Coast and Ghana because *Things Fall Apart* entered our consciousness in early independent and republican Ghana.[6]

This raises the question of reading him for solely literary insights and edification, as distinct from other ones. Should/could Professor Achebe be read for either or both reasons?

To think that in the early independent years, West African writers were just beginning to "enter" the "accepted" world cannon of the literature read by "educated" folks at home. That seems like another time and another place largely because, it could be posited, on account of his pioneering efforts and achievements.

How then was his work to be read, taught, thought and, eventually, assessed? In the first place, there must be ample room for interpretation and the ways and means of bringing his texts to life. If for example, there is an interest in getting critical glimpses into the historical moment in which African societies and polities responded forcefully in multiple ways to European colonial intrusions, it is critical to recognize the multiplicities of characters and actions which belie the imagining of any linear or simplistic centres. This offering alone helps to situate Continental Africa within a broader human framework. Of course, there is the persistent paradox of generalizing and particularizing about Africa. He had not set out to write about Africa. He wrote about a specific place and specific people and culture. In so doing, he provided a clear view into a part of Africa which then made both Africans and non-Africans begin to move from the specific to the general. It was a portrait which would make us all proud of an African community and its life and struggles. Briefly put, Okonkwo the man, the figure, the symbol could be imagined and re-imagined elsewhere on the continent because Professor Achebe was able to draw from the depths of observation, thinking and imagination to bring to life the complexity which was Okonkwo.

But, was Okonkwo just a one-time, one place figure? Are there his incarnations walking around today here, there, everywhere on the Continent? Of course, there is a simple answer which would not be totally satisfactory. He was a product of a historical time and place which no longer exist. But, are some of those issues still with us? To what extent can the individual successfully balance the challenges and tugs of self and community? What is the measure of success? Pride? Modesty? Conspicuous throwing around and display of the symbols of power? What about religion and its influences on generations of Africans? Missionaries and missionarising today?

This leads us into the realm of that very tricky question: what language to write in? The colonial one? An indigenous African one? This is not the place to re-visit that particular disputation, especially in the variant symbolized by Professors Achebe and Ngũgĩ wa Thiong'o.[7] In this language matter, the issue of exile comes to the fore. One is reminded of what the Uruguayan writer, Eduardo Galeano, once observed. That apart from the exile of living as an expatriate which had been the lot of many Latin American writers, there was another kind of exile, maybe even more profound, that is the fact that most Latin American writers are exiled from their countrymen and women who are unable to afford or read their books.[8] That offers some important food for thought for Africans, both writers and readers. Therein lies the import of the language question. Language and eloquence and the value placed on the ability to deploy these two with aplomb. Speaking is one thing. Capturing speech in writing becomes even more fascinating especially in view of the mediation of travelling from the indigenous language to the colonial one. His was the soft delivery, replete with proverbs and other signifiers which characterized his speech, both in individual conversation and in public ones. That, at least, is how this writer remembers Professor Achebe's use of language in different settings ranging from the 92nd Street Y in New York City to his office in Africana Studies at Brown University, at Commencement ceremonies in Africana Studies, and in the course of The Achebe Colloquium at Brown University.[9]

The last four years at Brown were a special bonus. For the community of students and faculty who were actively engaged in teaching and discussing his work, the mere fact that he was in his first floor office in Africana Studies meant that there was a feeling of ever-present connection to the whole history from *Things Fall Apart* onward. It was particularly pleasing to be able to inform a class on The Afro-Luso-Brazilian Triangle in May 2012 that, earlier that year, *A educacao de uma criança sob o Protetorado Britanico* had been published in Brazil.[10]

The story telling mode and the pointing in the direction of the interconnectedness of the moment to earlier historical ones and keeping eyes on the basic goodness and humanity of people, irrespective of the "Trouble" with past or present rulers of all stripes. His interest in the world around him informed his discourses. Readers might not readily or easily imagine him coming out on a cold-ish evening in May to wait for Ray Charles. But, that is what exactly transpired when he came to have an honorary degree conferred on him by Brown University in 1998. Ray Charles was billed to perform at the Pops Concert on the Saturday night before Monday's Commencement. He noted that a ticket for the Ray Charles Concert was a condition for accepting the honorary degree.[11] At the end of the concert, sometime after midnight, it was amazing to observe him responding to all those who were asking for autographs at that time.

If there were to be a discussion today of the world into which *Things Fall Apart* had first seen the light of day and its trajectory since then, there would be no gainsaying the fact that through that journey, Professor Achebe's commitment to telling the story and stories starting at the local level, moving to the national, keeping an eye on the continental and also the Diasporic and Transnational all culminate in a giant contribution to the appreciation of African humanity.

Not to put too fine a point on the Brazilian publication of *Arrow of God* but, its significance must be underscored. With the increasing asserting of Brazil's African-ness in the world today, to the point where Brazil's initiatives to connect to independent African countries beyond Portuguese-speaking African countries, a process both interesting and problematical to the extent that it is not often connected to the present predicament of people of African descent in Brazil, *Things Fall Apart* in Portuguese is likely to expand the boundaries of Continental African forms of knowledge to Brazilians. That is not a small matter.

There are discussions which, ideally speaking, could have been held about Continental and Diasporic relations, that is moving beyond official communiqués and looking at ways of augmenting direct exchanges among writers and "story tellers" from both sides. Since this is not something that Professor Achebe could be involved in, there is a case to be made for the serious exploration of a project under whose auspices the discussion of the continuing relevance of the road from *Things* to Nigeria and Africa can be further considered. That would be a fitting attention to the interconnectedness between paths and rivers and the matter of which comes first in the relationship. That he did himself not lay claim to being the singular voice of Nigeria or Africa does not in any way interfere with the universal acclaim accorded him as a most senior, if not the most senior in the pantheon of African writers. This said, it would be readily acknowledged by anyone who had the privilege of directly engaging with him that he was not preoccupied with matters of pedigree. But, he is, indeed, pedigree.

In *Anthills*, Beatrice and Elewa brought another dimension to "The Story," in the portrayal of two memorable women of different backgrounds who came together, eventually, to provide voices which would not have been found readily in the earlier "Story." As indicated above, the urban setting of *Anthills* and *Man* speak directly to those born and brought up in rough and tumble urban areas. Not that the rural origins of the new urban areas were totally out of mind. In those late days of colonial privilege urban life for its "freedom" to the point when rural areas were not considered "with it," to borrow a later expression, *Things* became culturally affirming in its educational value. *Things* provided the eyes and ears which came to be appreciated for the poignancy of the "story" told and the challenges it posed. Actually, it became a counterpoint to the town/city narrative of Cyprian Ekwensi's *People of the City* and his *Jagua Nana.*[12]

For this writer, Professor Achebe's "story" in *Anthills* has a particular resonance in the character of soldier Sam. Coming across him always brings to mind a particular general in that parade of generals who have occupied the "seat" of state. Why this is so can only be attributed to the strength of the characterization he offers. And, not to forget the obsequious Lawyer-Minister, more specifically, Attorney-General whose constant refrain of himself as an outsider in the matter of elite schools. If, in *Things* and *Man*, we see earlier forms of colonial education, as per Chief Nanga's relations with his former student, Odili, by *Anthills*, we have moved into university education and its rewards which are not necessarily predictable. Higher education did not necessarily trump gender roles.

Perhaps it is all about power, from *Things* all the way to *Anthills.* How to acquire it and its corroding influence on individuals and relationships. If your childhood days friend becomes the dictator in charge, are you duty-bound to address him as "Excellency" with a smile or a smirk? Does he suddenly acquire the right to interfere in your romantic life, ex officio? But even, maybe especially the military dictator has to treat foreign visitors in a special manner redounding to the prejudice of national women.

The impermanence of conditions and the constancy of the idea that no one climbs the ladder of death alone escape the attention of the foolhardy and the short sighted like the dictator Sam in *Anthills* who wreaks havoc on his old friends Chris and Ikem. But then, his own fate found him. Not that Professor Achebe put it that simply. He wove the story in all its complexity in a way that makes it easy to relate fiction to real life. Unless, of course, one took the position that between *The Trouble* and *Anthills*, there is a certain difficulty in separating developments in these books. That, arguably, is the real significance of his contribution to the enhancement of looking into and developing a better appreciation of stories, how they are composed and delivered and their continuing significance for African and Africana letters and thought.

A traveller's travel has come to an end, after a fashion but the road maker who followed the path cleared by ancestors has himself now become a path-clearer.[13] Clearing the path and travelling which open possibilities for seeing and seeing anew for more stories to be woven to cover and comfort us. That is the work Professor Achebe has wrought. We are all in his debt.

## Coda

The discussion continues apace in the matter of the "fatherhood" of African Literature. This ties into the very conceptualization and definition of Africa. Wole Soyinka has recently observed that Chinua Achebe himself had eschewed the "fatherhood" designation. Soyinka further observed that, given the multiplicities of languages, cultures, literary traditions to be found on the Continent, the designation is anything but helpful. That it plays into the hands of ignorant observers and commentators, with the occasional flights into exuberance even by those who know better.[14]

A writer in the Afro-Brazilian online publication of the Afro-Brazilian women's organization, Cidinha da Silva, reacted thus to hearing the news: "I have great difficulty in penning a few lines because this writer (Chinua Achebe), brought about a revolution in my head. He made me change the way I look at myself. I consider him vital for whosoever wants to do away with the colonialism that lives inside herself or himself. Chinua, my teacher, go in peace. May the creative and transformative forces receive you very well. There are good people waiting for you."[15]

## Chapter Twenty-Seven

# *In Memoriam*

# Morning, March 22, 2013, Charleston, South Carolina

*Maureen Ngozi Eke*

African Literature Association (ALA) Executive Council meeting

Messenger at the door
Someone approaches
I turn
Walk to the door
The messenger announces
We received word this morning that Chinua Achebe has passed. He was 82.
Stillness
I am frozen
A river runs down my face
Sounds defy me
Rivulets gush down my face tumbling down onto clothes
I contemplate a dirge, a scream
How do I lead home a father, brother, guardian, son of the land, his time now come?
How do I weave a narrative about a weaver of tales?
With whose voice do I sing for a praise singer?
Who greets a griot whose voice has grown silent?
What songs do I perform?
I know not what voice
With which to speak all that my tongue wishes to say
But holds back
O ancestors
What message do you send us on this day recalling our griot, our ogene, ekwe?
Who released our tongues...

Achebe gave us a unique voice in the face of centuries of assaults against our psyche. Those of us who met him even once were charmed by the humanity and humility of this modern day Prometheus, who chose to live among us and insisted on our right to be human, to be Africans and human. The publication of his first novel *Things Fall Apart* (1958) announced to the world that we, too, had the right to create narratives of ourselves as we wished – that we had something of importance to tell a world that did not seem too interested in our survival or that looked at us with "scorn." In his essay "Named for Victoria, Queen of England," Achebe asserts, "The nationalist movement in British West Africa after the Second World War brought about a mental revolution which began to reconcile us to ourselves. It suddenly seemed that we too might have a story to tell. *Rule Britannia!* to which we had marched so unself-consciously on Empire Day now stuck in our throat" (Ashcroft, Griffith and Tiffin 145). In defiance, he proclaimed to the world that Joseph Conrad and western writers like him did not fully understand us, refusing to concede that such writers could enunciate for us. How could Achebe be faulted for daring to hold such writers accountable for what they write? If a griot's responsibility is to his/her people, then, Achebe unmasked what he saw as "the desire... in Western psychology to set Africa up as a foil to Europe, as a place of negations at once remote and vaguely familiar, in comparison with which Europe's own state of spiritual grace will be manifest" (*Hopes and Impediments* 2-3). Indeed, *Things Fall Apart* signalled Achebe's battle cry and Achebe was the warrior, who recognized the power of language – words. Thus, in manipulating the English language, the colonial "tongue" which he inherited, to represent his people and culture in *Things Fall Apart*, Achebe initiated an unbridled anti-colonial war or protest against western discourses of representation deployed against Africans. "I believe that it is impossible to write anything in Africa without some kind of commitment, some kind of message, some kind of protest," he says in his memoir, *There Was a Country* (2012), adding, "In my definition I am a protest writer, with restraint" (58). This discourse of engagement, of protest "with restraint" and of re-repositioning Africa and Africans would be continued consciously or unconsciously by later generations of African writers in various forms.

For sure, Achebe's quarrel with Joseph Conrad and Joyce Cary was about writing Africa, but, his criticism underscored the significance of interrogating and consequently correcting the erasure of Africans by a discourse of imperialism which saw Africa and Africans only as objects of mercantile exchange – slavery or colonization. He has described his work as an "act of "atonement," stating, "Although I did not set about it consciously in that solemn way I now know that my first book, *Things Fall Apart*, was an act of atonement with my past, the ritual return and homage of a prodigal son"

(Ashcroft, Griffith and Tiffin 145). Really, Achebe could not have been incorrect in charging Conrad with racism in projecting an image of Africa as a place that was incapable of speaking for itself, an Africa that was simply to Marlow "a place of darkness," whose people passed him "without a glance," but "with that complete, deathlike indifference of unhappy savages" (Murfin 30). Truly, who asked the Africans if they defined or saw themselves as savages or barbarians before the Europeans arrived? How could a people with centuries of cultural, political and artistic history suddenly become savages with no history, language, or civilization? Really, who would blame Achebe for taking umbrage with such dehumanizing representation of his people, even, if Wilson Harris thinks that Conrad's narrative is a "frontier novel," standing "upon a threshold of capacity," and that Achebe's "judgement or dismissal of *Heart of Darkness* is a profoundly mistaken one" (qtd. in Murfin 110)? One might ask Harris if people live in his so-called "frontier" landscape and if those living there have a right to selfhood, history and/or to speech? Of course, history is replete with stories of what happened to those living in the "frontier." Take for instance the fate of the Arawak, the Carib/Kalinago, the Taino, various North American indigenous groups, as well as African and other indigenous nations whose cultures no longer exist or whose tongues have been symbolically severed because they were defined as "frontier peoples." In his novel *Waiting for the Barbarians* (1980), J.M. Coetzee calls attention to the playing out of the trauma of imperialism and its politics of domination, extermination and containment. Of course, Coetzee's novel challenges to investigate and engage the nature and construction of barbarism and who the barbarians may be. It seems that Achebe asks a similar question in his engagement with the discourse of colonial and western imaginations of Africans. But, he also recognizes the daunting task of correcting or contending with the spectral presence of racism in western representations of or dealings with Africa, when is says: "I am not so naïve as to think that I have slain the monster of racist habit with one stroke of the essay" (Achebe xiv). Invoking W.E.B. Du Bois' warning in his seminal book *The Souls of Black Folk* (1903) that "The problem of the 20th Century is the problem of the colour line" (qtd. in Achebe xiv), Achebe insists that Conrad, even if he were writing before the 20th Century should be held accountable for proffering a text which dehumanized the continent and its people. Really, as Achebe's prodding suggests, Conrad could not be completely unaware of Europe's racism or its discourse; otherwise, why write a book that Conrad's defenders claim takes issue with imperialism or the colonial project – a very "racist" project? Indeed, African and Postcolonial literary scholarship has vindicated Achebe, underscoring the significance of his palaver with Conrad. Critics such as Benita Parry and Susan Blake, for instance, have agreed with Achebe and point to other ways in which Conrad's narrative discursively invokes race and other inequities (Murfin 110).

I want to draw attention to the historical relevance of Achebe's engagement of Conrad and other colonialist writers like him. For indeed, were it not for Achebe, the discourse of Postcolonial literary studies and criticism or even cultural studies in relation to African literary scholarship may not have been as foregrounded as it became. Indeed, Achebe troubled and expanded, if not initiated, the discourse of what would become Postcolonial African literary studies. His influence on the field cannot be ignored, for clearly, the publication of *Things Fall Apart* did not only give birth to Heinemann Publications of the "African Writer's Series," but also it established the thematic tone of the series for decades. Like Olaudah Equiano's narrative, *The Interesting Narrative of the Life of Olaudah* Equiano (1789), which challenged European representation and imagination of Africans more than one century earlier, Achebe's *Things Fall Apart* troubled the consciousness of Europe and its imagination of Africa and Africans, serving as a counter-canonical text to a long standing European "master" narrative in which Africa could not be seen or heard. Achebe was simply confronting the historical trauma of colonization or imperialism and his novel represented that initial salvo, which shocked its audience out of complacency. For, really, how does one explain Okonkwo, who despite his flaws remains one of the most memorable characters in African and/or World literature(s)? Anyone who has taught *Things Fall Apart* must contend with Okonkwo's killing of his adopted son Ikemefuna and the protagonist's suicide at the end of the novel. Yet, readers are drawn to Okonkwo's character and often, readers empathize and are frustrated by his death and the irony of it all. In my teaching of this text over several decades, these incidents more than any other event in the narrative trouble the audience and tend to define the closing conversations about the narrative. Some readers ignore or accept Okonkwo's suicide, but cannot understand Ikemefuna's death, specifically Okonkwo's role in it. I have had teachers come up to me at gatherings seeking answers to this incident. What was Achebe trying to say or do? How should we accept or read Okonkwo? Is he a liberation fighter, a nationalist, a nativist or simply an unhinged malcontent? The issue is complex, yet, one might simply ask: How "truthfully" does one represent one's culture or understanding of it? Achebe seeks balance in his representation – the beauty and the ugliness, for clearly, we cannot be completely ugly and thus devoid of any beauty as those colonialist writers would want to see or define us. Geoffrey Winikur describes the function of *Things Fall Apart* best when he says, "*Things Fall Apart* [is] an extraordinary novel for teaching students critical thinking skills, learning to read from multicultural perspectives and for challenging assumptions that we make about other cultures." Winikur is not alone in noting the cross-cultural significance of Achebe's work, for Barbara Kingsolver would pay an homage to Achebe, acknowledging his influence in the "Author's Note" in her work, *The Poisonwood Bible* (1998). In this work, albeit fictional, Kingsolver, the "fortunate child of medical and public-health workers, whose compassion and curiosity led them to the Congo" (x), picks up the mantle from Achebe, presenting an Africa and Africans that Conrad refused to acknowledge. Whether or not critics agree with Kingsolver's representation or its accuracy is not my focus here.

As Mĩcere Gĩthae Mũgo informed us this afternoon, Achebe inspired many of us, serving as literary "god father" and model to several African and African Diaspora writers, women and men (from Octavia Butler to Toni Morrison and Chimamanda Ngozi Adichie). For those of us who study this discipline called African Literature, Achebe's anti-colonialist discourse helped to pave the path for our discipline. Some of us encountered him before becoming aware of a field called African literature. Indeed, Achebe was not the first African writer to be published. There were others before him, including Amos Tutuola (*The Palmwine Drinkard* 1952), Peter Abrahams (*Mine Boy* 1946) to mention a few. But, Achebe's work was unique, because of its attempt to recuperate African voices and cultures, its rendering of the narrative through African lenses. My first encounter with Achebe was through this familiar "African" narrative voice in his children's book, *Chike and the River* (1966) shortly after the Nigerian-Biafran war. Perhaps, it was even towards the end of the war. It was a gift from one of my teachers. Where he got the book I will never know. But, the book enchanted me, I suppose, because following the adventures of Chike as he tried to cross the river drew me into the world of the oral traditions and stories whose experiences we only imagined or to lost memories of eating suya (kebab), a privilege we could no longer afford during the Nigerian-Biafran war. Achebe would recreate this world of the oral tradition in several of his novels. Mensah Adinkrah, Professor of Sociology and a suicidologist who teaches criminology offered the following comments during a "Memorial Tribute" to Achebe at Central Michigan University, underscoring Achebe's influence not only on him, but also on generations of Africans: "Like many people of my generation growing up in Africa, the writings of Chinua Achebe made quite an impression on me. Of course, it started with Achebe's most celebrated and internationally acclaimed work *Things Fall Apart* [which] I first read in 1971." Adinkrah added that what impressed him most with Achebe "was the quality of the writing style and how vividly realistic the book portrayed life in my corner of the world." He was also "impressed by the boldness of Achebe in repudiating colonialism. His was an eloquent challenge to the presentation of colonialism as having a benign, benevolent influence on the colonized people and their institutions."

Indeed, as Adinkrah's comments affirm, above all else, Achebe was a man of the people, a son of the African soil, who like the griots of the past held our feet – individuals, national governments and/or collective of people, to the fire. He did not spare his own country Nigeria from his tongue lashing either. In his collection of short essays, *The Trouble with Nigeria* (1983), he holds the leadership accountable, insisting that the nation's problem "is simply and squarely a failure of leadership" (1). "There is nothing basically wrong with the Nigerian character," (1) Achebe asserts, adding that the problem is "the unwillingness or inability of its leaders to rise to the responsibility, to the challenge of personal example which are hallmarks of true leadership" (1). In many ways, this critique of the leadership is akin to his earlier criticism of the discourse of power as deployed by Conrad. Today, one would be hard pressed to disagree with Achebe, in light of the emergence of what has been described as a new form of terrorism represented by Boko Haram in the country, an increase in the escalation of various forms of violence against the citizenry and the disenfranchisement of indigenous groups such as those in the oil-producing Niger Delta. Achebe was correct in identifying the various ailments of a nation whose potential has been sapped by a failed leadership and the unwitting complicity of its citizens, who have not held their leaders and even themselves fully accountable and the unwitting complicity of the citizenry.

One is not surprised, therefore, when Achebe returned to the question of national and leadership accountability in his last book, *There Was a Country* (2012) to address the past, specifically, the issue of Biafra, justice for those traumatized by the civil strife. To date, Nigerian leadership has made very little attempt to examine the realities of Biafra: no truth and reconciliation processes have been undertaken to examine past atrocities committed against those areas that were part of the short-lived nation called Biafra. No serious inquiries into post-conflict punitive acts – neglect of those areas formerly under Biafra either in terms of resource distribution or development. Indeed, Achebe recognized the incompleteness of the national narrative about Biafra. While the Federal government of Nigeria denies and refuses to name the mass killings of Igbos and Biafrans during the war as genocide or pogrom, Achebe defines it as such, describing it as a precursor to Rwanda and Darfur "[a]lmost thirty years" earlier and "over two million people – mothers, children, babies, civilians – [who] lost their lives…(228). On "the question of genocide" against Biafrans, therefore, Achebe asks critical questions that remain unaddressed. As a writer who is also a victim of the carnage, he testifies to the trauma, for Achebe served as an emissary for Biafra, asserting that "As a writer I believe that it is fundamentally important, indeed essential to our humanity, to ask the hard questions, in order to better understand ourselves and our neighbours. Where there is justification for further investigation, then I believe justice should be served" (*There Was a Country,* 228). Should the nation – named Nigeria – be held accountable for a "thirty-month war" that left "perhaps three million dead…approximately 20 per cent of the entire population [of Biafra]"? (227). Achebe is also critical of the role of some Nigerian "intellectuals" or elites who colluded with the Nigerian federal government. Furthermore, Achebe questions the integrity of some regional and international organizations, such as the Organization of African Unity (OAU) now the African Union (AU) and the United Nations, respectively for failing to intervene or criticize the genocidal practices of the federal government of Nigeria. This memoir represents Achebe's final challenge to the world, a swansong and one performed with acute deftness, as an elder, a writer-griot-witness-seeker of truth-sojourner, but especially as a progeny of the soil.

This is a sad day. Yet, this too, is a day of celebration and remembrance. Perhaps, Achebe was prescient when he published his memoir *There Was a Country* less than one year ago, again nudging some of us, Nigerians in particular, to re-examine our memory of what we think we know about ourselves and/or our history, to confront the truth about ourselves, no matter what they may be so that we may safeguard the future. While we must leave this day with the awareness that our elder brother has left us, we are also gratified by his gift to us, his insistence on our humanity. Today, we sing him home:

The Iroko has fallen
And the world stands aghast
Shaken by reverberations of an avalanche
We did not foresee
In this year of memorials
In this place of rememory (at the Port of Charleston, where so
many enslaved Africans stepped
Onto the American soil for the first time)
Whose signs were laid centuries before us
We felt the great calling home
The journeying back of a son
A brother, father, griot to ancestors waiting
How quietly time meets us
How brazenly it mocks our illusions of grandeur
And fevered visions of certainty
Dear brother, elder, griot, may the ancestors guide your return
as they guided your visitation with us
As you become now one of the honoured
Laa n'udo, k'emesia (Go in peace till we meet again).

Chapter Twenty-Eight

# Chinua Achebe

## *The Passing of a Comet*

*Ernest N. Emenyonu*

When Chinua Achebe died on March 21, 2013, he was 82 years old. Since the middle of the 20th Century he had been the most important figure in the field of African Literature. Some scholars described him as the "creator/inventor" of African Literature, others called him "the grandfather" of Nigerian Literature, and yet others referred to him as the creative genius and pre-eminent African literary philosopher of the 20th Century. In the context of his pioneer contributions to African imaginative creativity and literary criticism, Chinua Achebe was perceived in a variety of other ways by people and organizations worldwide. *The Times* of London cited him as "one of the 1000 Makers of the 20th Century." Nuruddin Farah of Somalia, himself an accomplished prolific novelist and the 1998 winner of the prestigious Neustadt Literary Prize, referred to Achebe as "Africa's best novelist and craftsman and one of the world's greatest, living or dead." Toni Morrison, the 1993 Nobel Laureate for Literature, thanked Chinua Achebe for "doors which he opened figuratively for her…" James Brooks an eminent African American scholar described Achebe as the "necessary angel who restored for us (Africans in the Diaspora) something that slavery took from us." Achebe was held in such high esteem by the great African American writer, James Baldwin, that at Baldwin's death his family presented to Achebe, Baldwin's most priceless possession as a writer – his briefcase – believing that "he would have wanted you to have it."

In sum, Chinua Achebe was the world-acclaimed African writer who at 28 published in 1958, a first novel, *Things Fall Apart,* that went on to become a world classic that has been translated into sixty-five languages (with more in the pipeline), with over 12 million copies in sales. This anti-colonial novel told the inside story of European colonialism in Africa, and laid to rest centuries of European distortions of African precolonial life, history and reality. In essence,

*Things Fall Apart* is Africa's side of the story of the continent's encounter with the early Europeans who came to Africa at the turn of the 20th Century. Through the story, Achebe wanted to show the reader that the tactics of the early Europeans in their encounter with Africans were well-designed strategies for the fall of Africa. Furthermore, the story of the "falling apart" of Africa brought about by European colonization is vital in the understanding of the key issues in today's Africa – issues of cultural confusion and conflicts, the weakening effects of African development as a geo-cultural region and the psychology of imperial conquest and its implications.

Chinua Achebe was the inimitable pacesetter who gave Developing World writers of the 20th Century, not only an aggressive *message* but also an enduring medium to convey it. At his death he was Distinguished Professor and Writer-in-Residence at Brown University (one of America's Eight Ivy League Universities) in Providence, Rhode Island. For more than fifty years, Chinua Achebe ruled the world of African Literature, providing it stature, substance, structure, vitality; virtually dictating its pace and nurturing its vision and development.

In 1964, six years after the publication of *Things Fall Apart,* Achebe in an article titled "The Role of the Writer in a New Nation," issued a kind of blueprint for his contemporaries and other writers after them on what African imaginative writing at the time should be about. "This is my answer to those who say that a writer should be writing about contemporary issues – about politics in 1964, about city life, about the last *coup d'état.* Of course, these are all legitimate themes for the writer but as far as I am concerned the fundamental theme must first be disposed of. This theme, put quite simply, is that African people did not hear of culture for the first time from Europeans; that their societies were not mindless but frequently had a philosophy of great depth and value and beauty, that they had poetry and above all, they had dignity. It is this dignity that many African people all but lost during the colonial period and it is this that they must now regain. The worst thing that can happen to a people is the loss of their dignity and self-respect. The writer's duty is to help them regain it by showing them in human terms what happened to them, what they lost. There is a saying in Igbo that a man who can't tell where the rain began to beat him cannot know where he dried his body. The writer can tell the people where the rain began to beat them. After all, the writer's duty is not to beat this morning's headline in topicality; it is to explore in depth the human condition." For his contemporaries and others, this was a proposition, by no means binding; for Chinua Achebe, it was the only way to go, *a mission.* For, a year later in 1965, in a related article titled, "The Novelist as Teacher," he declared, "Here then is an adequate revolution for me to espouse – to help my society regain belief in itself and put away the complexes of the years of denigration and self-abasement. And it is essentially a question of education in the best sense of the word. Here, I think, my aims and the deepest aspirations of my society meet. For no thinking African can escape the pain of the wound in our soul. You have all heard of the African Personality; of African democracy, of the African way to socialism, of negritude, and so on. They are all props we have fashioned at different times to help us get on our feet again. Once we are up we shan't need any of them any more. But for the moment it is in the nature of things that we need to counter racism with what Jean-Paul Sartre has called an anti-racist racism, to announce not just that we are as good as the next man but that we are much better."

It is very necessary to quote these non-fictional statements in great length because that is the only way we can understand what Achebe's vocation as a writer truly entailed; for it is what separates him from not only his contemporaries but all other African writers before and after him. A writer must plead the cause of his society and if need be, take up arms to defend that cause. It is from these declarations that we understand Achebe's devotion and dedication as a writer. An African writer must be committed to his society and do battle for that society without thinking twice. Any wonder then that he denounced the so-called Western ideology of "art for art's sake," dubbing it "a deodorized dog-shit." Till death he was uncompromising in his belief in the social significance of art, and the artist's commitment to serve his/her society through imaginative creativity.

During the first decade after the publication of *Things Fall Apart*, Achebe wrote a series of articles showing how the African writer can make himself/herself relevant to the immediate society in much the same way that the artist in traditional African society identified with the society, had a clear conception of its problems and needs and when he performed for an audience, reflected those needs and addressed himself to specific human problems, projecting through the ethical formulas in his tales, a direction for his society and individuals caught in the dilemmas of humanity. The traditional artist saw this as an inviolable commitment for relevance and acceptance. So did Achebe and that is why the African Literature that he espoused was different from any other literature of its time. Achebe had clearly answered for the African continent the often asked question – *How is African Literature different from other literatures, particularly Western Literature?* He defined African Literature as a literature of socio-cultural relevance and the African writer in terms of his/her service to the community. He quoted the Ghanaian professor of philosophy, William Abraham to reinforce his position: "Just as African scientists undertake to solve some of the scientific problems of Africa, African historians go into the history of Africa, African political scientists concern themselves with the politics of Africa; why should African literary creators be exempted from the services that they themselves recognize as genuine?" It was at this point that Chinua Achebe clearly defined his mission as an African writer. Concluding his article on "The Novelist as Teacher," he maintained: "I for one would not wish to be excused. I would be quite satisfied if my novels (especially the ones I set in the past) did no more than teach my readers that their past – with all its imperfections – was not one long night of savagery from which the first Europeans acting on God's behalf delivered them. Perhaps what I write is applied art as distinct from pure. But who cares? Art is important but so is education of the kind I have in mind. And I don't see that the two need be mutually exclusive." To the best of my knowledge no other African writer dead or alive has articulated a mission statement so succinctly and precisely, setting a bar for the writer and holding him/her accountable to the society.

Achebe did not define African Literature by its theme of social relevance and the avowed commitment of the writer to his/her society only, he also addressed the issues of narrative techniques and linguistic particularities. He had no problem using English, the language of the ertswhile colonial oppressors, to communicate his African values and sensibilities, asserting that by so doing he was neither betraying his "Africanness," nor demeaning his Afrocentric integrity as an artist. He urged the African writer to "strip" the English language of its colonial rigidity and customize it to suit the needs of the African socio-cultural and linguistic environment. Said he in another 1965 article titled, "English and the African Writer": "The price a world language must be prepared to pay is submission to many different kinds of use. The African writer should aim to use English in a way that brings out his message best without altering the language to the extent that its value as a medium of international exchange will be lost. He should aim at fashioning out an English which is at once universal and able to carry his peculiar experience. I have in mind here the writer who has something new, something different to say. The nondescript writer has little to tell us, anyway, so he might as well tell it in conventional language and get it over with. If I may use an extravagant simile, he is like a man offering a small, nondescript routine sacrifice for which a chick or less will do. A serious writer must look for an animal whose blood can match the power of his offering." In essence, Chinua Achebe, in his role as "the novelist as teacher," has useful lessons for the African reader for the appreciation not only of his/her past but also to be proud of his/her cultural heritage. He also has important lessons for the teacher and critic of African literature in the oft asked question – *Are there African standards for the criticism of African Literaure?* And for the creative writer, the important lesson is to learn the techniques of "extending the frontiers of English so as to accommodate African thought-patterns." Like the thematic propositions, the stylistic techniques advocated are non-binding but we know that implementing such things as the incorporation of proverbs, sayings, songs and folktales into the novel helps to distinguish the African novel from novels elsewhere. It is clear to the perceptive reader and the resourceful critic that Achebe the writer is also Achebe the teacher, the social critic, the reformer, the revolutionary, the counsellor and the crusader.

Chinua Achebe was at the forefront of the crusade against European colonization of Africa and a major advocate for the dismantling of residual colonial institutions, artifacts and legacies that continue to militate against effective decolonization of African minds perverted by colonial mentality. Achebe took on the role of the 'Field Marshall' in the crusade, leading the way and charting the course for *activist* African writing, unequivocally asserting in his 1968 article, "The African Writer and the Biafran Cause": "It is clear to me that an African creative writer who tries to avoid the big social and political issues of contemporary Africa will end up being completely irrelevant – like that absurd man in the proverb who leaves his burning house to pursue a rat fleeing from the flames." Chinua Achebe lived what he preached.

This explains why he had no second thoughts with the joining ranks and playing the roles he played in Biafra during the Nigerian civil war. And characteristically, when he saw the dream fading and the Biafran leadership going off track, he took issues with those misadventures in his final testimony with Nigeria – *There Was a Country* (2012) – before his terminal "exit." The same unflinching integrity produced the polemics in *The Trouble with Nigeria* (1983) where he stated without mincing his words that the trouble with Nigeria was visionless and corrupt leadership. He returned to the issue of bad and senseless leadership over and over again in *There Was a Country* because with time bad leadership got worse instead of ameliorating. It is surprising that some people seem not to see the pattern of Achebe's consistency in seeking and 'preaching' the truth no matter whose ox is gored. He had written *A Man of the People* (1966) where he denounced a cabinet minister, Chief Honourable M.A. Nanga, Minister of Culture – flamboyant, sinister, corrupt to a fault; totally lacking in moral principles – whom Achebe had modelled after the typical corrupt politicians of the first decade of Nigerian independence in the 1960s.

"Chief Nanga was a born politician; he could get away with almost anything he said or did. And as long as men are swayed by their hearts and stomachs and not their heads, the Chief Nangas of this world will continue to get away with anything. He had that rare gift of making people feel – even while he was saying harsh things to them – that there was not a drop of ill will in his frame." (AMOP p.73). Nanga climbed to power ruthlessly without care as to who might get hurt. He "yapped and snarled for the meaty prize like a dog." In the race for positions, everything was possible. When bribery failed, politics was seen in its lowest form: killing opposing politicians or injuring them severely. Such was the political life of Nigeria where the leaders, the press, the military and the people were driven by the quest for power and wealth. So accurate was Achebe in the portrayal of the abysmal nature of politics at the time, predicting a fall of the government through a military overthrow of the civilian regime, that when that in reality happened the week Achebe's *A Man of the People* was released in 1966, soldiers went on a hunt for him to find out what he knew and how he knew so much!!

In *A Man of the People*, Achebe deals with life in Nigeria in the first decade of independence. The destiny of the new nation is in the hands of the Nigerians themselves. But sadly the promised fruits of independence were eluding the people and corruption was rampant as was the exploitation of the masses. Unlike in his previous novels, Achebe makes more direct comments on what was going on because, for the first time, he adopts an autobiographical style of narration. In the novel when the corrupt civilian government is toppled by the army and the frauds and criminals of the old regime are clamped into jail and political parties are abolished, there is a sudden rush of happiness by the masses. But Achebe is not fooled. The commentary he provides in response to the behavioural duplicity in the masses remains one of the strongest indictments of the masses in the contemporary African political environment. "Overnight everyone began to shake their heads at the excesses of the last regime, at its graft, oppression and corrupt government: newspapers, the radio, the hitherto silent intellectuals and civil servants – everybody said what a terrible lot; and it became public opinion the next morning. And these were the same people that only the other day had owned a thousand names of adulation, whom praise-singers followed with song and talking-drum wherever they went. Chief Koko in particular became a thief and murderer, while the people who had led him on – in my opinion the real culprits – took the legendary bath of the Hornbill and donned innocence." Achebe had never lacked the right words to describe events and situations and never was a person to close his eyes and restrain his pen from attacking injustice, corruption, hypocrisy, deception and exploitation of the less privileged. On October 18, 2012, five months before his death on March 21, 2013, Chinua Achebe released *There Was a Country: A Personal History of Biafra*, which must be seen now as his "last direct talk" without equivocation to Nigeria and Nigerians much like his "direct talk" about the Nigerian politicians, leaders and the masses almost 47 years ago in *A Man of The People*. The memoir provoked much controversy and vituperations in some parts of the country. People who cringed at his utterances in the book and called him names at his daring to say the things he said, must not know very much about Achebe the man, or Achebe the writer!

Chinua Achebe knew Nigeria like the palm of his hand. He knew what went on behind closed doors in government, the civil service, military establishments, in churches, in community assemblies, on university campuses, in market places etc. When he painstakingly wrote about what he knew, it sometimes created uproar in many souls.

Legendary writers like Chinua Achebe come perhaps once in a century. This is what Nigeria, Africa and the literary world lost at the Harvard University Teaching Hospital in Massachusetts, at 11.51 pm on Thursday, March 21, 2013.

Chinua Achebe will not come back, except metaphorically or by reincarnation as he once promised he would. And if he does, he would not be called Chinua Achebe; he would not write *Things Fall Apart, A Man of the People,* or *There Was a Country*! That is why Nigeria in particular and the literary world in general, must celebrate the life that the Chinua Achebe we knew lived and the legacies he bequeathed to humanity as a whole.

Since the death of Chinua Achebe, two questions have consistently featured in the media and other interviews namely: *What accounts for Chinua Achebe's world-wide fame as a writer?* and *What is it about Things Fall Apart that makes it resonate with readers all over the world?* The answers to these questions are encapsulated in two undeniable truths – (1) Chinua Achebe *happened* and World Literature was changed forever! (2) Chinua Achebe's *Things Fall Apart* **emerged** and the art of the novel was changed forever!

Chinua Achebe devoted his entire life to the development of African Literature and died at the beginning of the 21st Century. Did he have any ideas about the future of African Literature? On June 11, 2000, my wife and I visited Chinua Achebe at his home then at Bard College, Anandale-On-Hudson in New York State. Interviewing him that day, I asked him two pertinent questions about the future of African Literature. The first one: "What is your vision of African Literature in the 21st Century?" He answered: "Achievements since mid-20th Century can be categorized as setting the appropriate stage and nurturing the ground for the future. What now lies ahead is to establish the balance of stories between Africa and the West. The lack of balance is the burden that Africa has carried in the last 500 years since the continent encountered Europe. Europe created stories of Africa to make it possible for Europeans to enslave Africans and colonize them thereafter. What African writers of the 20th Century have done, has been to challenge these stories and show how their ancestors dreamed their world. We are still at the beginning of that task which has been appropriately defined. The 21st Century will move it forward and reduce the gap. We are one foot in the door. My hope is that the 21st Century will bring us fully into the arena of world literature and that we will witness the real flourishing of African Literature."

My second question to him was: "What is your message for young African writers in the new millennium?" He answered: "They should keep at it (writing). If you feel you have a story to tell, go ahead and tell it in writing. Every one has a story to tell but those who feel strongly about it, should go ahead and tell their stories. But remember, it is not easy. It is not as glamorous as it may seem on the surface. It requires a lot of hard work and sacrifice of time and energy. But if you feel the urge, keep working on it. You don't need anybody to tell you how to go about it. Write, edit and shape it and take full responsibility for the way it is. And when you have written your story, there will not be any need to chase it to explain what it is and why. Once the story is out of your hands, leave it to find its way. Don't be too concerned about current fashions of either the work or the conduct of the writer. Don't be distracted by issues of how an artist looks or the latest topics to write on. Don't be concerned with all that. Just go the way the spirit moves you. But this is not saying that there is no value in reading what others have written. Read widely to find out what is missing in the gallery of the world's (African) stories and make a contribution towards filling that gap."

Embodied in those two answers are Chinua Achebe's visions for both the African writer and African Literature in the 21st Century. There are challenges to both the discipline and the upcoming African writer. Achebe gave modern African Literature a recognizeable identity in its evolution and development for over 50 years. He played his role in ensuring the stability of African Literature today. He nurtured the ground for African Literature to grow and flourish. The greatest tribute that can be paid to him is to ensure that his vision for the future of African Literature is realized and excelled. In the life and death of Chinua Achebe, the literary world has witnessed the *passing* of a Comet!!!

Chapter Twenty-Nine

# Ugo Chara Acha Adighi Echu Echu

## The Path to Achebe's Undying Legacy

*Toyin Falola*

Perhaps no other figure represents the pride of Nigeria better than Chinua Achebe. As a writer, scholar and activist, Achebe brought to light both the colonial and postcolonial reality of Nigeria through his globally renowned writing, exposing the world to Africa in a way that no one has matched before or since.

Albert Chinualumogu Achebe was born on November 16, 1930, in the Igbo town of Ogidi, Eastern Nigeria. Born into a family that fully represented the complexities of the colonial experience, Achebe was raised by his parents, who were converts to the Protestant Church Mission Society, but who also respected the traditional religious and cultural customs of the Igbo people, including storytelling.

Achebe had a great-uncle who was a staunch believer in Igbo religion. He found himself attracted to his uncle's religion and spent as much time as he could spare talking with him. However, being the catechist's son, he had to suppress this interest. Thus was the world in which Achebe grew up. He was torn between two religious worldviews. This background proved vital for Achebe's career as a novelist and greatly influenced his early writings about Igboland and its encounter with colonial forces.

Achebe's inquisitiveness about customs and traditions did not cease even after he left home in search of formal education. His schooling began around 1936, at St. Philip's Central School, Ogidi. From there, he moved to Central School, Nekede and the prestigious Government College, Umuahia. While in Nekede, Achebe's interest in Igbo culture continued to grow and he sought informal education among the villagers who eagerly told him about legends and village deities. It was in this town that he became introduced to Mbari as art. This experience in Nekede left an indelible impression on him.

An excellent student, Achebe did well in secondary school and earned a scholarship for his university education. The University College, (now the University of Ibadan), was the first university in Nigeria, opened in 1948 in anticipation of Nigerian independence. There, Achebe started off as a student of medicine, but because of his already established interest in arts, diverted to English, history and theology after his first year at university, despite the fact that this move would cost him his scholarship.

It was while at university that Achebe began his career as a writer, developing essays and short stories and serving as an editor of the university's newspaper. A careful study of these early writings provides an insight into the maturation of his talent as the renowned writer and scholar that he became. It was also during this time that Achebe began to critically compare the religions of Christianity with African religions, as well as carefully examining European literature and colonialism.

These are the themes and ideas that surface in all of Achebe's works, beginning in 1958 with his seminal *Things Fall Apart*, followed a few years later by *No Longer at Ease*. The import of these works should not be understated. Often students' only exposure to African literature, even at university level, consists of Achebe's novels. His career as a writer led him to a profound meditation on the nature of African societies and their relationship with the wider world. Through Achebe, readers are exposed to some of the most poignant and important themes in African history.

Shortly after his university education, Achebe embarked on a path that further defined who he eventually became. He was employed by the Talks Department of the Nigerian Broadcasting Corporation to prepare scripts for broadcasting. He took advantage of the opportunity and improved his skill of writing realistic discourse, an ability that came in handy while writing his novels.

Achebe was once criticized for his use of the English language in his writings rather than his native Igbo. However, it is clear that his English is that of his homeland and not the British English of Nigeria's colonizers. By writing in English, Achebe was able to make his work available to a much wider audience, as well as fully demonstrate the complexities of the Nigerian colonial experience.

Achebe took controversial stances on other issues as well, such as the Biafran secession, which he publicly supported. He not only served in intellectually-oriented committees that contemplated the future of the newly created Biafra, but also became an unofficial envoy for the Biafran government. In collaboration with his friend, Christopher Okigbo, he established the Citadel Press and through African fables, notably *How the Leopard Got Its Claws*, articulated the Biafran story. His last work, *There Was a Country*, part history and part memoir, explores this turbulent period of Nigerian history, allowing Achebe to again fully realize his role as a historian, novelist and activist.

A car accident in 1990 left Achebe paralyzed, but this did not hamper his ability to continue to impact global understanding of Africa. After moving to the United States for better medical care, Achebe served as a Professor on various campuses (UMASS, Amherst, Dartmouth College, Bard College), and most recently at Brown University. Here he held the position of David and Marianna Fisher University Professor and Professor of Africana Studies, highlighting not only his prowess as a writer, but also as a scholar. In scholarship, Achebe is perhaps best known for his 1975 essay, "An Image of Africa: Racism in Conrad's Heart of Darkness," but, ultimately, his novels are as much scholarship as they are literature.

His book, *Home and Exile*, depicts Achebe's lifelong effort to develop the incomplete story of his own oppressed people. Through this, he hoped to regenerate an autonomous identity and reclaim the cultural power of his people, while encouraging others to follow suit – another critical aspect of his legacy. In a 2000 interview, he reflected on this pursuit: "This is really what I personally wish this century to see – a balance of stories where every people will be able to contribute to a definition of themselves, where we are not victims of other people's accounts. This is not to say that nobody should write about anybody else – I think they should, but those that have been written about should also participate in the making of these stories."

Achebe quite easily became an internationally recognized scholar, which is not to say that he did not face challenges very early in his career. For instance, his first novel, *Things Fall Apart,* was met with uncountable rejections and the manuscript was nearly lost but for the intervention of a British colleague. If this had happened, Achebe's history might have turned out differently and his journey might have moved away from the literary path. Ironically, the stone that the builders rejected eventually became the corner stone and *Things Fall Apart* became his most renowned contribution to African literature.

Beyond his career as a writer and academic, Achebe was also an activist whose role in promoting the interests of the continent did not go unrecognized. Many of the honours which came his way were not only in recognition of his forays into African literature but also of being a champion for African interests and economy. His immense harvest of recognitions and his universal appeal did not deter him from confronting the residual bigotry and insensitivity of the West to Africa. He was an intelligent observer of the impact of Structural Adjustment Policies on the economies of Africa and did not hesitate to condemn Western approaches to Africa – not as a continent of human beings but as a laboratory fit for intellectual abstraction. His status as a thinker and embodiment of knowledge and truth even earned him May 25, 1989, as Chinua Achebe Day in the borough of Manhattan.

When Achebe died in a Boston hospital at the age of 82, he left a legacy that has had far-reaching consequences. Modern African literature was legitimized in part through the popularity of his novels (*Things Fall Apart* alone has sold more than ten million copies in more than fifty languages). As early as 1986, the sales figures of Heinemann Educational Books showed that Achebe's novels accounted for 33 per cent of the combined revenue of the 270 titles in the African and Caribbean Writers Series. Thanks to Achebe's example, we now have a host of Nigerian and African authors beautifully portraying the reality that is and has been Africa. The course he charted for African history and literature can never be erased and for that he will be remembered for generations to come.

*Oke Osisi, Laa n'Udo*
The Giant Tree, Rest in Peace.

## Chapter Thirty

# A Wake For The Storyteller

## (For Chinua Achebe)

*Harry Oludare Garuba*

It was an evening of elegies
a night of tributes, this wake
for the storyteller who changed
the plot of the story and sang a new song

the story teller who resurrected in his tales
the multitude of voices unheard,
the many unknown and unsung
the silenced subjects
whose dawn he crowed,
whose days he crowned with sunlight
that their deeds never again be hidden
that the shroud of savagery that cloaked
the stories of their lives be lifted

In far away Charleston in South Carolina
The news came sombre as a slave song
Was it befitting that in the famed port of arrival
where flesh ceased to be human and men and women
were sold in the streets, the news came of the
death of the storyteller who told the story of the enslaved
in another land and clime? Was there a story here?

As the voices of the mourners rose one after the other
Each burdened with grief and a tale of loss

I swear

I saw the storyteller rise in rebuke,
raising a song for the newly enslaved,
a story for the many dispossessed
and disposable people of our new age
those whose stories await a new voice, a new plot
Wondering how many in the gathering had witnessed this wake,
this resurrection, I wakened with a story and a smile on my lips.

Chapter Thirty-One

# An Interview with Chinua Achebe

*Helon Habila*

In this rare interview with the late Nigerian author, published by *The Africa Report* and *Sable Lit Mag* in 2007, Achebe insisted to fellow Nigerian writer Helon Habila that although his country's situation seemed bleak and the public had to wait 10 years between his novels, he still had more to say and would keep working until his last day.

Award-winning author of such novels as *Waiting for an Angel* and *Measuring Time*, Helon Habila, was named a Chinua Achebe Scholar in 2005.

Habila was given the opportunity to interview his scholarship's namesake, renowned Nigerian author of *Things Fall Apart* and *Anthills of the Savannah*.

Achebe shares his insights on the problems that plague contemporary Nigeria, the politics of African literature and his own future as a novelist and writer of essays.

**Helon Habila: *In The Trouble with Nigeria*, you say that Nigeria's problem is leadership. It's been quoted so many times that it's almost become the accepted way of thinking in Nigeria. How do you compare the present leadership with others before, do you think we have managed to make progress?**

**Chinua Achebe**: No. I don't think we're getting there and that's a very sad thing to say after the very perilous escape we had, especially under Abacha.

One thought, OK, we'll see where certain trends lead and we mustn't be caught in this again and somehow that hope, that expectation, seems to me to have been dashed.

I was guilty if you like, maybe of misleading people, when President Obasanjo came in again, as many people were disappointed during his first term.

I found myself writing, "since, you know, the situation is tough, let's give the man a chance to err – maybe he has discovered that Nigeria's situation is worse than we thought and so he will need a little time."

And that was a mistake, because we should have seen from the beginning that this man was not a democrat – that's the number one disqualification.

He had many qualifications which I talked about; his experience in the military and the fact that he suffered under Abacha and he knew what it meant to come close to death and all that – these were great qualifications for him, but he has obviously not used that, from what is going on right now in the country.

**HH: Some say you can't have a perfect ruler and if you look at the few advances that he has made, putting the Chief of Police in prison and fighting corruption, isn't that some kind of hope we're getting there?**

**CA:** Well, it's not enough. Listen, Nigerians are not fools, you know.

If Nigerians saw genuine decision making from the leadership to change things, to do something about corruption, to... all kinds of things that need to be done – power supply and so on – if they saw that, Nigerians are generous enough to say: "Yeah, this man is trying."

But, if what is going on seems to me to be mere fiddling, you know, trying to be clever with things – instead of solving the problem... people are watching, who and who are being punished, watching how Obasanjo chooses between criminals.

If you go and catch a small criminal and lock up him up, and the big one is dining with you, people notice that – people are very concerned about fairness.

**HH: I was going to ask if you thought Nigeria has moved forward almost 40 years after the civil war, especially with regard to the position of the Igbo?**

**CA:** There have been small changes here and there, but basically, the Igbo are still not in the main action in Nigeria... and when they talk about marginalisation, there is truth in that – it is also true that after a civil war there will be repercussions, which affect especially those who lose the war, affect them badly, and sadly it happens everywhere, so it's not something totally unexpected.

But people who are sensible will know that you cannot go on in that kind of direction too long, because as long as you are excluding a significant section of the community and the life of that community, you are depriving the state of the full benefit of their talents – that by itself should tell any good leader that reconciliation is what is required after a bitter quarrel and not to aggravate this from time to time, to point to it and say, "You remember what you did?"

So we have made a little progress I would say, but not enough, because the mind of the leadership in Nigeria is not really on it.

**HH: So where do you see Nigeria in 15 years? There have been predictions that Nigeria is going to break up, like some of the Eastern European countries.**

**CA:** I have to confess to you that I am really quite superstitious. I hope Nigeria doesn't break up in 15 years, so I prefer not to prophesy (they laugh).

**HH: Do you think that the Heinemann African Writers Series was too protective of African writers? Heinemann delineated the market and did everything in that regard. Do you think that made the writers have similar thematic concerns which had to do mainly with the colonial engagement? Do you think that Heinemann encouraged that kind of style which became almost incestuous . . . writers, being over-determined thematically by books like *Things Fall Apart* for instance.**

**CA:** That's a very interesting question. I don't remember at any point in my career as a writer, any situation in which Heinemann went out of its way to protect anybody – except perhaps the fact that they encouraged large numbers of people to come into the writing market if you like – by publishing the person.

OK, now this book maybe looks a little like the one we published last year which sold well . . . so we'll also put this on the market; it's possible I think . . . quite natural given their business – that's marketing; you know.

I for one always resisted the idea that this is 'The Achebe School'. Personally, I didn't want a school at all and looking back at that generation and you not being aware what it was like to grow up in a situation in which you have no literature, in which you do not belong to the stories that are told, a period in which you went to school and passed through school and you did not hear anything about yourself throughout that period – unless you went through that, it will be difficult to understand why there was all this to-do about writing our own stories, crafting our own style and so on. And so perhaps, there is some truth, some justice in what you say, in that it then began to look like 'protecting,' like publishing people who would not have otherwise been published, giving them the opportunity to be published.

And people who never read anything found themselves reading – it was a whole revolution that hit a continent, therefore in retrospect, you'll find that it created a style, maybe . . . There were people, even while the African Writers Series was active and alive – I'm talking now about the people in England –

there were people, even within Heinemann itself; the younger ones – because there was a second generation even within Heinemann publishers – who were not so keen about what the first generation were doing and not in any strong, hostile way but, you know, critical. And this criticism boiled down to this: that the stories being produced about the colonial period had not done justice to the civilizing nation of Europe, to what their ancestors did; you know, that's the way they saw it.

Someone whom I thought was a friend of mine for a long time – finally, something happened and I discovered that he considered my work ungrateful.

There are many people walking around in Britain today who do not accept that the colonial period adventure was not fair to the people on whom it was unleashed.

**HH: You emphasize that in your writings, one could say that that's almost what your whole career is based on, 'telling our stories ourselves' – do you think that we've started achieving that? Do you think that the world just deliberately tries to look at only one side of Africa? Or is it that they don't understand that there are people, normal people in Africa, yet they only see starving babies. Is this still another way of trying to appropriate our stories?**

**CA:** There is quite a bit of that – the psychology – because I think the almost automatic response that people have when you mention Africa is something which has been fixed in the mind for a long time, so the tendency of the cameraman who goes to Africa is . . . he has something on his mind...about what real Africa is.

It doesn't mean that that particular picture he or she takes is false – it actually happens – but the point is, that there is something else happening also at that time and the choice that is left to the cameraman is determined by this long history of images.

There is still much work ahead of us . . . we must be ready, but I don't think we need worry unduly about that. What we should be worrying about is creating our own avenues for making these images.

You can place beside the image you don't like, the other image which is also real and true: if somebody tells a story about you which you don't like, tell another story about yourself that you like which is also true and stand your real story beside the other one – let's not talk about knocking down the other story, especially if it is true, but create a situation in which there is evenness.

We've got to do that kind of thing on a large scale – to change the dominant image of Africa which has been there for hundreds of years.

**HH: You haven't published a novel in a while and the last novel took you over 10 years, so are you working on a novel now? Or do you think writing essays is more effective for your purposes?**

**CA:** Well, I do have every form of writing on my table and in fact more than one novel on my table.

The question of when, I wish I could tell you. One of the problems: first of all, I don't write a lot, I don't speak a lot, so that's the first handicap. The second is that I don't feel the pressure that you must...that I must bring out a book every so often, simply because I work differently and what I consider my work in life contains more than just writing books.

There is a lot in my life that keeps me busy and the day is much shorter for me than it used to be. So when we put all these things together, I simply say: when we see, we will accept.

**HH: Some people say that maybe you have given up on Nigeria and you feel that there is really nothing that you can write that might make a change.**

**CA:** Sometimes I do feel, maybe that I've said everything I need to say, but I don't think so. I will keep attempting to speak in the hope that if the first time it didn't work, maybe the second time, it will work. But as I said, I have no other profession or interest in any other profession. So you must assume that I'll keep working at it to the last day.

Chapter Thirty-Two

# Chinua Achebe

## His Wondrous Passages

*Biodun Jeyifo*

Chinua Achebe had more than the standard allotted respect and fame for writers, including even those who in their lifetime achieve great acclaim. One of the most notable expressions of this respect bordering on adoration came from one who is himself a celebrity among celebrities, Nelson Mandela. In their long time in the prisons of the South African apartheid system, above all other writers it was Chinua Achebe's works that sustained the spirit of Mandela and the other giants of the anti-apartheid struggle. "The writer in whose company the prison walls fell:" That is how Mandela described the liberation of psyche and spirit that he and his mates felt when they encountered Achebe's brooding and insightful novels on colonialism and its complex legacies for Africa, the West and the rest of the world.

I had not yet read of Mandela's uncommon praise for Achebe's writings when, as a member of a volunteer team of professors of Cornell University that taught in both medium and maximum security prisons in Elmira and Auburn in upstate New York, I taught Achebe and Frantz Fanon to some inmates of these prisons. A disproportionately large number of these prisoners were African American and all were men. I think these factors account for the fact that more than all the other Cornell volunteers, the inmates felt a very special emotional bonding with me since I was the only African male in the group. But beyond this, Achebe, shall we say, provided the real fulcrum for that emotional bonding – Achebe in dialogue with Fanon. Fanon was not exactly a hard nut to crack for the prisoners, but the mix of flights of spellbinding psychoanalytic and philosophical musings with visionary and prophetic prose in his writings was a bit too abstruse for them.

With Achebe, things were different. His stories, his prose style and the depth of his wisdom made an apparently deep impact on the prisoners. With very little prompting from me, many of these prisoners – some of whom were lifers who were serving time for extremely violent crimes – used Achebe's works to throw further light on my explications on the more schematic or programmatic aspects of Fanon's theories of radical decolonization. One surprising thing in this was the fact that the two Achebe novels that I taught the prison inmates, *Things Fall Apart* and *Arrow of God*, told harrowingly tragic stories of the failures of anti-colonial revolt, whereas Fanon's books mapped difficult but ultimately victorious paths to decolonization. When I probed the sources of this deft move by the prisoners, they revealed their deep empathy with aspects of Achebe's novels that I had not at the time paid much attention to, aspects to which their own situation had apparently made them far more responsive. Chief among these was the startling fact that beneath and beyond the main plotlines of failed and tragically flawed nationalist revolt against colonialism, Achebe's novels told scores of mini stories of ordinary men and women whose humanity, resilience and self-empowerment were not crushed, could indeed not be crushed by the otherwise powerful and all-conquering forces of colonialism and imperialism. This experience, this revelation served as the catalyst for two of the most important among the half-dozen essays and monographs I have published on Achebe: "For Chinua Achebe: the Resilience and Predicament of Obierika" and "An African Cultural Modernity: Achebe, Fanon, Cabral and the Philosophy of Decolonization."

The passage from the heroic world of Mandela and his prison mates at Robben Island to the world of hardened criminals and other carceral subjects in America's prison colonies is typical of the centrality of passages between incredibly diverse spheres of sociality and community that Achebe as writer and public intellectual traversed in his life and career. One of the most portentous of these passages is the journey in his works in fiction and non-fiction into virtually all the literary languages of the world. He got extensive commendations, inquiries and plain "thank you and thank you again" correspondence from men and women, old and young, the highly literate and the modestly schooled. And these came from all the continents, all the regions of the world, and all stations in life.

This liminality, these wondrous passages into nearly every corner of the world of letters on the planet pose tremendous interpretive challenges to us. Achebe is one of two or three of the most popular, most widely read contemporary authors and yet he is a writers' writer, an author who was/is deeply respected by some of the most influential authors of the past half century like James Baldwin, Nadine Gordimer, Doris Lessing, Toni Morrison and Wole Soyinka. He is a towering pioneer figure in modern African literature but he is also in the front ranks of the rarefied canon of World Literature. He is a constant subject of discussion in the popular presses of Africa, Europe and

America but he is also an endless source of debate and controversy among literary scholars all over the world.

As much as these passages are constitutive of Achebe's fame and renown, they cannot be taken as self-evident or self-explanatory. Of course it is not the case that "explanations" that do not explain much, that are in fact rather tautological have not been proffered as interpretive keys for unlocking the enigma of these exemplary, border crossing passages of Achebe across the typically fragmented publics of writing and cultural production in the African continent, its Diasporas and the world at large. For instance, here is one such "explanation": Both the popular mind and the world of scholarly researchers and exegetes have focused almost exclusively on *Things Fall Apart*, ignoring other writings of the Nigerian author like the infinitely more complex *Arrow of God* and the fascinating and reflexive meta-narrative that is *Anthills of the Savannah*, thereby making the passage from the "high" to the "low" and back again to the "high" in the critical discourses on Achebe's writings a fairly easy one to make. Here is another "explanation": *Things Fall Apart* cemented Achebe's celebrity status among both "naïve" readers and the professoriate of letters because it enabled legitimacy for African writing in the upper stratospheres of academia to be tokenized without compromising that legitimacy with racial and cultural condescension which, for a long time in literary history, had been a constant, almost inevitable precondition for granting legitimacy for any intellectual or cultural production from our continent.

These "explanations" are neither false nor redundant. But they are external to writing qua writing. In other words, they do not even remotely engage the fact that both the passionate enthusiasts and the sometimes equally passionate if more politely and discretely self-restraining opponents of Achebe as an author base themselves on his *writing*. And on this central issue of writing and in particular on the nature and status of Achebe's writing, we are caught between two fundamentally opposed notions or traditions of writing. Writing, the best writing, must draw attention to itself, to its forms and modes of self-constitution: this is the fundamental article of faith of modernists and postmodernists alike, even if both camps differ in big ways on the specific modes and forms through which self-display and self-reference in writing can be achieved or manifested. Conversely, writing must not unduly draw attention to itself; it must find a balance, an equipoise between what needs to be expressed and the formal and linguistic means for its expression. That is the classical and much older but still extant tradition of writing to which – so goes the determination of the arbiters of taste in the contemporary world of letters – Achebe putatively belonged. I would personally argue that Achebe actually made the passage to and from these two seemingly opposed traditions in several of his writings in both fiction and non-fiction. But that was not the judgment of the border guards of modernist and postmodernist literary culture and thought. This, it seems to me, lies at the root of why the so-called "highest" prize, the Nobel Literature award, was denied him.

In all, I personally met Achebe only a few times, on four, perhaps five occasions, only one of which was at his home at the University of Nigeria, Nsukka when he taught and lived there. But among contemporary authors, he was among the select few to whom I felt a great closeness because I found myself returning again and again in the last four decades to his works. He was a master storyteller who had the quite unique gift for folding countless stories of ordinary women and men into the big, "world-historical" currents and forces of modern culture and society. In certain key areas of artistic vision and a radical-humanist cosmopolitanism that predates nearly all the currently fashionable expressions of that term, I think Achebe quite easily surpassed nearly all the other great novelists on colonialism – Conrad, Kipling, Forster, Ngũgĩ and Coetzee. First of all, Achebe took the humanity of both the colonizer and the colonized for granted; he neither deified nor demonized one or the other, colonizer and colonized. By contrast, most of these other great novelists of colonialism could not, or did not entirely escape this trap. Secondly, Achebe forcefully showed that both sides in the colonial divide were simultaneously subjects and objects of powerful forces whose outcomes they could neither control nor predict. And thirdly, Achebe had a deeply tragic sense of life and history that was however leavened by irony, wit, humour and a calm openness to the absurdities of existence. As perhaps the single most important historical force in the making and the unmaking of the modern world as a global community structured by and in interdependence and inequality, colonialism needed a master novelist and essayist whose works could resonate throughout the world in the West and the Non-West, among both the ex-colonizers and the ex-colonized. It was given to our own Chinua Achebe to be the novelist and essayist who rose to successfully engage that challenge.

With his recent death, another passage, perhaps the most significant of all, has taken place. I once joked that Achebe was second only to his own creation, Okonkwo, the protagonist of *Things Fall Apart*, as the most famous Igbo person in the world. But that was about half a decade ago, long before Achebe's demise. With the number and scale of the outpouring of a mixture of grief and celebration from all parts of the world that followed the notice of his transition, Achebe, it now appears, is second only to Nelson Mandela as the most famous African in the world. I don't think the near unanimous judgment that he has achieved immortality through his works is premature.

In due time, Achebe's works will undergo another passage, this time into the regime of *posthumous* commentary and debate, free of both the positive and negative consequences of imbrication in the towering presence and subjectivity of Achebe himself. I am thinking here in particular of his last published book, *There Was a Country*. The anger, the bitterness and the outrage caused in many quarters by some of the views and claims made in the book will stay with us for some time to come. To Nigerians in particular, the book is a deeply ambiguous last offering from one about whom, in comparison with the other titans of his generational cohort like Soyinka, Clark and Okigbo, there had hitherto been only the faintest echoes of controversy or disputation. There was of course the controversy generated by what can be described as "the Conrad affair" when establishmentarian Western critics took great umbrage at Achebe's forceful and eloquent charge of racism of the basest kind against the writer of that icon of the modern European novel on colonialism and imperialism, *Heart of Darkness*. But that was nothing in comparison with the strident and rancorous debate sparked by *There Was a Country* in Nigeria. In one fell swoop, that last book launched Achebe into the territory of a raging critical firestorm that Soyinka in particular and Clark also had many times been subjected to by their country's literary intelligentsia. Speaking for myself, it took everything I had learnt over many decades as a reader and critic to write the long review of the book that ran for six weeks in my weekly column in one of Nigeria's major newspapers, *The Guardian*. I can now confess that I wrote that series as much for Achebe himself as for the community of the national literati, hoping that one day, I would get a response, no matter how indirect, from the old master himself. Alas, this was not to be.

That said, I personally see no portent at all in the fact that this last book was the most controversial among all of Achebe's writings. His legacy is much vaster than the controversies engendered by that book, just as it is also absolutely unconstrained by the Nobel Prize that was not awarded to him. Speaking about the loss of another great Nigerian, Wole Soyinka once remarked that that personage will walk tall among the ancestors. With an unabashed rationalist and humanistic idealism, I read that benediction as meaning that the departed had entered the hallowed ranks of the true immortals of all ages. So let it be with Chinua Achebe.

Chapter Thirty-Three

# Memories of Chinua Achebe

*G. Douglas Killam*

I first met Chinua Achebe in 1964, at Leeds University, during the first Commonwealth Literature Conference, attended by some 60 writers, academics, and others from various countries – people like George Lamming, A. K. Narayan and V. S. Naipaul. Professor Derry Jeffares, Head of the School of English at Leeds, convened this conference to recognize the rich body of writing in the English-speaking world, most of which then came from countries in the British Commonwealth – like South Africa, Canada, Australia, New Zealand – but also from other areas – countries like Sierra Leone, Nigeria, India, Ghana – where English was being used to establish literary conventions which reflected their cultural environments. This conference helped launch the notion of Commonwealth Literature as an academic discipline. At the conference in Leeds, Chinua read a paper entitled "The Novelist as Teacher," a paper which became very influential in the field; it dealt with the effect of writers in the Commonwealth using the English language when they were attempting to discover their own national voices.

Chinua's publishing and academic relationships with James Currey, Alan Hill, Keith Sambrook, Landeg White and others and his life as artist, broadcaster, spokesperson for the growing field of the production, promotion and study of African Literature has been fully documented elsewhere and is not the purpose of this brief memoir. I seek rather to remember Chinua as we became friends over the barriers of distance and time, snatching at the opportunities which time presented.

We met in Africa, the United Kingdom, India, Australia, New Zealand and of course Canada. We discovered that we had been born only two months apart – he in Nigeria, I in British Columbia. We noted the coincidence that Canadian and African literatures were getting well established at about the same time in our respective countries.

Our friendship was beginning to blossom when I was in Lagos in the late 1960s and I remember being startled when Chinua offered to loan me his Jaguar sports car for my research travels in the country. However, he then dropped the startling fact that as there were only three jaguars in Nigeria and since Chinua saw himself as a "wanted man" it might not be such a safe vehicle. We laughingly decided against it.

In my years of teaching and working in Africa – in Nigeria, Sierra Leone, Tanzania, Cameroon – as well as in my years back in Canada, I watched his influence grow. Chinua noted in the early pages of his final book, *There Was a Country* (2012) that two Canadians figured early in the recognition of his writing. First, the Canadian writer, Margaret Laurence, talked about *Things Fall Apart* (1958) in *Long Drums and Cannons* (1968). Laurence's own novel, *This Side Jordan* (1960), her short stories, *The Tomorrow Tamer and Other Stories* (1960), her travel book, *The Prophet's Camel Bell* (1963), and her collection of Somali poetry and prose, *A Tree for Poverty* (1954), are all set in Africa. Second, I published the first critical study of Chinua's work, *The Novels of Chinua Achebe*, in 1969 in the UK.

After Leeds we next met a few years later at the annual conference of the American Association for African Studies being held for the first time outside American borders at the Queen Elizabeth Hotel in Montreal. We had breakfast together and talked about African writing. By this time, I had finished a PhD thesis on the fiction set in Africa written mostly by church people, traders, colonial civil servants and administrators and I had taught in several African universities. I mentioned that I was preparing a book devoted to his novels and he seemed modestly – or perhaps cautiously – interested that a Canadian was undertaking the task. It is an indication of the quality of our friendship that over the years he always allowed me my own opinions and we never once spoke of his response to my early critique or my later writing about African literature.

That study (*The Novels of Chinua Achebe*) was originally meant to be a volume in *The Writers' and Critics' Series*, published by Oliver Boyd and edited by Robin Lorimer. I had done most of the first draft of the book when Robin reluctantly cancelled the series. Because it was half finished, I decided to finish it. I sent the completed manuscript to several publishers, without luck. Someone at Longmans suggested I send it to Chinua's publisher. I did this and received an immediate response from Keith Sambrook and James Currey, with the offer to publish. It was published in 1969 in the UK, the first of its kind, representing the beginning of 50 years of publication in the African Writers' Series with Heinemann Educational Books. In 1977, I expanded and retitled it for Heinemann as *The Writings of Chinua Achebe*.

In 1969, when *The Novels of Chinua Achebe* came out with Africana Publishing Corporation in New York, I was pleased and surprised to have a note from Hans Zell, editor of the series, that it was being reviewed in the *Library Journal*, the all-important book review. It did sufficiently well that, when I was introduced to Alan Hill, he looked up from his desk, and said, "We are very pleased with your book…" Then, with his amusing eccentricity, he looked at James Currey and inquired earnestly, seemingly as an afterthought: "*Aren't we*, James?" The day ended with a fine dinner at the Garrick Club.

I continued to meet Chinua at scholarly meetings over the years, including his visits to the Canadian Learned Society's meetings in the late 1960s and at a conference convened by Professor Rowland Smith at Dalhousie University which included some thirty African writers and noted African literature scholars. At conferences or in the presence of people he did not know, Chinua was reserved, always courteous and kind, always responded if spoken to, but he would never monopolize any public space, even when he was a featured speaker. He was quiet, self-effacing and genuine. In dress he favoured the distinctive African style in the rich and endlessly varied patterns of "adire" cloth.

Chinua read from his short stories at Harbourfront in Toronto for impressario Greg Gatenby. His performances were muted but warm, conveying in particular his passion for his characters. I later collected a group of his short stories which were published as *Girls at War* in 1973.

The Achebe-Killam friendship was cemented when he came to the University of Guelph on a Senior Visiting Practitioner's Award for a three-month period in 1984. In the same year, he received an honorary PhD from the University of Guelph, where I chaired the English Department from 1977 to 1988. He gave the convocation speech, which was very short, as was customary at our university. His address, devoted to consideration of the environment, expressed his grave concern over pollutions of various kinds. He closed by saying if we didn't take action now, we would be left with a "dead world."

The President's luncheon following the Convocation produced the appearance of the Director of Athletics, Dr "X," who, to everyone's astonishment, arrived fully kitted out in African bush attire (including khaki shirt and shorts, knee length hose and bush hat), rather like Sir Henry Morton Stanley or David Livingstone would have worn when exploring in Africa. He informed Chinua that he had spent quite a few years in West Africa, and loftily explained to all who were listening that he was wearing what he would have worn then. He then added, seriously and to inform his listeners, especially Chinua, "Whenever I went into a village that was new to me, I always said to the first villager I met, 'Take me to your *witch doctor*.'" Chinua's surprised response to that was a bemused and genial, "*Is that so*?"

This "witch doctor" episode became quite a joke between us. As we travelled around Southern Ontario, keeping various speaking appointments – to Wilfrid Laurier University, the University of Waterloo, the University of Western Ontario, York University and the Marshall McLuhan Institute in Toronto – if we got lost in an unfamiliar environment, we would turn to one another, chuckling, "Take me to your *witch doctor*."

There were other times I had seen Chinua patronized with racial clichés – first in 1964 when a young British academic at Derry Jeffares' reception had informed him that blacks were "coming along quite well" in their development and he had actually seen one attending a recent theatre performance. Chinua always handled these comments with admirable restraint.

Once when Chinua and I had met in James Currey's office at Russell Square in London we were caught in heavy rain while waiting for a cab to take us to dinner. We took cover in a courtyard, where we were joined by a third person who turned out to be an Englishman lecturing at the School of Oriental and African Studies. Serious conversational topics came up as we waited and when discussing South Africa, this man dogmatically asserted that Nelson Mandela should be held in prison for the rest of his life. On this occasion, Chinua was ready to do battle with the man, but decided that caught in the middle of a cloudburst was not the right time and place. In his visits to Guelph over the years, he had read plenary papers at three different international conferences – The Canadian Association for Commonwealth Literature and Language Studies (CACLALS), Canadian Association of African Studies (CAAS), and the International Federation for Modern Languages and Literatures (FILLM). We had many good times, together with my wife, Shelagh and children, Sach and Sarah and guests we invited into our home to meet him. Chinua had many skills. He was, for example, an excellent cook, having learned cooking as a boy when he was expected, as customary, to make meals for the older children who in turn looked after his father and mother. He deftly prepared gris-gris, cassava, pounded yam, goat and other meats for gatherings in my home.

At Guelph there was a gathering of teachers and university professors, among them was Bernard Fonlon from University of Yaoundé, Cameroon. Dr Fonlon had met Chinua Achebe on many occasions and they enjoyed these meetings to pick up on where their lives had been leading. Dr Fonlon said that he had written the first review of *Things Fall Apart* in French and published it in *Présence Africaine* in 1958.

While Chinua was in Guelph, he wanted to go to Winnipeg to meet an anthropologist who had spent a full university term at the University of Nsukka in Nigeria, and who also had worked among the Inuit in Canada. After much research in Nigeria that had been undertaken on a sabbatical leave, she had written a paper of such authority that Chinua said when he set off to Winnipeg on a bus to meet her, "She knows more about Ezeulu than I do."

Peter Gzowski ran a very popular morning programme called "Morningside" on the Canadian Broadcasting Company network from 9-12, five days a week, commenting on current subjects, politics, literature, music and culture. Peter, like Chinua, had been awarded an honorary doctorate by the University of Guelph and the morning after Chinua's convocation speech, I drove him to Toronto to meet Gzowski for an interview on "Morningside." We waited a while for Gzowski to appear, and when he rushed in, he called out to Chinua, jokingly, "*My* convocation speech was longer than *your* convocation speech." The light-hearted tone of this introduction soon gave way to very serious questions. This was the time of the Biafra-Nigerian War and its aftermath. Peter had read *The Trouble With Nigeria* (1983) in which Chinua was hard on his own people and country. Gzowski brought all of this out in the interview. Many people phoned to express their thanks for the complex discussions of the troubles in Nigeria better than the local media had done.

The second of Chinua's "Morningside" interviews dealt with the surrender at the close of the Biafran War and its consequences for Nigeria – subjects which he has now written about in *There Was a Country* (2012).

In another CBC segment, Chinua read his "Letter from Canada to Nigeria." It was taped in Toronto by Aldo Marchini who had come up from Montréal to direct this 20-minute segment for Radio-Canada International. Aldo asked if they "could time the item" before they taped it. He was amazed when the piece came out to an exact 20 minutes, neither a second more or less. He had not known that Achebe had been a radio broadcaster in Nigeria.

Chinua also became very involved in the activities of the Guelph-Yaoundé Project (called "The Association for Creative Teaching" or "ACT" in short form). This project of ours, generously funded by the Canadian International Development Project (CIDA) and administered by the University of Guelph, was managed in Canada by Elizabeth Cockburn and by Patrick Mbunwe in Cameroon. Patrick had a brilliant and quick mind and to match it, a quick temper. He was shot dead in his own house when he tried to drive thieves away. His wife, Mary, has continued to be involved, along with Patrick's colleagues, with ACT activities in Cameroon.

Chinua took a healthy interest in what the project's aims and objectives were (establishing a writing programme in English-speaking Cameroon which recorded oral history and used it for teaching purposes). When a discussion arose in Canada about the many mechanical and electronic teaching materials that might be used, he pointed out that they were too sophisticated for impoverished schools in Cameroon and were therefore impractical. "All one needs to make a school room is a blank wall, a tin of black paint and a piece of chalk – then you have a blackboard, which is the most adequate of teaching tools."

When Chinua returned home to Africa from Guelph, he took many, many books. But he also had a practical side and one day asked if I could get him a working transmission for a Ford Marquis that awaited his return to Nigeria. A mechanic I knew acquired a certified used transmission and it disappeared into the bundle of things awaiting transportation to Nigeria. His daughter later told me that it had been installed but unfortunately it never worked.

Chinua arranged for his oldest daughter, Chinelo, to take her MA in English at Guelph. When he telephoned me from Lagos, saying she was on her way to Guelph, he said, "Chinelo is now your Nigerian daughter." On one occasion Chinelo asked me and my wife, Shelagh, if she could use our home to put on a reception for her father. Many people attended, mostly from local universities in Southern Ontario, but one Nigerian medical student drove all the way from St. John's, Newfoundland, over 3,000 kilometres each way, to shake Chinua's hand. Our gathering was interrupted by our aged Siamese cat, who walked into the living room to seek out its regular resting spot, saw the crowd and let out a howl that stopped all conversation. It died the next morning. Chinua was nonplussed.

One Nigerian who attended this party was Dr Ayo Banjo, then Chancellor at the University of Ibadan. Dr Banjo, a Yoruba, was married to an Ibo woman and probably had to tread softly when the Biafran War was on. By the time Chinua and Ayo met in my home, the war was over, but all Nigerians were concerned with the future fate of their country. Chinua and Ayo had much to talk about.

My next visit was to a conference and celebration honouring Chinua's 60th birthday held in Nsukka, Eastern Nigeria. Chinelo met me at Enugu Airport and drove me the sixty miles to the campus at Nsukka where I had asked to be put up in faculty housing I had used many years before. It had deteriorated badly and I awoke from my first night with my face covered in soot and filth. A very angry Chinua put that right and I ended up the next night in a plush hypermodern motel. I also remember the banquet at that event with many African writers and scholars who dined with one of their colleagues, writer Ken Saro-Wiwa, who would later be arrested and eventually hanged in 1995 by the Nigerian military dictatorship headed by Sani Abacha.

After his 1990 car accident in Nigeria, when he was left paralyzed and in a wheelchair, Chinua left Africa for a faculty position at Bard College on the Hudson River north of New York City. Several years later, my wife and I attended Chinelo's wedding at Bard, I remember my feelings of shock and sadness when Chinua entered the chapel last on that occasion, the first time I had seen him in a wheelchair. After a Christian marriage ceremony Chinua presided over a traditional Igbo language ceremony to see that "my Nigerian daughter" and her husband, Tosan Ejueyitchie, were fully and properly married. We made another visit to Bard College in 1994 and met the Achebe family members.

Our last visit with him occurred when he celebrated his 70th birthday at Bard. By this time, he was everywhere recognized as the most important figure in the development of Nigerian – and indeed in all African literature. He had given so much to the world in a general way, but in personal ways his wisdom, modesty and honesty have touched many more than could ever be counted.

Chapter Thirty-Four

# Achebe in Texas

*Bernth Lindfors*

I first met Chinua Achebe more than half a century ago. It was in the fall of 1961, when I was in my first term of teaching at Kisii School, a boys' boarding school in Western Kenya. Out of curiosity, I had started reading books by African authors and Achebe's *Things Fall Apart* was one of the first and certainly the best that I came across.

As I read more by him and other emerging African writers during the two years I spent at Kisii, I did not want to stop. I had been planning to return to graduate school to work towards a doctorate in English, so I started looking for a programme flexible enough to allow me to write a dissertation on this exciting new literature. The University of California at Los Angeles was building a big African Studies Centre at the time and the English Department there was one of only two in the United States willing to permit such an exception provided I jump all the usual disciplinary hurdles towards a normal PhD in their programme. I ended up writing my dissertation on Nigerian fiction. *Things Fall Apart* had helped things come together for me.

I first met Achebe in person in my first term of teaching at the University of Texas at Austin in the fall of 1969, when he was touring the US as a spokesman and fundraiser for Biafra. I was put in charge of the schedule for his day in Austin, which included newspaper and television interviews, meetings with two African literature classes and a public lecture he delivered on "The Writer and the African Revolution."

As I followed him around, listening to him field numerous questions about war, revolution, literature and the role of the writer in such turbulent times, I was struck by the intelligence, lucidity, grace and educational force of his responses. He immediately sensed what a questioner did not know about a subject and replied with a stream of information that would help that person understand the matter better. Even ignorant questions by undergraduates were handled in a polite manner that did not embarrass them but did much to enlighten them. It was clear that he was an excellent teacher.

One example may suffice. When asked, "Do you believe literature should carry a social or political message?" he responded by saying:

> Yes, I believe it's impossible to write anything about Africa without some kind of commitment, some kind of message, some kind of protest. Even those early novels that look like very gentle recreations of the past – what they were saying, in effect, was that we had a past. That was protest, because there were people who thought we didn't have a past. What we were doing was to say politely that we *did* – here it is. So commitment is nothing new. Commitment runs right through our work. In fact, I should say all our writers, whether they are aware of it or not, are committed writers. The whole pattern of life demanded that you should protest, that you should put in a word for your history, your traditions, your religion and so on.
>
> One big message, of the many that I try to put across, is that Africa was not a vacuum before the coming of Europe, that culture was not unknown in Africa, that culture was not brought to Africa by the white world. You would have thought it was obvious that everybody had a past, but there were people who came to Africa and said, "You have no history, you have no civilization, you have no culture, you have no religion. You are lucky we are here. Now you are hearing about these things from us for the first time." Well, you know, we didn't just drop from the sky. We too had our own history, traditions, cultures, civilizations. It is not possible for one culture to come to another and say, "I am the way, the truth and the life; there is nothing else but me." If you say this, you are guilty of irreverence or arrogance. You are also stupid. And this is really my concern.[1]

This was a memorable way of describing the political commitment of the earliest African writers, himself included.

But in his lecture on "The Writer and the African Revolution" Achebe made it clear that the situation in Africa had changed, so writers there now had a new problem to address:

> While the African intellectual was busy displaying the past culture of his people, the past culture of Africa, the peoples of Africa themselves, people caught in new emergencies, in new predicaments, were already creating new revolutionary cultures – cultures which take into account

> their present condition… This has been the problem of the African intellectual, the African artist: he has been left far behind by the people who make culture and he must hurry, he must now hurry and catch up with the people, catch up with them in that zone – to borrow a beautiful expression of Fanon – that zone of occult instability where people dwell. It is there, at that zone, that customs die and cultures are born. It is there that the regenerative powers of the people are most potent. These powers are manifest today in the African revolution, a revolution that aims towards true independence, as opposed to phony independence, formal independence; a revolution that moves towards the creation of modern states in place of the neocolonial enclaves we have today, a revolution that is informed with African ideologies.[2]

Here was a perceptive analysis of the role of African writers in a rapidly changing world. Achebe was warning them that they must move with the times or risk becoming irrelevant.

He was invited to campus many times thereafter, once to a poetry festival after his *Beware, Soul Brother and Other Poems* was published, another time to launch the American edition of *Anthills of the Savannah*, but most notably to speak at the inaugural African Literature Conference in 1975 and at the 24th annual African Literature Association Conference in 1998, in both of which he made seminal contributions. At the 1975 conference, placed on a panel alongside Keorapetse Kgositsile, Dennis Brutus and Ali Mazrui to discuss "Literature and Commitment in South Africa," Achebe made the argument that:

> It's not a question of whether or not there is commitment. It's a question of on whose side. Societies are varied. African societies are different from European societies; they are different again from American society. But if you take your society and look at it, you usually find there is one group sitting on another. There are two sides: wherever something stands, something else will stand beside it. There is the oppressor and the oppressed. And as a writer, all that you can do is ask yourself, "Am I going to be on the side of the oppressor or the side of the oppressed?" It sounds very stark and mechanical, but really, that's all that there is to it.[3]

He went on to describe art for art's sake as a "very deeply political position," one that says, "The political situation is all right. Don't upset it." Such writers, by attempting to avoid taking sides on important issues, are actually supporting the *status quo*, the oppressors.[4]

He then spoke of the dangers of using the word *commitment* as a cliché, without examining exactly what a writer is committed to. Here he took exception to works by certain West African writers – Ayi Kwei Armah, Yambo Ouologuem, J.P. Clark and Ken Saro-Wiwa – works that he felt did not exhibit a clear understanding of what was going on in Africa. These works were bad because "you cannot write untruth well... You can write truth badly, but there's no way you can make a lie into good literature."[5]

At the African Literature Association Conference in 1998, Achebe spoke on "Africa's Tarnished Name," reviving a theme he had explored many times previously – namely, the perpetuation of derogatory images of Africa and Africans in Western media, particularly 19th Century fiction but also the pernicious stereotypes that linger in contemporary cinema, journalism, as well as in certain varieties of anthropology, humanitarianism and even missionary work. His principal target was the racism evident in Joseph Conrad's depiction of Africans in *Heart of Darkness*, on which he had written a famous controversial essay some years before.[6] In a sense he was now answering his critics by going over the same ground in further detail, but this time he was expanding the range of reference to include other phenomena of the same type in a wider array of commentary and pictorial imagery. He conceded that much progress had been made in recent times in improving media coverage of Africa, but his message was that "when we are comfortable and inattentive, we run the risk of committing grave injustices absent-mindedly."[7]

Like his other addresses in Austin, this one was expressed with the same grace, dignity, cogency, humour and profundity of insight that have long been recognized as hallmarks of his expository style. It was always a privilege and pleasure to listen to him. It was like sitting at the feet of a very wise guru, drinking in new ideas.

Achebe soon grew to have an avid local following and his appearances drew large crowds. When we launched *Anthills of the Savannah* in 1988, the University Coop held a book-signing event for him and students and faculty lined up for more than two hours to get his signature. The manager there said the turnout was better than at any previous book signing the University Coop had organized. And when he spoke at the African Literature Association Conference in 1998, we had to book the largest hall on campus, an auditorium at the Lyndon Baines Johnson Presidential Library, to accommodate as many as we thought might want to hear him. But still there was not enough room for everyone who came. School teachers brought their students who were reading *Things Fall Apart*. Black Studies programmes at neighbouring universities sent their representatives. Nigerians from every corner of Texas streamed in. The hall was overflowing. Those who could not find seats either stood throughout his entire lecture, sat in the aisles, or moved to other rooms where they could listen and watch the proceedings on closed-circuit television. Needless to say, when Achebe finished speaking, he got a huge, Texas-size ovation.

Throughout his remarkable career, Achebe remained an articulate spokesman for Africa, but having read and taught his books for many years and having heard him express himself orally on numerous occasions, I believe he will be remembered best, on stage and on the page, for the sheer eloquence and elegance of his spoken and written words. He was a master craftsman who knew how to frame an argument and tell a story in memorable language.

Chapter Thirty-Five

# *Things Fall Apart* Revisited

## The Poetry and the Prose

*Ali A. Mazrui*

There are at least three genres of literature within which *Things Fall Apart* may be located. One school is the literature of postcoloniality. Although the book was published two years before Nigeria's own independence, it is a work which evaluates colonialism by describing what kind of Africa the imperialists encountered on their first arrival.

Achebe himself has often spoken of *Things Fall Apart* as a response to the white racism imbedded in such works as Joseph Conrad's *Heart of Darkness.*

Another genre to which the novel might be placed is a school of what has more recently been designated as the genre of clash of civilizations. It overlaps with the literature of imperialism and postcoloniality – but imperialism was only one illustration of civilizations in conflict.

Joseph Conrad's book *Heart of Darkness* was one such overlap between the literature of imperialism and the literature of clash of civilizations.

Chinua Achebe has himself held very strong views about Conrad, especially on the issue of race. Most recent examples of clash of civilizations concern the escalating conflict between Islam and the Western World, especially between the United States and such radical Islamic movements as Al-Qaeda.

Okonkwo in *Things Fall Apart* is of course a defender of his own civilization against the encroachment of British colonization.

Is *Things Fall Apart* a celebration of traditional Igbo culture? Or is it *de facto* an apology for westernization? Is westernization an answer to such Igbo flaws as the caste system?

There are Igbo traditions portrayed in the novel which the author knew were repugnant to western sensibilities, such as Igbo mutilation of a dead child to deny the child's spirit a re-entry back into this life. And was the killing of Ikemefuma by Okonkwo "The Father" who he trusted an act of barbarism?

Or was Okonkwo playing "God" The Father" facilitating the "crucifixion" of his own son? Was Ikemefuma's last thought after being stabbed by Okonkwo "Father, Father, Why Have You Forsaken Me?"

Did the dying child look at his Dad in a shocked state of incomprehension?

Does *Things Fall Apart* have more in common with Joseph Conrad's *Heart of Darkness* than Chinua Achebe has been prepared to acknowledge?

Achebe's Chancellor's Lecture at Amherst in February 1975 condemned Conrad as "a thorough going racist." Achebe accused Conrad's novel *The Congo* of Negrophobia and of dehumanizing Africans.

Others have defended Conrad's novel about the Congo as being anti-imperialist rather than racist. Would *Things Fall Apart* have been accused of racism had it been written by a white man? Does *Things Fall Apart* share with *Heart of Darkness* the quality of ambivalence between viewing the white man as intrusive and viewing the black man as primitive?

A novel portraying a religion negatively is sometimes more offensive to believers if the novelist originally belonged to that religion. On the other hand, a novel portraying a race negatively is often less offensive if the novelist is of the race he or she criticizes.

The *Satanic Verses* was written by someone who was brought up a Muslim. The novel was therefore much more offensive to Muslims than if Salmon Rushdie had been a Hindu. Among South Asians, negative writing by Hindus about Islam were commonplace. But a blasphemous diatribe by a Muslim against Islam verges on cultural treason. It was because Salman Rushdie was once a Muslim that *The Satanic Verses* was so profoundly offensive to Muslims worldwide.

With regard to a novel about ethnicity or race, a reverse phenomenon is often true. A novel by an African which portrays a seriously flawed African culture is far less offensive than a novel about such an African culture written by a white man.

A major reason why the whole world has saluted *Things Fall Apart* as a work of total cultural integrity is partly because the gifted author is an Igbo who was ready to write about his own people's mores, principles, scars and all.

We have saluted Chinua Achebe not because the Igbo did not leave newly born twins to cry themselves to death in the forest, or did not mutilate the body of a child who had just died a natural death at home, but because pre-Christianized Igbo did do precisely those things.

We are appalled in *Things Fall Apart* about domestic violence and spouse abuse, about an oracle that demands the death of a child and is granted the sacrifice.

Of course, Chinua Achebe tells us about those negative things concerning his people with understanding and empathy. But what saves the novel from being denounced as racist is that it is a view from within – both ethnically and racially. *Things Fall Apart* is a work of ethnic and racial candour and honesty. But had it been written by a white man, it would probably have been widely condemned and would never have been accepted as a great contribution to world literature.

Such a situation is of course not the fault of the real author, Chinua Achebe, nor does it detract from the singular brilliance of *Things Fall Apart*. The situation is a consequence of the history of racism and of the long record of negative portrayal of Africa and black people in so much of European and Caucasian literature across the centuries.

In reality Achebe's first novel is less about issues of race, even of culture conflict and more about the passing of traditional society. The relevant analogue in English literature is not Joseph Conrad, but more the 18th Century English Poets who lamented the demise of the traditional English village in the wake of first the Agrarian Revolution and later the Industrial Revolution. *Things Fall Apart* is about the pains of systemic change and the agonies of paradigm shifts in society.

In his first novel, Chinua Achebe is more concerned with the arrival of Christianity in Igboland than with the arrival of capitalism – although in reality colonialism was more inspired by the lure of wealth than the quest for salvation. On the other hand, 18th Century English and Irish Poets attributed the passing of traditional society in their own country to the new preoccupation with the pursuit of riches.

Achebe's lament for the passing of traditional society lies somewhere between Oliver Goldsmith's *The Deserted Village* (1770) and George Crabbe's *The Village* (1783). But while Chinua Achebe is minimally sentimental about what pre-colonial Igbo culture was like, Oliver Goldsmith seems deeply pained by the disappearance of the English village in the wake of agrarian and industrial change.

Achebe is resigned to the Christian penetration of Igboland, while Goldsmith is disturbed by the relentless pursuit of wealth in the new English society. Goldsmith's lamentation is most famously captured in the following lines:

> Ill fares the land, to hastening ills a prey
> Where wealth accumulates, and men decay;
> Princes and Lords may flourish, or may fade;
> A breath can make them, as a breath has made.
> But a bold peasantry, their county's pride,
> When once destroy'd, can never be supplied.

Imagine Okonkwo's grandson from the novel *No Longer At Ease*, becoming a product of the English village of Auburn instead of the Igbo of Umuofia, going to a more urban civilization and then returning to a desolate Umuofia. Would Okonkwo's grandson have lamented the disappearance of the old Umuofia in terms like the following?

> Remembrance wakes with all her busy train
> Swells at my breast, and turns the past to pain
> In all my wond'rings round this world of care
> In all my griefs – and God has give my share
> I still had hopes, my latest hours to crown.
> Amidst these humble bowers to lay my down
> To husband out life's taper at the close,
> And keep the flame from wasting my repose.
>
> I still had hopes, for pride attends us still
> Amidst the swains to show my book-learned skill;
> Around my fire an evening group to draw
> And tell of all I felt and all I saw
> And as a hare, whom hounds and horns pursue,
> Pants to the place from whence at first she flew,
> I still had hope, my long vexations passed,
> Here to return, Umuofia, and die at home at last.

In fact, such sentimentality about Umuofia would have been totally alien to Obi, the protagonist in *No Longer At East* and grandson of Okonkwo from *Things Fall Apart.*

Indeed, Chinua Achebe himself is far less sentimental about the past than Oliver Goldsmith was. Achebe is much closer to that other British poet of rural life, George Crabbe (1754–1832). Just as Achebe has been prepared to confront some of the great imperfections of Igbo rural life in the 19th Century, George Crabbe in 1783 explicitly rejected Goldsmith's idealization of English village life.

> I grant indeed that fields and flocks have charms
> For him that grazes or for him that farms,
> But when amid such pleasing scenes I trace
> The poor labourious native of the place,
> And see the mid-day sun, with fervid ray,
> On their bare heads and dewy temples play;
> While some with feebler heads and fainter hears,
> Deplore their fortune, yet sustain their parts,
> Then shall I dare these real ills to hide
> In tinsel trappings of poetic bride?

*[These remarks were originally written as part of the celebration of the 50th Anniversary of Chinua Achebe's classical novel, "Things Fall Apart" (1958). Part of the celebration was held at the Library of Congress in Washington, DC in 2008.]*

Chapter Thirty-Six

# Celebrating Achebe's *Utu* and Creative Genius in Oracy, Orature and Literature

*Mĩcere Gĩthae Mũgo*

In commemorating Chinua Achebe, I will actively draw upon African oracy, orature and orate skills in memory of the orate artist that this great son of Nigeria, Africa and the world was. "Oracy," "orature" and "orate" are used here as defined by Pio Zirimu and Austin Bukenya in their now famous piece, "Oracy as a Skill and as a Tool for African Development," originally delivered at the colloquium of the Second Black World Festival of Arts and Cultures in Lagos, Nigeria, 1977 (FESTAC 77) and since then published in *The Arts and Civilization of Black and African People.*[1] According to Zirimu and Bukenya, oracy is mastery in the effective use of the spoken word, while orature is the highest manifestation of oracy in action: imaginative compositions, transmitted through "verbal art" and ideally, culminating in performance. Thus, a person who is orate is versed in the basic skills of oracy and can use them to great effect, while an orator is a specialist and often, well-trained professional in the art of speech-making. Chinua Achebe was a skilful artist in all these media. He was a writer whose works celebrated African oracy; an orate craftsman who drew inspiration from his people's orature and an orator, to wit. No justification is thus needed to describe Chinua Achebe as an African orate-literate *griot par excellence*, for he epitomized the very best in both heritages. Indeed, Achebe traversed and crisscrossed the imaginative landscapes of orature and literature with unmatched ease, "bending and twisting" the very English language itself when need be in order to make it do his artistic bidding.

The first part, entitled, *"At the hearth[2]: First Encounter with the Master of the Word,"* will be a story-narrating session covering a long anecdote, reliving my very first meeting with Chinua Achebe in 1973, just before I defended my doctorate. This is some risky undertaking because I am at an age when senior moments are often upon me and so actual details of this unique and memorable experience might not be as sharp as they should be.

The second part is a long epic-style narrative praise poem, entitled: *"An Orature Poem in Praise of Chinualumogu Achebe."*

## Part 1: "At the hearth: First Encounter with the Master of the Word."

*Ancestors Rescue an Elusive Dream…*

Twi proverbial orature counsels that "dreams are voices of the ancestors." In hindsight, I believe that ancestral intervention had everything to do with the way I first met Chinua Achebe, a life dream that had eluded me for almost two years. Here is the story of how the dream was born and how it nearly withered before the ancestors said, "*Ashe!*"

*Crick! Crack!*

While working on my creative writing master's thesis at the University of New Brunswick, in Fredericton, Canada (1969-I971), I developed a voracious appetite for reading African, African American, Caribbean and Canadian writers. The appetite fanned my nerd tendencies and by the end of 1971, I had read so much "Commonwealth" literature that I could confidently hold my own in any literary discussion touching on most authors of the heritage. In all transparency, though, this achievement was not such a remarkable feat as I was a thoroughly spoilt, fully-funded Commonwealth scholar, enjoying a fellowship that not only covered all my expenses but gave me a monthly stipend. With no responsibility as a graduate assistant, I had all the time in the world for reading and there were weeks when I would actually demolish three to four books.

Chinua Achebe was among the writers whose works I read in total during this period, including his essays, interviews and statements he had made on literature and writing – anything that I could lay hands on by the *guru* of the word. His writing fascinated, engaged and absorbed me so completely that by the time I had defended my MA thesis in 1971, I had already decided to research on him (along with Ngũgĩ wa Thiong'o) for my doctoral dissertation.[3] As it eventually happened, I ended up with a much larger project that dealt with the works of Chinua Achebe, Ngũgĩ wa Thiong'o, Margaret Lawrence and Elspeth Huxley, later published as *Visions of Africa.*[4]

During the summer of 1971, I travelled to Kenya to interview Ngũgĩ and to research on Elspeth Huxley. Ambitiously, I had hoped to travel to Nigeria, locate Chinua Achebe and interview him as well; but however hard I tried, every time the trail would end up in a *cul de sac* and I would start all over again – with no added luck. This was the period just after the Nigerian Civil War and the debacle of Biafra (1967–1970). It is indeed good to be young, because thinking about the whole thing now, it is difficult to fathom how I was hoping to travel to a country where the sound of gun fire had barely died down, let alone conduct research. The dream of interviewing Achebe was even crazier, especially considering how deeply involved he was in the Biafran struggle during which he also lost one of his dearest friends, Christopher Okigbo, the celebrated poet.

Nonetheless, fanned by the optimism of *mageria nomo mahota*,[5] from the fall 1971 right through the summer of 1972, I sent out letter after letter to Chinua Achebe seeking an interview, but never heard back. Still, I refused to give up. As the fall semester of 1972 approached, however, I knew that my obstinacy needed to give way to realism seeing that the first draft of my dissertation was almost complete and my dissertation due for defence in the spring. I was getting ready to throw in the towel when I found out that Chinua Achebe had taken up a Visiting Professorship in the Department of Afro-American Studies at the University of Massachusetts, Amherst. Immediately, I sent out another letter and this time spent extra time refining it into a masterpiece, just in case my earlier attempts had failed to meet the mark. I waited breathlessly.

Sometime during the third week in November – and I remember this clearly because it was just after Achebe's birthday on November 16 – I received a letter with a Massachusetts postal stamp. Chinua Achebe had at long last written back – to me! However, instead of shouting with joy, I was hit by panic, fearful that the response might be negative. I do not recall now, but I probably first made a cup of tea to calm down my nerves before sitting down to open the letter, as is my habit when either anxious, or licking wounds. Whatever the case, Chinua Achebe had agreed to grant me an interview in January 1973. I was elated. No. I was actually beside myself. I could not believe that I was holding a letter from Chinua Achebe in my hands!

When I shared the news with my doctoral student colleagues, I could tell from their cynical looks that they were saying under their breath: "Yeah, right!" On learning about it, my advisor's first concern was that the January 1973 interview would delay the submission of my final draft, the deadline of which was early March. In my view, this was not an issue since I was a year ahead in completing the dissertation. I explained to him that I'd rather delay my graduation than miss interviewing Achebe. The only struggle within me was that the reason I had been rushing to finish early was because I had promised Ngũgĩ wa Thiong'o, Head of the Literature Department at the University of Nairobi[6], Kenya, that I would return home as soon as I could after defending my dissertation in order to join in the work of building the new department.

*Crick! Crack!*

"Journey" is an important as well instructive *motif* in African orature and as any orate person knows, the good traveller is he or she who makes a good start and then completes the journey arriving back wiser having managed to survive all adversity. In this regard, my chances were slim, for, anyone who knows about winters in Fredericton, New Brunswick, understands it when I say that making a trip by road in January is a wild idea. Certainly, the possibility of starting the journey wisely was almost nil and so all I could do was hope to arrive back successfully. Thanks to the indomitable energy of youth, I was undaunted.

I believe I took the Greyhound bus that used to go through Bangor, Maine and made my three-day trip to either Boston, or New York City, before heading to Amherst, Massachusetts.

*Crick! Crack!*

Now, if you want to hear about my meeting with the *Novelist as Teacher,* don't ask me awkward questions such as how I managed for showers because, frankly, I don't remember. I am not anxious to remember. All I recall is that on eventually arriving at the Amherst guesthouse where I had reserved a room, I slept for one and half days. This I remember too: there was both a bathroom as well as a shower there! Luckily, I had planned the trip such that I would be in Amherst a whole two days before the interview, as I could not afford to have anything go wrong. So anxious was I not to make any mistake that I took a walk around the neighbourhood where the Achebe's lived the evening before the interview to locate the address.

I can still see myself standing at the front door of the Achebe family residence ringing the bell in trepidation. I do not remember whether they lived in a house or in an apartment. However, I clearly remember it had a downstairs where I was ushered in by a young girl of about ten to twelve years who behaved older than her age. She offered me a chair and then nimbly ran up a staircase. I now wonder whether this could have been Chinelo – now Dr Chinelo Achebe-Ejeyueitche. Anyhow, as I sat down fidgeting but pretending to be rubbing my hands to ward off the cold I had just emerged from – the proverbial flies fluttering in my stomach – I looked towards the staircase and saw a figure that had become familiar from pictures I had seen coming down the steps. Chinua Achebe, the icon, was descending. I remember – no senior moment here – promptly standing up in confusion and mumbling something to the effect, "Good morning, Sir!"

Achebe must have noticed how very thoroughly I had managed to intimidate myself and said something to the effect, "That is not necessary," (obviously referring to my siring him). "Please sit down."

I thanked him, laughed self-consciously and then decided to hide behind the mask of humour, noting that I had grown up under settler colonialism in Kenya where "sir" was drilled into us. This seemed to have amused him and much later on, when I came to know him better, he would always remind me of it, explaining that initially he had wanted to point out that he was not a settler and then had decided to spare me. Anyone who has been at the sharp edge of Achebe's wit, or sarcasm would readily join me, even this many years later, in thanking him for having spared me the razor.

At any rate, the brief exchange had humanized the deity I had constructed in Achebe and had made me start to feel at home with the person in front of me.

In a lot of indigenous African orature ethics, the ideal person is he/she who has the ability touch others with ***utu,*** the essence of being human. Somehow, Achebe had, almost instantly, managed to do that with me. The terrifying "big man" I had conjured and intimidated myself with was gone. Achebe had emerged. He was tallish and I have always been short; but at no time did he tower over me. As he had walked down the staircase, his descent had appeared unhurried, measured, unobtrusive, but purposeful. His face had a no-nonsense, serious, reflective, but at the same time magnanimous appearance. Unless my imagination was playing me tricks, his eyes had a searching look that seemed to be seeing right through me and that made me conscious of the icon I was standing before. Once Achebe opened his mouth, however, his gentle, caring, unassuming and assuring manner of speaking carved out for me a comfort zone that lasted throughout the interview. Even though he spoke with natural authority, he did not "silence" me. All in all, Achebe had a general calmness and gentleness that made me both secure and comfortable.

Achebe proceeded to ask me about myself, Jomo Kenyatta and Kenya in general. When I explained that before Kenyatta's detention, the former Kenyan first president and my father were good friends, he teased me about being well-connected. However, not quite sure whether this was a compliment or a chiding, I made myself a mental note to avoid sounding as if I was name-dropping in whatever I said next. Achebe then asked me about Tom Mboya and the circumstances surrounding his assassination and I could not resist "name-dropping" here. On explaining the situation, I added that historically, Mboya and others had advocated for the de-racialization (I don't believe I knew the word then) of education in Kenya and because of this I had become the first African to be admitted into a whites-only high school, Limuru Girls' School. I don't believe I boasted that I knew the Mboyas personally.

He went on to ask whether I knew Ngũgĩ, another name I readily "dropped," elaborating on our Alliance Girls'/Boys' High school and Makerere University connections. I must have mentioned as well that Ngũgĩ was one of the writers whose works my dissertation was analysing and that I had interviewed him in 1971. Just in case this made him wonder why I had left his interview till the last minute, I recall explaining how desperately I had looked for him for about two years, confessing that I had nearly given up. He chuckled and quipped something to the tune that I did not look like the type that easily gives up. That was an accurate character analysis I have never forgotten because I am notorious for my persistence. I also clearly recall Achebe asking me if I was at Makerere in 1962 during the first African writers' conference.[7] I explained that I was in high school then doing my "A" levels and did not enter Makerere until 1963. He asked me about my Limuru Girls' School experience and then about my studies at the University of New Brunswick, Fredericton. All in all, we must have spent at least half an hour on these preliminaries and by then I was feeling completely at home with my literary idol. His warm welcome and humility had completely affirmed me and by then I knew I would have a good interview.

Rehashing that memorable interview would be redundant as a summarized form of it has been available through *Visions of Africa* since 1973, but I feel the need to briefly describe the way it unfolded. Achebe allowed me all the time I needed to pose my questions – some of them rather long and convoluted now that I think of it. He was patient, attentive, engaged and alert throughout, never giving me a sense of being rushed, or even time-constrained. Known for being on point, focused, concise and lucid, Achebe would often respond to my lengthy questions such that I would be sitting there waiting for more long after he was done. Luckily, I am a quick study and learnt fast when to wait for more and when to proceed to the next business on the agenda. Achebe was gracious, affirming and generous in responding to my graduate student questions. He is one of the best listeners that I have ever encountered, patiently "hearing" the interviewer's questions and observations with studied attentiveness, then, sensitively entering the space to enrich the discourse. At the same time, he did not hesitate to give a firm clue when he either did not want to take up certain issues or go into details. For instance, when I asked him about his role in the Biafran war, he paused and then simply remarked that it was a long story. Going into a reflective mode he then said that all I needed know was that from the way things had unfolded he had "fought on the wrong side." He was done. It was time to move on to another issue.

An exchange I will never forget was when, trying to be graduate-student-clever, I asked him why he had "killed" Okonkwo in *Things Fall Apart*. Laughing, he retorted, "Why not? He is my character," or some such words and then laughed some more. He then asked me, "If he had been your character what would you have done with him?" The question caught me by surprise and I prayed for divine intervention to give a coherent answer. At the time, I was evolving a theory that with all due to respect to Igbo philosophy and cultural wisdom, Okonkwo's decision to commit suicide was neither a shame, nor an abomination, but an act of resistance against a form of "silencing" (I believe I called it emasculation at the time) that was tantamount to "death" anyway. Thus by killing himself, Okonkwo was taking back "power" from the colonialists and making a conscious choice to "determine" his own life. In this sense, then, suicide on Okonkwo's part was an act of heroism and a triumph. I posited the thesis to Achebe and waited in trepidation. Surprisingly, he seemed impressed and commended me for my original thinking. However, he also impressed upon me the importance of interpreting the episode within the context of Igbo cultural philosophy. I remember being so happy that I wanted to bring the interview to a close before anything went wrong. This "theory" on Okonkwo's suicide remains one of the most debated ideas in *Visions of Africa.* I will be forever grateful to Achebe for encouraging me to evolve the thesis. More so, I will always appreciate the fact that even though he disagreed with me, he did not squash my unconventional interpretation of Okonkwo's suicide as an act of resistance against colonialist strangulation.

In the "Acknowledgments" page of *Visions of Africa,* I thank Achebe and Ngũgĩ "…for allowing me the privilege of interviewing them," adding: "Mr Achebe was particularly kind in answering numberless questions from me and in supplying me with material to which I would not have otherwise had access."[8] The ancestors had indeed not just rescued my elusive dream, but had found me a mentor for life. The "Introduction" to *Daughter of My People, Sing!* also pays tribute to Chinua Achebe, "…who went through the manuscript painstakingly suggesting improvements here and there."[9] Achebe was indeed instrumental to the publication of *Daughter of My People, Sing!* – my very first book. As if he had not already done enough for me, soon after I joined the University of Nairobi in 1973, Achebe wrote to me explaining that he wanted to include young scholars on the editorial board of *Okike* and wondered whether I would be interested in being a member. Of course I jumped at the offer – an honour that few young scholars have had the privilege of even dreaming about.

The 1973 interview had given me not just a mentor, but a revered and precious friend whose family members have also become valued friends.

## Part II: An Orature Narrative Poem in Praise of Chinualumogu Achebe

The *iroko* tree that stood at the entrance of the orature homestead has fallen
The drought-immune baobab tree with a giant trunk of oracy wisdom is gone
The mighty mahogany that held the secrets of mastery
word-weaving is no more
The evergreen cedar of imagination that birthed African writing has been felled
The *mugumo* tree that towered the ceremonial creative grove no longer lives
Its dark-green foliage has shrivelled, but left behind still growing metaphors of life
Where is the brown soil to fill the gaping holes in the desert of our bereavement?
Where is the rain of words to soften the parched earth of our emotional drought?

Unstoppable rivers of tears flood the shifting ground upon which we stand, threatening us with drowning…
The words of a Kiswahili proverb ring sharply in our minds
*Muti mukuu ukianguka, ndege huhangaika*:
(When a mighty tree falls, the birds wander aimlessly)

Suddenly, a rainbow draped in stunning colours curves across the sky
its beauty making a mockery of now retreating oceans of tears
its glamour lighting the sky for the birds to sail through the clouds
aiming at a new destination, their wings afloat a stream of fresh wind
Long nights of mourning yield to the breaking of a new dawn
calling for remembrance in the spirit of *Sankofa*
as we bask in the sunshine of celebration, commemorating
the life of a novelist, poet, essayist, philosopher, scholar, activist
storyteller, orature artist, master of the spoken and written word
griot unsurpassed: Chinualumogu Achebe, the "Novelist as Teacher…"
Husband, father, grandfather, uncle: Baba Chinua Achebe
We salute you, Elder Chinualumogu Achebe!
We salute you, son of the soil!
We salute you, son of Africa!

The ***iroko*** tree fell but was not uprooted
the ***mugumo*** tree left roots still anchored
so deep in the fertile soil of an indestructible past that

it will never die
but obstinately send baby shoots out of the yielding soil
giving birth to a new breed of indigenous trees
that will defy the drought of droughts.
For ever green, the cedar tree will thrive again
and never die
Reborn, the baobab will thrust out powerful branches
refusing to die
and the mahogany tree will stand tall in eternal splendor
forever celebrating life
We salute you, Elder Chinualumogu Achebe!
We salute, son of the soil!
We salute you, son of Africa!

You, who fathered the African novel
You, who gifted literature with *Things Fall Apart*
Writer, whose pen had the precision of a surgeon's knife,
Molder of words, sharp with cutting irony
Magician with language, entrancing as a spell
Seer who foretold the demise of the British Empire
upon which the sun did ultimately set
having made occupied worlds *fall apart*
leaving their cultures *no longer at ease*
opening wider the cracks through which the rain had begun to beat
Mother Africa's house
dismantling the walls of the original home of homosapiens
leaving ruins out of which mushroomed human ogres
dressed in Franco-German-Anglo-American suits
each one, a self-appointed Messiah: *man of the people*
Chief Nangas of Africa at whom the *arrow of God* will
forever remain pointed as *girls at war and other stories*
uncover ugly, indicting, oppositional narratives
damning these molesters and abductors of history
greedy hyenas, ravenous vultures, vampire warlords
that rule the Kongas of Africa through the power of the gun
reducing African peoples and nations to *anthills of the savannah*

For being the seer who foresaw this falling apart of Africa
For being the prophet who warned of *the trouble with Nigeria*
For being the visionary who rose above
the diet of false myths you were fed

under *the education of a British-protected child*
We salute you, Chinualumogu Achebe!
We salute you, son of the soil!
We salute you son of Africa!

You, the ultimate orature artist possessed with the eloquence of a griot
You, the bard who taught us to find poetry in the green branches of the palm tree
You, the elder who bequeathed us an overflowing granary of proverbial utterance
reminding us to turn them into the palm oil with which we eat our words
You, the griot who told stories that whet the appetites of young and old alike
setting their imagination on fire; transporting them to magical lands inhabited
by new breeds of beings, animals, birds and wonders of nature
hearing tales about:

> *Chike and the River*
> *How the Leopard Got His Claws*
> *The Sacrificial Egg and Other Stories*
> *The Flute*

charming the audience with the wooing artistry of *African short stories*
and the magnetic grip of *winds of change.*
holding us under the spell of the orate tapestry of your imaginative creations

For being the griot of African oracy
for being the grand master of the orate
and supreme keeper of verbal art

We salute you, Chinualumogu Achebe!
We salute you, son of the soil!
We salute you, son of Africa!

We salute you, yet again, father of African literature
We salute you, writer whose pen never dried of ink
moulder of words, sharp with cutting irony, ticklish with mischievous
humour magician with language, entrancing like a spell
Creator whose imagination the ancestors gifted with
rare artistic creativity; profound utterance and

stunning beauty of language that flows through every page
of your fictional genius:
*Things Fall Apart; No Longer at Ease; Arrow of God;*
*A Man of the People; Anthills of the Savannah*
Artistic genius eclipsing the ugliness of imperialist mega narratives
that aimed at stopping the heart-beat of the soul of Africa
through the strangulating myth of Conrad's heart of darkness
a dark heart with arteries that pumped dark blood that
later flowed through the veins of Cary's *Mister Johnson*

For shattering these imperialist myths and burying them
in the graveyard of Western colonial history's heart of darkness
for rebuilding the homestead whose walls had collapsed and
digging up people's stories long buried in the rubble

We salute you, Chinualumogu Achebe!
We salute you, son of the soil!
We salute you son of Africa!

You, the probing poet of
*Beware, Soul Brother* who penned
*Christmas in Biafra and Other Poems*
You, the essayist of *Morning Yet on Creation Day*
*Hopes and Impediments…*
*An Image of Africa*
You the orator-conversationalist of
*Conversations with Chinua Achebe*
And the sojourner of *Home and Exile;*
You, the communal historian of
*There Was a Country:* a memoir of re-membering a broken history
excavating national ruins in which homes and countries are buried
You, the mastermind of the Achebe Conferences on Africa
obstinately pursuing continental and international dialogue,
diligently seeking to understand "where the rain began to beat us"
Optimistically searching for peace, healing and human-affirmation

For being tireless champion of *utu/Ubuntu*
affirming the essence of being human
We salute you, Elder Chinualumogu Achebe!
We salute you, son of the soil!
We salute you son of Africa!

You, who left us and went well, surely arrived just as well.
So, listen to the welcoming orchestra of music and voices
and instruments that drown mourning
Listen!
Master drummers from every corner of Africa are here
to celebrate your life, weaver of narratives
Listen to the booming sound of the *udu*, the *ekwe* and the *igba*
Hear the *ashiko*, the delirious *atenteben* and the thundering *djembe*
Let the master drummers, drum till they grow dizzy
Let them drum till the earth shakes in rhythm with their drumming
Nothing will silence these breakers of silence
Listen!
The drumming has reached a frenzied peak
Our nimble feet refuse to touch the ground
choosing to dance in the air
as other instruments take up the challenge of the drums:
the xylophone and violin
the trumpet and the ivory horn
the accordion and saxophone
the *marimba* and the *marimbula*
the *akonting* and the guitar
the *nyatiti* and the *kora*
Listen!

Not to be beaten, the shy instruments join the chorus:
the flute and the *kayamba*
the *mbira* and the *wand nd*
the *njingiri* and the *shekere…*
Feeling upstaged, the whistle and the *vuvuzela* now pierce the air
transforming the dancers
into entranced mediums
under musical possession
as the multitudinous crowd breaks into wild, wild ululation

Overcome by the power of this *Ashe* moment,
streams of delirious tears
freely flow down our faces
and we let them

As we celebrate you: husband, father, grandfather, uncle
Baba Chinua Achebe

Saying, with renewed assertion:

We salute you, Elder Chinualumogu Achebe!
We salute you, son of the soil!
We salute you, son of Africa!

Chapter Thirty-Seven

# Reading Chinua Achebe

## Footholds in the Flood of History

*Njabulo S. Ndebele*

## I

When *Things Fall Apart* first drifted into my ears, it made little impact on my mind. The book entered my intellectual life in casual fragments of information, some directly related to it, others through incidental associations. Then, I was a high school student at St Christopher's High School for boys in Swaziland. It was probably in my last three years of boarding school between 1964 and 1966 that I heard about the book. Students at some school, I heard, were studying a novel by that name. The book preceded its author as a literary phenomenon.

In the vagueness of my encounter with it, the novel was said to be a book "about Africa." A little later, it took shape as real when I spotted someone at school reading a battered copy of it. *Things Fall Apart,* I read and remembered. From an earlier, casual auditory encounter, the book became a visual reality. I do not recall many details of my first sight of the novel, but I do remember to this day, the iconic orange and white cover that I would later recognize as signifying novels of the African Writers Series.

My next encounter with a book "about Africa" has some firmer contours of memory. A boy from Springs, a town some fifteen miles from my home town of Nigel in the East Rand, walked around the school with a brown and black covered book. While I had been curious about the copy of *Things Fall Apart,* I was bolder with the holder of this next book. Without a word, I reached out to grab the book in Dudley Ngcobo's hand. He let go. He was a friend. *The African Image* was the title of the book in his hand.

The name of its author struck me more than its title. "Mphahlele" was a very South African surname. Although I had not heard of him before, my recognition of a familiar African name as the author of a book in English

Mphahlele's struck an unforgettable chord of possibility. A black South African, from among oppressed people, had written a book in English! Such a possibility was until then very distant.

Little did I know that I would later have a more significant encounter with Mphahlele in my own home. The more I heard about him, the more inspired I got. Here was a remarkable man from my own country who was the first black South African to earn a Masters Degree in English with distinction, from the University of South Africa, a distance education institution in apartheid South Africa.[1] Fortuitously, we heard around that time about another South African who was in exile in Swaziland, and taught at a school in Manzini. This man reputedly spoke English with amazing command, using big words we called "terms." Can Temba was his name. A walking dictionary," he was awesomely described.

But what was I reading at the time? Frankly, I was preoccupied with an English literature syllabus dominated by Dickens, Hardy, Wordsworth, Keats, Tennyson, Shakespeare and others we had to read and study for the Cambridge Overseas School Certificate Examination. *English Today* and *The Student's Companion* claimed my required attention.

During the week at the boarding school, we had to speak English among ourselves. Prefects enforced the school rule. Various forms of punishment awaited culprits reported to the school principal. Weekends were fun. We spoke in all available languages among us. But I do remember how even over weekends we argued fiercely in English.

It was also around that time that I saw a picture of Nelson Mandela with Ahmed Ben Bella, President of newly independent, revolutionary Algeria. It could have been from *Newsweek* or *Time Magazine* but it did the rounds among us. Few things extended my view of the world beyond South Africa than that picture. Many years in the 1980s I would remember that picture when I first watched the movie *The Battle of Algiers*. The painful yet heroic history recalled by that movie provided a world of context to a single picture of Ben Bella with Mandela. A memory circle closed.

There was another more immediate, more personal context to that picture. It underscored the broader meaning of the presence of Nelson Mandela's and Walter Sisulu's sons at my school. Our parents sent us all to Swaziland probably for the same reason: to escape from Bantu Education, the system of education in South Africa designed by white people for the black people they oppressed. There was something affirming about the extraordinary, global resonance of the Mandela and Sisulu names and the ordinary proximity of their sons to me and other boys at school. History felt both awesomely remote and casually accessible.

I remember many reading moments in my own home during school holidays. Magazines lay around in the living room. My mother and father read

*Bona*, and *Drum*, *Huisgenoot*, *Africa South*, and *The Classic*, I noticed were additionally read by my father. I was quietly curious why my father subscribed to *Huisgenoot*, an Afrikaans magazine that seemed to be about farming. But I paged through *Africa South* and *The Classic* with an interest I could not articulate. I remember paintings of Gerald Sekoto hanging on our walls as a constant presence in the room.

In the mix were 78, 45 and 33.3 rpm vinyl records of township music, jazz and classical music. Of township music I would play The Dark City Sisters, Spokes Mashiyane, Lemmy "Special" Mabaso and music from the opera, King Kong. Of Jazz, my father's home offerings were The Oscar Peterson Trio, Thelonious Monk, Ahmad Jamal, Benny Golson, Sammy Davis, The Platters, and the South African Chris McGregor. Of classical music he frequently played Brahms, Rachmaninov, Tchaikovsky, Beethoven, Mozart, Mendelsshon, Bach, Chopin, Schumann and operas of Gilbert and Sullivan. I heard a great deal of music I did not really understand.

It was really this casual, un-reading reading and un-listening listening, this seeing un-seeing that countered or augmented in informal ways over time the prescribed reading of the school curriculum in a country, Swaziland, known at the time as a British Protectorate.

I remember our history teacher, who was also the school chaplain, an Englishman who loved a drink. He would hold forth with cruel glee about African tribes who sharpened their teeth. I began to dislike the image of African people portrayed as savages in some of the history books we studied at the time and presented by Father Johnson. To this day, I do not remember anything else about those tribes or even their names, except that they sharpened their teeth, or walked around naked, or engaged in endless conflict and "cattle stealing" or "raiding."

In the preface to my book of essays *Fine Lines from the Box: Further Thoughts About Our Country*, I recall how I discovered banned books hidden in a wooden box in my father's garage. In my gap year, I clandestinely read many of them. They were South African classics published in the early 1960s reflecting South African life in the 1950s. I found *Down Second Avenue* by Ezekiel Mphahlele; *Road to Ghana* by Alfred Hutchinson; *Blame Me on History* by Bloke Modisane; *Naught for Your Comfort* by Trevor Huddleston; *Wild Conquest* by Peter Abrahams; *Splendid Sunday* by James Ambrose Brown; *Transvaal Episode* by Harry Bloom; *Chocolates for My Wife*, by Todd Matshikiza; *The Struggle for a Birthright* by Mary Benson; *The Ochre People* by Noni Jabavu; *Ghana: The Autobiography of Kwame Nkrumah*; *Let My People Go* by Albert Luthuli; and *Go Well, Stay Well* by Hannah Stanton.

Of *Down Second Avenue* and *Blame Me on History* I wrote: "I still remember clearly the thrill of reading these two books and beginning to discuss them with myself. How different they were from each other, conveying different aspects of the same overriding political and social reality! It struck me then that no matter how much black people suffered under apartheid they did not experience oppression in the same way. They did not evoke the pain of oppression in the same way. It struck me then that oppressed people were far more complex than the collective suffering that sought to reduce them to a single state of pain."[2]

Finally, I read what had up to then been items of casual presence in a home: those magazines. They brought to me Nadine Gordimer, Nat Nakasa, Lewis Nkosi, Casey Motsisi, Dugmore Boeti, Bernado Honwana; artists Ezrom Legae and Sydney Khumalo; actors Barney Simon and Athol Fugard; photographers John Cohen and David Gloldbatt. I now bought my own copies of new editions of *Classic*, *The Purple Renoster* and *Contrast.* These purchases represented my first investment in literature.

1967 and 1968 were my two gap years between high school and university. That was when most of this reading took place. I now look back to those years as when my experience of the world exposed me to the informal, incrementally educative life of the everyday as a personal journey of growth that countered, sometimes augmented, the official world of school learning.

It was in that period of my life that I read books not in response to the demands of a curriculum, but to the urgings of my expanding curiosity and the personal excitement of new worlds opening up. My awareness grew at my own instance. I began to chart the course of my own intellectual growth in ways that I planned, saving money for books and records, or accidental learning that occurred from unintended opportunities made possible as a result of prior intentions to extend my reading in some way.

I am led to think that the full impact of education, public or private, can never be fully planned. Basic conditions do need to be carefully laid. They are vital. Laying such conditions for a young nation is a huge foundational step in the growth and nurturing of the young. It must enjoy the most intelligent, rigorous and caring policies that any country can develop and implement. Such a planned foundational environment increases opportunities for unplanned casual encounters with educative moments in the broader social realm.

Young people ought to be stimulated to learn everywhere. Education then ceases to be only about school and university campuses. It becomes an experience of encounters with echoes of learning that go in both directions between the formal and the informal. Nations that experience themselves as going through critical moments of change ought to regard the entire social realm as an expanded world of learning. Achieving such conditions is a historic challenge to the entire social imagination of a people. All countries in Africa are at various stages of meeting this challenge.

The import of this understanding is that up to the time that I registered as a first year student at the then University of Botswana, Lesotho and Swaziland at the Roma campus in Lesotho, I had learned on my own far more about my immediate world than five years of a formal curriculum at boarding school in Swaziland.

The bulk of my formal learning was orientated away from my most formative social world. In fact, the official world of my formal learning rendered as informal and largely illegitimate the world of my informal upbringing that in reality should have constituted the content of my formal education. When African writers I was to encounter in my first year of study in Lesotho suddenly filled my world, many of them articulated this insight clearly for me where I had only intuited it.

It was in this context that in 1969, Obi Okonkwo and his girl friend Clara knocked on the door of my awareness with the full reality of their lives well before Obi's grandfather Ogbuefi Okonkwo did in *Things Fall Apart.* Thus it came to be that I read and studied Achebe's *No Longer at Ease* in the formal setting of a university syllabus. If the novel sneaked up on me in this manner, it was because I had not expected it. But when it came my way I was ready for it. Required formal reading and study in a formal setting suddenly supported the world of my own discoveries. The impact of my informal literary experiences of earlier years began to assume a presence, validity, and a degree of ascendency in my intellectual growth. It was a stimulating and exhilarating confluence.

As I look back now it feels as if in my early years I was caught in a flood of history that carried me away and that in my gap years, I began to stretch my feet, feeling with my big toes for any ground beneath where I could land. My toes were my expanding awareness, the growth of my consciousness.

## II

*No Longer at Ease* was the first full-length novel I read, which was written in English, by an African writer. It was my first sustained entry in English into an engrossing imagined African world. It drew me in immediately with an imaginative intimacy I had never experienced before. My first literary lover, *No Longer at Ease*, embraced me with firm, warm arms. My own arms around her would tighten without let to this day.

There was something in the reading of *No Longer at Ease* that was different from my reading of the autobiographies of Mphahlele, Hutchinson, Modisane, and Nkrumah. While the novel shared with the autobiographies an embracing sense of authenticity, the impact of its imaginative world worked without the kind of expository intent one senses running through the recalled and recreated life of autobiography.

In *No Longer at Ease* the drift of the world and some of its insidious moments came across in subtle ways. In the very first page of my treasured copy that cost me sixty South African cents in 1969 is an almost throwaway reference to "some civil servants" in Lagos who "paid as much as ten shillings and sixpence to obtain a doctor's certificate of illness for the day" so as not to miss the case of Obi Okonkwo on trial for corruption. How many of the corrupt, were there in court to witness a trial in which their very own conduct was under scrutiny and that they seemed unaware of the irony in which they too were on trial and that their own behaviour was as reprehensible as the accused's whose public disrobing they had come to witness?

I remember the assignment topic: "'Real tragedy is never resolved. It goes on hopelessly for ever. Conventional tragedy is too easy. The hero dies and we feel a purging of the emotions. A real tragedy takes place in a corner, in an untidy spot, to quote W. H. Auden. The rest of the world is unaware of it.'[3] Discuss."

Obi Okonkwo's perspective on tragedy may underscore the aesthetic conception of the novel that tells his story. In *No Longer at Ease* Achebe created a world without postured messages of self-justification, self-proclamation, or censure and reproach. Instead, it had something far more elemental in its social wisdom. He portrayed a self-validating, self-referential world at a level of literary rendering I had not experienced before. Here was a world in which I felt I did not have to justify living in it, nor did I feel any pressure to abandon it for other worlds whose power over me demanded that I aspire towards them, away from my own. I belonged to Obi Okonkwo's Umuofia, to his Lagos and its Ikoyi and to Clara's Yaba. And it was not a romantic world, as Obi's "mummy wagon" journey to Umuofia depicted. It could be as hilarious as it could be sad.[4]

My imagined world whirled on its own orbit in a vast universe, one that could exert, with cosmic indifference, significant influence on a human moral or ethical order. Within that very universe human beings were doomed to create ethical and moral markers with which to both sustain their own order as well as navigate within it. Human beings were entirely responsible for the world they created. In it they made decisions that made or unmade them.

In this context the most immediate causes of success or failure of human effort, such as conquests and invasions leading to colonial and imperial occupation and strong human feelings spurred on by them, could never be sufficient and final causes in the determination of Africa's destiny. In the total scheme of history, such immediate causes hold temporary sway, urgent for the times in which they dominate. In order to overcome the onerous restrictions of the logic of colonialism, Africans must place themselves in a universe of awareness outside of colonial determinations.

I make this observation to suggest that the critique of Africa's colonial history as a definitive cause of the continent's historical misfortunes has held centre stage for too long. More vital now is not what has been lost than what needs to be created, and even more urgently, how to create it.

The discourse of what was lost up to the era of Africa's independence from colonialism ought now to retain significance only as a historic point of reference, while being replaced by a transformative discourse of what needs to be done in the present for the future.

For half a century since Africa's independence from Europe began, what Africa lost has been sharply contrasted with a future to be gained, as that hoped for future was captured in declarations of independence and constitutions of aspiration. Many were designed to yank Africa "into the modern world." Being dragged into history, sometimes an inescapable experience, is vastly different from creating it. The decision to create history is indeed, a decision. And Africa did make some decisions. They were not always the best ones. But they were all African decisions, nevertheless, even when they were decisions to let others make decisions for Africa. There is no escape from responsibility and accountability. It all comes with the terrain to decide to make history.

The dominant decisions of the 1970s and the 1980s had much to do with notions of Obi Okonkwo's "Augean stable." "Where does one begin?" he mused. "With the masses? Educate the masses? Not a chance there. It would take centuries. A handful of men at the top. Or even one man with vision – an enlightened dictator. People are scared of the word nowadays. But what kind of democracy can exist side by side with so much corruption and ignorance? Perhaps a half-way house – a sort of compromise. When Obi's reasoning reached this point he reminded himself that England had been as corrupt not so very long ago. He was not really in the mood for consecutive reasoning. His mind was impatient to roam in more pleasant landscape."

The era of impatience was the era of failed attempts: military coups and nationalization of strategic assets. They swept across the continent like a tidal wave. Seeking to make the new African state stronger, they only weakened it. A desire to acquire traction through a centralized state led to the tendency to miss the vital middle point between a current sense of malaise and the end point of aspiration. There was hell and heaven, and no life in between to live.

It is as if Africa sought to emulate and reproduce the effects of imperial energy at the point of its subjugating impact than at its enabling source in the colonizing country. Perhaps there was something inevitable about this behaviour. The colonial and imperial enterprises were about funnelling local energies at home towards meeting focused imperial objectives away from home in the local colonial space. Thus, in the colony there was a levelling and a marshalling that made very few, or crude if any, distinctions between phenomena, human and non-human, in the local colonial environment.

Thus military coups as a mechanism to achieve some form of local autonomy became a continuation in their effects of the objectification, by imperial powers, of the colonial environment in its totality. As a single energy of intervention, military coups amplified the single focus of imperial design even where such coups, as Sankara's of Burkina Faso were driven by a radical intention to empower a mass population base. The resulting structure of governance was inherently constrictive even when it sought to achieve expansive effects.

Africa needs to restore the vital sense of its diversity, human and non-human, as a fundamental source of it being in the universe, and then to turn that diversity into a source for fresh social, political, and economic visions.

When Obi Okonkwo pondered above the condition of England he started a thought he did not complete. The external and single, laser focused energy of imperial design was fed by a large measure of diversity of the United Kingdom as a state: an economic, cultural, social, and political space with a history of coalescing effects. The energy of diversity and its inventiveness at home fed a singularity of purpose away from home. The colony was confronted by singularity and was wont to mistake it as a primary mechanism for social effort. It was unable to recognize that a local single source of national effort could not be as strong as the emulated external source of energy focused on its acquisitive objectives, but creatively diverse at its own origins.

Centralized government, whether military or civilian, combined with nationalization of assets contributed significantly towards some unintended consequences: corruption; crime; mass poverty; and a deterioration of public systems, and an overall decline in state capability. Those located at the centre of an incapable state will work not for the common good but for themselves. Coherence for the whole achieved by individuals that have, formally or informally, taken advantage of opportunities created by the state has generally failed to take root. These are Obi Okwokwo's "handful of men at the top. Or even one man with vision – an enlightened dictator." They are not the lasting answer.

African countries need to unlock and begin to benefit from the genius of their local diversity. Without a diverse national energy to feed from, the centre of a centralized African state often goes on its own without the genius of its people. That genius lies in an overall self-organizing capability and a commitment to build strong institutions. We learn from the human condition as explored in various explorations of the tragic impulse in world literature and drama that human beings require institutions to provide both a permissive and restrictive environment within which to give play to human impulses.

*No Longer at Ease* may not be the greatest of Achebe's novels, but it was formative for me in a life-changing manner. Thereafter, I read A *Man of the People*, then *Things Fall Apart* and *Arrow of God* in that order. I like to think that *Arrow of God* captured more comprehensively for me the integrity of a world that began to see its end after Obi Okonkwo's grandfather in a fit of anger steeped in past glory struck a man down who had brought a message from the new British administration. His tribe did not rally behind him to follow through with the support he assumed he would receive. The larger society senses the end as much as it can sense a beginning.

The power of a wider universe bearing down on Okonkwo's people was much greater than their collective capabilities at that point. Okonkwo's people intuited this understanding. It required that individual character give way to reconstituting its habitual expectations with knowledge of a new environment. Until that condition was achieved, they would be swept by a flood whose power I still felt when I went to university in Lesotho where I felt with my toes the bottom of a swirling river.

My feet landed when the literature syllabus opened up more worlds and I discovered that my feet stood astride the opening of a spring. African waters broke in worlds created by Wole Soyinka, Ayi Kwei Armah, Nuruddin Farah, Ngũgĩ wa Thiong'o, Ama Ata Aidoo, Ola Rotimi, Buchi Emecheta, Dambudzo Marechera, Cheikh Hamidou Kane, Alex La Guma, Mariama Bâ, Gabriel Okara, Dennis Brutus, Mongo Beti, Amos Tutuola, Tchikaya U Tam'si, Elechi Amadi, Christopher Okigbo, Agonstinho Neto, Aminata Sow Fall, Taban Lo Liyong, Okot p'Bitek, Ferdinand Oyono, Ali Mazrui, Flora Nwapa, Yambo Ouologuem, Cyprian Ekwensi, Tayeb Salih, Mazisi Kunene, Leopold Sedar Senghor, Camara Laye, Ousmane Sembène, Cyprian Ekwensi, Festus Iyayi, Kole Omotoso, Odia Ofeimun, Pepetela and so many others who came out of the spring.

Many years later in South Africa in 2013, I look at where Africa is today and at my own country South Africa. I am struck by two historic trends. One is the historical moment that produced the African writers and their world that I encountered in my undergraduate days and how the curriculum at the university validated my sense of an African arrival in my own life. I do not have the sense that that formative world lasted long. The historic FESTAC '77 in Nigeria seemed to mark the apex of that period. What characterized it for me was the congruence of political and cultural resurgence. In retrospect, both were evocative. They were acts of self-assertion, evoking a future. But the future required a self-conscious and purposeful present, continuously rigorous in its intent.

The second trend is the period in South Africa just before freedom in 1994. What I experienced in Lesotho twenty years earlier was beginning to set in, in

South Africa. Projects such as the History Workshop at the University of the Witwatersrand produced new knowledge of previously suppressed histories. Many of the books in my father's box were unbanned. The cannon of English Literature was challenged and called upon to change and be replaced eventually by African and South African literature such that it would not take twenty-one years before a young African could read an African novel. Predominant religious thinking practices were challenged. Eventually, South Africa was free and one more constitution in Africa was added to the history of continental aspiration.

Twenty years later after 1994, that nascent, creative energy does not appear to have been sustained and embedded in national life. Departments of English that were under a pre-1994 siege, appear to have recovered to continue to conserve the colonial heritage that created and sustained them. The new state appears to have abandoned its formative, radical aspirations. Perhaps it is more accurate to say that if it has not abandoned those aspirations, it has certainly not been rigorously attentive in its day-to-day politics to the means of sustaining a historical quest *in the doing* instead of overwhelmingly in the aspiring. It sees a future out there but not in a rigorous presence of its current choices and actions.

If in one case an entire continent ground to a halt, and in the other, a country about which there was so much hope, is seriously faltering, I can see some hope in four factors. In the first it is generally acknowledged that Africa has in the last twenty years enjoyed relative peace in the marked reduction of debilitating wars. In the second, the decline in inter-state wars may have seen an increase in intrastate contestation. This is to be expected where electoral democracy has become a more accepted way of choosing political leaders. Even if elections can be rigged in sophisticated ways, the subversion by hidden means is a tacit acknowledgement of the desirable ideal situation.

The third factor is the growth and strengthening of market economies across Africa. This factor, together with the steady consolidation of electoral democracy, speaks to a steady, if historic, acknowledgement of diversity and the necessity to learn how to live with it purposefully and creatively. Electoral democracy begins to appear more like a home-grown historic necessity than a seeming imposition from somewhere else.

The time has come for African people to elect leaders who are not embarrassed by principled value and who are not wont to reject policies and practices that make sense, if only they did not appear to have colonial origins. There are very few things in the world today that can claim purity of origins. In this regard, leaders in the Southern African Development Community have an established tendency to adopt agreements, particularly in relation to Zimbabwe, that do not make any sense because they do not want to be seen to be taking positions accommodative of "white" European powers. They seem to prefer meaningless solidarities to sound principle for the greater good of their people.

The last factor is the demographic trend towards a youthful continent. In some countries 60% of their population are 35 years old and younger. We have a smaller part of the population that has accumulated experience and is looking back, and a larger one with limited experience and is looking ahead. For much of the day, these two population segments converge in Africa's thousands of schools. What is it that the older generations give? And how do they give it? What is it that the younger generations look forward to. How do they see the future? Why should any of them read their first African novel at twenty-one? By then they should have read so many that have become part of the foundation of their identities; part of an assumed world that is nevertheless ever subject to their critical intellects.

A few months before Achebe's death, frustrated by my own country, I reread his polemic, *The Trouble with Nigeria.* It was as fresh as ever. It could have been *The Trouble with Africa.* But in the light of the four scenarios just contemplated, there should be a book soon with the title *The Promise of Africa.* Somewhere along the line in modern African history, politics was divorced from a strategic awareness of the social sphere as its very embodiment. The opportunity for reconnection seems at hand.

If many of us, and I suspect it is most of us, learn through things drifting into their awareness, then an abundance of positive stimuli in the social realm promise opportunities for endless learning. There is then the promise of an intimate affinity between people in their countless individualities and the physical and social world they live in. They share together what they experience individually in a continuum of social mutuality. Where I found little of such consonance between my immediate world and I, the young of my continent deserve better. Things should not always be falling apart, but they should never be at ease either, precisely because "real tragedy is never resolved": so says my first love in the reading of novels. My toes tire from stretching and feeling for a foothold. I want to land on my feet in the river of history astride its African springs, augmenting the flood and shaping it.

Chapter Thirty-Eight

# Chinua Achebe

## A Legend and Master Storyteller

*Okey Ndibe*

The death on March 21, 2013 of Professor Chinua Achebe meant the dimming of one of the world's brightest literary stars. Yet Mr Achebe, whose works included the inimitable *Things Fall Apart* and four other highly celebrated novels as well as four collections of essays, a short story collection, several children's books and last year's widely debated memoir, *There Was a Country: A Personal History of Biafra*, was in person one of the most approachable men I ever met. His personal modesty sometimes masked the fact he was a writer of such staggering talent, ambitious range and intellectual power. His surpassing gifts as a writer as well as his admirable personal attributes will combine to make him – one can confidently predict – an imperishable presence in global letters and life.

I had the rare honour and luck of being close to the revered Achebe for some thirty years. In that time, he was an inspiration, model, beacon of moral clarity and intellectual integrity as well as my teacher in the best, broadest sense of that word.

I first met Achebe when I was a young journalist at the now defunct *African Concord* magazine. My first major assignment was to interview him at his office then at the Institute of African Studies at the University of Nigeria, Nsukka. The encounter taught me something about the man's genial and generous nature – and the depth of his humanity. I will get to that first encounter later, but must recall a more recent memory.

Five years ago, I drove from my home in central Connecticut to the quiescent country precincts of Annandale-on-Hudson to visit Chinua Achebe, who then held a prestigious endowed Professorial Chair at Bard College and whose novel *Things Fall Apart* was enjoying a cheery 50th anniversary.

Achebe's self-effacing, soft-spoken personality was always in ironic contrast with the exuberant celebration that erupted around his first – and most widely read and translated – novel. I was in his home to coax him to look back on 50 years of his book's extraordinary journey. Achebe disclosed that I was one of perhaps more than a hundred interviewers he'd hosted that year. Even so, I dared convince myself that there was something special about my interview with him.

Let me explain.

I had interviewed Achebe several times in the past – first in 1983, when I was a rookie correspondent for the now defunct *African Concord*, the last time in 1987, shortly after the publication of his latest novel, *Anthills of the Savannah*. That first interview set a mood for my relationship with the author. Quite simply, he saved my career.

I met Achebe by sheer serendipity. It was 1983 and I had just graduated from college. Visiting Ogidi, his hometown, to see my girlfriend at the time, I raved and raved about Achebe and *Things Fall Apart*. The young woman listened for a while, a bemused smile creasing her cheeks. Then she said: "Achebe is my uncle. His house is a short walk away. And he happens to be home this weekend. Do you want to visit him?" Did I ever!

The Achebe I met in his country home personified grace. I still remember that he served us biscuits and chilled Coca-Cola. He regarded me with penetrating eyes as I gushed about his novels, his short stories, his essays, even reciting favourite lines I had memorized from years of devoted reading. I told him I had just got a job with the *Concord* and would be honoured to interview him. He gave me his telephone number at Nsukka, the university town where he lived and ran the Institute of African Studies. A week later I flew to Lagos, reported for work and told the weekly magazine's editor that I had Achebe's telephone number – and a standing commitment that he would give me an interview. Elated, the editor dispatched me on that assignment. It was my first real task as a correspondent.

Achebe and I retreated to his book-lined office at the institute. The air in the office seemed flavoured with the scent of books stretching and heaving. Five minutes into the interview I paused and rewound the tape. The recording sounded fine and our interview continued for another two hours. Afterwards Achebe told me it was one of the most exhaustive interviews he'd ever done. I took leave of him and heady with excitement, took a cab to the local bus stop where I paid the fare for a bus headed for Enugu – the state capital where I had booked a hotel.

That evening several of my friends gathered in my hotel room. They asked questions about Achebe and then said they wanted to hear his voice. Happy to oblige them, I fetched the tape recorder and pressed its play button. We waited – not a word! I put in two other tapes, the same futile result. How was I going to explain this mishap to my editor who had scheduled the interview as a forthcoming cover?

I phoned Achebe's home in panic. In a desperate tone I begged that he let me return the next day for a short retake. "Thirty minutes – even twenty – would do", I pleaded. I half-expected him to scold me for lack of professional fastidiousness and hang up, leaving me to stew in my distress. Instead he calmly explained that he had commitments for the next day. If I could return the day after, he'd be delighted to grant me another interview. And he gave me permission to make the next session as elaborate as the first.

Two days later we were back in his office for my second chance. This time I paused every few minutes to check on the equipment. I stretched the interview to an hour-and-a-half before guilt – mixed with gratitude – compelled me to stop. It was not as exhaustive as the first outing, nor did it have the spontaneity of our first interview, but it gave me – and the readers of the magazine – a prized harvest. My friends got a chance to savour Achebe's voice, with its mix of faint lisps and accentuated locutions.

That interview happened thirty years ago. It had been followed by several other encounters with Achebe, but it still stands out in my mind. I had admired the man from a distance, in awe of his extraordinary powers as a writer. After he saved my career, I was inspired by his uncommon generosity.

I was so impressed by Achebe's example that I became something of a lifelong student of his work, my PhD dissertation focusing partly on his deployment of history and memory in his writing.

In 2009, Brown University lured Achebe away from Bard College, scoring a major transfer of intellectual assets. At the Ivy League Brown, Achebe assumed the chair of the David and Marianna Fisher University Professor of Africana Studies and Literary Arts. With his blessing, Brown University also invited me to take up a visiting appointment.

Achebe was a widely honoured and highly decorated writer, winning some of the most prestigious literary prizes, including the Man Booker for the sustained excellence of his oeuvre. In 2010, he was awarded the Gish Prize, established in 1994 as a bequest of two sisters, Dorothy and Lillian. The $300,000 prize is bestowed each year on "a man or woman who has made an outstanding contribution to the beauty of the world and to mankind's enjoyment and understanding of life." Part of Achebe's particular contribution was his insistence to speak courageously to power, to bear truthful witness. His genius lay also, I suggest, in his signature clarity of language and brevity of utterance. He did not seek to confound. And he respected language too much to indulge in superfluity. Among us lived a man who for eighty-two years never wasted a word!

The sentiment behind the Gish Prize sums up, for me, the essence of Achebe the man, writer and citizen. He strove in his own quiet, stubborn way to make the world more beautiful. I was blessed to have known him at close quarters, ennobled by his extraordinary example as a writer and human being and ever indebted for the opportunity to learn at his feet.

Chapter Thirty-Nine

# The Achebe Thread

*Alastair Niven*

In early 1966 I was thinking ahead. When one is a student this is a fairly unfamiliar exercise. On a Friday, one might idly speculate about which pub one would visit on Saturday and with whom. Occasionally conscience would demand that an essay should be completed no more than a day or two late. Otherwise life was virtually unplanned until that sudden realisation, on a cold late January morning in one's final year at university that this life was not forever and that one would need to think of the aftermath.

A notice caught my eye in a corridor I seldom frequented. 'Commonwealth Scholarships for British Postgraduates Abroad.' It seemed that the closing date for applications was the next day. In an uncharacteristic burst of purposefulness I went back to my college room and wrote out an application to study West African literature for an MA at the University of Ghana. Why Ghana and not Guyana, Fiji or Hong Kong, I have no idea. I knew I wanted to see somewhere outside Europe, but I could have named any Commonwealth country where literature was researched at postgraduate level.

I was given a fierce interview in London a few months later, not realising that the panel was secretly delighted that a British person had come forward to study in West Africa. Outgoing Commonwealth Scholars from the United Kingdom usually went to Australia or Canada. I must have had some plausibility because I was offered what was then an extremely generous award and so found myself at the Legon campus, just outside Accra, only a few weeks later. There on the first day I met my future wife, Helen Trow, but that is another story. I also had my first serious encounter with African scholarship. The professor in the English department, where I was to be based, asked me what I thought of *Things Fall Apart.* "By Yeats, do you mean?" I asked. Long pause. "It's the name of a novel by Chinua Achebe," came the reply. Thus it was that I heard Achebe's name for the first time. Today I imagine, and hope, that it would be impossible for anyone to be given a high level prestigious scholarship when as ignorant and as thoughtlessly unprepared as I was. Then apparently it was, as a result of which I had three years in Africa that were more educative than any I had had at Cambridge, which allowed me a perspective on my own country that I could only gain by being outside it, and which not only provided me with my life-long partner but with some shreds of insight into other worlds every bit as richly endowed as the one in which hitherto I had been monolingually and homogeneously residing.

As a postgraduate student I was let loose on some first year teaching. There was a programme called the First University Examination (FUE), which over three semesters required the students to look at contemporary fiction, drama and poetry from all round the world. English literature courses in Anglophone African universities were still dominated by the Leavisite canon of Cambridge and London Universities. Even my MA programme on African literature, for which I was the only candidate, included a specialist paper on Henry James. I found myself teaching obscure contemporary works by Ivy Compton-Burnett and Christopher Fry, along with a couple of African novels, Achebe's *No Longer At Ease* and James Ngũgĩ's *Weep Not, Child.* Ngũgĩ had not yet started publishing as Ngũgĩ wa Thiong'o and had not yet set out his case for African writers to use indigenous languages if they were to seek to be authentic. The assumption, however, that literature was something that took place in another continent was beginning to be under attack. The inclusion of Achebe and Ngũgĩ may have started off tokenistically, but the strength of their writing, as well as irresistible changes in the university sector all round the world, changed the nature of student expectations. Now they were starting to want to know about themselves as well as other people.

I embarked on a thesis looking at the first critical responses to African fiction. Obviously it meant not only reading the publications in which these appeared, but also the novels upon which they commented. I immersed myself in modern African literature, often reading books as they were published. I recall obtaining Ayi Kwei Armah's *The Beautyful Ones are Not Yet Born* on its first day of publication and discovering as I did so that I was instantly popular, because everyone at the University of Ghana wanted to read it. Achebe featured centrally. *Things Fall Apart, No Longer at Ease* and *Arrow of God* had been published between 1958 and 1966. The last of the linked quartet, *A Man of the People,* with its prescient description of a coup obliterating democratic prospects in Nigeria, came out just as I arrived in West Africa. Chinua Achebe's work became the centre of my studies, at a time when many people in Europe, hearing that I was going to spend a few years researching on African literature, would regularly ask me if there was any?

Only three years before I began reading Achebe's works, the best known British historian of the day, Hugh Trevor-Roper, had written 'Perhaps in the future there will be some African history to teach. But at present there is none, or very little: there is only the history of Europe in Africa.' Achebe's novels portrayed the precise opposite, telling African readers in particular that their past was not one long night of savagery redeemed by the light of European traders and fervent missionaries. His message was heard at once. In my hall of residence at Legon the section containing contemporary African authors was much the most visited part of the library. Copies of *Things Fall Apart* were themselves literally falling apart because so many students read them.

I stayed three years in Ghana, moving from student to lecturer. In that time the literature syllabuses were substantially Africanised, a process that gathered pace after I left. When I returned to Britain in 1969 to work on my PhD thesis, which was a comparative study of African, Asian and Caribbean fiction in English, there was an obvious centre at which to base myself, the University of Leeds. Both Ngũgĩ and Wole Soyinka had passed through. It was by now the pre-eminent university in England and some would say in the world, for the study of Commonwealth literature, which had not yet transmogrified into postcolonial studies. Achebe was venerated. Only eleven years before he had been an unknown Nigerian naively chancing his one manuscript copy of his first novel to the vagaries of the post and a publisher's slush pile. Now he was the Editorial Adviser to the Heinemann African Writers Series, very nearly, at the age of forty, the *doyen* of Anglophone African novelists. Later, as he became even more in demand elsewhere, he gave up actual editorial work on the Series, but to its end his name presided over it as its Founding Editor. We think of Achebe today as the paramount African novelist of his generation, but it is vital to remember too that it was through his advocacy and resolution, which saw the publication of the work of so many new authors, who then went on to have literary careers almost as distinguished as his own. Achebe was the most uncompetitive of novelists, always delighting in the success of other writers.

He had an unexpected success himself in 1972 when he was the Joint Winner with the Irish Canadian writer George McWhirter of the Commonwealth Poetry Prize. I was later to chair the Prize's advisory committee for many years, but at this stage I was just an onlooker. I was delighted, however, that *Beware, Soul Brother* did so well and I later included four of its poems in an anthology I edited.

Through most of the 1970s I taught at the University of Stirling in Scotland. Without exception, everyone in the department of English Studies there had worked outside Britain. Our cast of mind was internationalist. My task of building up the Commonwealth and African courses was made much easier because of this. The medievalist in the department, Felicity Riddy, had written a very sound article on *No Longer At Ease* for *The Journal of Commonwealth Literature.* The professor, Tommy Dunn, had held chairs at both the University of Ghana and the University of Lagos, where he had not only taught Chinua Achebe's novels but, had known the author himself. Robin Mayhead, Senior Lecturer, was yet another 'Legonite', as familiar with the new West African authors as he was with John Keats and Henry James.

First year Scottish students, encountering *Things Fall Apart* and Africa for the first time, often commented on the resonances they felt in reading about a society undergoing great change amid cultural tension. Some of what they felt about Scotland matched what they read in Achebe's works. Meanwhile postgraduate students were recruited from West Africa, writing theses that linked their own nascent literatures with British novelists recording transitional societies, such as Thomas Hardy and D.H. Lawrence. There was huge excitement among us all at reading, teaching and writing about authors around whom a body of canonised respectability had not yet accrued. I recall Iain Banks, who later emerged as one of Scotland's greatest modern writers, saying to me, when I asked why he could get good grades when writing undergraduate essays about Chinua Achebe and only modest ones when Shakespeare and Jane Austen were his topics, "I can say what I believe about Achebe and Wilson Harris. If I were to slag off Austen you would have my guts for garters." He was probably right.

In 1974 the University of Stirling decided to award an honorary degree to Chinua Achebe. It was only the third he had ever received, the others being at Dartmouth College, USA in 1972 and the University of Southampton, also in 1974. He went on to receive another 38. Honorary degrees are a two-way street, probably conferring more honour on the giver than the receiver. Achebe's reputation was now worldwide and by agreeing to be one of Stirling's honorary doctors he implicitly endorsed what we were doing in the fields of African literature and history. As his reputation was by now international it marked a crucial moment of rehabilitation for a university that had suffered a devastating blow to its esteem when three years earlier Queen Elizabeth had been seriously jostled during a visit to the campus.

I recall the social side of Achebe's visit to Stirling more than the academic. On 21st April 1975 he and his wife Christie came to dinner with my wife and I. I recall Joyce Dunn, the professor's wife, asking how the rainy season had been. "Wet, I suppose," was Chinua's answer, this most courteous and expressive of men momentarily silenced by the banality of the question.

I left Stirling in 1978 to become Director General of the Africa Centre in London. This was the main focal point in London for African affairs. It had a famous restaurant serving only African cuisine. It ran adult education classes in Swahili. It had wonderful nights of African music and dance. There was a small library there and during my time we opened an African art gallery. Above all, it organised a programme of about a hundred lectures and discussions every year. There was hardly an African writer of note who had not been there. Ngũgĩ, now exiled from Kenya, made the Africa Centre a second home and it was here in 1984 that he directed the Wazalendo Players in *The Trial of Dedan Kimathi*, a play he had written with Mĩcere Gĩthae Mũgo.

Achebe's relationship with the Centre was necessarily more distant because he was still living in Nigeria and was only occasionally in London. From time to time, however, he would drop in. I particularly recall him being there shortly after the publication of *The Trouble with Nigeria* in 1984. He gave me a copy of the book and we talked about how corrupt leadership percolates down. A nation does not get the ruler it deserves, but a bad ruler poisons his nation. It was a Shakespearian view of the world, in which if a Claudius gets the upper hand rather than a Hamlet then the country will suffer bitterly. 'Denmark's a prison.' Achebe's understanding of how nations run began and ended with his understanding of people. He knew that powerful heads of government have huge moral authority and the ability to steer those they rule towards a good or a selfish end. Among his many books of essays, this slight volume has exerted a special influence, distilling in its simple form and direct language the essence of Africa's post-independence political dichotomies.

In 1990 I went to Nsukka in Nigeria for the *Eagle Over Iroko* celebrations of Chinua Achebe's 60th birthday. The event was nearly a day late in starting because the Governor of the state had other matters in hand and nothing could start until he turned up. I had been allocated fifty minutes to give my paper, but as I stood up to deliver it the chairman of the session leant over and explained that I should cut it to five as the conference was running late. My abiding memory is not of any particular talk given at the gathering, but of Chinua's own hospitality. I went to say goodbye to him on my last day and took a photograph of him standing at the entrance to his house, dressed in an elegant pink lace *agbada*. It was to be the last time I saw him upright, because a short while afterwards came his appalling accident. Being driven to the airport to catch a flight to the United States, the axle of the car broke and Achebe was thrown out. He came to England first for months of medical treatment and then settled in upper New York State, where Bard College became his home for many years. There is a special poignancy about the Iroko conference, not just because of what happened to Chinua, but because the woman who put this ambitious and wide-ranging tribute together and who later edited its proceedings, Edith Ihekweazu, herself died the following year.

Because he had to restrict the amount of travelling he could now undertake, meeting Achebe became a rare event for those of us not living near him. I was greatly privileged in 1999 to chair a discussion between him, Wole Soyinka and

Derek Walcott at the Hackney Empire Theatre in London. Billed as 'Two Nobel Laureates and a Legend,' this was the hottest ticket in town that week. No one in the audience would have known that the organisers of the event had not really understood the nature of Chinua's disability. He and Christie Achebe had arrived in England on an overnight flight and since then had been in four different hotels before one was found that could accommodate him properly. His discontent with what he had been offered was not the vanity of a pampered celebrity, but rather a cry of pain by a badly injured man. How he rose above his anger to speak so humbly and cleverly that night I shall never know.

One year on Achebe, by now well settled at Bard College, was the object of massive praise and affection as he reached the age of seventy. I was again present at the celebrations. This time, the great and the good of American letters were present to honour him. So too was Ngũgĩ wa Thiong'o and African writers and scholars living in the United States. It was a massively well-supported occasion. Achebe himself was droll, wise and erudite. He watched from his wheelchair, missing nothing, smiling modestly at the tributes, never a man to be blown away by praise poets.

His international standing was confirmed not by the Nobel Prize for Literature, as almost everyone familiar with his work felt should have been the case, but by the award of the second Man Booker International Prize for Fiction in 2007. He was a popular choice, beating Carlos Fuentes, Doris Lessing and other luminaries on the short list. Sadly he was not well enough to come to Oxford in June that year to receive the prize in person, though a video link allowed him to speak to us on screen. The award ceremony took place in the Sheldonian Theatre, where the most eminent scholars have addressed the University of Oxford. Achebe's graceful manners and obvious delight in being recognised in this way made up a little for the gathering frailty projected before us.

Then the Man Booker team had the brilliant idea of inviting Achebe over to Britain the following year, when he was well enough to come. He gave readings and signed books. The highlight was a luncheon given in his honour at the House of Lords. Lord Baker (Kenneth Baker), a former Minister in Margaret Thatcher's government, presided. It was a mellow and dignified event, with generous speeches. As it came to a close, however, I realised that neither Chinua nor Christie Achebe had been given the chance to look around the Parliament building. Out of courtesy to his disability, he had been brought into the dining room by a side entrance. Now he was about to be led out by the same way. I whispered to Kenneth Baker that it might be nice to show the Achebes a bit more of their surroundings. He took the point at once. Thus the five of us, two Achebes, two Nivens and our host, looked round first the House of Lords and then the House of Commons. Parliament was not sitting. To my amazement

Chinua was permitted to wheel himself into the main chamber of the Commons, with the rest of us in tow. There for a few minutes he commanded the floor. The Empire had struck back in the most elegant manner. Of all my memories of the great writer, it is this image, historically ironic and witty, which resonates the most.

Achebe's eightieth birthday passed with less fuss than the sixtieth and the seventieth, but three days after it he came to England to deliver a lecture at the University of Cambridge. It was the first lecture in a projected annual series to commemorate Audrey Richards, who had founded the Centre of African Studies at Cambridge. The occasion was packed out, with people crouching in every aisle. Most of them were young. In truth it was not Achebe's best lecture. It went on too long and occasionally it seemed to veer uncharacteristically towards bitterness as he set out his familiar position on the nature of Nigerian leadership. One felt that it would be a last appearance in Britain and so it turned out to be. The students, however, were enchanted, as wide-eyed as though they were at a pop concert. Afterwards Sir Leszek Borysiewicz, the Vice-Chancellor of the university, gave a dinner for a large number of guests, a happy and informal occasion.

I saw Chinua once more. In December 2011 he invited me to Brown University, Rhode Island, where he was now installed in a specially created Chair. He had put together a brilliant symposium to examine the position of Africa in the world today. It was not only a literary event but, a searching analysis of governance, social inequities and environmental change. I was asked to take the chair for the final panel discussion, which was the only session of the gathering in which Achebe himself spoke. Dressed in charcoal grey, with a red beret, he once again charmed and alerted his audience with the precision of his remarks.

I was present at his funeral at Ogidi on 23rd May 2013. Although the Archbishop of Canterbury sent his personal representative to the funeral, the British government was not represented, the only major nation associated with Achebe's career not to be. When I wrote to the Foreign and Commonwealth Secretary to ask how this had come about, a minion replied that they had not received an invitation. It was a frail excuse for an obvious embarrassment. The service managed to be both intimate, with Christie Achebe at one point leading a Christian singsong and a national event, honoured by the presence of two Presidents; Nigeria's Goodluck Jonathan and John Dramani Mahama from neighbouring Ghana. There were around four thousand mourners in Ogidi that day. Chinua was laid to rest in the newly built mausoleum beside his home. He had passed, as they say in that part of the world. But in my mind's eye he is a living being. He is the finest man I have ever known and on your page and mine, one of the greatest writers of our time.

Chapter Forty

# For Chinua Achebe*

*Odia Ofeimun*

You say your hurricane lamp can issue
no more the perfunctory flame
of artistic innocence
(Ostrich mentalities, you have seen,
will not help the situation)
I raise my fists to your guts

The strafing reports, the 'assault and battery'
of questions which splinter our snail-shells
decide us in their maledictory exercise
for, none can afford the lyrical sanity
of the hermit when his clothes are on fire

I raise my fist to your guts

But, then, when troubadours become matchets
in the frenzy of storms they must underline,
their finest truths are iron banners
for wrapping the corpses of fleeting slogans

And, Compatriot, this is my concern...

I suppose you can break the kernel of these days
better than my poor plastic slab will allow
You know the intricate weave of the barbwire-roost
into which you must plunge

Oh my concern overpowers me
I do not know how to escape from
such wind as bear you, now, away
from your once unruffled waters

*Poem taken from *The Poet Lied* by Odia Ofeimun: Hornbill House of Arts, Lagos, 2008.

Chapter Forty-One

# What Chinua Achebe Never Heard From Me

*Kole Omotoso*

It is not an exaggeration to say that Chinua Achebe's life and literary career has done more for my life and literary career than any other writer in Nigeria, bar none. I read his books at Harman's House at Kings College. I agonized over his choice of Anglicised Igbo as a choice of a working tool. In spite of *No Longer at Ease* being supposed to be insubstantial as a novel, I came to like it more than any of his other novels. Perhaps this short novel made it for me because it is the first and perhaps the only Nigerian novel that mentions Akure my hometown, other than my own novels. His other fiction, a short story, to speak to me, is his civil war "Sugar Baby."

On a personal level, one of the confusions that one faces wanting to be a writer was never about the writing but about how you carry yourself as a writer. Are you the un-acknowledged legislator of the world? Or that artist in *A Man of the People* by Chinua Achebe, who not only cuts his own clothes but also sews them as well? Or would you like to be a gentleman writer, who holds down a job, is a good husband, a caring father and a loyal friend? Anyone familiar with the life of Chinua Achebe knows which of these he was. His example became an inspiration for me to follow.

My literary life began with the publication of my first novel in the African Writers Series by Heinemann Educational Books. The second novel had a more difficult time with the Editor of the African Writers Series, Mr Chinua Achebe. *The Combat* was conceived as a mockery of the behaviour of adults during those thirty months of madness called the Nigeria-Biafra War. Month after month I asked if it would be published and no answer came. Then, one day, a letter came and said that Mr Achebe had given his imprimatur!

After returning to the country in 1972 I taught and wrote and organised anything to do with writing, writers and publishers. From 1980 onwards I worked with Professor Chinua Achebe on the Association of Nigerian Authors and thought more and more on the oeuvres of Chinua Achebe. My conclusion came very soon and I do not think that he liked that conclusion. So when he said if someone does not like his stories, they should go and write their own I knew that was a challenge I had to take up.

In 1980 Professor Chinua Achebe invited some Nigerian writers to the University of Nsukka to deliberate on the need for an association of Nigerian writers. He, Christopher Okigbo, Wole Soyinka, Francesca Emmanuel, J.P. Clark, T.M. Aluko and Amos Tutuola had been part of a fledgling collection of writers who came together in Ibadan in the early 1960s. By 1964, the political crisis that saw Obafemi Awolowo imprisoned, the Western Region in flames and finally the military in politics, had scattered these writers into wildernesses within Nigeria and without. A younger crop of Nigerian writers had come into being between the end of the civil war and the oil boom years going into the 1980s. We trooped to Nsukka and listened to the Oracle of Ogidi pronounce on the necessity of our togetherness. We applauded and joined him in bringing to life the Association of Nigerian Authors. He was elected President and I was elected the General Secretary. Other officers took their places and what today is one of the strongest writers organisations began to build institutions. There would be branches of ANA in every university campus committed to frequent meetings and readings. There would be branches of ANA in every state capital in the country dedicated to frequent meetings and readings. These readings became known as Okigbo Nights after the poet Christopher Okigbo. The constitution would prescribe a term of two years each for office holders and an annual ANA gathering on the first weekend of November every year. Perhaps the most important institutional arrangement that we put in place was the annual literary prizes in every area of literary endeavour. The sums awarded were modest but very soon winners of ANA literary prizes began to win prizes around the world.

We had a campaign which had begun in the 1970s for Nigerian newspapers to devote at least one page a week to literary matters instead of using every unused page to carry the picture of the current Head of State. There are at least, at any time in Nigeria, twenty-six or so daily newspapers. We pressured these papers, big and small, to carry literary reviews of books, interviews with writers and publishers and arguments among writers. Today in Nigeria, unlike many African countries, newspapers – dailies, weekenders and Sundays – carry copious pages of not just entertainment such as Nollywood but also of writers, writings and publishing news.

It was exciting working with Professor Achebe. I would drive to Nsukka to consult with him and then drive all over the country, inaugurating the branches and making contacts with writers. At the Lagos ANA conference of 1986 I was elected President of the Association of Nigerian Authors as successor to a reluctant Professor Chinua Achebe. Odia Ofeimun was the General Secretary.

There had been a concerted effort to publish in Nigeria first and then publish abroad. We also wanted our older writers to also publish in Nigeria. It was not true that Nigerians did not read. We, as writers, needed to find out what they read. It was at this time that publishing houses like Onibon-Oje Publishers, Fagbamigbe Publishers, Fountain Publishers, Fourth Dimension Publishers, New Horn Press and many others came into being. And one must not forget the Pace Setters Series set up by MacMillan Publishers of Nigeria. There was also Spectrum Books of Ibadan. All this time, older, British originated publishing companies such as Heinemann Educational Books, Evans Publishing Company and MacMillan were also present in the country.

My own writing continued to be experimental and not particularly appealing to Professor Achebe as editor of *Okike* to which I sent a short story. Professor Achebe did not think that the short story worked but still he let *Okike* publish it. But the story that I did not send to him *The Return of Oduche* dealt with the detritus consequent on societies in contact through colonization, through trade and through cultural exchanges. No society could avoid these. That the Umuofia Progressive Union would pray that only the good of such encounters and contacts should come to them as they earned a living in Lagos while the evil goes to those who own the land (and know which gods to appease) was not only wrong-headed but also inhumane. Oduche would bring the good from the Christianising British. But he would also bring what up to then was a taboo. That story was later published in the University of Stirling journal during my year in that university as a Visiting Professor in the Department of English Studies.

The destruction of the physical infrastructure of Nigeria by the military holding political power with the help of self-serving civilians went hand in hand with the destruction of the moral foundation of the country as it had existed for a short time from about 1955 and 1962, perhaps the years of possibilities for the emerging Nigerian polity. We did not have the arms to take on the Nigerian military but we could at least write. This led to the publication of my *Just Before Dawn* in 1988. Professor Achebe let me know that there was nothing like the Ibo State Union although, with the help of Ken Saro-Wiwa, I had come across the minutes of their meetings covering the years from 1948 to 1958. There was also the accusation that it seemed only the Yoruba political leader was a good person in my writing about the political history of Nigeria's first one hundred years.

At least once a year I would re-read *No Longer at Ease.* Sometimes I would read it alone. At other times I would read it as part of the trilogy of *Things Fall Apart, No Longer at Ease* and *Arrow of God.* For me, Chinua Achebe's failure as an artist is his inability to follow the logic of his calling as an artist. It happens in *No Longer at Ease.* Mr Obi Okonkwo, BA (Hons) London in English meets Clara, an *osu*, a qualified nurse, on the boat returning to Lagos from Liverpool. They get involved and continue to see each other on their settling into Lagos. First the Umuofia Progressive Union, Lagos Branch, and then Obi's parents back home, object to the relationship and Obi's mother begs her son to let her die first before he marries Clara or else accept responsibility for her death when he marries her.

In the meantime Clara is pregnant. Obi Okonkwo caves in, gives up and abandons Clara and her pregnancy. For me, Chinua Achebe abandons humanity and fails to make a promise of a better future to that unborn child. Clara goes through a painful abortion and we never hear from or about her again. By the time I was finishing my year at the University of Stirling I had made up my mind to write a book about Chinua Achebe's writing. Hans Zell gave me the opportunity and the result is *Achebe or Soyinka: A Study in Contrasts.* One issue which the book did not attend to is the issue of suicide in Chinua Achebe's writings in relation to the definition of tragedy. At Obi Okonkwo's interview for the civil service job, he makes the comment that the end of Graham Greene's *The Heart of the Matter,* is not tragic simply because the police chief commits suicide. In fact he calls it a happy ending. This makes the chair of the interview sit up and question Obi Okonkwo about which book he was talking about. Obi Okonkwo concedes that happy ending was too strong but tragedy, according to a man in his village was like a bowl of wormwood from which one drank world without end. Does this mean that Okonkwo Senior's suicide at the end of *Things Fall Apart* makes it a book with a happy ending?

The lives and writings of Leo Tolstoy and Fyodor Dostoyevsky provided the example to follow. The case against Chinua Achebe is that he fails to write towards a community of Nigerian sensibilities. He fails to do this because he fails to uphold the ultimate commitment of art: the commitment to humanity above everything else, especially above nationality and above ethnicity, the commitment to life only. Art is for the sake of Art. Art is humanity asserting and re-asserting itself as the detritus of living drags it downwards. Art lifts humanity up, forward, towards hope in the future. Chinua Achebe's last book *There Was a Country: A Personal History of Biafra* confirmed for me Chinua Achebe's ordinariness.

If there is nothing to add, there are some people who would say, one should shut up. But, for writers, when there is nothing to add, is when they are at their best in saying something new. A harvest of the reviews and responses to Chinua Achebe's *There Was a Country* across the globe makes more interesting reading than the book itself. The responses can be divided into three categories. There are those from writers of Igbo origin, Achebe's nationality, which cannot even pretend to be anything but praise-singers of their idol. There are those from writers of Yoruba origin, the nationality of Achebe's bête noir, Obafemi Awolowo. Chinua Achebe blames all the woes of the Igbo in Nigeria on Obafemi Awolowo. The third group of responses comes from outsiders simply interested in the health of Chinua Achebe's writing.

Chinua Achebe's book makes the point that Obafemi Awolowo prevented Nnamdi Azikiwe from becoming the Premier of the Western Region in 1951 by encouraging some members of Azikiwe's party to cross over to Awolowo's party. My very personal response to this piece of misreading of history is that it was a good thing, in fact a great thing that Azikiwe did not become the Premier of the Western Region. This is mainly because Azikiwe could never have done for the Western Region what Awolowo did for the region.

The second point that Chinua Achebe makes is that Awolowo organised the genocide of the Igbo people by insisting that hunger was a legitimate weapon of war. As the Ndigbo in Lagos, Chinua Achebe's own people have pointed out in their response to the controversy that their kinsman's book has generated, Awolowo explained things back in 1983 and his explanation should have closed the issue but not for Chinua Achebe. The Yoruba responses have been simply to point out, as the Ndigbo in Lagos have pointed out, that Awolowo had responded to this particular accusation and others years ago and Chinua Achebe is simply flogging a dead horse.

A reviewer in the South African *Mail and Guardian* wondered if it was right for an elder to not represent the truth as it is. He praises Chinua Achebe's pioneering novel *Things Fall Apart*. Everybody does. But why would he want to publish this now, especially when most of the material is already available in his other publications? Chinua Achebe reproduces material from his Cape Town Steve Biko lecture at the end of this book. It is possible to say that just as many of the essays of Chinua Achebe have been published in different collections with different titles, perhaps his other writings are to be repackaged in different collections under different titles.

The review that appears in the London *Financial Times*, written by William Wallis, FT's Africa editor, is, for me, one of the most interesting. It is worth quoting at length from this review. Here goes: "Achebe's prognosis for his country is grim. 'Corruption in Nigeria has passed the alarming and entered the fatal stage and Nigeria will die if we continue to pretend that she is only slightly indisposed,' he writes. Before arriving at that bleak conclusion, however, he stitches his story together joltingly, moving from the autobiographical to the historical and ending with something of a rant. There is an eclectic range of insights and fascinating anecdotes buried here and there, but this is not a book that will add much to the understanding of the war, nor one that will go down among Achebe's great works."

Personally, two things bother me about this book. The first is its timing. The second has to do with the issue of mediocrity. Why is Chinua Achebe publishing this book now, after the death of Ojukwu the leader and President of Biafra? Ojukwu is not the hero of the book as one would have expected. After all he was the driving force and the face of Biafra. Except for the anaemic *Because I am Involved,* Ojukwu himself wrote nothing during his lifetime to state the rationale for his declaration of Biafra. Chinua Achebe does not provide any intellectual arguments that placed Biafra over Nigeria in terms of superiority of intention, compactness of development alternative agenda and clarity of national vision for the people of Biafra, of Nigeria and of Africa. For me this is the great failure of this book. There was a country but other than the anger about the killings in Northern Nigeria there was no justification for declaring a state of Biafra that had nothing over the Nigeria that Chinua Achebe left behind to work for Biafra.

Mediocrity is one of the problems which Chinua Achebe identifies as bedevilling Nigeria. Was Biafra devoid of mediocrity? One of the sins of Nigerian intellectuals, including Chinua Achebe, is their readiness to tolerate mediocrity in the politics of their country, be the country Nigeria or Biafra. What superior argument did Chinua Achebe provide to justify or to counter the secession of Biafra? We live with the consequences of mediocrity today and nobody wants to know!

The last time we met was when he was in South Africa to give the Steve Biko lecture and accept an honorary degree at the University of Cape Town. It was at a private dinner given to him, his wife and their entourage in the Vice Chancellor's Lodge by our friends Professor and Mrs Njabulo Ndebele. There was silence between us over so many issues and there was politeness over those issues we bothered to speak about.

Professor Chinua Achebe had had an accident in Nigeria and was now permanently in a wheel chair. He had continued to be critical of the Nigerian government and even refused a national honour although he accepted an award worth one million naira made by Minister for Culture, Dr Ojo Madueke, under President Olusegun Obasanjo, sometime later. While it was not difficult to fault his selective criticism of the governments of Nigeria, it would have been insane to contradict him in his criticism of the governments.

He sent his condolences when Maggie passed on in 2003 through our mutual friend Nuruddin Farah. Would I have felt better if he had communicated directly with me?

I am grateful for his life and works and consider myself enriched by my contact with him.

Akure, Ondo State, Nigeria.
August 2013

Chapter Forty-Two

# The Discombobulation of a Rookie Patriot

## A Stage Adaptation of Chinua Achebe's *A Man of the People*

*Femi Osofisan*

**Note:** *This play was written on commission by the Port Harcourt Rainbow Book Club, though it was not eventually performed owing to some political reasons. It is therefore only a Working Script. It cannot be quoted or used in any form without prior permission from the author.*

### CAST

Odili Samaru (The Narrator)
Nurse
Barrister Max Kulamo
Chief Nanga The Honourable Minister of Culture
Edna Odo
James a Journalist
Pa Samalu Father Of Odili
Edna's Mother
Man in Uniform
Councillor "Couple"
Crowd
Journalist
Odili Samalu (The Actor)
Eunice His Fiancée
Mr Nwege The School Principal
Mrs John, MP
Mr Odo Father of Edna
Mama, Pa Samalu's Eldest Wife
Old Man
Three Local Government Policemen
Towncrier (Unseen)

*The stage consists of two playing areas: one, where the interview between Odili the Narrator and the Journalist takes place (which can be 'mobile'); and the other for the various Flashbacks.*

## The discombobulation of a fledgling patriot

### PART ONE
### Scene 1

*Highlife music, of the early 1960s, welcomes us into the Scene.*

*Lights come up on* **Odili** *The Narrator, on his hospital bed.*

*(NOTE: this could also be a wheel chair, which would enable the Director move* **Odili** *around to different locations on stage and within the theatre during the performance).*

*His turbaned head and various bandages indicate his position as a convalescent.*

*He is about to begin an interview with the Journalist, who will record his responses on a tape as well as make notes on his pad.*

*With them now is the* **Nurse**.

*(The music fades as the play begins, but should always be in the background for these scenes where* **Odili** *the Narrator appears).*

**NURSE.** *(Leaving).* Right, I'll leave you now. But please remember what the doctor said – You must not excite yourself. I'll be just outside there if you need me.

**JOURNALIST.** I promise, Nurse, I won't stress him. I know he's not fully recovered yet.

**ODILI-NARRATOR.** Thanks, I'll be good, don't worry.

*(Nurse goes).*

**JOURNALIST.** So, we'll start now. Ready? *(***Odili** *nods). (Talking into tape).* Can you please give us your name, sir?

**ODILI-NARRATOR.** Odili Samalu. I was the candidate for the CPC in the Anita Federal Constituency in the last general elections.

**JOURNALIST.** Thank you. *(To tape).* Mr Samalu was viciously attacked during the last election campaigns and is still recuperating on his hospital bed. *(To him).* How long have you been here now?

**ODILI-NARRATOR.** They tell me for about nine weeks. I don't remember clearly. For most of it I was in a coma.

**JOURNALIST.** Awfully sorry, sir. Hope you're better now?

**ODILI-NARRATOR.** Much better, thank you. At least I can talk now and move around a bit by myself.

**JOURNALIST.** So can you tell us, how it happened?

**ODILI-NARRATOR.** Well, how shall I begin?... I suppose you could say it all started the day I decided to join politics and run for the seat of Anita in the Eastern region. By then the seat had more or less become the property of Chief Nanga, member of the POP and current Minister of Culture. I remember the day very clearly. In fact, I'd just left Chief Nanga's ministerial mansion, in the capital city of Bori, where I had been staying as his guest. I had moved out to stay instead with an old mate of mine in the university, who is now a lawyer, Barrister Max Kulamo. We had not seen each other for a long time....

## Scene 2

*Flashback as lights transfer us to* **Max's** *modest apartment. The place is Bori, a place like Lagos in the early 1960s. The time is early evening.* **Max** *has just ushered* **Odili Samalu** *into his guest room. The* **Odili** *in these Flashback Scenes, it is understood, will be played by another actor).*

**MAX.** *(shouting, as he shakes his hand violently).* Good gracious! Dili-Diligent! Na your eye be this?

**ODILI.** 'Cool Max!' The campus Poet! How good to see you again, man!

*(They laugh).*

**MAX.** Odili the Great! You rascal! So you've been in this town for a whole month and you didn't call me!

**ODILI.** Sorry, it's –

**MAX.** I know. You couldn't reach me, yes. This bloody phone they won't give me. You won't believe how many months now I've been on the waiting list for one! But I'm not going to give bribe to anybody!

**ODILI.** Still the old Max!

**MAX.** You know me! So, Dili Diligent, where have you been staying?

**ODILI.** You won't believe it – with Chief Nanga!

**MAX.** What! That corrupt, empty-headed, illiterate politician!

**ODILI.** Hey, he's your Minister of Culture!

**MAX.** Isn't that the tragedy of our nation? To be ruled by ministers who cannot even spell their name!

**ODILI.** Are you telling me! What I saw and heard in those four weeks I was with him! These people will ruin the country!

**MAX.** But how did you...I mean, I didn't know you were so close to the man.

**ODILI.** No, I'm not. He'd been my teacher in the primary school, that was all. Long ago, before he went into politics. But as it turned out, the man has an uncanny memory, quite apart from his charisma. It's one of his assets.

**MAX.** Yes I can well imagine. If you stole so much money from the country, I bet you'd have a lot of 'charisma' and other assets too!

**ODILI.** Max-Max, the 'Angry-Young-Man'! No doubt you're right. But I tell you...to think that the man would not only remember me after all these years, but also invite me to be his guest! Can you imagine? You see, he'd been invited to pay an official visit to the village grammar school by our Principal, Mr Nwege –

**MAX.** Nwege? The same Nwege, Mr Push-Me-Down?

**ODILI.** Ah, you too, you never forget anything, do you?

**MAX.** How can one forget those rib-cracking stories you used to tell us back there on campus! So the man's still alive!

**ODILI.** Very much so my friend! Very much so!

**MAX.** And still riding his bicycle?

**ODILI.** For where? He owns the village grammar school and is a rich man now. One of the local heavyweights. That's why he invited Chief Nanga over to the school, so as to ingratiate himself with the Minister and win some contract or other from his ministry!

**MAX.** Not to supply bicycles, I hope?

**ODILI.** *(Laughing).* Ah my friend, you should have been there!

**MAX.** Go on, what happened! Nack me the 'tory!

**ODILI.** Well, the minister arrived and as you would expect, the usual din began. Dancers hurling themselves across the sand; hunters shooting their guns; praise singers blowing horns. At last, when everybody was seated, our friend, Mr Nwege got up to speak. 'My dear friends, ladies and gentlemen,' he began, 'the distinguished guest, as you know, needs no introduction, so I will be brief...' And then he launched into this 'brief' speech that went on and on, for almost the next hour –

**MAX.** Typical!

**ODILI.** The crowd became restless. Nwege did not notice! Even the Minister was looking at his watch. A loud grumble began among the audience. But our friend, Mr Nwege would not stop. Soon some daring voices started shouting, asking him to sit down, to let the minister they had come to hear talk. But Nwege either ignored, or did not hear a word of these warnings –

**MAX.** He was enjoying his own voice so much!

**ODILI.** A more insensitive man you never saw! Then – you know what happened? One young man from the village, one of the tough young men, jumped up suddenly and shouted: 'It is enough, Principal, or I shall push you down and take three pence.'

**MAX.** (*Laughing*). Ah!

**ODILI.** The laughter that went up must have been heard a mile away!

**MAX.** They'll never let him forget that incident of his past, will they!

**ODILI.** He asked for it. Otherwise he'd probably have gone on forever!

**MAX.** *Anikilija* wasn't it, the name you said they called his old bicycle?

**ODILI.** *Anikilija-kilija-kilija!* Ah, that was the noise the rickety thing!

**MAX.** And it had no brakes!

**ODILI.** 'No brake, no jam, *anikiliia*!'

**MAX.** I always see his picture vividly, each time you narrate the story, the poor man riding down the slope that day. Going down merrily, whistling to himself. And then suddenly looking up, to find a lorry rolling towards him from the opposite direction–

**ODILI.** *Eziokwu*! It was the day Nwege entered the folklore of the village forever. There was the lorry coming towards him, at a furious speed! And Nwege applied the brake of his bicycle. But there was no answer! Again, to no avail! *Anikilija kilija!* He pumped it again; the bicycle would not stop! Again, and again, but the horrible thing went rolling on! A head-on meeting was coming on the bridge. Yeah, shouted Nwege, this is Death coming! Help! He was crying to passing pedestrians – *Help* in the name of God! Somebody, push me down!

**MAX.** *(Acting the part too and cranking furiously at the brake)*. 'Push me down, I beg now! *Nna*, push me down!'

**ODILI.** *Anikilija* ! No one intervened! Nwege, desperate now, decided quickly to add an inducement. 'Push me down, I beg, he cried, push me down – and take my three pence!'

**MAX.** 'Push me down and take three pence! *Nna*, push me down and take three pence! And then – *bagam bagam crassshhh!*

*(They collapse in laughter).*

**ODILI.** He'll never live down that joke in Anata, it's sure! It will go down with him to his grave!

**MAX.** So, the minister – ? What did he do?

**ODILI.** He burst out laughing too of course like everybody, shaking his head at his hapless host. Which I thought rather uncharitable of him!

**MAX.** Can't say I blame him! But you were saying that he invited you to his house?

**ODILI.** Yes, that was before the speech. There we were, we teachers, waiting in line to shake his hand. I must say I was quite unhappy to have to line up like that, like the pupils. In fact I was frowning when he came to me. Our hands met. I looked him straight in the face. Then… what happened completely astonished me –

## Scene 3

(**Odili** *walks to the scene on another part of the stage).*

**Nanga** *appears, conducted by a fawning* **Nwege**. *The Minister is wearing damask and gold chains and acknowledging cheers with a fan of animal skin. He is indisputably handsome and youthful looking. His entourage includes James, the Journalist and two females,* **Edna** *and* **Mrs John**.

*(As he reaches* **Odili**, *the Minister stops, puzzled).*

**NWEGE.** *(Effusive, beginning the introduction).* Honourabe Minister, sir, I have the honour to introduce –

**NANGA.** *(Waving his hand impatiently to stop* **Nwege** *as his smile slowly creases up into lines of thought).* Just a moment, Mr Principal. *(Then his face brightens).* Yes, of course! That's right, you are Odili, aren't you? Odili Samalu!

**ODILI.** *(Pleasantly surprised).* Yes, sir.

**NANGA.** *(Throwing his arms round* **Odili** *and smothering him in his voluminous damask).* Yes, of course! I remember! Odili the Great!

**ODILI.** What! Wonderful, sir! It's at least fifteen years since –

**NANGA.** Yes, fifteen years! Time passes, doesn't it! Ah, Odili the Great!

*(Turning to announce it proudly).* You know, my people, I taught this young man in, er... –

**ODILI.** Standard three, sir.

**NANGA.** *(Excitedly).* That's right! Standard three!

**NWEGE.** Ah sir, so you taught him! No wonder, he is one of the pillars of this school, sir! He is –

**NANGA.** (*to* **Nwege**). Thank you, thank you! *(Boyishly and still out of breath).* Odili, the great! That's what I called him. Ah my boy, where have you been all this time?

**ODILI.** I've been to the University, sir and then, when I came out, I joined the staff here. I've been teaching here for the last eighteen months.

**NANGA.** Good boy. I knew you would go to a university and become a doctor! Yes, I used to tell the other boys in the class that Odili will one day be a great man and they will be answering him sir, sir. That he'll be as great as Shakespeare, Mills and Boons, Tarzan and Michael West! All these wonderful writers! But why did you not tell me when you left the University? That's very bad of you, you know.

**ODILI.** Well, I know how busy a minister can –

**NANGA.** Busy? Hear him my people! Busy! Don't you know that minister means servant? That busy or no busy he must see his master, people like you?

*(A loud applause).*

**NANGA.** Yes, my dear boy! Servants, that's what we are! Sometimes I tell you, I use to regret ever leaving the teaching field. For although I am a minister today I can swear to God that I am not as happy as when I was a teacher. True to God who made me, I used to regret it. Teaching is a very noble profession. Ask Mr Nwege here!

*(Everybody collapses with laughter, including* **Nwege** *and the Minister).*

**NANGA.** Yes, I tell you, you can rest assured that those of us in the Cabinet who were once teachers know that, 'Once a teacher –

**VOICES.** Always a teacher!'

**NANGA.** There is no better profession than this! And the proof is what we see today! For only teachers can make this excellent arrangement *(Turns to the newspaper correspondent in his party)*... See, Mr Journalist? It is a mammoth crowd. Mammoth! Write it down! M-A-M-O-T!

*(The journalist whips out his note-book and begins to write).*

**NWEGE.** Sir, it is an unprecedented crowd in the annals of Anata!

**NANGA.** You hear that, James?

**JAMES THE JOURNALIST.** No, sir, what is it?'

**ODILI.** *(Tongue in cheek).* Our Principal says it is the most unprecedented crowd in the annals of Anata.

**NANGA.** Write it down! Quick! On-pres'dent! Good gracious, on-pres'dent!

**JAMES THE JOURNALIST.** Got it, sir! Please, what is the gentleman's name?'

**NWEGE.** Nwege. N-W-E-G-E! Principal and Proprietor of Anata Grammar School'. *(Turning to the Minister, proudly).* These big crowds, sir, I had to visit every section of the village personally to tell them of your – I mean to say, of the Minister's – visit.

**NANGA.** Thank you very much, thank you, sir.

**MRS JOHN.** *(Glad to get a word in).* You see? You see wetin h-I de talk. How many minister fit h-answer *sir* to h-any Tom, Dick h-and Harry wey senior them for h-age? I h-ask you how many?'

**MANY VOICES.** Na true o! Dis minister is different. Na our son! A man of high position who still dey give respect to age!

**NANGA.** Of course! Wetin! My people, minister or no minister, a man who is my senior must still be my senior. Other ministers and other people may do otherwise but, as you know, my motto is: '*Do the right thing, and –*'

**VOICES.** '*– Shame the Devil!*'

*(General applause).*

**NWEGE.** I'm not surprised. The Minister's excellent behaviour, is due to the sound education he had here, in those days when education *was* education.

**NANGA.** 'Yes, sir! That's what I use to tell them, that standard six in those days is more than Cambridge today.

**NWEGE.** Cambridge? Cambridge? Who dash frog coat? You mean it is equal to BA today – if not more?

**NANGA.** My private secretary has BA from Oxford. Yes, Oxford and Cambridge together, my Secretary who carries my files! He should have come with me on this tour but I had some office work for him to do. And… By the way, Odili, I think you are wasting your talent here. I want you to come to the capital and take up a strategic post in the civil service. We shouldn't leave everything to the highland tribes. My secretary is from there; but as they say, charity begins at home. Our people must begin to press for their fair share of the national cake.

*(A loud and prolonged applause).*

**ODILI.** Thanks, sir, but –

**NANGA.** No buts! It's decided! You will –

**ODILI.** I mean to say, sir, that I have applied for a post-graduate scholarship already, to bring myself up to Mr Nwege's expectations!

*(General astonishment. The beautiful girl in the Minister's party turns round to look at* **Odili** *and their eyes meet. But she quickly turns away again, though not before the Minister has noticed).*

**NANGA.** What! That's even better! It's settled then. You will see me at the end of this reception to take my address and all the details, you hear? It's an order! If you fail, I will send my orderly to arrest you. You will come and spend your holidays with me in the capital and while you are there I will try and find out from my Cabinet colleague, the Honourable Minister of Overseas Training, who's my friend, what he's doing with your application.

*(General applause again. Some come to shake* **Odili's** *hand).*

**NANGA.** If you come as soon as you close, you can stay in my guest-room with everything complete – bedroom, parlour, bathroom, latrine, everything – self-contained. You can live by yourself and do *anything* you like there, it's all yours.

**MRS JOHN.** *(Again quickly interposing to be noticed).* Make you no min' h-am, o, my young man! H-I kin see say you na good boy. Make you no gree h-am spoil you. Me h-I no de for dis bedroom and bathroom business o.

*(General laughter).*

**NANGA.** Eleanor, why you no wan my friend to come enjoy him own share of national cake too? Odili, it is important you come at once as I am planning to go to the United States in about two months. *(Confidentially to him, but loud enough for everybody to hear).* You see, I have to go, because they are going to give me doctorate degree in America. Doctor of Laws, LD.

*(A roar of admiration all around).*

**ODILI.** That's great, sir! Congratulations.

**NANGA.** Thank you, my brother.

**JAMES THE JOURNALIST.** So the Minister will become "Chief the Honourable Doctor M. A. Nanga!"

*(General cheer).*

**NANGA.** Na so my brother! You no see say the title fit my name *pem!*

*(General noise of agreement).*

**MRS JOHN.** "Chief the Honourable Dr M. H-Ay. Nanga, MP, LLD." Na wah! Nothing fit passam...

**NANGA.** You see? Odili the great, take, this is my card, with my residential address in the capital. I will be expecting you. Mr Principal, *o ya*, let's go and see the other things you want to show us!

**NWEGE.** Follow me sir.

*(The whole crowd goes.* **Odili** *walks back to* **Max's** *house).*

## Scene 4

**ODILI.** Yes. I suppose now, with hindsight, that I should have been warned by all that display of vulgarity. But I must tell you, I was genuinely taken by the man's charisma and his generous offer. And then, there was something else...

**MAX.** Don't tell me – The girl!

**ODILI.** I knew you would guess! Cool Max, Terror of Women on Campus!

**MAX.** Oh I've changed, man. But you apparently haven't. So who was she?

**ODILI.** That's what I tried to find out. One moment, when I saw the journalist standing alone, I quickly drew him aside and whispered in his ear:

## Scene 5

*(***Odili** *goes to meet him, as* **James** *re- appears)*

**ODILI.** Who is the young lady?

**JAMES.** *(His mouth wide open for a while as a danger signal).* Ah, make you no go near am-o. My hand no de for inside!

**ODILI.** Ah-ha, yousef! I no dey go near am now! I just de ask who she be.

**JAMES.** 'The Minister no dey introduce am to anybody. But dem talk say na im cousin.

**ODILI.** Cousin! I see.

**JAMES.** My friend, make I confess, meself I done lookam, lookam, lookam sotay I tire. I no go tell you lie! Dese girls for this una part of de kontri sabi fine-o. God Almighty!

**ODILI.** So you tink say na de Minister im cousin true-true?

**JAMES.** Hen, some people talk so. But – *(Draws closer, changing to normal English)* – it's a lie. I know for sure that she's his girl friend.

**ODILI.** Oh!

**JAMES.** Actually it's more than that. He is planning to marry her soon according to native law and custom.

**ODILI.** What! You are sure?

**JAMES.** Don't say I told you! They say his present wife is too "bush" for his present position, so he wants a bright new "parlour-wife," to play hostess at his parties.

**ODILI.** Who told you all this?'

**JAMES.** You forget I am a journalist! That's why he doesn't introduce her. He knows his wife won't like it and may want to cause trouble for him.

**ODILI.** Oh she will all right. I know Mrs Nanga –

**JAMES.** I don't think she will cause any trouble at all. She will still be number 1 after all.

**ODILI.** You're probably right. She won't want to stop being Madam Minister's Wife!

**JAMES.** For where? If you were the one, *nko*?

**ODILI.** Too bad! I mean, for the girl. At her age, and with her looks, she deserves to be somebody's first wife not an old man's mistress.

**JAMES.** He sent her to a Women's Training College, you know. So he has been planning it for a few years at least.

**ODILI.** I feel sorry for her.

**JAMES.** Feel sorry for yourself! You don't know these girls of nowadays? I'm sure she's already dreaming of all the things she will be enjoying as a minister's wife. Money and luxury! That's all they care about now, these girls! Imagine such a beautiful thing wasting herself on such an empty-headed ass.

**ODILI.** Ah-ha! But… you too, you were showering praises on him just now!

**JAMES.** My daily bread, man! Make I no chop? How I go collect my own share of the national cake if I no praise am, praise am!

*(He goes off, laughing.* **Odili** *walks back to* **Max***).*

## Scene 6

**MAX.** So have you seen the girl since then?

**ODILI.** No. But I intend to now.

**MAX.** In spite of her being engaged to the minister

**ODILI.** In fact, ***because*** of her being engaged to him!

**MAX.** Ah-ha?! And what about Elsie then, the one you said you were planning to marry?

**ODILI.** Ah, Elsie! What will you say if I tell you she's the reason I am going after Edna!

**MAX.** Oh she left you?

**ODILI.** Yes, she left me – for the Minister. Nanga snatched her from me!

**MAX.** You don't mean it!

**ODILI.** That's why I'm anxious to go back to our village. I must have my own back!

**MAX.** I see!

**ODILI.** But it's a long story. Maybe when you're back. Go to your meeting now. Or didn't you say you are meeting some people?

**MAX.** Oh yes! What's the time? *(Looking at his watch)* Ah, thanks for reminding me, I must go now. We'll talk later.

**ODILI.** Yes, we will. There's still a lot to say!

**MAX.** Meanwhile make yourself at home. And if you like, when you have settled down and freshened up a bit, you can come and join us. The meeting's downstairs and food will be ready then.

**ODILI.** Ok then. I'll join you.

**MAX.** There'll be a number of people you haven't met before. Although you may have heard their names on the radio, or read about them in the newspapers. We are, I don't mind telling you, trying to form a political party–

**ODILI.** You, a political party!?

**MAX.** Are you surprised? So am I too with myself! But with all the rot going on around us, none of us can afford to sit on the fence any longer, don't you think? Otherwise these locusts will ruin the country for us!

**ODILI.** That's what the meeting is about? OK then, I'll come and listen.

**MAX.** The people coming are the core members. Come to the dining room when you are ready. Who knows, you may become our newest recruit?

**ODILI.** Right, we'll see about that!

*(As* **Max** *goes, Blackout).*

## Scene 7

*(***Odili*** the Narrator is speaking to the Journalist).*

**ODILI-NARRATOR.** I went to the meeting and listened quietly as they talked. And, I must confess, I was immediately taken with the idea of their new party, the Common Peoples Convention. It was after they had broken up, when I was left with Max and his fiancée, that the conversation began that would lead me to my important decision…

*(The scene lights up, showing* **Odili** *the Actor with* **Max** *and* **Eunice***).*

## Scene 8

**MAX.** Well, what do you think, Odili?

**ODILI.** I like your ideas, but I must say that I find it somewhat odd that a party calling itself the 'Common Peoples' Convention' should be made up of only professional men and women!

**MAX.** That is not entirely accurate, Odili. What you saw here just now is only the vanguard, the planning stage. Once we are ready we shall draw in the worker, the farmer, the blacksmith, the carpenter.

**EUNICE***: (A young and beautiful woman lady with a somewhat intimidating confidence).* And the unemployed, of course. But I'd like to take our friend up on a purely historical point. I want to remind him that the great revolutions of history were started by intellectuals, not the common people. Karl Marx was not a common man; he wasn't even a Russian.

**MAX.** True, Eunice, but I can't say that I am surprised Odili made that point. He's always been a stickler for thoroughness. That's why at school we called him Diligent!

**ODILI.** And you? Look if you don't know yet, Eunice, *his* name was Cool Max. That should be a warning to you. Because he always played it cool with the girls.

**EUNICE.** *(with a wink at him).* Oh he still does.

**MAX.** *(protesting playfully).* I beg your pardon! Anyhow, lady and gentleman, or is it, gentleman and lady, as Odili says –

**EUNICE.** *(protesting in mock outrage).* Max! Why not simply say 'Comrades' – as our Trade Union friend keeps saying?

**MAX.** No. As I've said several times before, I don't want anybody to say we are communists. We can't afford the label. It would simply finish us. Our opponents would point at us and say, "Look at those crazy people who want to have everything in common including their wives" and that would be the end of everything. That's the plain fact.

**EUNICE.** I think I agree with you. But our friend the Trade Unionist's reply, as you know, is that our trouble in this country is that we are too nervous. We say we are neutral but as soon as we hear communist we begin to shake and piss in our trousers!

**MAX.** Yes I know. The other day, when somebody asked him why he went to Russia last January, he answered – It's because if you look only in one direction your neck will become stiff…

*(They laugh).*

**EUNICE.** Well, I am sure you guys still have a lot to talk about. But, me, I am already worn out, I want to turn in. So, Odili, if you'll excuse me –

**ODILI.** Oh please, go in. Thank you for all this. Good night and see you tomorrow morning then –

**EUNICE.** *(Giving him a peck).* OK, Max.

**MAX.** Good night, dear.

*(She goes.* **Max** *pours out another drink).*

**ODILI.** Excuse my saying so, Max, but this new party you people are setting up, how many months to the elections. How do you think you can win?

**MAX.** Of course, we can't. That's fairly obvious, isn't it?

**ODILI.** What! You mean, you –

**MAX.** There are too many mushroom political parties springing up, prophesying a landslide victory for themselves. Soon, we know, they'll all shrivel up again.

**ODILI.** Ah, so you know that!

**MAX.** But what we must do, what we're trying to do, is get something going, something truly different, however small, while we wait for the blow-up. For it's bound to come. I don't know how or when but a blow-up's got to come. You simply cannot have this stagnation and corruption going on indefinitely.

**ODILI.** OK, but also, tell me, how do you propose to get the money?

**MAX.** (*smiling*). We will get some, don't worry, at least enough to finance ordinary election expenses. We will leave mass bribing of the electors to POP and PAP. We will simply drop cats among their pigeons here and there and stand aside and watch. And, this will perhaps surprise you, but do you know that one of the junior ministers in the Government is behind our new party?

**ODILI.** I don't like that. What is he doing in the Government if he is so dissatisfied with it? Why doesn't he resign?

**MAX.** *(Laughing)*. Resign! Where do you think you are – Britain or something? Don't be funny, Odili.

**ODILI.** *(Hotly)*. I am not being funny: I know very well and need no reminder that we are not in Britain or something, that when a man resigns in our country it is invariably with an eye on the main chance – as when a few years ago ten newly elected PAP Members of Parliament switched parties at the opening of the session and gave the POP a comfortable majority overnight in return for ministerial appointments plus – if one believes the rumours – a little cash prize each as well. All that is well known, but I would have thought it was better to start our new party clean, with a different kind of philosophy?

**MAX.** I know how you feel. I felt like that at first. But we must face certain facts. You take a man like Nanga now on a salary of four thousand plus all the – you know, the perquisites. You know what his salary was as an elementary school teacher? Perhaps not more than eight pounds a month. Now do you expect a man like that to resign on a little matter of principle?

**ODILI.** Assuming, that is, that he can recognize principle when he sees it!

**MAX.** Well, exactly. I am not saying, mark you, that our man is like Nanga. *He* is a true nationalist and would not hesitate to resign if he felt it was really necessary. But as he himself points out, do we commit suicide every day we feel unhappy with the state of the world?

**ODILI.** It's hardly the same thing.

**MAX.** Well, I know. But having a man like him right in the Government is very essential, I can assure you. He tells me all that goes on.

**ODILI.** In that sense I suppose you are right. As the saying goes it is only when you are close to a man that you can begin to smell his breath.

**MAX.** Well, exactly.

**ODILI.** Max the Political Strategist! Strange role for you! Do you still write poetry?

**MAX.** Oh of course. Now and then.

**ODILI.** I remember the lines you wrote many years ago to the tunes of that famous highlife music. You remember? The one I believe you called 'A Dance Offering to the Earth Mother'...

**MAX.** That was the poem I wrote during the intoxicating months of high hope soon after Independence. What a coincidence! Only this morning I was reading it to Eunice. You want to hear it? Wait. *(He fishes out a piece of paper).* Now listen:

*(He begins to sing, tapping his foot to the highlife rhythm).*

I will return home to her – many centuries have I wandered –

And I will make my offering at the feet of my lovely Mother:

I will rebuild her house, the holy places they raped and plundered,

And I will make it fine with black wood, bronzes and terra-cotta...

**ODILI.** Poor black mother! Waiting so long for her infant son to come of age and comfort her and repay her for the years of shame and neglect. And the son she has pinned so much hope on turning out to be a Chief Nanga!

**MAX.** Poor black mother.

**ODILI.** Only seven years ago, when you first sang it. Then it was filled with gaiety and high promise. Now that time seems like more than seven lifetimes away; and as you sing, it sounds so much like a dirge, I almost want to cry.

**MAX.** *(A long pause. Then he turns to* **Odili** *abruptly).* You know, Odili, I don't believe in Providence and all that kind of stuff. But your arrival just at this very moment seems to me to be most fortunate. You see, our plan is to appoint able and dynamic organizing secretaries in each of the regions very soon. You say you're going back home, to avenge yourself on Nanga. So how about going back for something more noble, standing as our candidate in the southeast?

**ODILI.** What! You really mean that? –

**MAX.** It will be killing a bird with two stones, if you agree. You fight Nanga for the girl. And you also fight him on our behalf for his constituency!

**ODILI.** What a marvellous idea! I'll do it, Max!

## Scene 9

**ODILI-NARRATOR.** So I returned to Anata on 23rd December, after Max and his fiancée, Eunice, had tried in vain to make me spend Christmas in Bori. As soon as I returned, I got busy with my plans. The first thing to do, I thought, was to first get close to Edna, before announcing my entry into politics. That proved to be more difficult than I thought. I didn't even know where to find her. Fortunately however, Chief Nanga had sent his wife and children to the village to spend the Christmas as he did every year. I went to visit her and gradually steered her on to the subject of a rival coming to disrupt her family. Then, on the pretext of going to Edna to dissuade her from the marriage, I got Mrs Nanga to give me her address. But what I had not reckoned with was the girl's greedy father, when I went calling…

## Scene 10

(**Odo's** *house of red earth and thatched roof).*

*He is sitting in his front room making the rope used for tying yams on to erect poles in the barn. The short pieces of fibre from which he works lie beside him in three bundles, one of which has become loose at the girdle from depletion. The rope he has made so far is rolled up in a ball lying between his feet; he holds its free end in his hand and ties new lengths of fibre to it.*

*As* **Odili** *enters* **Odo** *is strengthening the last knot by pulling hard at it across his chest, exposing his locked teeth in the action. He is a big man with an enormous, shining stomach sitting on the rolled-up portion of his loin-cloth. His eyes are bloodshot and his hair greying.*

*(They shake hands and* **Odili** *sits on a chair facing him and backing the approaches to the house).*

**ODO.** *(Re-tying knot that had just come undone under his pull).* Welcome, my son. Welcome. But, please forgive me, I must carry the debt of a kolanut. It got finished only this morning.

**ODILI.** Don't worry about kolanut. You do not know me, I'm sure. I am one of the teachers at the Grammar School.

**ODO.** *(looking up).* Yes, I knew it was a face I had seen. *(Shakes his hands again).* Welcome and I apologize once more for not having kolanuts.

**ODILI.** Oh I understand. It's not every time that people have kolanuts nowadays.

**ODO.** It's just that, since the woman of the house went into hospital there hasn't been anyone to look after these things.

**ODILI.** I hope she will become well again soon.

**ODO.** We are looking on the Man Above.

**ODILI.** *(After a suitable pause).* How's Edna?

**ODO.** *(coldly).* Edna? She is cooking the food to take to the hospital.

**ODILI.** I have a message for her from my friend Chief Nanga.

**ODO.** You are a friend of my in-law? Why did you not tell me so? Have you come from Bori, then?

**ODILI.** Yes. I came back just a few days ago.

**ODO** True? How was he when you left him?

**ODILI.** He was well.

**ODO** *(Turning round on his seat, towards a door leading into inner rooms and raising his voice).* Edna! Come and salute our guest.

**ODILI.** *(Making a special effort to look as casual as possible).* Has your wife been in the hospital a long time?

**ODO.** Since three weeks. But her body has not been hers since the beginning of the rainy season.

**ODILI.** God will hear our prayers.

**ODO.** Amen. He holds the knife and He holds the yam.

*(Edna comes into the middle room. She is wiping her face, as she approaches, with a corner of her lappa, which she drops as soon as she sees Odili. She is wearing a loose blouse over her lappa and an old silken head-tie. She is now a beautiful young woman in contrast to the girl looking as though she was waiting to be taken back to her convent at her first appearance).*

**ODILI.** *(Springing to his feet like some Englishman).* I am a teacher at the Grammar School. We met the day Chief Nanga lectured...

**EDNA.** *(Screwing up her face slightly in an effort to remember).* Oh yes, it is true! You are...er, Mr Samalu.

**ODILI.** That's right! You have a good memory – *(dropping his voice)* – on top of your beauty!

**EDNA.** *(Smiling).* Thank you.

**ODO.** Sit down, teacher? *(Turning to his daughter).* He says he has a message from Bori.

**ODILI.** *(A little embarrassed).* Oh nothing really. Chief Nanga just said I should come and greet you and find out about your mother.

**ODO**. *(In a most unpleasant tone).* You may tell him she is still in the hospital, and that her medicine costs money and that she planted neither cassava nor cocoyam this year.

**EDNA.** Don't listen to him. *(Turning on her father).* Did he not send you something through his wife?

**ODO.** *(To* **Odili***).* Listen to her! Because your mother ate yesterday she won't eat today? No, my daughter. This is the time to enjoy an in-law, not when he has claimed his wife and gone away. Our people say: if you fail to takeaway a strong man's sword when he is on the ground, will you do it when he gets up? No, my daughter. Leave me and my in-law. He will bring and bring and bring and I will eat and eat until I am tired. And thanks to the Man Above he does not lack what to bring.

**EDNA.** Excuse me, but I must go now and finish packing the lunch I am taking to her. If I don't get there before one o'clock, the nurses would not let me in. *(Pausing at the door).* Father, have you given the stranger a kolanut?

**ODO.** I have none. If you have, bring it and we will eat.

**ODILI.** Oh don't bother, I'm OK. By the way, I hope you don't mind if I come with you to see your mother? Now that I am here, I think I ought to go and see her so that when next I write to Chief Nanga I shall have something to report.

**EDNA.** That's very kind of you.

**ODILI.** And I can also give you a ride on my bicycle, if you wish.

**EDNA.** Oh yes! Thank you! Then I can get to the hospital quicker. Let's go.

**ODILI.** Goodbye, sir.

**ODO.** Goodbye. And don't heed what my daughter says. When you get back to Bori, tell my in-law that the treatment of his wife's mother is costing me water and firewood.

**ODILI.** I shall certainly say so.

## Scene 11

**ODILI-NARRATOR.** So far so good, I told myself! Edna was obviously the trusting type – which augured well for my plans. I mounted the vehicle with the can on the back and Edna climbed on the bar sitting sideways; and I pushed off. You can imagine my excitement at having her so close within my arms and the perfume of her hair in my nose! The road to the hospital turned out to be quite hilly, steep enough to take the wind out of one; but, with the kind of passenger I had, I didn't care to admit too readily to being tired. So I raced up all the little hillocks until my heart raged like a bonfire. Then, as I pedalled freely down one small, friendly descent – it was not a lorry this time, like Mr Nwege's! A stupid sheep and her four or five lambs rushed out of the roadside on my left. I braked sharply. The bicycle pitched forward and I crashed down on the road. Edna was thrown farther up the road. I got up and rushed to help her to her feet again. Then we both saw the *foofoo* and soup in the sandy road…

*(Lights transfer us to the scene).*

## Scene 12

*(***Edna** *bends down and picks up the travelling-can and began to wipe away the sand and the spilt soup with green leaves).*

**EDNA.** Oh my mother! She will die of hunger today.

**ODILI.** Edna, I'm sorry.

**EDNA.** It was not your fault, I know.

**ODILI.** Can she manage bread and corned beef? We could buy some outside the hospital.

**EDNA.** I haven't brought any money.

**ODILI.** *(Relieved).* Oh I have enough on me, don't worry about that. *(He notices that she has grazed her knee on the road).* Your knee!

**EDNA.** It's not serious, let's go and buy the bread.

**ODILI.** We'll also get some disinfectant for your knee. I'm terribly sorry, my dear.

**EDNA.** *(Suddenly bursting into laughter).* It was the stupid sheep. And you too, look at you!

*(Still laughing, she goes to dust his shoulder where his new white shirt carries a thick patch of red-earth. He starts laughing too).*

**ODILI.** Oh dear, Edna, thank you.

**EDNA.** Ah, you were eating all the hills like yam!

**ODILI** *(Boastfully).* Which hills? I didn't notice any hills!

**EDNA.** Strong man!

**ODILI.** That's me!

**EDNA.** Brought down however by mere sheep!

*(They laugh and he decides to seize the opportunity of this sudden intimacy).*

**ODILI.** Edna, listen, there is something I want to tell you.

**EDNA.** Me?

**ODILI.** Yes, I want to give you a piece of advice – as one who has seen more of the world and as a friend.

**EDNA.** Yes, go on.

**ODILI.** You may say it's not my business, but you will be making a big and serious mistake if you allow anyone to rush you into marriage now. Honestly, you are too young to be rushed into marrying now and especially a polygamist.

**EDNA.** Is that what Mama asked you to tell me?

**ODILI.** Who is Mama? Oh, Mrs Nanga, I see. Why? Why should she ask me to tell you anything? No, Edna, nobody has sent me. In your own interest, I'm begging you. Don't go and spoil your life.

**EDNA.** What is your business in it?

**ODILI.** None whatever. Except that I think a beautiful young girl like you deserves better than to marry an ancient polygamist.

**EDNA.** You told my father he was your friend!

**ODILI.** Even if he was my brother or my father . . . Edna, give yourself a chance. The man's son is almost your age. And –

**EDNA.** (*Resignedly*). That is the world of women. It's what we have to accept.

**ODILI.** Rubbish! An educated girl like you saying a thing like that! Are you a Moslem or something?

**EDNA.** He paid for me to go to the College.

**ODILI.** So what? Come –

*(Goes and tries to put an arm round her waist. She swings round and pushes him away in one alarmed movement. For a while they stand looking at each other. Then her eyes fall).*

**EDNA.** Are you angry?

**ODILI.** You know, that very first time I saw you, I... *(Sighs resignedly)*. Forget it, everything I've said. You are right, it's none of my business.

**EDNA.** *(After a long pause)*. I am sorry, Odili.

**ODILI.** (*Glumly*). Sorry for what? Let us go...

## Scene 13

**ODILI-NARRATOR.** I was defeated. That would have been the end of the whole matter, I confess. But do you know what happened? As soon as I got home, my boy Peter handed me a blue envelope. A boy had brought it on a bicycle, he said.

The writing was beautifully rounded; without doubt a woman's hand.

Feverishly, I opened it... and it *was* Edna!

(**Edna** *appears in a spotlight, reading over her letter):*

**EDNA.** "Dear Odili, I cannot adequately express my deep sense of gratitude for your brotherly piece of advice. It is just a pity that I answered you the way I did. I feel like going on a bended knee to beg forgiveness. I know that you are so noble and kind-hearted to forgive me before I even ask (Smile!). I have thought carefully over all that you said about my marriage. But really, you should pity poor me, Odili. I am in a jam about the whole thing. If I develop cold feet now my father will almost kill me. Where is he going to find all the money the man has paid on my head? So it is not so much that I want to be called a minister's wife but a matter of can't help. What cannot be avoided must therefore be borne. What I pray for is happiness. If God says that I will be happy in any man's house I know I will be happy. I hope however we will always be friends. For yesterday is but a dream and tomorrow is only a vision. But today's friendship makes every yesterday a dream of happiness and every tomorrow a vision of hope. Good-bye and sweet dreams. Yours very truly, Edna Odo."

*(Lights die on the spotlight).*

**ODILI-NARRATOR.** I read the letter standing up, then sitting down and finally lying on the bed, flat on my back. I analysed it word by word, phrase by phrase. And I realized at last what I had not wanted to admit to myself – I was not just playing with Edna because of Chief Nanga. I was deeply in love with her! I wanted her for myself, at all costs! And now, I felt even bolder to launch my offensive against Chief Nanga.

*(The* **Nurse** *enters).*

**NURSE.** I'm afraid I'll have to stop you now. That's enough strain for today. You can continue tomorrow.

**JOURNALIST.** All right, thank you. We'll continue tomorrow then.

*(He rises. LIGHTS. End of PART ONE. An INTERMISSION is suggested here).*

Chapter Forty-Three

# Chinua Achebe

## Death, Where Are Thy Claws?

*Niyi Osundare*

Chinua Achebe is one of those epically unique individuals whose lives have been so full, so purposeful and so impactful that we begin to pray that they will never die. But who doesn't know that that is mere wishful thinking? To be sure, the Eagle on Iroko didn't die young, but he left when we still need him urgently and acutely. He has gone, but he left so much of himself behind...

Achebe shook up the literary world with *Things Fall Apart* when he was barely in his late twenties. He told Africa's story and gave humanity a song. Since that day in 1958, when that epochal novel intruded upon the world to this very day, hardly a week has passed without the author's name being mentioned somewhere in this world of books and ideas.

But if the sheer force and range of Achebe's fiction gave Africa a voice, the fearless truth of his critical interventions challenged so many myths and deliberate falsehoods about the most misrepresented and recklessly abused continent in the world. Achebe knew and he tried to get us to know that Africans will remain mere objects of the stories told by others, until they, the Africans themselves have started to tell their stories their own way - without shutting out the rest of the world. Achebe challenged the 20th Century philosophy of fiction as a pretty *object d'art,* arriving with works that foregrounded the human condition and told the wondering world that the clotheless Emperor was, indeed, naked! He entered a plea for the urgent necessity of an entity called 'applied art' and emboldened us to look triumphalist formalism in the face and demand to see its passport. Yes, Achebe told a world sold to the art-for-art's-sake mystique that it is, indeed, possible to be an accomplished novelist who is also a teacher.

Controversy hardly ever parts company with a writer and thinker of his brand. He took almost as much criticism as he gave; for he was a man who never ran from a fight.

The world celebrates the LIFE of this distinguished storyteller and thinker. (Yes, ***celebrate***, for to mourn is to concede supremacy to Death – and Oblivion, its Mephistophelean factotum).

Rest well, Chinualomogu. Rest well, Obierika, the man who thought about things. Posterity will never let you die. We regret your passing.

We celebrate your Life.

New Orleans, March 22, 2013.

Chapter Forty-Four

# A Tribute to Chinua Achebe

## The Father of Modern African Literature

*Eustace Palmer*

With the passing of Chinua Achebe, Africa lost one of her mightiest sons and the world lost one of the greatest literary artists of our times. The occasion of his death was one of those earth-shattering moments of which it will be asked of everyone, where were you when it happened, where were you when the news was announced, where were you when it was first whispered in unbelievable tones and then magnified in words we did not expect to hear, where were you when it was confirmed that the great Chinua Achebe, the greatest of the heroes, the greatest of the champions of human dignity and the dignity of the African personality, who represented all that is best in African life past and present, who in his life took so many titles, titles that his African community or that the world could give him, titles that were, indeed, far below what he deserved, was no more? Though he achieved the grand old age of eighty-two, we had come to assume, somehow, that his wisdom would be with us forever. In his traditional Igboland the cannon would have boomed and "shattered the silence" and the magnificent Ekwe talking drum would have started the communication of the unbelievable news, plucking at the heartstrings of an awed people anxiously and breathlessly awaiting the naming of the fallen champion, as they did for Ezeudu of old, naming first the community which, in this case would be both local and universal, before mentioning to expressions of disbelief, sorrow and anguish the mighty name of Chinua Achebe.

Chinua Achebe was undoubtedly the doyen, the mighty man of African letters and the father modern of African literature. In his own words, he showed us where the rain began to beat us; he showed us Africans where we have come from, where we are and who and where we ought to be. More than arguably any other African writer, his work, taken as a whole, celebrated the totality, not just of the Nigerian experience, but of the whole African experience: the grandeur and authenticity of the African traditional past in refutation of those, who for various reasons, wanted to put us down and he did it without, in his own words, "glossing over inconvenient facts;" the clash between that traditional and vibrant culture and the new methods and values introduced by an, at times, ignorant, arrogant and uncomprehending imperialist onslaught; the temptations and, indeed, the complexity of the problems facing the new educated African elite as they prepared to take their countries to independence; the strains and stresses in African life during the immediate post-independence era as African nations sought to rediscover themselves, redefine their values and respond to problems that were partly the legacies of colonialism and partly the consequences of the depredations of corrupt and incompetent leaders; the sufferings of the African peoples under repressive military and authoritarian regimes and during brutal civil wars; and the hope of a glorious future in which all segments of the society, including students, workers and women in particular, will play their rightful part and where the path will never close. And he did it all while manifesting the most consummate artistry and superbly blending form and content in a way that had never been done before by any African writer. It is probably the most egregious lack of awareness of this that prevented the Nobel Committee from awarding him the Nobel prize for literature, a prize, that, according to any reasonable criteria, he more than richly deserved. It is for this reason that this essay will largely concentrate on the majestic achievement of the first novel, *Things Fall Apart* and the last, *Anthills of the Savannah.*

Above everything else, *Things Fall Apart* was a magnificent and much needed exercise in cultural and historical reclamation. Fully rising to all the demands of his role as both novelist and teacher, Achebe sought to teach, not only Europeans and the West in general, but also Africans who lacked knowledge of their history, of the grandeur, dignity, majesty and order of traditional African life. Let us take our minds back to the date of the publication of *Things Fall Apart*, 1958. Intensive research into African history and culture was only just beginning. This was the time when respected historians, like Hugh Trevor Roper, the Regius Professor of History at Oxford University, could make the appalling statement that Africa has no history. A number of people in the West, their imaginations having been fuelled by the sensationalized accounts of earlier travellers like Henry Morton Stanley, Rider Haggard and others, still thought that Africa was a disorganized, benighted, backward place inhabited by dirty, lazy, pagan peoples incapable of rational thought or of participating in certain disciplines and who had to be rescued from the consequences of their own barbarism by the blessings of imperialism. Of course the real truth was quite different. Diversified historical methodology, the use of non-Western Arabic sources like those of Al-Bakri and Al-Idris and the result of linguistic and archaeological research have given us quite a different view of the African past and of traditional African culture and society. In the fifties the process was just beginning and Achebe's *Things Fall Apart* played a gigantic role.

In particular, we know that Achebe was reacting to the works of two writers who had presented a particularly jaundiced view of traditional African life: Joseph Conrad and Joyce Cary. Conrad, as a result of his journey up the then river Congo at the turn of the 20th Century had all but presented Africans, in his celebrated novel *Heart of Darkness,* as cannibalistic individuals indulging in the most ghastly rituals and capable of corrupting enlightened Europeans like the exemplary Mr Kurtz. The very choice of a title – Heart of Darkness – speaks volumes. Whatever critics might say about the artistry of that novel, there can be no doubt that Conrad was pandering to the equation, in the Western imagination since medieval days, between blackness and darkness on the one hand and evil on the other. Achebe's celebrated riposte in which he accused Conrad of racism is now well known. Joyce Cary, for his part, had presented, in the novel *Mister Johnson,* which was set in Northern Nigeria, a foolish and laughable protagonist whom quite a few African intellectuals, including Achebe, saw as a caricature of the African. Achebe therefore sought to set the record straight and to present not just a fair picture of traditional African society in the representation of Umuofia, but also a portrait of a genuine African gentleman in Okonkwo.

The traditional society that Achebe presents in *Things Fall Apart* is a highly organized and religious society, with its own social and judicial structures: a far cry from the chaos that African detractors would have us believe the imperialists found. If by a religious people we mean people who believe in the existence of a supreme supernatural being or beings, who obey that being or those beings and allow their entire lives to be regulated by the dictates of those beings, then there could be no more religious people than the inhabitants of Umuofia. Apart from the complex hierarchy of gods and deities, major and minor, like Ani, Ojukwu, and Ifejioku, their entire lives are regulated by the need to obey the dictates of the gods, however harsh those dictates may be. Indeed, what some might consider the harshest and worst aspects of the society are occasioned precisely by the need to adhere to the dictates of the gods. Thus, if a god's oracle says that an innocent fourteen year old boy from another clan who has been living with the clan as a hostage must be killed, they feel they have no alternative but to do so; if the goddess Ani says that twins are an abomination and must be thrown alive into the evil forest or that anyone who has the swelling sickness should not be allowed to die in the village but must be taken alive to the evil forest and abandoned to die there, so be it. The case of Ikemefuna is interesting, because it has an almost exact parallel in the Judaeo-Christian tradition, a parallel about which those who condemn the brutality of this society seem to be oblivious of. In the Old Testament, the patriarch Abraham is asked by God to take his son Isaac to a makeshift altar in the wilds and kill him. Does Abraham refuse? Not a bit of it. He obeys unquestioningly and is about to cut off the boy's head when God stops him and says he was only testing him to see whether he would obey his behests. He then shows him a sheep that he asks him to sacrifice instead, thus giving rise to a number of rituals in more than one religion. Abraham demonstrates his religiousity, his faith and belief in God by his unquestioning obedience. The case of the Umuofians is no different.

One of the most interesting passages in *Things Fall Apart* is that in which the missionary Mr Brown visits the elder Akunna and they discuss theological matters:

> "You say there is one supreme God who made heaven and earth," said Akuna on one of Mr Brown's visits. "We also believe in Him and call Him Chukwu. He made all the world and the other gods."
>
> "There are no other gods," said Mr Brown. "Chukwu is the only God and all the Others are false. You carve a piece of wood – like that one" (he pointed at the rafters from which Akunna's carved *ikenga* hung), "and you call it a god. But it is still a piece of wood."
>
> "Yes," said Akunna. "It is indeed a piece of wood. The tree from which it came was made by Chukwu, as indeed all minor gods were. But he made them for his messengers so that we could approach him through them…" (179)

What is being demonstrated here is the essential similarity between Christianity and the traditional religion of the Umuofians. Though there is a plurality of gods, there is one supreme being who created everything else, as is the case with Christian belief. And there are some Christian sects who make wooden and other representations of holy figures through whom they pray to the supreme being.

The elaborate social and administrative structure of the Umuofians ensures fair play and it is a system that works. The various social and administrative units like the family, the lineage groups, the age groups, the council of elders and the oracles all play their part and the religious, social and judicial systems are interconnected. One of the great set pieces in the novel is that in which nine elders of the clan, wearing the masks of the nine ancestors, form a kind of Supreme Court (consisting of nine elders like the United States Supreme Court) and sit in judgment on the most difficult cases. The sanctions for those who transgress the laws are set and no exceptions are made no matter what the status of the transgressor might be. Thus the mighty Okonkwo is exiled to his motherland for seven years for the accidental killing of a kinsman and he has to pay a severe penalty for breaking the week of peace. Wouldn't it be splendid if every contemporary nation could set aside a week of peace every year during which everyone has to be nice to their neighbours?

This is a society also that shows tremendous concern for the observation of the proper protocols and modes of behaviour. Thus visitors are offered kolanuts before conversation and other business proceed. When Okonkwo goes to Nwakibie to ask for seed yams he takes a pot of palm wine. Neighbours are called in to witness this and it is the youngest man in the group who pours out the palm wine. The first cup must go to Okonkwo to ensure that it is not poisoned and then the other men drink in order of seniority. When the men have drunk, it is the turn of the women, but they, too, cannot just drink in any order. Nwakibie's senior wife must drink first and the other wives have to wait until she arrives. But, again, she doesn't just drink in any haphazard fashion: "She walked up to her husband and accepted the horn from him. She then went down on one knee, drank a little and handed back the horn. She rose, called him by his name and went back to her hut. The other wives drank in the same way in their proper order and went away." (20) This tremendous delicacy in relationships and concern for protocol must come as a shock to many foreign travellers to Africa who still believe that African society is happy-go-lucky and slap-dash. This is also a society that shows tremendous tolerance and consideration for strangers. It is interesting that although the British missionaries and administrators take advantage of their position, they are initially welcomed by the people and allowed to stay as long as they behave themselves. This is remarkable at a time when we, in the United States, are concerned about immigration and there are so many groups that are anxious to keep immigrants out.

Achebe and some other African writers have been criticized for their presentation of women in their early works. The accusation is that they have not done justice to the totality of the female experience in Africa and have confined themselves to the presentation of stereotypes: the woman as mother or girlfriend, witch or prostitute. Florence Stratton, in particular, accused Achebe of depriving women of their voices in *Things Fall Apart* and not giving them a role in the political affairs of Umuofia. This is an unfair accusation. Achebe's intention was to present a fair and objective picture of his society. He could not give women a share in the political affairs of Umuofia if at the time of which he was writing they did not have such a role. Of course, research has shown that in many parts of precolonial Africa, women played very important political roles and even in the areas where the men were in charge politically the women's role was substantial. It is the latter that Achebe presents in his depiction of Umuofia. Women might not be among the nine egwugwu who put on the ancestral masks and form the highest court of the land, they might not have been allowed to see the inside of the hut from which the egwugwu emerged, but all the evidence suggests that they were highly respected and played their own roles in their own particular age groups. Indeed, it is Okonkwo's failure to see the subtle nuances in his society's attitude towards and treatment of women that constitutes one of his weaknesses and leads to his doom. Contrary to some of the simplistic generalizations one sometimes finds in some students' essays, Okonkwo is the only Umuofian we see beating his wives and he is severely reprimanded for it. When Ogbuefi Ndulue dies, his senior wife dies immediately after and we are told:

> "He could not do anything without telling her."
>
> "I did not know that," said Okonkwo. "I thought he was a strong man in his youth."
>
> "He was indeed," said Ofoedu.
>
> Okonkwo shook his head doubtfully.
>
> "He led Umuofia to war in those days," said Obierika. (68)

Achebe included this interlude in the novel for a particular reason: to show that Okonkwo is out of step with his society in his attitude towards women. It is Okonkwo who feels that strong men should not consult their wives. Here we have the example of a very strong man, one who was, in his day, as brave a warrior as Okonkwo himself and led his clan to war, consulting his wife in everything and being so close to her that she dies immediately after he does. In fact, as Iyasere and others have pointed out, a strong female principle exists in Umuofia that ensures that although women do not wield the political power, they are nevertheless highly respected and not subjugated or mistreated. It is not incidental that one of the most powerful deities in Umuofia is female – the goddess Ani. When Okonkwo accidentally kills his kinsman, he is exiled to his motherland to live among a clan that he considers rather feminine and he starts brooding. But his uncle Uchendu summons him and gives him a lecture, explaining why one of the commonest names given to female children is Nneka, meaning "mother is supreme." Men might wield political power and yet "mother is supreme." Mother provides refuge and protection.

Of course, Achebe had said that, in his presentation of this traditional African society, he would not gloss over inconvenient facts, and he doesn't. Unlike the Negritude writers, he does not over-idealize this society; he is objective, presenting both the strengths and the weaknesses. There is the case of the osus whom the rest of the clan ostracize and consider as outcasts; there is the case of twins who are considered an abomination to the Earth goddess and have to be abandoned in the evil forest and there are the people who suffer from the swelling sickness and are not allowed to die in their beds in the village. It is a society that might not look too favourably on those who do not measure up to its very high standards, like Unoka, Okonkwo's father and Nwoye, Okonkwo's son. Indeed, the new religion introduced by the white man is able to make inroads into Umuofia society precisely by shrewdly exploiting the weaknesses of this society. Nevertheless, true to his original intention, Achebe is able to present in *Things Fall Apart*, a traditional African society of great dignity and beauty and one that possesses an essence that is of value.

One of the reasons why *Things Fall apart* has become the seminal African novel, the most popular African literary work ever, is that it is a perfect blend of form and content, subject matter and artistry and one of Achebe's great achievements is that he pointed the way for other African writers as to how this could be done. The novel could so easily have become a sociological document, but Achebe prevents this from happening by linking all the sociological information of that lengthy first part of the novel, which gives the picture of traditional society, with some aspect of Okonkwo's, the protagonist's, character. The very first word in the novel is "Okonkwo": "Okonkwo was well known throughout the nine villages and even beyond." Chapter one then goes on to tell us about Okonkwo's skill as a wrestler and how he threw Amalinze, "the Cat." Wrestling is thus seen as one of the major pastimes of this society and this great set piece goes on to describe the wrestling contest. Interestingly, it would seem, superficially, as if the chapter is mainly about Unoka, Okonkwo's father and the values the society holds dear, but it comes back at the end to Okonkwo and his determination to be everything that his father was not. Unlike his father, Okonkwo had lived up to those values: "Age was respected among his people, but achievement was revered. As the elders said, 'if a child washed his hands he could eat with kings'. Okonkwo had clearly washed his hands and so he ate with kings and elders." Shrewdly making use of a very relevant proverb, Achebe blends sociological information with character development and adopts the tone of a village elder telling a story. Chapter two is about the preparation of Umuofia for war against the clan Mbaino that had killed a daughter of Umuofia and it tells us a lot about Umuofia's political arrangements and the process of decision-making; but it comes round in the end to Okonkwo who, because of his achievements and leadership qualities, is the emissary chosen to take Umuofia's ultimatum to Mbaino. When Mbaino decides to comply with the ultimatum and hand over a virgin and the young boy Ikemefuna to Umuofia, it is Okonkwo who is chosen to be Ikemefuna's guardian. Chapter three is about Unoka's consultation of the oracle to find out why he is not successful and his subsequent shameful death of the swelling sickness. It is full of sociological information of the values and protocols of this society and laden with well-chosen proverbs, but it is firmly centred on Okonkwo and his capacity for hard work, which makes him a success unlike his father. Chapter four is largely about the observation of the week of peace, but once more Okonkwo is solidly at the centre, since he breaks the week of peace by severely beating one of his wives and having to be reprimanded by the High priest. Chapter five is largely about the celebration of the New Yam Festival, but it also presents Okonkwo's restless energy, his lack of enthusiasm for such celebrations and his subsequent senseless beating and near murder of another wife. Chapter six is about another wrestling contest. It is not only reminiscent of Okonkwo's throwing of the Cat, but a preliminary contest between two young wrestlers reminds Okonkwo of his own prowess as a young man.

The extremely important chapter seven starts almost innocently with the description of the locusts and the people's joy as they collect them for food. Superficially, it might seem as just another attempt to present these people and their environment. But it is while Okonkwo and his sons are happily crunching locusts that the blow falls; the news arrives that the Oracle has decided that Ikemefuna must be killed and Okonkwo is faced with one of the most difficult decisions of his life: whether or not to be involved in the killing of Ikemefuna. The ogbanje chapters nine and eleven show a soft side of Okonkwo, revealing that he is capable of tender feelings for an individual, in this case, his ogbanje daughter Ezinma. Chapter ten, the trial scene, is about the clan's judicial processes, but, again, it is riveted on Okonkwo who is one of the nine judges or egwugwu wearing the masks of the ancestors. Chapter 13 is about the clan's funeral customs; it presents the funeral ceremonies for the mighty warrior Ezeudu, but it is during these ceremonies that Okonkwo's gun goes off accidentally and kills a kinsman, and for this he has to be exiled to his motherland for seven years. It is the climax of the first part of the novel in which Achebe has been concerned with the presentation of the nature of this traditional society, but he has also cleverly linked this with the development of Okonkwo's character.

One of Achebe's major achievements in *Things Fall Apart* is to demonstrate for the benefit of later writers how they could communicate their insights and present a genuine African environment while still using one or other of the metropolitan languages. He has been at the centre of the discourse regarding the use of the English language by African writers. He could have written in his native Igbo, but then *Things Fall Apart* would certainly not have gained the worldwide audience that it has done and we must remember that one of Achebe's purposes was to educate non-Africans about Africa. Still, he realized that the African writer could not use the English language in the same way in which the native speaker of the language does, especially as the African writer had to use language to present a genuine African environment. Quite perceptively, he saw that the African writer had to bend the language he was forced to write in, but he also saw, as he himself has said, that the African writer must do so from a position of strength, not from a position of weakness. In other words, before bending the language, the African writer must achieve mastery in it and his work must show that he has achieved this mastery. So Achebe's work gives us dazzling passages of tremendous majesty, lucidity and grandeur in which he shows he is completely at home with this alien medium, but he also shows tremendous adroitness in bending it when it suits his purpose to reflect the nature of the society and the characters he presents.

One of the ways in which he bends the language is his copious use of the oral tradition. Indeed, Achebe's novels, particularly *Things Fall Apart* and *Arrow of God*, can be used as object lessons in how the oral tradition can be incorporated into novels. It is in *Things Fall Apart* that he makes the engaging statement that, 'among the Igbo, proverbs are the palm oil with which words are eaten'. No other African writer has been able to equal his skill at the relevant use of proverbs to illuminate character and theme. Let us just refer to the use of two proverbs in *Things Fall Apart*. The first is "let the kite perch and let the egret perch; if one says no to the other, may his wing break." This surely refers to the people's tolerance and their desire for peaceful co-existence, co-existence that is initially extended to the intruding British missionaries and administrators. The other is the one about the bird Eneke Nti Oba who was asked why he was always flying without landing on a twig. His reply is that since men of today have learnt to shoot without missing, he has learnt to fly without perching. In other words, in order to survive one must be able to adapt to a changing situation. This is precisely what Okonkwo is unable to do. For good or for ill the white man had come with a new religion and a new administration and the society had to adapt to the changing situation; at least, new methods were called for to handle the white man and there is evidence in the novel that quite a few people are changing. Indeed, for most of the time the talk is about change. Okonkwo, however, is incapable of change. He still keeps using the old language of war and invoking the masculine standards and values, this is why he is destroyed.

Achebe's last novel, *Anthills of the Savannah*, shows that he himself was capable of change and of responding quite positively to the views of his readers, his admirers and his critics. This massive novel, written about twenty years after the publication of the fourth, *A Man of the People*, was partly in response to those who wanted to hear Achebe's views about the disastrous events that had happened in Africa between the 1960s and the 1980s when the entire continent, including Achebe's own country of Nigeria, was held in the nefarious grip of one party authoritarian regimes and brutal military dictatorships. Achebe had become the sage, the grand old man of African letters and his views were important and sought after. To a certain extent these were given in *The Trouble with Nigeria*, published in Nigeria in by Fourth Dimension 1983 and Heinemann in 1984 respectively. *Anthills of the Savannah*, first published in 1987, can be regarded as his artistic response and goes over some of the territory covered in *The Trouble with Nigeria*. It was also partly his response to those feminist critics like Carole Boyce Davies, Kirsten Holst Petersen and Merun Nasser who had accused Achebe of failing to present portraits of modern African women engaged in jobs outside the home. In a determined effort to rectify this deficiency, Achebe creates in Beatrice, the modern pioneering African career woman who meets the men on her own terms and is more than a match for them. This essay will now briefly discuss three aspects of this remarkable novel: the narrative technique, the presentation of Beatrice and the exploration of the role of the writer.

It will not be too much of an exaggeration to say that *Anthills of the Savannah* is a post-*The Interpreters* novel in which Achebe abandons the linear method of narration he had employed in his earlier four novels for one that is similar to Soyinka's. In this, he shows he is responsive to the new trends in the African novel during the last quarter of the 20th Century when many novelists sought to devise new strategies to reflect the disillusionment and uncertainties inherent in the current African realities. As with *The Interpreters*, the narrative perspective shifts from one major character to another and, in the first section of the novel at least, Achebe makes little attempt to preserve a linear chronological sequence. Where Soyinka calls his own leading characters interpreters, Achebe calls his own leading characters/narrators "witnesses," and the effect is almost as though they are giving evidence in a court of law or during an investigation into the nation's affairs. The reader becomes a juror, as it were, in a court of law listening to several versions of events with varying degrees of authenticity, reliability and truth, and he himself has to come to a vision of the real truth through a resolution of all the conflicting versions. After giving narrations by the various narrators in the first seven chapters of the novel, Achebe switches in chapter eight to the first person "we" making the narrative issue out of the collective consciousness of the Nigerian people. The narrator now sounds like the ordinary Nigerian citizen speaking from the vantage point of his people and their traditions. He makes reference to the oral tradition at this point in a manner reminiscent of Soyinka in *The Interpreters*, presenting us with the story of the female Igbo deity Idemili who in this novel is closely associated with Beatrice. From now onward, the third person omniscient is used right up to the end of the novel, although Achebe keeps us very close to the consciousness of some of the leading characters like Chris and Beatrice. Achebe's "witnesses" are all highly educated, articulate and intelligent young individuals who are conscious of their role in bringing about the transformation of society. On the whole, they possess much greater moral integrity than Soyinka's Interpreters and they are all morally superior to the rest of society. It is largely through their eyes that we see the prevailing corruption, decadence and brutality.

Beatrice is one of the "witnesses" and she is one of the most compelling women in the whole corpus of the African novel. Her boyfriend Chris's comments on her suggest how Achebe himself regards her: "Beatrice is a perfect embodiment of my ideal woman, beautiful without being glamorous. Peaceful but very strong. Very very strong. I love her and will go at whatever pace she dictates"(58). Presented as one of the most brilliant people of her generation in Nigeria, she is remarkably perceptive, level-headed and sane and can see things that her boyfriend and the other men cannot. It is not surprising that towards the end of the novel Achebe refers to her as a "captain" with a "company." Achebe uses this, as well as the mythological associations that surround her, to suggest the leadership position that woman should be permitted to wield in Africa for the good of the entire continent. In the context in which the reference to Beatrice as "captain" emerges, we see her functioning as a real leader who is sensitive to the peculiar needs of her people. This is what the erstwhile leaders, who were military men, should have done. The mythological context also reinforces the new notion of leadership. This is the significance of the association between Beatrice and the Igbo goddess Idemili. Achebe uses her in chapter eight of the novel to suggest that power and authority, which constitute one of the major themes of the novel, should be based on morality and be clothed in modesty and peace. In other words, leaders need not be arrogant, corrupt and brutal as His Excellency is in *Anthills.* Beatrice, as the perceptive and brilliant Ikem realizes, is the modern equivalent of Idemili, although she herself does not realize it. Beatrice is therefore used to suggest that power, especially the kind of power possessed and wielded by such males as His Excellency, should be moderated by morality, modesty and peace. These are among Beatrice's leading attributes. Idemili was also a nourisher who sent water to her thirsting people, the water that, according to legend, eventually became the Niger. Idemili seems to have done the opposite of what the sun did in Ikem's "Hymn to the Sun."

> Great Carrier of Sacrifice to the Almighty: Single Eye of God! Why have you brought this on us? What hideous abomination forbidden and forbidden and forbidden seven times have we committed or else condoned, what error that no reparation can hope to erase?
>
> Look, our forlorn prayers, our offerings of conciliation lie scattered about your floor where you cast them disdainfully away; and every dawn you pile up your long basket of day with the tools and emblems of death.
>
> Wide-eyed insomniac, you go out at cock-crow spitting malediction at a beaten recumbent world. Your crimson torches fire the furnaces of heaven and the roaring holocaust of your vengeance fills the skies...
>
> The trees had become hydra-headed bronze statues so ancient that only blunt residual features remained on their faces, like anthills surviving to tell the new grass of the savannah about last year's brush fires. (28)

The title of the novel occurs here in this poem which, on the surface, is a plea to the sun to relent in its merciless torture of mankind. It is the sun that has caused the drought that has plagued the people of Abazon. On a deeper symbolic level, however, the poem refers to the general suffering the leaders have inflicted on the people. Idemili's influence is the reverse. Where the sun doomed the people to ages of relentless drought, Idemili gives them water and nourishes them. As Idemili and therefore nourisher and the embodiment of morality, modesty and peace, Beatrice plays an extremely important role in the novel, particularly in exposing the brutality and corruption of the regime in general and His Excellency in particular and in highlighting the theme of African womanhood.

Ikem Osodi is the moral centre of *Anthills of the Savannah.* He is crucial to the social comment in the novel and the exposure of the brutality and decadence not only of the leaders, but the society as a whole. He can be regarded as the spokesman for Achebe, elucidating his views on revolution and change, the role and attitude of the students and the masses and the degradation that the leaders bring on the people. But Ikem is also a journalist and writer and as such, he is used by Achebe to elucidate, quite compellingly, the novelist's views on the role of the writer in society. Two episodes are worthy of note here: the meeting in which the Old Man of Abazon gives a remarkable speech and Ikem's lecture to students at the university. Making extensive use of the oral tradition and thus highlighting the struggle against tyranny and the abuse of power and authority, the Old Man talks at length of the importance of "story" in the lives of the people. Story here means, not just the oral tradition, or history, but writing or literature in general. Achebe obviously intends the Old Man's speech to be one of the centrepieces of the novel and he invests this illiterate old man with tremendous moral and intellectual stature. Highlighting his compelling voice and personality, he points to the tremendous hold the Old Man has on his audience, literate and illiterate alike, during his undoubtedly brilliant speech, which dwells on the importance and primacy of "story." In a sense, the Old Man is talking about the importance of the oral tradition in African life, but, in another sense, he is also talking about Ikem's profession, that of the writer who writes the story of the country. Let us recollect that the Old Man's speech had emerged out of a context in which he set out to defend Ikem against the criticism of the Master of Ceremonies who had upbraided Ikem for not attending the meetings and activities of the descendants of Abazon in Lagos. The Old Man stresses that Ikem, as a journalist and writer, is brilliantly doing a job that is vital to the health of the nation; it is a job that no one else can do and he must be left to do it in peace. But above all, the Old Man and Achebe himself are talking about the importance of the writer in society, an importance that a good many do not recognize:

> "When we are young and without experience we all imagine that the story of the land is easy and that every one of us can get up and tell it. But that is not so. True, we all have our little scraps of tale bubbling in us. But what we tell is like the middle of a mighty boa which a foolish forester mistakes for a tree trunk and settles upon to take his snuff... Yes, we lay into our little tale with wide eyes and a vigorous tongue. Then, one day Agwu comes along and knocks it out of our mouth and our jaw out of shape for our audacity and hands over the story to a man of his choice... Agwu does not call a meeting to choose his seers and diviners and artists; Agwu, the god of healers; Agwu, brother to Madness! But though born from the same womb he and Madness were not created by the same *Chi*. Agwu is the right hand a man extends to his fellows; Madness, the forbidden hand. Madness unleashes and rides his man roughly into the wild savannah. Agwu possesses his own just as securely but has him corralled to serve the compound. Agwu picks his disciple, rings his eye with white chalk and dips his tongue, willing or not, in the brew of prophecy; and right away the man will speak and put head and tail back to the severed trunk of our tale." (114–115)

The force of Agwu to which the Old Man refers is obviously the force of genius or power of inspiration that possesses the writer and forces him to tell his tale. It is akin to madness, but also quite different from it in its method of operation and effects. The writer is like the Old Testament prophets who were inspired to prophesy and who some might have thought were mad. The writer or storyteller is like a prophet possessed, with white chalk ringed around his eye. He not only tells his tale, but he also sees into things. In other words, the writer is not only an artist, but also a seer or prophet or diviner who not only tells his people the story of their land, but also warns them of impending disasters and shows them how to mend their ways. This is, of course, Ikem's role in society: to sensitize his people to the extent of their wrongdoing and decadence; and he does it most effectively, suggesting that almost every segment of society is involved in the corruption and decadence. And this is, of course, the role that Achebe himself has played.

Some critics attacked Achebe for not suggesting solutions to the daunting problems he so convincingly analyses. He responded quite effectively in *Anthills of the Savannah* during Ikem's meeting with the students. When the chairman in his concluding statement asserts, rather fulsomely, that writers must "move to the higher responsibility of proffering prescriptions," Ikem shouts, "Writers don't give prescriptions…they give headaches." (148) However, in *Anthills of the Savannah* at least Achebe holds out the possibility of hope for the future and the hope resides with women and children, the next generation. At the end of the novel, the leading women – Beatrice and Elewa – meet with others to name Ikem's and Elewa's daughter. Beatrice takes upon herself what should have been a man's job: naming the child. It's a sign of the changing times and the growing importance of women. The name they give to the child, who is a girl, is a man's name: Amaechina – which means "may the path never close." The name suggests not only the continuation of Ikem's line (appropriately through a girl and not a boy), but also of his vision and the baby suggests hope for the future. It is also significant that the gathering brings together almost every segment of society: the Senior Assistant Secretary, the army captain, the university student, the illiterate salesgirl, the maidservant Agatha and the taxi driver. Various tribes are represented and so are the major religions: Christianity, Islam and traditional African religion. The scene holds out the hope that in spite of the ravages of the past the whole of Nigeria will go forward together in hope. This is Achebe's final word; it is one of reconciliation and togetherness.

It must be said that Achebe was the perfect gentleman. He taught us the values of humility and unpretentiousness in spite of his gargantuan achievements, a humility and unpretentiousness that are reflected even in his style. He spoke to us vibrantly in language we could all understand and, being the wise man he was, he communicated values we could all endorse. Nevertheless, he did not avoid the controversial issues and he did not shrink from coming to the defence of those who had been unfairly treated. I remember the first time I met him; it was at the annual conference of the African Literature Association in Gainesville, Florida, in 1980. He was one of the featured speakers and another was the novelist James Baldwin. During James Baldwin's speech some hoodlum, making use of the latest technology, kept interrupting the speech from the outside through the loudspeaker system, using racial epithets, referring to Baldwin's sexual orientation and generally making the most ribald comments. Achebe, in his own remarks that immediately followed, robustly came to Baldwin's defence, publicly rebuking the interrupter and letting him know that such conduct was most unseemly and certainly not in the African tradition.

Finally, we must celebrate Achebe, not only as a great literary artist, but as one of Africa's great intellectuals who, like Obierika and Ezeulu, thought about things. Like some of his characters who could get to the heart of an issue or argument by making use of a pithy proverb, he had the remarkable ability of quietly surveying all aspects of an issue and then giving an irrefutable judgment in a few well-chosen words. I also recall that at that ALA conference in Gainesville which was devoted to an exploration and definition of the African aesthetic, a rather blurred issue at the time, we academics had been struggling with the issue for days, giving various opinions and failing to arrive at a consensus. But then came Achebe and in his own inimitable way and in a few well-chosen sentences gave a definition that was universally accepted. It was a definition that revolved around the concept of morality, a concept that is central to all his own works. He may not have won the Nobel Prize for literature, but, in a sense, he did not need the validation of the Nobel Prize. His validation remains in the works themselves and in the hearts and minds of scholars, students, teachers and writers all over the world who are grateful that such a mighty man of valour was allowed to live among them.

And so, he has gone to join the ancestors and we know that from the realm of existence he will continue to regard us his children with his usual benevolence and tolerance. We mourn him, but we also celebrate his life, his example, and his incalculable contribution to humanity as a whole. We place him right up their with other heroes like Mandela and others who have demonstrated the best that African life, that human life, ought to be, and we say, as he himself would put it, "May the path that he has charged never close."

Chapter Forty-Five

# Chinua Achebe and the Literary Compass

*Ato Quayson*

Like most educated Ghanaians of my generation, I was first introduced to *Things Fall Apart* as a student in high school. Boarding high school was very popular at the time and being heavily state-subsidized ended up a commonly educational shared rite-of-passage for many youth in the country. At mine the authorities got the bright idea of putting all of us 15-year-olds on the same block of dormitories above a newly constructed classroom complex separated from the standard Houses. The converted dormitories were destined to become classrooms some two years later, but for some reason not quite clear to anyone but the authorities, all Form 3 boys were asked to move from their allotted Houses to be segregated at this new location. It did not take us long to see the stupendous opportunities this provided for mischief and the testing of boundaries and we proceeded to heartily create a fortress that none of the seniors or indeed the masters could easily access without triggering an elaborate but invisible early-warning system. Reality and high fantasy of freedom were completely blurred for us in those days and it was into this heady adolescent vortex that Achebe's novel was first introduced.

The exact phase in which we read Achebe also meant that he was inserted into concerns that had little to do with our studies at all, never mind with literature. It was the habit then for all boys and some girls to either adopt or be given a nickname, the more colourful, the better: Watermelon, Asanka, Kofi Monrovia, Bangladesh, Rasta Pee, Calabash, Sheikh Bujibur Rahman, Don Kpiti Mattoya, Kakalika. The primary interest of *Things Fall Apart* for us, then, was as a fresh source of nicknames. Thus an *efulefu* was shy and not good with the girls. An Obierika was a nerd. An Ogbuefi Ezeudu was likely a slightly older student who behaved like a wise man. Ezinma was a smart and unattainable girl that more than one boy built their dreams on, while an Okonkwo was the envy of us all, as he was supposed to be strong, bold and a royal pain to the authorities. Everyone was an object of fun and some derision and some nicknames could quickly trade places depending on memorable circumstances. But there was one other aspect of *Things Fall Apart* that seized our interest. By virtue of most of us having been brought up as city kids, we had a mixture of reverence and bewilderment for all things considered rural. What we admired most by far was the rural use of language and anyone that could weave speech through the language of proverbs had our complete attention. We took Achebe's saying that 'proverbs are the palm-oil with which words are eaten' completely too seriously, the poignancy of it being further augmented for us by the fact that many of our number declared *fufu* and *abenkwan* (palm-nut soup) to be our favourite meal. It was Achebe then that gave us city kids the first route into understanding the rhetorical magic of proverbs and it was his novel that gave many of us the early practice of quoting them, sometimes inappropriately, well before we came to understand our own local-language proverbs. Among my favourites from both *Things Fall Apart* and his other novels that I have subsequently put to variant use I count:

> "A toad does not run in the day time for nothing; when you see it you must know that something is after its life."
>
> "The earth is like a mask dancing, you cannot see it properly by standing still."
>
> "When Eneke the bird was asked why she was always on the wing she said: 'Now that men have learned to shoot without missing I have also learned to fly without perching.'"
>
> "The lizard that fell from the tall iroko tree nodded, saying 'If no one will praise me, I will praise myself.'"
>
> "The eye is not harmed by sleep."
>
> "If a man returns from a long journey and no one says *nno* (welcome) to him, he feels like one who has not arrived."

Going to University to study English Literature predictably brought me into contact with Achebe again, but this time as an African writer. For some reason his Africanness had not been the emphasis in high school so we were left to engage him with the same spirit of amazement and wonder with which we viewed Shakespeare, Chaucer, the Brontës, The Metaphysical Poets and

Wordsworth, among the various other writers we were exposed to, many of whose worlds seemed exciting yet confusingly distant from our own. In university at Legon, Achebe was a different proposition; we had to understand how he was related to Wole Soyinka and Ngũgĩ wa Thiong'o and Kofi Awoonor and Amos Tutuola and Ama Ata Aidoo and many other African writers. Apart from *Things Fall Apart*, which I studied practically every year at University, we were also introduced to selections from his short story collection, *Girls at War*. The title story made a special impression on me and even though it was not as memorable as Ring Lardner's "Haircut," which I still immodestly hold to be one of the best short stories ever written, I quietly added Achebe's to the list of ones I was to re-read many times later in my career. "Haircut" always put me in mind of Jeebo (a nickname) with whom I used to run away from boarding school to the beach in town most Tuesdays to read poetry and eat bananas with canned sardines. Jeebo was just a grade above me, but that didn't prevent me from seeing him as by far the most advanced consciousness in the entire school and even greater than our teachers. Jeebo read everything including Karl Marx but was especially interested in poetry and the short story, which he promoted with the idea that you could pack more of them into a day than you could novels. I was completely persuaded by that idea, taking it with me well into adulthood and have forever been on the lookout for good short stories to add to my collection. Achebe's made the list, as much later did Leila Aboulela's "The Museum", Yvonne Vera's "Without a Name" and Marechera's "House of Hunger" (both the last two strictly speaking more novellas than short stories) and several by Ben Okri. It was at University too, studying phenomenology of religions that I first came to wonder about the significance of the *chi* concept in *Things Fall Apart.* Despite the fact that the *chi* had no material manifestation, I considered it to carry much more phenomenological and indeed social significance than even the *egwugwu* that manifested themselves in such ritual grandeur in the novel. And even though at the time I had no clear evidence for this conclusion I always wrestled with the *chi* somewhere at the back of my mind.

Cambridge for the PhD threw up a completely unanticipated set of questions, the most recalcitrant of which was why I had decided to study Nigerian literature instead of the literature of my own homeland. The question baffled me greatly since to my mind being Ghanaian and African were one and the same thing, especially if the latter category allowed me to celebrate the achievement of all Africans and not just that of my compatriots. The announcement of Soyinka's Nobel Prize in 1986 and of Naguib Mahfouz's in 1988 were for example, met with spontaneous celebrations across campus at Legon and, when in 1990 we learned of Achebe's bad accident that left him paralysed many were those that said a quiet prayer for his recovery. (By the way, prayers had also been said for Nelson Mandela at church every Sunday throughout my time at boarding school. Mandela represented The Prisoner for whom prayers routinely had to be said, along with special ones for the sick, the hungry, our politicians and so on before we could come to thank God for forgiving us our trespasses and delivering us from many evils. It was a Methodist service and the sequence of the prayer was firm and abiding). At Cambridge I never managed to persuade anyone apart from Tim Cribb, my supervisor, with my reasons for pursuing Nigerian literary history and just trudged along making up weaker and weaker excuses as the dissertation progressed. I had started out originally interested in Achebe and it was indeed a lengthy piece on the realism of *Things Fall Apart* that I submitted for my registration at the end of the probationary year of the PhD. The essay opened with an Akan proverb: "No matter how well the hen dances, it cannot please the hawk," which of course was a reprisal of the proverbial knowhow that had originally started out with Achebe in high school.[1] And yet Achebe was in the end only to serve as a gateway for thinking about Nigerian literary history, for he ended up not featuring in the dissertation at all as it came to focus on Rev. Samuel Johnson, Amos Tutuola, Wole Soyinka, Ben Okri and the Yoruba literary tradition.[2]

Later, when I returned as a Lecturer in the Faculty of English, Achebe came to take a completely new turn in concerns. It was teaching the Tragedy paper for the English Tripos that radically transformed my understanding not just of him but of African Literature in general. The Tragedy paper is one of two obligatory papers at the 3rd year of the English Studies at Cambridge and covers all aspects of tragedy from the Greeks to the present day. The Greeks and Shakespeare are obligatory but after that anything can be introduced. And the concept is not restricted exclusively to literature either but encompasses everything from religion, ritual, sociology, economy and politics, each of which has to have some bearing on the literary and aesthetic domains. I still felt that the Tragedy paper was a more comprehensive education for me than it was for my students and I count my entrance into teaching that paper as one of the most significant of my career, even though at the time I spent many sleepless nights wondering what I had gotten myself into. When asked by the amiable Colin Wilcockson, the then Director of Studies in English at Pembroke College if I would like to join him in sharing the teaching of the paper I said yes more out of embarrassment than conviction. At the time the only Greek play I knew in any detail was *Oedipus Rex* and even then the relationship between the structure of the myth and the painful unfolding of Oedipus's self-knowledge that was Sophocles's real object baffled me greatly. It was all I could do in my first year of teaching the paper to remain some five pages ahead of my students, with my notion of what constituted tragedy evolving week by week and changing radically over the decade that I taught it. Perhaps the most significant effect engaging Tragedy was that I came to take seriously Antonio Gramsci's maxim of "Pessimism of the intellect and optimism of the will." I detect a dimension of tragedy in almost everything I have read subsequently, even though I do not allow this understanding to deaden my optimism for living.

Exposing my students to the little that I knew about Tragedy meant crafting a process of restless translation between the Greeks, Shakespeare and African Literature, among many other things. This turned out to be extremely productive for in this way, I managed to see hidden connections between say Soyinka's *Death and the King's Horseman*, Aeschylus's *Prometheus Bound*, Sophocles' *Philoctetes* and Beckett's *Endgame* in terms of the dialectic of stasis and mobility that silently undergirds all these plays yet would have remained invisible if I had not been able to set them each other. Another fascinating thread was the place of anger that is to be found in *Oedipus Rex*, *Coriolanus*, Mahfouz's *Midaq Alley*, and Achebe's *Arrow of God*, for example. In all these works anger is not just a visceral quality shared by all the characters but also seems to harbour a lesson about the constrictions of historical processes that, while invisible, yet generate conditions for the visceral anger in the first place. Such connections were many and completely unplanned and often generated from the quirky creativity of my students. It was also in teaching the Tragedy paper that my old interest in the *chi* concept came to fruition, for it helped me to re-think from an African Literature perspective what might be meant by the contradiction between determinism and free will that was so prominent among the Greeks. I concluded after a while that perhaps the most important epistemological conundrum that a novel like *Things Fall Apart* presents us with has to do with the place of the *chi* in the Igbos' self-perception and the connections that this concept has with the ethos of historical unfoldment that is presented us in the novel. The *chi* concept points to the belief in a personal god, personal fate if you will, but in such a way as to defy easy explanation even to the people of the fictional Umuofia. When Okonkwo's gun goes off at Ogbuefi Ezeudu's funeral and kills the dead man's son to trigger his exile from the clan, it seems that his *chi* began to say "no" to his self-affirming "yes." It raises in a stark way the issue of individual autonomy. Since the *chi* is not a visible physical entity, the culture's understanding of it is expressed through a variety of proverbs and ritual dispositions. But I thought that for the implications of the *chi* to be fully grasped and thus differentiated from Greek concepts of determinism, a whole range of socio-cultural relations had to be understood as laid out in the novel: the hierarchical relations between men and women, the relations of exchange and reciprocity, the link between a proverbial language of cultural certitudes and a rapidly changing world, the economy of exclusions that peripheralise certain constituencies within the culture despite the essentially meritocratic impulses upon which it has been constructed (*osus*, twins, "effeminate" men etc). In other words, Achebe suggests that the question of autonomy as articulated by the *chi* cannot be grasped except through a form of embedding that takes the whole range of possible and potential socio-cultural relations into account.[3]

And yet on closer examination from a different perspective the concept of *chi* in the novel also serves to raise a question about the ultimate unknowability of History. This seems to place the *chi* at a certain remove from the Greek example. The utter elusiveness of the *chi* that we find in *Things Fall Apart* parallels to an uncanny degree the problematic status of the historical processes that affect the culture and lead things to fall apart. When the white man first comes to Umuofia in the form of the early missionaries he is perceived as easily explainable within the conceptual scheme then available within the culture. What are these but a bunch of "clucking hens" as Okonwko asserts derisively? They are *efulefu*, effeminate men who can do no harm and who should either be chased away immediately or just tolerated as a nuisance that would hopefully vanish in due course and without a trace. The Umuofians of course turn out to be tragically wrong. In my view, however, the significance of their misinterpretation is not that they failed to recognize History when it walked into their midst in the form of the white man, but that this potential for misrecognition inheres in any human encounter with universal historical processes as such. For the universal is a deception until after it successfully gains a society's acquiescence through the defeat of alternatives that are set up against it. This is far from straightforward, and sometimes requires bloodshed. But the universal is more subtle and insidious when it does not require bloodshed but conscripts historical processes themselves to gain it dominance. In the novel the ultimate unknowability of historical processes as they unfold is paralleled by the elusiveness of the *chi* concept. There is a certain homology in the discursive conceptual structure of the novel that is only discernible when the *chi* is seen as the parallel of the unknowable face of a tragic History. For Aristotle this tragic face is revealed through the sudden *peripateia* (reversal) of the hero or heroine's fortunes but which for the truly complex tragic plot has to be tied to *anagnorisis* (recognition/knowledge). For Achebe, on the other hand, the face of tragic history is encapsulated in the *chi*'s unanticipated no to the hero's insistent yes that is revealed first as an accident (the shooting of Ezeudu's son) and then as an irritating historical wrinkle (the arrival of the Christians). One might venture even further to argue that the *chi* is actually a historicizing concept which the culture, however, deploys to explain personal fortune and culpability rather than wider details of historical process. For, as we see in the novel, all the major thresholds of the plot turn on the actions of the great men in the novel, with Okonkwo at the very epicentre of all such turns. (As an aside, it is important to contrast Achebe's novel to say Tsitsi Dangarembga's *Nervous Conditions* in which, though it also has a rural setting places all the plot thresholds firmly within the domain of the private sphere. If *Things Fall Apart* is an exemplary novel of the public sphere of epic action then *Nervous Conditions* must be driven by the private domain of domesticity. And each has a different and in many respects diametrically opposed conception of historical processes and the protagonists' place in them). Both the *chi* concept and History, then, might be thought to raise identical epistemological questions, the first articulated at the level of the personal, the other at the level of historical unfoldment but both inextricably interconnected.

So far I have conveyed the impression that *Things Fall Apart* was the most important of Achebe's novels for the formation of my own literary compass. However, the compass image also helps me correct this impression, for what has happened over the decades in which I have read and taught his work is that this novel has shifted across its ambit, being central at certain points yet moving steadily and sometimes even suddenly to alter its status as it got recombined with other concerns and interests. This flickering movement has also affected the way I see it in relation to the rest of Achebe's work, to the point that I now boldly join those that declare *Arrow of God* to be his best novel and not *Things Fall Apart*, as might previously have been assumed from what I have said thus far. The shift for me occurred sometime in the last four or five years and with respect to a long-standing interest in the concept of alienation that also developed from my days at Cambridge. My understanding of alienation itself has changed dramatically in this period, but I have settled on it as referring not just to the separation from one's labour (the Marxian view), or the separation from the dominant mores of society (the Werberian view), but rather as generated from the difficulties produced in the way of giving a proper account of oneself.[4] While both Foucault and Judith Butler have had a hand in this new understanding, it is really my reading of Fanon, especially his *Black Skin, White Masks*, that brought the matter to some clarity for me. In brief, alienation entails the contamination of the instruments by which one might provide a coherent account of oneself. This contamination is potentially produced by various factors, among which might be included the historical contradictions generated by the encounter between a culture and its negation (colonialism, military invasion, etc.), the rise of internal constituencies that were hitherto marginalized and supressed and the recognition that the cultural past no longer provides a viable prologue for understanding the personal and/or collective future. Critical to my notion of alienation is that these contradictions have to be felt in the mind of the protagonist and must generate a certain degree of ambiguity with respect to their culture. And the ambiguity must be such that it produces two warring kinds of absolutes: one to do with acquiescence and the other to do with critical inquiry but held together in an unresolvable bind. Finally, the ambiguity produces a problem of moral choice, for it is no longer self-evident what the terms of ethical action might be without serious and sometimes even devastating consequences for the self. My interest in alienation has developed alongside a larger interest with the relationship between literary history and history itself, particularly since I moved to the University of Toronto and began working on diaspora and transnational studies. With these emerging concerns, *Arrow of God* has come to provide a much richer entry into the questions than has *Things Fall Apart*, highlighting for me also the much more sophisticated fit between the objective world of social facts and the internal workings of the protagonist's consciousness. While Okonkwo is clearly a vividly conceived character, the one thing he rarely displays in the course of the novel is any form of internal contradiction. This is definitely not the case with his equally vividly conceived counterpart Ezeulu in *Arrow of God.* Like *Things Fall Apart Arrow of God* also has a largely rural setting but the story is placed in a period of colonialism among the Igbo much later than what we find in the earlier novel. And yet at the same time nothing could be more different than in the earlier offering. To Umuofia's unanimism is set Umuaro's lack of communal consensus. In place of Okonkwo, "a man who was well known throughout the nine villages and even beyond" (3) is contrasted Ezeulu, Chief Priest of Ulu who though also well-known throughout the six tribes that make up Umuaro is from the start met with a mixture of reluctant respect and uncomprehending revulsion by his own people. And the Chief Priest does not love them unconditionally either. It is the way in which *Arrow of God* thematises transition and assimilates its vagaries to the consciousness of Ezeulu that registers the novel as a supreme example of the literature of alienation.

The complex set of events that lead to Ezeulu's invitation by the white district commissioner to become a Warrant Chief and his outright refusal serve to focus the entire apparatus of ambiguation that is expressed at various points in the novel. When early on the clan ignore his advice and send out an irascible emissary who provokes war with Okperi the white man steps in, collects all their guns and destroys them, by this earning for himself the redoubtable epithet of "Breaker of Guns." When Captain Wintabota (Winterbottom) tries to ascertain the cause of the war between the people of Umuaro and Okperi, Ezeulu is the only truthsayer, telling Captain Wintabota the facts of the matter according to his perspective. Ezeulu's testimony is responsible for Wintabota deciding the case in favour of Okperi. Rumours after that are that Ezeulu has become the white man's "friend" and some powerful elders of the clan progressively distance themselves from him to the point where towards the end of the novel when he is invited by Wintabota to Okperi for a consultation, his elders can barely conceal their disgust. "Now it is not clear to me whether it is wrong for a man to ask his friend to visit him. When we have a feast do we not send for our friends in other clans to come and share it with us and do they not also ask us to their own celebrations?. . . Or does Ezeulu think that their friendship should stop short of entering each other's houses?" (143) are what Nwaka, thorn in Ezeulu's flesh from the very beginning, asks on this occasion. Ezeulu's implacable disdain for the self-made Nwaka and indeed those that follow him in the clan is balanced by his absolute dedication to the service of their collective god Ulu. His admiration of the white man's mission school, to which he sends his youngest son Uduche as his "eyes and ears" and earns himself further enmity, is a purely pragmatic measure of counter-surveillance so he can know and anticipate what the white man is bringing to his world. When on his arrival at Okperi, he is offered the opportunity to be crowned chief of his traditionally acephalous society as part of the well-known and highly controversial colonial policy of Indirect Rule, Ezeulu's response is quick and unequivocal: he does not serve anyone but Ulu. He is promptly thrown into jail for his troubles. Whilst shunning the profane incredulity of the white man Ezeulu preoccupies himself with planning a terrible punishment for his people in reaction to their derisive and sceptical to his predicament. In this he makes the serious mistake of extrapolating from the mischievous indifference of the elders of Umuaro to generalize the fate of all his people, something for which he is made to suffer at the end of the novel. Ezeulu has been shown throughout to be an anchorite, alone with the burden of comprehending the complex nature of his sacred mission alongside the historical transformations that are taking place in his clan. As the novel unfolds he recognizes that his solitude is not a mere necessity enjoined by his priestly vocation but that limitations have been set on the actions and judgments of the priesthood of Ulu due to the changes in opinion that have taken place within his society. Ezeulu recognizes that the power of instituting social reform that had been the purview of his grandfather had by his own day contracted to the mere tending of the rituals of Ulu, an intolerable abbreviation of his own identification as Chief Priest and servant of the god and his people. While in the white man's jail he has a nightmare in which first his grandfather and then he are almost lynched by the elders of the clan. The historical diminution in the social role of the priesthood is registered for Ezeulu almost as a psychosomatic re-ordering of his very being. Thus when he reflects upon the unsettled position he now seems to occupy among the tribes he is frequently stung by anger, as though by a "black ant" (*Arrow of God* 3; also 159-161). His reaction is simultaneously psychological *and* physical. Thus the ambit of ethical judgment (is it right to go to war, to inform on his people to the white man, or to respond to the white man's invitation to become a chief?) is intricately tied to questions of action but in such a way as to ensure that any action that he might undertake will, while seeming authentic in his own eyes, remain decisively inauthentic in the eyes of his own people. His existential condition is that of being the victim of an alienating world whilst being a central and indispensable part of it.

And thus it is that the old order changeth, yielding place to the new. But at each stage of evolution as a literary scholar the work has been there somewhere, ebbing and flowing in and out of my interests and helping to continually order and re-order my sensibilities. To close, another proverb of his: "He who has people is richer than he who has money." I have Achebe.

Chapter Forty-Six

# An Entire Star Has Left Us

## Chinua Achebe, *In Memoriam*

*Tijan M. Sallah*

I will miss Chinua Achebe. His passing away is as if an entire constellation-star has collapsed. It is monumental, weighty, concerning, depriving and sad.

It is monumental because it is difficult to imagine African literature without Achebe. He was one of African literature's most ardent champions and undoubtedly one of its great contemporary voices. Achebe is by no means the first African novelist; there have been antecedent novelists like the South African Thomas Mofolo, who wrote *Pitseng* (1910) and *Chaka* (1925). He is not the first Nigerian novelist; there has been Amos Tutuola, who wrote *The Palm Wine Drinkard* (1953), which the Irish poet, Dylan Thomas, described as a "grisly and bewitching story, written in young English by a West African." Dylan Thomas was alluding, in typical imperial condescension, to Tutuola's story being "primitive" and his English as "young" – it still had some way to grow. If one goes narrower, Achebe is not even the first Igbo novelist; there has been Peter Nwana, who wrote *Omenuko* (1933) in Igbo, which won the all-Africa contest in indigenous African languages. Achebe is not even the first Igbo novelist who wrote in English; there has been Cyprian Ekwensi, who published *People of the City* (1954). The significance of Achebe, I would argue, is that he was a cultural revolutionary figure in the same way that Einstein was revolutionary for science. He led a paradigm change in African literature, which was that Africans did not have to imitate Europeans to tell their own stories. They could use European languages to expand their audience base, but they must tell their stories as Africans in the same way that Europeans tell their stories as Europeans. Chinweizu and his Bolekaja group of critics put it succinctly: "And Achebe's *Things Fall Apart* was, as he himself has often said, a deliberate (and successful effort) to recreate a pre-Westernized African reality, using authentic Igbo characters, situations, values and religious concepts, bending the English Language to express Igbo proverbs and idioms (*Towards the Decolonization of African Literature*, pp. 288–289)". Achebe set the foundations for an African storytelling that was to be done as simply and unapologetically truthful as possible, drawing on the rich repertoire of Africa's traditions and environment and using and bending European languages only as tools to facilitate the conveying of our stories, but not getting trapped or seduced by their self-alienating aspects.

And there rests the monumental greatness of Achebe. That a young man in his late twenties in 1958 would, through the singular effort of his first novel, *Things Fall Apart*, eclipse artistically all his predecessors and switch the curiosity of a world that has been long accustomed to Europeans or Arabs defining Africans, to Africans now defining themselves with a language that was laced with existential profundity, marrying comedy and tragedy and conveying deep oral traditional richness. Achebe has often said that one of the things he has tried to do in his work was to switch Europe's long domineering monologue into a dialogue. Europe has been talking, talking for a long time. Europe has been talking to non-Europeans everywhere and often talking down to them. Europe has been interpreting the histories of non-Europeans and defining others through its self-aggrandizing frame of reference. Achebe saw this as problematic. The rest of the world did not only have ears to take orders, they also had mouths to express themselves. It was important to force Europe to pause from its long, uninterrupted speech and listen. Achebe's *Things Fall Apart* was a brave and successful effort in that direction. It was the Empire writing back. It was the Empire speaking back not as a defensive response as Negritude uncritically became but as a parallel conversation. You have your stories; we have ours. We can learn from each other's stories.

Many Africans identify with Okonkwo, Achebe's tragic protagonist, in *Things Fall Apart*, because Okonkwo spoke something deep about African's inner sensibilities. He stood up for the right to defend the indigenous autochtonous. He remained firm, despite the fact that his village accommodated and made compromises with the invader and eventually abandoned him in the lurch. Although Achebe sees Okonkwo's inflexibilities to adapt to the intrusion of empire as what eventually led to his downfall, he makes us love and admire this indigenous hero. He eulogizes Okonkwo through Obierika, "That man was one of the greatest men of Umuofia. You drove him to kill himself and now he will be buried like a dog…" Colonialism reversed the social order of indigenous African communities; the great got socially demoted and the not-so-great got elevated. Colonialism also injured the African mind and spirit, but Africa is far too resilient to go down. Africans have cultural roots deep as the Baobab's. They mustered the ability to heal and rebuild. Speech was part of the rebuilding. Achebe's storytelling was, in short, that of a freedom fighter. Like the Jamaican Reggae world Star, Bob Marley, who surreptitiously graced us in his songs, "Get up, Stand Up. Stand Up for Your Rights," Achebe graced us in his stories to speak out about what is valuable in our midst.

Achebe is monumental because he believed in speech – especially by and for Africans and saw how peoples who are speech-deprived or have others speaking on their behalf can find themselves mentally slaving in the alphabet soup of the dispossessor. All free peoples have to reclaim their stories and speak for themselves. Achebe was clear about this in his 2002 speech as winner of the German Peace Prize, awarded by the German Book Trade. He concluded: "The Africa I write about is not inhabited by people without speech. I grew up hearing sometimes magnificent and always efficient, language in my community. I did not hear the grunts and the screeches that savages were supposed to use instead of speech. So I wrote what I did hear, in a translation that accorded equal respect to the two languages I have." (p. 42, Literature and Peace). And Achebe is right. My people, the Wolof, have a saying, "*Wakh moi nit*" or literarily, "Speech is the person."

It is irrefutable that the whole project of empire was partly based on the propagation of myths of superiority through stories and partly on deeds, some of it based on violence or the threat of violence in the event of native resistance. Natives were classified into a hierarchy of beings. Those with written narratives were superior to those strictly oral. The latter were considered primitive and without history. Hugh Trevor-Roper, then Regius Professor of History at Oxford, one of the more learned men of Europe at the time was not learned enough to give Africa its due appraisal. The manuscripts of the civilizations of ancient Mali/Timbuktu, the *Kibre Negest* and other geis manuscripts of Ethiopia, etc., were all not within his zone of awareness, or were deliberately ignored, to result in his ignorant assertion in his 1964 book, *The Rise of Christian Europe*: "Undergraduates, seduced, as always, by the changing breath of journalistic fashion, demand that they should be taught the history of black Africa. Perhaps, in the future, there will be some African history to teach. But at present there is none, or very little: there is only the history of Europeans in Africa. The rest is largely darkness... And darkness is not a subject for history." (Trevor-Roper, p. 9)

Trevor-Roper did not moderate his sins with informed scholarship; he rode on his imperial high-horse with the scholarship of a maxim gun: "If all history is equal... we may neglect our own history and amuse ourselves with the unrewarding gyrations of barbarous tribes in picturesque but irrelevant corners of the globe..." (Trevor-Roper, p. 9). But, in retrospect, should we not amuse ourselves with the scholarship of Trevor-Roper? For, if scholarship is about truth finding and truth telling, should it not have occurred to a seemingly bright mind as Trevor-Roper to search deeper for evidence to back his arguments? Is scholarship about making untutored speculative claims? The magnificence of Achebe is that he challenged such European storytellers and mythmakers as Hugh Trevor-Roper, Joseph Conrad, Count Gobineau and Hegel. They were bright men but limited by the prejudices of their education and their environment. They were raised during the period of the great European imperialisms and bought into the imperial project; hence they became facilitators or propagators of narratives of denigration of the "other." They spread not truth and understanding but self-serving narratives and myths of cultural superiority.

I will miss Achebe because his passing away is weighty. Achebe is not, by any means, a prolific writer; 5 novels and 1 collection of short stories is a lean harvest for a major writer. However, Achebe's achievement is not in the quantity of his oeuvres but in their quality. I have noted in our biography on him, *Chinua Achebe: Teacher of Light*, that his works are, "deceptively simple and accessible and so richly interlaced with Igbo proverbs that they have the rare classical elegance of Biblical parables." Achebe saw himself first and foremost as a teacher, but not your "beat me down" teacher of today's crash schools but a great teacher, like a Gandhi or Confucius, of African and Developing World literatures. This is because of the sheer moral weight of Achebe's literary productions. Achebe's writings have an enduring, pedagogic quality. My good friend, the late Professor Emmanuel Obiechina (Achebe's friend also) and one of the most humble and decent Nigerians I have ever encountered once remarked to me about the weight of Achebe's moral authority in the popular discourse of Nigerians; "Many a time in popular palaver that only Nigerians know how – Chinua Achebe is quoted to support or illustrate a point. His words are like the palm oil with which words are eaten."

Achebe's contribution to early development of modern African literature is not only qualitatively enormous, but hinges on the legendary. When his first novel, *Things Fall Apart*, made a breakthrough with Heinemann publishers in 1958, Heinemann made him the founding editor of the Heinemann African Writers Series, in which he oversaw the development of the entire African continent's literature. He edited the first 100 titles. His enormous self-sacrifice in reviewing and commenting on even the worst manuscripts took much valuable time from his own creative work, but undoubtedly helped in the shaping of the continent's literature. Even after editing his last title for Heinemann, Achebe continued to mentor and encourage young writers through his University of Nigeria-Nsukka literary publication, *Okike* and other avenues. As Achebe became an elder and began to cope with a debilitating physical condition, he began to understandably cut down on his social engagements. In 2003, I made a phone request to Achebe about writing a blurb for a promising first novel by a young Nigerian novelist. In his characteristic polite and forthright manner, Achebe replied, "Thank you. But I have already done my national service." We laughed over the matter – especially the use of the term "national service" –reflecting the mandatory youth service by the Nigerian government. I reflected on the response and said, yes, he was right. He had sacrificed enough in the course of Africa's literary good and it was his time to rest. Others now needed to step in and fill the void.

Achebe's legendary status accompanied the popularity of his novels. I recall a two-hour evening encounter with the Egyptian Arab and winner of the 1988 Nobel Laureate, Naguib Mahfouz in 1998 at Farah Boat in Cairo, Egypt. The meeting was organized by Amr Shaarawi, Professor of Electrical Engineering at Cairo University, who had been a graduate school friend of mine. Amr, I later learned, was the grandson of Huda Shaarawi, the first Egyptian woman feminist to remove the veil. Huda Shaarawi has a street named after her near the currently fabled pro-democratic protests venue, Tahrir Square. In any case, when we met Mahfouz, he wore dark glasses and seemed to continuously smile and stare up, in the manner of African American singer Ray Charles, as if he was blind. I asked Mahfouz whether he was familiar with African literature south of the Sahara. He gave a bemused response, noting that he remembered in the sixties, when Gamal Abdel Nasser championed Pan Africanism (with his friend Osagyefo Kwame Nkrumah) that he read a fascinating book written by a Nigerian which the translator noted as, "*When Things Go Down.*" He was referring to *Things Fall Apart.* Achebe's novel was famous, even in Egypt. I informed Achebe about this encounter and he seemed amused by the twist in the title of his novel. We laughed about it over the phone.

Achebe's passing away is weighty in another respect. He was not only a great writer; he was a builder of African cultural institutions. In 1989, I received a letter from him, asking me to serve on the Editorial Board of *African Commentary: A Journal of People of African Descent*, a new Pan African magazine that he founded while he was a visiting professor at the University of Massachusetts in Amherst. I accepted the invitation. The core drivers of the magazine were the distinguished Nigerian engineer, Bartholomew Nnaji, who was then Director of the Automation and Robotics Lab at the University of Massachussetts – - and who later became the Minister of Science and Technology in the short-lived Nigeria government of Ernest Shonekan and then subsequently served as Minister of Energy in the Federal government of President Goodluck Jonathan. Bart Nnaji had been a graduate school colleague and friend. The editorial board also included the journalist, Okey Ndibe; Chudi Uwazurike, Obi Nnaemeka; John Maxwell; Michael Mbabuike and C. Don Adinuba and such intellectual/public heavyweights as columnists: Ali A. Mazrui, Dennis Brutus, A.M. Babu, Leonard Jeffries, Nadine Gordimer,

Olusegun Obasanjo; Michael Thelwell, Chinweizu, Ibrahim Gambari and Fela Anikulapo-Kuti. What was Achebe's vision with this magazine, which had debut editions pitched at such high level of journalism and so impressive that the magazine was even compared to *The New Yorker*? Achebe's vision for the magazine was part Africa gloriana, part restoration, but more importantly it was a forum for Africans and people of African descent to reflect and devise joint solutions to the current ills confronting the continent. Achebe's editorial in the debut edition sums it all up:

> Africa is more than a geographic reality; it is a spiritual phenomenon, born truly enough, of a painful history – the history of slavery – but it is a history which binds every Black person to Africa. It is for this reason that *African Commentary* is 'a journal of people of African descent' – whether they are African Americans, or Africans in Europe, the Caribbean, or in the homeland.
>
> It is not too long to the 21st Century: we are indeed running out of time. The goal of *African Commentary* is, in part, to ensure that Africa and the rest of the Black world step into the next century, with dignity and a restored sense of initiative. In the decades since many African nations became independent, the question of forging African unity has often been raised and sabotaged by African leaders themselves. With just about ten years to the 21st Century, it is clear for us that Africa cannot make it on the individual steam of the diverse countries.
>
> *African Commentary* is committed to reclaiming the rich heritage of Africa and re-drawing the contours of African history. Beyond reclaiming the African past, the pages of African Commentary will be open to some of the best minds in Africa and the Black world to ponder the question of Africa's and its descendants place in the world today.

With this preamble, Achebe was on an ambitious intellectual project. The high quality of the essays in the magazine were difficult to sustain without resources. Unfortunately, *African Commentary* lasted between1989–1992 and then morphed into *African World* in 1993 and then went defunct due to inadequate funding. The thin subscription base, the weak advertisement mobilization and the inability to develop an endowment aborted its growth.

The bug to build cultural institutions, however, has continued in Achebe's eldest son, Ike, a Cambridge University doctorate, who has quietly continued to do many important cultural projects for the development of Africa. Ike, for example, was a major force in having Rosen Publishing House of New York start the Library of African Peoples, a series of monographs on Africa's major ethnic groups targeted at young adults. In fact, through Ike's foresight, I was asked and I wrote an ethnography on the Wolof peoples of Senegal and the Gambia, which appeared in the Rosen series. Moreover, Ike has been busy developing the Chinua Achebe Foundation as well as leading a project for the preparation of an Igbo Archival Dictionary. Although funding for this has been tough to come by, Ike has been persistent and is slowly making headway.

It has been my puzzle about Africa about how so little Africans with money support the development of African cultural institutions. Whereas America, in its early development, has seen the Vanderbilts, the Dukes, the Carnegies, the Mellons, the Fords and the Rockefellers use their largesse to support higher educational, scientific and artistic institutions; in Africa, the capitalist class has continued to be largely and shortsightedly parasitic and only a few are visionary and philanthropic. One could point to a few like the late Nigerian Chief Bashorun Abiola, who financed African magazines, such as the *African Concord* and supported chairs in universities and lectureships in academic associations, such as the African Studies Association and perhaps, the Sudanese Mo Ibrahim, who sponsors the Mo Ibrahim Index and governance indicators and the Mo Ibrahim Prize for African leaders who practice good governance and exit power voluntarily. But even these well-meaning efforts can be questioned. Why do Mo Ibrahim and other monied Africans like him not use their money to support African thinkers, writers, scientists; that is – have an African Nobel, rather than give this money to African leaders who are at the very heart of Africa's contemporary problems? Why does Africa's rich not use their money to support African publishing to get books written by Africans to African schools? The answer is, of course, it is their money. And I respect that it is their money. Of course, Mo Ibrahim, in particular, is already doing a great job as a philanthropist – we need more like him to perhaps follow that path and fill the vacuum in other areas.

I will miss Achebe because his passing away is worrying. Achebe was an able spokesperson for Africa and he did so with an unrivalled moral authority. On June 17, 1998, we invited him to give a James D. Wolfensohn Presidential Lecture at the World Bank. Before his invitation, Nigeria's current Finance Minister, Ngozi Okonjo-Iweala, who was then a Director in the World Bank and I conspired to make the case that Achebe be invited. Initially, the Pakistani Tariq Hussain, who was then in charge of the Presidential Lecture series, was ambivalent, wondering how a writer might fare in an environment of hard-nosed bankers. Achebe proved him wrong and vindicated us. He came and gave a lecture titled, "Africa is People" and the room was packed to standing room capacity. Even President Wolfensohn, so amazed by the attendance, quipped, "With this, maybe you should be president." And Achebe gave a brilliant speech. He argued for the cancellation of debt owed by the poorest countries. He also argued for the World Bank to convince commercial institutions of the developed world to return stolen wealth stashed away by corrupt leaders from developing countries. He cited Wolfensohn's statistic, "You will be staggered to know, as I was, that 37 per cent of African private wealth is held outside of Africa, whereas for Asia, the share is 3 per cent and for Latin America, it is 17 per cent." Achebe went on to note: "It would be a great pity if the world were to sit back in the face of this tragedy and do nothing, merely to preserve codes of banking etiquette and confidentially formulated for quite other times." Achebe was making a revolutionary plea and Wolfensohn sympathized with the message and indeed did take heed later to champion a debt cancellation/forgiveness initiative known as the Highly Indebted Poor Countries (HIPC) initiative and also the Stolen Asset Recovery Initiative (STAR), from which many African countries benefitted.

Achebe was a man of integrity. I will give one anecdote that startled me. In 1996, the Indian economist, Ajay Chhibber was leading a team of World Bank economists to produce the 1997 World Development Report, titled, *The State in a Changing World.* The World Development Report (WDR) is the most important publication annually by the World Bank. Ajay Chhibber, knowing my connections with Achebe, asked me to approach him to write a paragraph on his thoughts about the "state" in Africa. Chhibber had read Achebe's *The Trouble with Nigeria* and was impressed by its self-indicting sober wisdom. Chhibber promised to pay US$5,000 for the paragraph. I took up the mission and approached Achebe tactfully – first, explaining the WDR and second, making the request. Achebe responded, in his usual polite, but frank manner: "Well, thank you for thinking about me. Sometimes you have to learn to say – no. Aha… But thank you for thinking about me…" I conveyed the response to Chhibber, but reflected that this was a man who believed in his word. He was not ready to sell it for a quick buck. Also, in many a conversation with Achebe on the phone about publishing, he would despairingly comment that; "publishing has been taken over by bookkeepers." He felt that over obsession with what sells has taken many a publishing house on the wrong path of not taking up valuable material, but material that would generate the quick buck. He would nostalgically recount his early days with Heinemann when publishers took interest in both the writer and the work.

I will miss Achebe because his passing away is depriving and sad. His life was a consequential life – which deeply touched many – and offended few. I have tried in this paper not to rehash too much of the existing literature on Achebe for his writings have spawned an entire industry. I have tried, instead, only to recount a few memorable anecdotes and encounters.

I will miss Achebe – our brother, our teacher. My feelings about his passing are best described in verse below. May the wisdom he has left us be the pillow of peace on which his soul rests.

## Dear Teacher

Dear Teacher
As we ponder your Exit;
We know a weighty star in our sky has left us.
Our bruised hopes seek your soaring light,
At the edge of clouds. We stare. We mourn.

Dear teacher, it cannot be the same.
You were the luminous light from Ogidi.
We drew to you because we believed your lore.
In this, our twilight of loss, that Fate,
So cruel, stole you, when unexpected.

We will remember you for your dreams to make Africa fly.
Your light to illuminate the untruths about Africa.
We will remember your integrity and your spine.

Now that you are suddenly gone, dear brother,
Who will tell us where the rain began to beat us?
Who will give us cultural hope to overcome our impediments?

Dear teacher, now that we have lost you,
Someone else must bear your weight.
And, now, as we ponder your Exit.
A heavy sadness squats in our hearts.
We will not let it go –
Until Africa awakes to your wisdom.

Chapter Forty-Seven

# Chinua Achebe's Legacy*

*Véronique Tadjo*

I saw Chinua Achebe at various conferences on African literature but always from a distance. The last time was in 2008. He was led onto the platform by his son who pushed him in a wheelchair onto the stage to a welcoming standing ovation even before he had said a word. Just seeing him there, his face was radiant and there was warmth emanating from his presence. He read from his work in a careful and soft voice yet totally assured. He laughed easily. After the event, he went on to autograph his books. The public immediately surrounded him, like a movie star, everybody trying to get his attention. The signing went on for such a long time that he literally had to be extracted from the crowd and taken to the private function that had been organized in his honour.

For me, Achebe was not only an accomplished writer but also a man who was close to his readers and who had the precious gift of being a wonderful communicator. You did not feel that he was talking down at you, on the contrary, that he was talking to *you*.

In his writing, it was also the same. His language was accessible to all, yet powerful. His use of Igbo words in his narratives revolutionized our relationship with our linguistic heritage from colonization. He showed us that art was universal and that no language was private property; that languages were rather tools that could be used by anybody who wished to in order to render his or her contemporary experience. No big theories with Achebe but an approach to life that was down to earth and constructive. He was deeply rooted in his African culture and at the same time a citizen of the world able to look at his own culture, history and society with the distance necessary to be a great writer.

He created complex characters – neither just bad nor good; neither just strong nor weak. He chose to emphasize their human traits above all. For him fiction had a level of truth which was more profound than journalism or history.

I discovered Chinua Achebe's writing when I as a schoolgirl in Abidjan in Côte d'Ivoire. *Things Fall Apart* translated into French formed part of our curriculum. The story of Okonkwo, the protagonist had resonance in our lives, not just because Nigeria is our big neighbour, but mainly because we could identify with the characters in the novel. In the story, Okonkwo lives in a village very similar to the villages that existed in many parts of Africa and especially in West Africa. The conflict between tradition and modernity was predominant in our part of the world, too. Even though I lived in the capital city, I had ample opportunities to go to my father's village where I could experience rural life and observe the rapid transformation that was going on there. Yet, like many of my friends we thought the pace of change was too slow. But one thing was for sure, our life was a constant battle with compromise, trying to find a balance between our grandparents' past and our parents' present. We did not know how much faster we could go. Nevertheless, we knew instinctively that it would fall on us, very soon, to assess our cultural heritage and decide what we should keep and what we should abandon. At stake was our position in "The world arena" or as Léopold Sédar Senghor, the great Senegalese poet of the Negritude movement used to call it, "The concert of nations."

The French translation of *Things Fall Apart* was brought out in 1966 by Présence Africaine in Paris and very quickly it also became a classic in our part of the world. Présence Africaine was a Pan African cultural, political and literary review founded in 1947 by Alioune Diop, a Senegalese writer and professor of Philosophy. He collaborated closely with writers and thinkers from Africa, Europe and the US among whom were the two founders of the Negritude movement, Léopold Sédar Senghor and Aimé Césaire. A publishing house and a bookstore were later added. As a literary review, Présence Africaine was highly influential in the struggle for decolonisation from France. The ambition of its editors was to create a platform of expression, using literature as a cultural weapon against colonial oppression.

In 1956, Présence Africaine organised the First International Congress of Black Writers and Artists (Premier Congrès international des écrivains et artistes noirs) in Paris. Jacques Rabémananjara, Cheikh Anta Diop and Frantz Fanon joined the other writers of the Négritude movement; and Pablo Picasso, who had been interested in African art since before World War I, designed the poster for the occasion. In this spirit, Présence published the most important Francophone African writers of the 20th Century and were pioneers in bringing out French translations of the works of Anglophone writers such as Wole Soyinka and Ngũgĩ wa Thiong'o in addition to Chinua Achebe and other key Lusophone writers.

Senghor, who was one of the originators of the concept of Négritude, defined it as "the totality of the values – economic and political, intellectual and moral, artistic and social – not only of the peoples of Black Africa, but also of those of the minorities of Black America and even of Asia and the Ocean islands" (Biondi, 146, my translation). His conception of Négritude was different from that of Aimé Césaire, who was known to be more radical in his fight against French racism and imperialism. His long poem *Return to my Native Land* is a perfect illustration of his revolutionary writing. Senghor was more preoccupied with the meeting of cultures and the idea of universality. However, both agreed that their shared black heritage was a rallying force in the fight against French political, economic and intellectual oppression.

To my mind this literary movement among Francophone Africans and their supporters applies to *Things Fall Apart* as well. On numerous occasions, Achebe has stated that, at the time (the fifties) his intention in writing the book was a response to European cultural domination. For him, a novel like *Heart of Darkness* by Joseph Conrad "projects the image of Africa as the 'other world,' the antithesis of Europe and therefore of civilization, a place where man's vaunted intelligence and refinement are finally mocked by triumphant bestiality" (*Hopes…* 3). *Things Fall Apart* successfully challenges the colonialist discourse of the time by showing the complexity and richness of Igbo life and customs. Achebe sought to put an end to a Eurocentric way of telling Africa's story. The novel takes place at that moment in the 19th Century which marked the end of one time and the beginning of another.

In this sense, one can say that the importance of *Things Fall Apart* lies in the fact that it is a text grounded in paradox. Indeed, Achebe's novel is striking for its realistic style, which is rooted in a specific historical and social context to such extent that it could be considered as a documentary or an eyewitness's account of traditional Africa and of Igbo culture in particular.

The village of Umuofia located in Igboland where the story takes place is a world unto itself. It appears totally cut off from the outside world having its own rules, laws and religion. In this closed environment, Okwonko lives entirely for his clan, seeing himself as a defender of his society against outside influences. Yet despite this very specific, localised subject matter, the novel has been translated into more than fifty languages and has sold over twelve million copies worldwide. As a result, it can be claimed that, more than any other novel, *Things Fall Apart*, illustrates that art is a universal medium.

The paradox here is that the more you dive into a particular culture, the more it is possible to attain a universal level of meaning because the human dimension needs truth and authenticity to be fully realized. Okwonko exemplifies the tragedy of transition, of the old order being replaced by the new. Every society has experienced this situation at some point or the other.

What we are as human beings is defined by our past. But what is left of it? The precolonial African way of life is no more. In *Things Fall Apart* we become, as readers, the witnesses of this destruction.

But the novel is also remarkable because it recounts the downfall of Okonkwo, an ambitious man who all his life strove to become influential in his society, but who was ultimately defeated by his own demons and ended up miserable and rejected by his clan. Underestimating the apocalyptic clash of civilization brought by the arrival of Europeans and of the Christian religion, he stuck to the old ways even when they did not make sense anymore in the new order.

The worldwide success of this novel is unmistakably due to yet another factor: Achebe's creative use of language. In an interview, he stated: "When I decided to write a novel which would deal with the colonizing presence of Britain in my life and in my country, I realized I had to start a conversation between these two languages, which is how the book was conceived. I knew that in some way the meeting of these two languages would define my literary identity (Interview). Achebe freely uses untranslated Igbo words and phrases. In *Things Fall Apart* one of the characters Okoye speaks in proverbs and explains the Igbo art of communication in these terms: "… proverbs are the palm-oil with which words are eaten" (4). Achebe uses the same principle in his writing in order to better render the flavour of Igbo society and culture. "In fact, it is not one language – English – that Achebe uses but a series of languages with which he explores new frontiers. He does that in order to accommodate new realities in the social experience." (Anohu 9)

Although English was the language of the colonialists, Achebe understood the power of the English language as a weapon in furthering Africa's agenda. Through his inclusion of proverbs, folktales and songs translated from the Igbo language, Achebe managed to capture and convey the rhythms, structures, cadences and beauty of the Igbo language. His approach was revolutionary and it brought about a real liberation of the English language from the shackles of its oppressive historical past as a medium for change.

It is interesting to note that during the Négritude movement, language was also at the heart of the issue of liberation and Senghor and Césaire had a strong bond with words. Having chosen French as their medium of expression they used it in a very personal and imaginative way bending it to serve their purpose. It gave rise to a powerful new form of language, combative for Césaire and lyrical for Senghor.

Then, when most of the former French colonies became independent in the sixties, it was a time of euphoria and great hope for the future of Africa. Less than a decade later, however, a period of disillusion followed. Neocolonialism took hold of most economies and the political elites proved too greedy to honour the promises they had made at independence. Military dictatorship governments rose in Sub Saharan Africa and the novel that best illustrates this post-independence disenchantment in francophone Africa is without doubt, *Les soleils des indépendances* (*The Suns of Independence*) by Ahmadou Kourouma from Côte d'Ivoire. When Kourouma submitted his manuscript for publication, it was refused by publishers in both France and Africa on the grounds that it was written in "incorrect" French. The manuscript found itself passed around before it ended up in Canada where it was finally published in 1968. It became an instant bestseller and was subsequently bought by a prestigious Parisian publisher, Le Seuil, in 1970. Cheaper editions were produced for the African market and the book was read by millions of school children as part of the syllabus for decades where it is still being taught today.

What was revolutionary in Kourouma's novel was the fact that for the first time a writer attempted to recreate the way common people really expressed themselves in Africa. He fused French with his Malinke mother tongue. French syntax and grammar were twisted and some words took on a whole new meaning. His language ignored basic rules. The style was exuberant and full of raw sensuality. With this book, Kourouma showed that French wasn't just the language of the former oppressors but that it could also be used to serve our purposes and render our contemporary African experience. Achebe's "conversation" between the English language and Igbo defined a new literary identity for the generations of African writers that followed. Achebe left us with an important message: every writer who uses a European language in an innovative way reveals to the whole world the richness of his or her cultural heritage in its capacity to reshape a given medium.

In reference to the more recent argument of Ngũgĩ wa Thiong'o in *Decolonising the Mind* (2006) which says that there is nothing "African" in contemporary African literature because it is written in European languages, Achebe has stated his position clearly:

"Theatricalities aside, the difference between Ngũgĩ and myself on the issue of indigenous or European languages for African writers is that while Ngũgĩ now believes it is *either/or*, I have always thought it was *both*" (Achebe 97).

For Achebe, it is only through a creative use of language that a writer can begin to approach "truth." And in his case, this search led him to tell the story of Igbo traditional society in all its grandeur as well as in all its weakness. Many critics have pointed out Achebe's courage as a writer because he chose to include in his story the dark side of Igbo customs. If he was skillful enough not to turn this into a denunciation, he was nevertheless clear-sighted in his portrayal of the village of Umuofia with some of its gruesome ritual killings and negative beliefs. At no time does Achebe fall into a nostalgic recounting of the past. This is unusual because occupying such a position at the time required a *distancing* much more difficult to achieve than today.

Okonkwo is a tragic figure whose weakness lies in his inability to understand the winds of change. He wages havoc in his society because of his intransigence and refusal to bring about the necessary changes that could have saved his society from defeat and domination. Had he been a different kind of hero, he would have been able to integrate the new and to make it work for the good of the community.

When I look back at my own life as a writer, I can say that *Things Fall Apart* was a great inspiration as far as my work is concerned. It was certainly at the back of my mind when in 2006, I wrote my novel, *Reine Pokou* (*Queen Pokou*). It is the retelling of a well-known legend/myth. Pokou was the founder of the Baoulé kingdom located in present-day Côte d'Ivoire. According to the 18th Century legend the queen, originally from the Ashanti kingdom (present-day Ghana), had to sacrifice her only son in order to save her people from a fratricidal war. The kingdom was named after the words Ba-ou-li, (the child is dead) pronounced by the sorrow-stricken queen.

This being said, as a woman writer/reader I found *Things Fall Apart* a bit problematic in some aspects. Okonkwo, Achebe's most famous character, for example, illustrates varying interpretations of masculinity. Because of his failed relationship with his father whom he considered weak, Okonkwo adopts a violent and harsh manner towards people he perceives as being in a lower position than him. Consequently, he rejects anything that might appear feminine or too compassionate. Masculinity is therefore linked with force and brute authority. He beats his wives and even threatens to kill the youngest in fits of rage because she has been "unruly." Moreover, Okonkwo chooses to participate in the ritual killing of the boy who, over time, had become like an adoptive son to him. He even gives him the fatal blow so as to avoid being seen as too soft or showing signs of vulnerability. In this sense, Pokou, by committing an infanticide, is not unlike Okonkwo who as a leader and an influential person in his community who bows to tradition and does what is expected of him instead of bringing much needed reforms.

It is fitting to conclude with the words of Chinua Achebe himself with a quote from his collection of essays *Hopes and Impediments,* published in 1988:

"The matter is really quite simple. Literature, whether handed down by word of mouth or in print, gives us a second handle on reality; enabling us to encounter in the safe, manageable dimensions of make-believe the very same threats to integrity that may assail the psyche of real life; and at the same time providing through the self-discovery which it imparts, a veritable weapon for coping with these threats whether they are found in problematic and incoherent selves or in the world around us. What better preparation can a people desire as they begin their journey into the strange, revolutionary world of modernization?" (*Hopes*...170)

Most of us are still in one way or other, in the throes of transformation at the national and/or personal levels of our lives. And this is why Chinua Achebe's work remains so relevant to us. To this we can add, his depiction of what exile really means. When asked during an interview what he missed most about living in the United States, after his tragic car accident, he gave a heartfelt reply:

"What I miss most is a true work atmosphere where everybody would be on the same page. The other day, the mayor of my hometown (in Nigeria) wrote to me to ask if I could help in setting up a new library. Nobody here, in the state of New York is going to come and ask me: 'We are building a new library, can you help us?' What I miss is the fact that I am not where I am most needed." (Interview)

Chapter Forty-Eight

# In Memory of Chinua Achebe

*Patrick Wilmot*

Although Chinua Achebe refused the title of 'Father of African Literature' this does not reduce the importance of his contribution, not just to African, but to world literature. Achebe was a great man and great men are humble, because they do not need to inflate their egos by lies, boasting, pomp or heraldry. Achebe was not just a writer whose words could be understood by children, however.

Like Mandela, Neto, Cabral and Machel, Achebe was a simple man who could be approached by other men, women or children without consideration of rank, status, fame, wealth or reputation. He was one of the greatest writers who ever lived, whose books sold millions of copies, were translated into dozens of languages and he should have added the Nobel Prize to his many honours.

Yet, when I was a very junior lecturer at Ahmadu Bello University in Zaria, Northen Nigeria and sent poems and short stories to *Okike* which he edited at Nsukka, he treated me as an equal, even though I was a complete nonentity. To his students and colleagues in Nigeria and the US, he was simply a man who could be approached and consulted. In a profession where mediocrities preened like divas, he was a rarity.

The stories he published in *Okike* could have encouraged me to take writing more seriously but I was a full time academic and activist and somehow the liberation of Southern and part of West Africa seemed more urgent at the time than becoming a full time writer. But now that I have retired, I hope someday to produce work worthy of his memory and genius.

It is a tribute to his achievements that great writers who followed him acknowledge the debt they owe to his pioneering work. Ngũgĩ wa Thiong'o, Ousmane Sembène, Wole Soyinka, Kofi Awoonor, Dambudzo Marechera and others paid tribute to Achebe through work that highlighted the spiritual magnificence of the African reality and personality. But writers on other continents admired him too.

*Things Fall Apart,* his most famous book, is rightly acclaimed as a masterpiece, a work which will continue to be recognised and appreciated by unknown generations to come, just as the work of Sophocles, Shakespeare and Pushkin continue to dazzle and bewitch us today. It was a tale of a simple Igbo villager, caught up in forces he confronted but could not understand or accept.

It was not Anthropology or folklore, however, but Art, the phenomenon which transforms the individual, particular, ordinary and transient into the universal, permanent and immortal. Like Oedipus, the exiled king who achieved immortality through the genius of Sophocles, Okonkwo the African villager became greater than the colonialists who destroyed him, through Achebe's talent.

The work of colonialism was annihilation, the destruction of the economy, political system, culture and religion of the other, the enslaved and colonised. In politics Fanon and other anti-colonial writers exhibited the process through which the colonised was negated, in which his or her identity was substituted by that of the Master, the bringer of death into the existence and soul of the other.

The Igbo and fellow peoples of Africa and other continents existed as long as, or far longer than the English, French, Spanish, Portuguese, German or other Europeans. Yet the colonialists did not take this longevity into account, they did not recognise the humanity of the people to be colonised. Their mission was not appreciation of human values, or a confluence of civilisations, but destruction.

Colonialism was mass murder, the suppression of the way of life of peoples labelled as alien and subhuman, even though extinction was cloaked in the slogan of the 'civilising mission' and the 'white man's burden.' Despite their skills in plot, character and narrative, writers who followed the colonial script could never create great literature because they negated the humanity of their creations.

Kipling, Conrad, Naipaul and other writers who accepted colonialism as civilization and extermination as culture, could never produce world literature because, no matter their technical abilities, their assumption of the racial superiority of European values rendered their work derivative and apologetic, and served as glorification for inhumanity and barbarism.

Modern European writers who present their shallow, homogenized, middle-class existence as universal and expect Africans to copy them slavishly, are more subtle than their imperial forebears, but more pernicious for that matter. Achebe was courageous enough to refuse the accolade of becoming an 'African' Conrad or Kipling.

*Things Fall Apart* was a work of genius because it affirmed the humanity of Okonkwo and his people, their language, traditions, culture and religion. Despite the colonial declaration of the universality of its values, in total opposition to the values of the people it suppressed, the art of Achebe elevated the villager to the rank of Hero, superior to colonial mediocrity, racism and genocidal pragmatism.

That Achebe spent the last years of his life away from his own country was testimony to how far the Nigerian leadership absorbed the colonial ethos, the belief that their people were subhuman, with no right to the resources necessary to ensure life, liberty and the pursuit of happiness. While the wealthy luxuriate, the people cannot enjoy stability, welfare or a future for their children.

To young people who share Achebe's anti-colonial philosophy and wish to follow in his giant footsteps, his work is not an inspiration to construct political tracts. Political theory and tract making have their rightful places but works of literature are not wholly, or primarily, concerned with the organisation or use of power, including force and violence. Art transcends the ordinary and banal.

Agostinho Neto, who was a poet as well as President of Angola, did not construct his poems as political tracts, to be used to mobilise his people. His poems were used as songs for militants of the MPLA, but that was because they were properly constructed art works, with the correct rhythmic and metaphorical structures. The power of *Things Fall Apart* was its success as literary masterpiece.

In his cell on Robben Island, where he was confined by a despicable form of colonialism, Mandela spoke of Achebe's work crumbling the walls of his prison. This work of literature had a greater impact on the greatest politician of the past several centuries than the political tracts and analyses of theorists and agitators. This simple writer was political dynamite, a true freedom fighter.

Despite his greatness, however, Achebe never had the claim to fame and fortune of the 'heavy weights,' the 'men of timber and calibre' he mercilessly parodied in *A Man of the People. Things Fall Apart* was a tribute to the heroism of ordinary people, in the face of their denigration by a colonial power which regarded them as nonentities. Our present Big Men and Women are the new colonialists.

For the young and the not so young, Achebe's work is an affirmation of the need to struggle, a confirmation that the work of the freedom fighters who sacrificed for independence is not complete. His heroes and heroines acknowledge themselves as members of a community, units in a whole that is Africa and the continents of all oppressed people who suffer cruelty, poverty and indignity.

We who survive must honour Achebe's memory by remembering that we cannot be free as long as the poorest and most downtrodden among us suffer the pain and loss of poverty and disinheritance. His quiet voice condemns those deluded advocates of mindless violence who bolster imperialism by murdering Kofi Awoonor and other innocent victims of colonial murder.

Like Mandela who acknowledged the limitations of power, glory and possessions, we preserve his memory by imitating his humility and quiet industry. We become true men and women of the people by never forgetting them, by identifying with their abandonment, their pain, deprivation and loss. We honour Achebe by continuing to embody his values of humanity, simplicity and humility.

May his soul rest in perfect peace and may we who still live not rest till his great work is complete.

Chapter Forty-Nine

# How To Write About Africa

*Binyavanga Wainaina*

Always use the word "Africa" or "Darkness" or "Safari" in your title. Subtitles may include the words "Zanzibar", "Masai", "Zulu", "Zambezi", "Congo", "Nile", "Big", "Sky", "Shadow", "Drum", "Sun" or "Bygone." Also useful are words such as "Guerrillas", "Timeless", "Primordial" and "Tribal". Note that "People" means Africans who are not black, while "The People" means black Africans.

Never have a picture of a well-adjusted African on the cover of your book, or in it, unless that African has won the Nobel Prize. An AK-47, prominent ribs, naked breasts: use these. If you must include an African, make sure you get one in Masai or Zulu or Dogon dress.

In your text, treat Africa as if it were one country. It is hot and dusty with rolling grasslands and huge herds of animals and tall, thin people who are starving. Or it is hot and steamy with very short people who eat primates. Don't get bogged down with precise descriptions. Africa is big: fifty-four countries, 900 million people who are too busy starving and dying and warring and emigrating to read your book. The continent is full of deserts, jungles, highlands, savannahs and many other things, but your reader doesn't care about all that, so keep your descriptions romantic and evocative and unparticular.

Make sure you show how Africans have music and rhythm deep in their souls, and eat things no other humans eat. Do not mention rice and beef and wheat; monkey-brain is an African's cuisine of choice, along with goat, snake, worms and grubs and all manner of game meat. Make sure you show that you are able to eat such food without flinching and describe how you learn to enjoy it – because you care.

Taboo subjects: ordinary domestic scenes, love between Africans (unless a death is involved), references to African writers or intellectuals, mention of school-going children who are not suffering from yaws or Ebola fever or female genital mutilation.

Throughout the book, adopt a *sotto* voice, in conspiracy with the reader and a sad *I-expected-so-much* tone. Establish early on that your liberalism is impeccable, and mention near the beginning how much you love Africa, how you fell in love with the place and can't live without her. Africa is the only continent you can love – take advantage of this. If you are a man, thrust yourself into her warm virgin forests. If you are a woman, treat Africa as a man who wears a bush jacket and disappears off into the sunset. Africa is to be pitied, worshipped or dominated. Whichever angle you take, be sure to leave the strong impression that without your intervention and your important book, Africa is doomed.

Your African characters may include naked warriors, loyal servants, diviners and seers, ancient wise men living in hermitic splendour. Or corrupt politicians, inept polygamous travel-guides and prostitutes you have slept with. The Loyal Servant always behaves like a seven-year-old and needs a firm hand; he is scared of snakes, good with children and always involving you in his complex domestic dramas. The Ancient Wise Man always comes from a noble tribe (not the money-grubbing tribes like the Gikuyu, the Igbo or the Shona). He has rheumy eyes and is close to the Earth. The Modern African is a fat man who steals and works in the visa office, refusing to give work permits to qualified Westerners who really care about Africa. He is an enemy of development, always using his government job to make it difficult for pragmatic and good-hearted expats to set up NGOs or Legal Conservation Areas. Or he is an Oxford-educated intellectual turned serial-killing politician in a Savile Row suit. He is a cannibal who likes Cristal champagne and his mother is a rich witch-doctor who really runs the country.

Among your characters you must always include The Starving African, who wanders the refugee camp nearly naked and waits for the benevolence of the West. Her children have flies on their eyelids and pot bellies and her breasts are flat and empty. She must look utterly helpless. She can have no past, no history; such diversions ruin the dramatic moment. Moans are good. She must never say anything about herself in the dialogue except to speak of her (unspeakable) suffering. Also be sure to include a warm and motherly woman who has a rolling laugh and who is concerned for your well-being. Just call her Mama. Her children are all delinquent. These characters should buzz around your main hero, making him look good. Your hero can teach them, bathe them, feed them; he carries lots of babies and has seen Death. Your hero is you (if reportage), or a beautiful, tragic international celebrity/aristocrat who now cares for animals (if fiction).

Bad Western characters may include children of Tory cabinet ministers,

Afrikaners, employees of the World Bank. When talking about exploitation by foreigners mention the Chinese and Indian traders. Blame the West for Africa's situation. But do not be too specific.

Broad brushstrokes throughout are good. Avoid having the African characters laugh, or struggle to educate their kids, or just make do in mundane circumstances. Have them illuminate something about Europe or America in Africa. African characters should be colourful, exotic, larger than life – but empty inside, with no dialogue, no conflicts or resolutions in their stories, no depth or quirks to confuse the cause.

Describe, in detail, naked breasts (young, old, conservative, recently raped, big, small) or mutilated genitals, or enhanced genitals. Or any kind of genitals. And dead bodies. Or, better, naked dead bodies. And especially rotting naked dead bodies. Remember, any work you submit in which people look filthy and miserable will be referred to as the 'real Africa' and you want that on your dust jacket. Do not feel queasy about this: you are trying to help them to get aid from the West. The biggest taboo in writing about Africa is to describe or show dead or suffering white people.

Animals, on the other hand, must be treated as well-rounded, complex characters. They speak (or grunt while tossing their manes proudly) and have names, ambitions and desires. They also have family values: *see how lions teach their children?* Elephants are caring and are good feminists or dignified patriarchs. So are gorillas. Never, ever say anything negative about an elephant or a gorilla. Elephants may attack people's property, destroy their crops and even kill them. Always take the side of the elephant. Big cats have public-school accents. Hyenas are fair game and have vaguely Middle Eastern accents. Any short Africans who live in the jungle or desert may be portrayed with good humour (unless they are in conflict with an elephant or chimpanzee or gorilla, in which case they are pure evil).

After celebrity activists and aid workers, conservationists are Africa's most important people. Do not offend them. You need them to invite you to their 30,000-acre game ranch or 'conservation area' and this is the only way you will get to interview the celebrity activist. Often a book cover with a heroic-looking conservationist on it works magic for sales. Anybody white, tanned and wearing khaki who once had a pet antelope or a farm is a conservationist, one who is preserving Africa's rich heritage. When interviewing him or her, do not ask how much funding they have; do not ask how much money they make off their game. Never ask how much they pay their employees.

Readers will be put off if you don't mention the light in Africa. And sunsets, the African sunset is a must. It is always big and red. There is always a big sky. Wide empty spaces and game are critical – Africa is the Land of Wide Empty Spaces. When writing about the plight of flora and fauna, make sure you mention that Africa is overpopulated. When your main character is in a desert or jungle living with indigenous peoples (anybody short) it is OK to mention that Africa has been severely depopulated by Aids and War (use caps).

You'll also need a nightclub called Tropicana, where mercenaries, evil nouveau riche Africans and prostitutes and guerrillas and expats hang out.

Always end your book with Nelson Mandela saying something about rainbows or renaissances. Because you care.

# Notes on Contributors

**Lyn Innes** is Professor Emerita of Postcolonial Literatures at the University of Kent, Canterbury, where she taught African, African American and Caribbean Studies, Australian and Irish literature. Before coming to Kent in 1975, she taught at the University of Massachusetts, Amherst, where Chinua Achebe was Professor of African Literatures and became Associate Editor of *OKIKE Magazine: A Journal of African Creative Writing*, which Chinua Achebe founded. Her publications include two collections of African short stories co-edited with Chinua Achebe and a critical book, Chinua Achebe (1990). Her other books are *The Devil's Own Mirror: the Irish and the African in Modern Literature* (1990); *Woman and Nation in Irish Literature and Society*, 1880-1935 (1993); *A History of Black and South Asian Writing in Britain, 2nd Edition* (2008); *The Cambridge Introduction to Postcolonial Literatures in English* (2007); and *Ned Kelly* (2008). Her annotated edition of Francis Fedric's 1863 narrative *Fifty Years a Slave in Virginia and Kentucky* was published by Louisiana State University Press in 2010.

**Maya Jaggi** is an award-winning critic and cultural journalist in Britain, who received an honorary doctorate in 2012 from The Open University – the UK's largest higher education institution – for her 'outstanding contribution to education and culture', especially in 'extending the map of international writing'. A long-form profile writer and book critic for *The Guardian* for more than a decade (her profile of Achebe was cited by the judges in his 2007 International Man Booker Prize win), she has interviewed 12 Nobel prizewinners in literature and also writes for the *Financial Times*, *Independent*, *Newsweek* and *Literary Review* (London) and appears on BBC radio and television. She chaired the Man Asian Literary Prize jury in Hong Kong in 2013 and has been a judge of many other literary awards, including the Orange Prize, Commonwealth Writers Prize and International Impac Dublin Literary Award. Educated at Oxford University and the London School of Economics, she is an Associate Fellow of Warwick University.

**Wole Soyinka** is a Nigerian writer, playwright, poet and activist and the author of numerous plays including *The Lion and the Jewel* (1963), *The Trials of Brother Jero* (1963), *Kongi's Harvest* (1967), *Death and the King's Horseman* (1975), *The Beautification of Area Boy* (1995). From 1960 to 1964 he was co-editor of *Black Orpheus* an important literary journal. His poetry includes *Mandela's Earth & Other Poems* (1988) and *Samarkand and Other Markets I Have Known* (2002). His prison writing includes *The Man Died* (1972) an account of his arrest and imprisonment in Nigeria. His principle critical work is *Myth, Literature and the African World* (1976) a collection of essays in which he examines the role of the artist in the light of Yoruba mythology and symbolism. His work has continued to address Africa's ills and Western responsibility in *The Open Sore of a Continent* (1996) and *The Burden of Memory, the Muse of Forgiveness* (1999). He published his autobiography *Aké: The Years of Childhood* (1981) and another memoir, *You Must Set Forth At Dawn* (2006). He has long been a proponent of Nigerian democracy. His decades of political activism have included periods of imprisonment and exile. Soyinka was the first black African to be awarded the Nobel Prize for Literature in 1986. Since winning the Nobel Prize, he has been greatly sought after as a university lecturer in Nigeria, Europe and the US. Many of his lectures have been published – notably the Reith Lectures as *Climate of Fear* (2004).

**Toni Morrison** is an African American novelist, literary critic and editor and currently Robert F. Goheen Professor in the Humanities at the Lewis Centre for the Arts at Princeton University. She previously taught at Yale and Howard Universities. Morrison won the Nobel Prize for Literature in 1993, and both the Pulitzer Prize for Fiction and Anisfield – Wolf Book Award in 1988 for her novel, *Beloved* (1987), which has also been produced as a film starring Oprah Winfrey and Danny Glover. In 2012 she received the US Presidential Medal of Freedom, the highest civilian honour in America. Her other novels include: *Song of Solomon* (1977), which received the National Book Critics Circle Award, *Tar Baby* (1981); *Jazz* (1992); *Paradise* (1997) and *Home* (2012). She has also received an honorary Doctor of Letters from Oxford University (2005), the Commander of Arts and Letters, Paris (1993) and the Robert F. Kennedy Award (1988). Like Soyinka, Morrison believes in the blending of the arts and created in 1994 the *Princeton Atelier* an arts curriculum project of composers, musicians, poets and writers. Morrison's works with *Atelier* have included the lyrics, *Honey and Rue* commissioned by Carnegie Hall and *Four Songs* and *Sweet Talk.*

**Nadine Gordimer** is a South African novelist, founder of the Congress of South African Writers and an African National Congress activist during the anti-Apartheid era. Among her 15 novels are: *A Guest of Honour* (1970); *Burger's Daughter* (1979); *July's People* (1981); *My Son's Story*; and *None to Accompany Me* (1994). Gordimer received in 1961 the W.H. Smith Commonwealth Literary Award and won the Booker Prize in 1974 for *The Conservationist.* Her non-fiction works include *The Essential Gesture*; *On The Mines* and *The Black Interpreters.* She was awarded the Nobel Prize for Literature in 1991.

**Henry Chakava** is a renowned East African Publisher and Chairman of East African Educational Publishers Limited (EAEP) in Nairobi, Kenya established in 1992. In 1972, he was appointed an Editor in the Nairobi office of Heinemann, the multinational publisher. In addition to developing a thriving local list, he was a key player in the growth and success of the African Writers Series. He bought Heinemann in East Africa to set up his own company and has established branches in Uganda and Tanzania and is ranked as one of the leading indigenous publishers on the continent. Chakava has been involved in book and publishing politics for many years, sometimes at the expense of his own life and career. In the 1970s and 1980s, he published renowned Kenyan writer Ngũgĩ wa Thiong'o when no local publisher would have dared touch him. Between 1982 and 1992, as a long serving Chairman of the Kenya Publishers Association, he locked horns with the Kenya Government over many issues and is largely credited for having ended the state monopoly in textbook publishing in Kenya and the East African region. He is a founding member and Chairman, East African Book Development Association, a founder member of the African Publishers Network and the African Books Collective, a long serving member on the International Committee of the International Publishers Association. He has written or contributed to 15 books, written more than 100 papers, over 30 that have been published in learned journals. His book *Publishing in Africa: One Man's Perspective* addresses a wide range of pertinent and urgent publishing issues in Africa. Chakava is currently involved in setting up an international centre for the advancement of African Languages and Literatures to be based in Nairobi, Kenya.

**Ngũgĩ wa Thiong'o** is the Director of the International Centre for Writing and Translation, University of California Irvine, where he is also a Distinguished

Professor of English. Before then, he was Visiting Professor at New York University (1989-92), Yale University (1988) and at Amherst, Mount Holyoke, New Hampshire, Smith and East Massachusetts, Northwestern University and earlier in his career, a Fellow in Creative Writing at Makerere University in Uganda and Lecturer at the University of Nairobi. A social activist and critic, he suffered detention in Kenya for his writings and especially for his peasants and workers stage play, *Ngaahika Ndeenda (I Will Marry When I Want,* 1977); Ngũgĩ's famous and award-winning publications include, *Weep Not, Child* (1964); *A Grain of Wheat* (1967); *Petals of Blood* (1977); *Devil on the Cross* (1982); *Matigari* (1986); *Wizard of the Crow* (2006); *Something Torn and New: An African Renaissance* (2009); *Dreams in a Time of War. A Childhood Memoir* (2010). A many-sided intellectual, he is novelist, essayist, playwright, journalist, editor, academic and social activist.

**Simon Gikandi** is Robert Schirmer Professor of English at Princeton University and editor of *PMLA*, the official journal of the Modern Languages Association (MLA). He was born in Kenya and graduated with a BA [First Class Honors] in Literature from the University of Nairobi. He was a British Council Scholar at the University of Edinburgh in Scotland from which he graduated with an MLitt. in English Studies. He has a PhD. in English from Northwestern University. He is the author of many books and articles including *Writing in Limbo: Modernism and Caribbean Literature, Maps of Englishness: Writing Identity in the Culture of Colonialism*, and *Ngũgĩ wa Thiong'o* (2009), which was a Choice Outstanding Academic Publication for 2004, and co-author of *The Columbia Guide to East African Literature in English Since 1945.* He is the co-editor of *The Cambridge History of African and Caribbean Literature* and the editor of the *Routledge Encyclopedia of African Literature.* His latest book, *Slavery and the Culture of Taste* (Princeton University Press, Spring 2011) was the co-winner of the James Russell Lowell Award given to the best book by a member of the Modern Languages Association and of the Melville J. Herskovits Award for the most important scholarly work in African studies published in English (2011).

**Ama Ata Aidoo's** literary career dates from when, as an undergraduate, she wrote her first play, *The Dilemma Of A Ghost* (1964), which was subsequently produced and published. She followed that up with *Anowa* (drama 1970). Since then, she has published novels, including *Changes* (1991), volumes of poetry and short stories including *An Angry Letter In January & Other Poems* (1992) and *The Girl Who Can & Other Stories* (1997). Her third collection of short stories; *Diplomatic Pounds & Other Stories* (2012). She also edited the prize-winning, *African Love Stories Anthology*, (2006). Her books for children include *Birds & Other Poems* (2002) and *The Days* (2010). She has taught at colleges and universities in Ghana and the United States including the University of Cape Coast and Brown University. Aidoo's many awards include the Nelson Mandela Prize for Poetry in 1987 for *Someone Talking to Sometime* and the Commonwealth Writers' Prize for *Changes* in 1992. During the 1980s, she served as the first female Secretary for education in the Rawlings government. Aidoo currently lives in Ghana and is the Executive Director of Mbaasem, a foundation she founded to promote the work of Ghanaian and African women writers.

**Emmanuel Akyeampong** is Professor of History and of African and African American Studies at Harvard University. He is a Fellow of the Ghana Academy of Arts and Sciences and a Corresponding Fellow of the Royal Historical Society (UK). He is a co-founder and director of the International Institute for the Advanced Study of Cultures, Institutions and Economic Enterprise based in Accra, Ghana. He is the author of several books and articles including *Drink, Power, and Cultural Change: A Social History of Alcohol in Ghana, c.1800 to Recent Times* (1996); and *Between the Sea and the Lagoon: An Eco-Social History of the Anlo of Southeastern Ghana* (2001). He served as co-chief editor with Henry Louis Gates, Jr., for the *Dictionary of African Biography*, 6 vols. (2012). Akyeampong has been a co-editor of the *Journal of African History*, of *African Diaspora* and serves on the editorial board of *African Arguments*.

**Anne V. Adams** is Professor Emerita of Africana Studies and Comparative Literature from Cornell University, specializing in African literature, Black women's writing and Afro-German cultural studies. Following retirement, she served for five years as Director of the W.E.B. Du Bois Memorial Centre for Pan-African Culture, in Accra, Ghana. She has held visiting professorships at universities in Congo Republic, Germany and Ghana. She served as Headquarters Director and as President of the African Literature Association. Her publications in African literature include *Ngambika: Studies of Women in African Literature* (with Carole Boyce Davies), *The Legacy of Efua Sutherland* (with Esi Sutherland Addy), *Essays in Honour of Ama Ata Aidoo at 70*. Her Afro-German publications include the translations from German of *Showing Our Colours: Afro-German Women Speak Out* by K. Oguntoye, M. Opitz and D. Schultz; and *Blues in Black and White* by M. Ayim.

**Chimamanda Ngozi Adichie** was born in Nigeria. She is the author of four books, including the novels *Half of a Yellow Sun* (2007) and *Americanah* (2013).

**Akin Adesokan** is Associate Professor of Comparative Literature at Indiana University, Bloomington. His books include *Roots in the Sky*, a novel, and *Postcolonial Artists and Global Aesthetics.* His recent writings have appeared in *AGNI, Screen, Textual Practice, Social Dynamics, Research in African Literatures, CityScapes, World Literature Today* and *African Affairs.* He is a Contributing Editor of *Chimurenga.*"

**Margaret Busby, OBE** was born in Ghana and educated in Britain. She co-founded the publishing company Allison & Busby, of which she was Editorial Director for 20 years and was subsequently Editorial Director of Earthscan Publications. A writer, editor, critic and broadcaster, she has served as a judge for several literary awards – including the Independent Foreign Fiction Prize, the Caine Prize for African Writing, the Bocas Prize for Caribbean Literature, the Orange Prize, the SI Leeds Literary Award (for unpublished fiction by UK-based Black and Asian women) and the Commonwealth Book Prize – and has been associated with many cultural ventures internationally in the fields of literature, music, art and theatre. She edited the pioneering *Daughters of Africa: An International Anthology of Words and Writing by Women of African Descent*, contributes to many publications (such as the *Guardian, Observer, Independent* and the *New Statesman* and *Wasafiri* magazine), and has also written prize-winning drama for BBC radio and for the stage, including *Yaa Asantewaa – Warrior Queen* (2001-2) and *African Cargo* (2007).

**Zaynab Alkali** is a multiple award-winning, author, teacher and women's rights advocate. Alikali has published six novels and some short stories, some of which have been translated into French, German, Japanese, Spanish and Arabic. Her 29 awards include those of Association of Nigerian Authors (ANA) and Spectrum Books. She has spent most of her working life in the university system, except for a brief spell between the years 2000 – 2003, when she joined the Ministry of Health and was appointed Deputy Director and Editor of a Health magazine at the Ministry's arm, National Health Care Development Agency. (NPHCDA). In September 2003, she returned to academia as a Professor of English. From 2006-2007, she was Acting Vice Chancellor in the absence of the substantive Vice Chancellor She is currently a Visiting Professor of English at the Bayero University, Kano where she teaches African literature and creative writing and supervises undergraduate and postgraduate programmes in African literature. She lives in Keffi, Nasarawa State in Nigeria.

**Kwame Anthony Appiah** teaches philosophy at New York University, where he is Professor of Philosophy and Law. Born in London and raised in Ghana, he has taught in Europe, Africa and the Americas. He is the author of *In My*

*Father's House: Africa in the Philosophy of Culture, Cosmopolitanism: Ethics in a World of Strangers,* as well as of three novels and more than a dozen other books.

**Ibrahim Bello-Kano** is Professor of English at Bayero University, and a Visiting Professor at Ahmadu Bello University, Zaria and Umaru Musa Yaradua University, Katsina. He was a visiting scholar at the University of Delaware in 1997–98, and is a member of the Editorial Board of the African Humanities Publications Series, in conjunction with the University of South Africa Press. He has published on various topics in literary theory, aesthetics, the novel, life and travel writing, and, recently, poetry. He is currently working on subjects involving Fredric Nietzsche, Matthew Arnold, and Jacques Derrida. His new book, *Travel, Narration, and the Fiction of Exploration*, is forthcoming from Ahmadu Bello University Press.

**Carole Boyce Davies** is an African Diaspora Studies scholar and Professor of Africana Studies and English at Cornell University. She is author of *Caribbean Spaces: Escape Routes from Twilight Zones* (University of Illinois Press, 2013); *Left of Karl Marx. The Political Life of Black Communist Claudia Jones* (Duke University Press, 2008) and *Black Women, Writing and Identity: Migrations of the Subject* (Routledge, 1994) that is considered a theoretical base for many studies in the field of black feminist literary theory and the writing of migration. In addition to numerous scholarly articles, Davies has also published the following critical editions*: Ngambika. Studies of Women in African Literature* (Africa World Press, 1986); *Out of the Kumbla. Caribbean Women and Literature* (Africa World Press, 1990); a two-volume collection of critical and creative writing entitled *Moving Beyond Boundaries* (New York University Press, 1995*): International Dimensions of Black Women's Writing* (volume 1), and *Black Women's Diasporas* (volume 2). She is co-editor with Ali Mazrui and Isidore Okpewho of *The African Diaspora: African Origins and New World Identities* (Indiana University Press, 1999) and *Decolonizing the Academy: African Diaspora Studies* (Africa World Press, 2003). She is general editor of the 3-volume *The Encyclopedia of the African Diaspora* (Oxford: ABC-CLIO, 2008). She recently published a collection of the writings of Claudia Jones titled *Beyond Containment: Claudia Jones: Autobiographical Reflections and Essays* (Ayebia, 2011).

**Abena P. A. Busia** is Associate Professor and Chair of Women's and Gender Studies, Rutgers School of Arts and Sciences, The State University of New Jersey where she has taught for over 30 years. She has been Senior Research Fellow and Visiting Professor at the Universities of Ghana and Cape Coast and earlier in her career, a Visiting Lecturer at the Department of African and Afro-American Studies, Yale University and an External Tutor, Ruskin College, Oxford. Her teachings have been influenced by being a black woman in the diverse migrant exile communities of Africa, Europe and America. She became President of the African Literature Association of the United States between 1993-94; a Member of the Board of Directors of the African Studies Association of the United States (1992-93) and Executive Committee Chair, Modern Languages Association (Division on African Literature). Busia has received many international academic honours, awards and grants. Publications include: *Testimonies of Exile* (1990); co-editor of *Theorizing Black Feminisms: The Visionary Pragmatism of Black Women* (1993); *Song in a Strange Land; Narrative and Rituals of Remembrance in the Novels of Black Women of Africa and the African Diaspora* (forthcoming) and *Traces of a Life – A Collection of Elegies and Praise Poems* (2008).

**Helen Chukwuma** is a feminist scholar and the first female to be made a Professor at the University of Port Harcourt, Rivers State, Nigeria in 1993. From 1991–92, she was a Fulbright Research Fellow at the University of Cincinnati in Ohio. She is Professor of English in the Department of English and Modern Foreign Languages in Jackson State University, Jackson, Mississippi, US. Chukwuma has written or edited seven books and has served as the editor of the *Journal of Women's Studies in Africa*. Her academic areas of interest are African literature, oral and written, African fiction, feminist theory in literature, contemporary English and American literature, African and African-American women authors and women's studies. Chukwuma's current research focuses on indigenous African feminism and meeting points in Black women's literature. She is currently editing a text on M*eeting Points in Black Africana Women's Literature.* Her publications include *Achebe's Women: Imagism and Power* (2012); *Accents on the African Novel*, 2nd edn. (1991); Ed. *Feminism in African Literature*, 2nd edn. (1994); *Women Writing: Feminism and National Development in Nigeria*, Inaugural Lecture, University of Port Harcourt (2004).

**John Pepper Clark-Bekederemo** is a Nigerian playwright and poet born in 1935 of Ijaw parents. Along with Wole Soyinka, he is one of the most articulate and proficient literary artists from Africa. Clark and a group of fellow students founded the *Horn*, a publication for which Clark served as editor and where he began to publish his poetry. In 1960 Clark wrote his first dramatic work, *Song of a Goat*, which was staged in Ibadan the following year. After graduation, Clark worked as a journalist, editor and feature writer in Lagos for *Express* newspapers. His success as a journalist resulted in his being awarded a fellowship to study at Princeton University in the United States. Clark returned to Nigeria to teach English at the University of Lagos. In 1964 he published *America, Their America,* which chronicles his experiences and impressions of American society. Clark served as the Department Head of English at the University of Lagos until his retirement in 1980. His published works include *A Reed in the Tide* (1965), *Casualties: Poems* (1970), *A Decade of Tongues* (1981), *State of the Union* (1981), *Mandela and Other Poems* (1988), among others. In 1991, he was awarded the *Nigerian National Merit Award* for literary excellence and the publication by Howard University of his two definite volumes, *The Ozidi Saga and Collected Plays and Poems*, 1958-1988.

**Anani Dzidzienyo** is a Professor in the Departments of Africana Studies and Portuguese and Brazilian Studies, Brown University. His research focuses on Afro-Brazilians and Afro-Latin Americans in Latin America as well as contemporary relations of Africa and Latin America. He has written on Blacks in Brazilian Society, specifically on the ways historical and contemporary meanings of blackness impact on the polity. More specifically, he has focused on a study of Abdias Nascimento as a metaphor of Afro-Brazilian political activities. His publications include, *The Position of Blacks in Brazilian Society, 'The African Connection* and *Afro-Brazilian Social Mobility, Coming to Terms with the African Connection in Latino Studies, Afro-Latin Americans within the Changing Global Order. Africa e Diaspora; Lentes Contemporaneas, Vistas Brasileiras e Afro-Brasileiras.* He is co-editor of, *Neither Enemies Nor Friends; Latinos, Blacks, Afro-Latinos.*

**Maureen Ngozi Eke** has a PhD and MA in Comparative Literature from Indiana University, Bloomington. She is currently a Professor of English at Central Michigan University, where she teaches courses in African Diaspora Literatures, Postcolonial Literatures & Theory, World Literature, Women Writers, and the Literary Dimensions of film. She has also served as the Associate Vice President for Diversity and International Education at Central Michigan University. She is a Past President of the African Literature Association (ALA) and current editor of the ALA's Series. Her publications include four co-edited volumes: Cross-Rhythms; *African Images: Recent Studies and Texts in Cinema* (2000); *Gender and Sexuality in African Literature and Film (2007)*; and *Emerging Perspectives on Nawal El Saadawi (2010)*; and *Literature, the Visual Arts and globalization in Africa and its Diaspora* (2011). She has published numerous articles on African Literature and cinema. Some of her articles have appeared in *Research in African Literatures, Callaloo, Visual Anthropology*, and *South African Theatre Journal.* She serves on the editorial boards of several international publications, including *Critical Arts*; *Journal of*

*African Cinema*; and *Africa Literature Today*. She recently co-edited a special collection of essays in *Research in African Literatures* (RAL) on "Memory/History, Violence and Reconciliation." Eke is the convener of a biennial conference on Human Rights, Literature, the Arts and Social Sciences (HRLASS).

**Ernest N. Emenyonu** is a Fellow of the Nigerian Academy of Letters, Nigerian Academy of Education and a member of the Board of Trustees of the Association of Nigerian. He is Professor of Africana Studies, University of Michigan-Flint. A specialist in African Literature, he has taught African Literature in various universities in Nigeria and the United States and published several journal articles and works of criticism on African Literature as well as fiction. His recent publications include *Emerging Perspectives on China Achebe* Vols. 1 & 2 (2004), *Emerging Perspectives on Nawal El Saadawi* (2009), a collection of short stories, *Tales of our Motherland* (1999), and a number of children's books including *Uzoechi: a story of African Childhood* (2012). He is the Series Editor of the journal, *African Literature Today.*

**Toyin Falola** is the Jacob and Frances Sanger Mossiker Chair in the Humanities and University Distinguished Teaching Professor at the University of Texas at Austin. A recipient of three honorary doctorates and over 20 lifetime career awards, he is currently the Vice President of the African Studies Association. His forthcoming memoir, *Counting the Tiger's Teeth,* narrates his years as a teenager.

**Harry Oludare Garuba** teaches at the Centre for African Studies, University of Cape Town, with a joint appointment in the English Department. He has published widely in the area of African and postcolonial literary studies. In the recent past, he has been a Mandela Fellow at the W.E.B. Du Bois Institute, Harvard University, a Mellon Fellow at the Harry Ransom Humanities Research Centre at the University of Texas at Austin, and has recently been a Visiting Research Fellow at Emory University, among others. Garuba has published a volume of poetry, *Shadow and Dreams and Other Poems*, an anthology of Nigerian poetry *Voices from the Fringe* and edited the African Section of the special issue on English language poetry across the world in *Poetry International* 7/8. He is currently working on a new volume of poetry entitled "Animist Chants and Memorials."

**Helon Habila** was born in Nigeria. He worked in Lagos as a journalist before moving to England in 2002 for a writing fellowship at the University of East Anglia. In 2001 his short story, "Love Poems" won the Caine Prize and in 2002 his first novel, *Waiting for an Angel* was published. The novel went on to win the Commonwealth Prize for Best First Novel (Africa Section) in 2003. In 2006 he co-edited the British Council's anthology, *New Writing 14.*

In 2005-2006 Habila was the first Chinua Achebe Fellow at Bard College, New York. He stayed on in America as a professor of Creative Writing at George Mason University in Virginia. In 2007 his second novel, *Measuring Time,* was published. The novel won the Virginia Library Foundation's fiction award in 2008. In the same year Habila's short story, "The Hotel Malogo" won the Emily Balch Prize. "The Hotel Malogo" was also selected by the Best American Non-Required Anthology, edited by Dave Eggers. Habila's third novel, *Oil on Water,* which deals with environmental pollution in the oil rich Niger Delta, was published in 2010 and shortlisted for the Commonwealth Writers Prize (2011) and the Orion Book Award (2012). It was also a runner up for the PEN Open Book Award (2012). In 2011 Habila edited *The Granta Book of the African Short Story.* Habila has been a contributing editor for the *Virginia Quarterly Review* since 2004. From July 2013 to June 2014, Habila will be a DAAD fellow in Berlin. He lives in Virginia with his wife and three children.

**F. Abiola Irele** is currently Provost of the College of Humanities, Kwara State University, Malete, Nigeria. He was formerly Professor of French and Head, Department of Modern Languages, University of Ibadan. He has taught at various universities in Africa and the USA, including the University of Ghana, the Ohio State University, Tulane University and Harvard. He has also held a visiting fellowship at Churchill College, University of Cambridge. His publications include *The Cambridge History of African and Caribbean Literature* (edited with Simon Gikandi) published in 2004, and four collections of essays: *The African Experience in Literature and Ideology* (1981, rpt 1990) *The African Imagination: Literature in Africa and the Black Diaspora* (2001), *Négritude et Condition Africaine* (2008), and *The Négritude Moment: Explorations in Francophone African Literature and Thought* (2011). He has also published annotated editions of Selected Poems by Léopold Sédar Senghor (1978) and Aimé Césaire's *Cahier d'un retour au pays natal* (1994; second edition, 1999). His edition of Chinua *Achebe's Things Fall Apart* was published in the Norton Critical Series in 2008, and *The Cambridge Companion to the African Novel* under his editorship appeared in 2009. His latest publication is *The Oxford Encyclopedia of African Thought,* co-edited with Biodun Jeyifo (2010).

**Biodun Jeyifo** is Emeritus Professor of English at Cornell University. Since 2006 he has been Professor of African and African American Studies and

Professor of Comparative Literature at Harvard University. He has published widely in the fields of postcolonial theory, literary and cultural studies; drama and theatre; and Anglophone African and Caribbean Studies. He has served as External Examiner at several Canadian, European, African and South Asian Universities and has also lectured widely in major universities in Africa, Western Europe, the Caribbean and China. The two-volume *Oxford Encyclopedia of African Thought* (OUP) that he co-edited with Abiola Irele was published in 2010.

[**Gordon**] **Douglas Killam** was educated in Canada and University College, London. In Africa, he taught in Sierra Leone, Nigeria and Tanzania during the 1960s and 1970s. He has published books and articles on African and Canadian literature and was a visiting lecturer in Cameroon, Australia, India, the USA and the South Pacific. In Canada, he taught in British Columbia (University of British Columbia), Alberta (the University of Alberta), Nova Scotia (Acadia University) and Ontario (York University in Toronto where he was also founding master of Bethune College; and the University of Guelph, from which he retired in 1995). From Guelph, he co-directed (with Elizabeth Cockburn) the Education Project, ACT (Association of Creative Teaching) in Cameroon.

**Bernth Lindfors** is Professor Emeritus of English and African Literatures at the University of Texas at Austin. He has written and edited a number of books on Anglophone African literatures. He is currently working on a multi-volume biography of Ira Aldridge (1807–1867), a black Shakespearean actor who performed in Europe.

**Ali A. Mazrui** was born in Mombasa, Kenya and now holds the following positions: Albert Schweitzer Professor in the Humanities and Director of the Institute of Global Cultural Studies, State University of New York at Binghamton, NY; Senior Scholar in Africana Studies and Andrew D. White Professor-at-Large Emeritus, Cornell University, Ithaca, NY; Albert Luthuli Professor-at-Large, University of Jos, Nigeria; Chancellor Emeritus, Jomo Kenyatta University of Agriculture and Technology, Nairobi, Kenya; Prince Alwaleed bin Talal Senior Fellow, Georgetown University, Washington DC; Member of the Board of Trustees, Oxford Centre for Islamic Studies, Oxford, England. Mazrui was previously Professor of Political Science and Dean of Social Sciences, Makerere University in Uganda. He has published more than thirty books and numerous of articles. He is best known internationally for his television and video series, *The Africans: A Triple Heritage* (PBS/BBC/NTA, 1986). A book by the same title was published in the same year. The TV series has been translated into several languages. He also delivered the six BBC Radio Reith Lectures in 1979. Mazrui has a doctorate from Oxford University. He also holds honorary doctorates awarded by multiple universities.

**Mĩcere Gĩthae Mũgo** is currently Meredith Professor for Teaching Excellence and Professor of African American Studies at Syracuse University. She is a poet, playwright and literary critic and community activist who has published 6 books, co-edited 8 supplementary school readers, 3 monographs and edited the journal, *Third World in Perspective.* Her works include: *Writing and Speaking from the Heart of my Mind* (selected essays and speeches); *Art, Artists and the Flowering of Pan-Africana Liberated Zones* (monograph); *My Mother's Poem and Other Songs* (poetry); *The Long Illness of Ex-Chief Kiti* (play); *Daughter of My People, Sing!* (poetry); *Visions of Africa* (literary criticism), *African Orature and Human Rights* (monograph); *Gikũyũ, Shona and Ndebele Ethics and Aesthetics* (monograph); *Mũthoni wa Kĩrĩma – Mau Mau Woman Field Marshal: Interrogating Silencing, Erasure and Manipulation of Female Combatants' Texts* (monograph) and *The Trial of Dedan Kimathi* (play, co-authored with Ngũgĩ wa Thiong'o). Mĩcere is a recipient of numerous honors, including the following: Distinguished Mwalimu Julius Nyerere Award from the University of Dar es Salaam; College of Arts and Sciences Award for Excellence in Master Level Teaching and Distinguished Africanist Award from the New York African Studies Association for her contribution to scholarship. At the Kenya 50th jubilee in December 2013, she was awarded the Elder of the Burning Spear and in November 2002, *The East African Standard Century* listed her among "The Top 100: They Influenced Kenya Most During the 20th Century."

**Njabulo S. Ndebele** has served in higher education as teacher and executive leader for three decades, last serving as Vice-Chancellor of the University of Cape Town. His fiction includes *Fools and Other Stories*, joint-winner of the NOMA Award, Africa's highest literary award for the best book published in Africa in 1983 and the highly acclaimed *The Cry of Winnie Mandela.* His expository writings include the influential *Rediscovery of the Ordinary: South African Literature and Culture* and *Fine Lines from the Box: Further Thoughts on our Country* which won the 2008 Sello Duiker Memorial Award for Literature. Regarded as a public thinker, he writes incisive critiques on the public space in contemporary South Africa. A Fellow of the University of Cape Town, Honorary Fellow of Churchill College Cambridge and the Chancellor of the University of Johannesburg, he has received honorary doctorates from universities in Europe, Japan, UK, United States and South Africa. He chairs the Nelson Mandela Foundation.

**Okey Ndibe** is the author of the acclaimed *Arrows of Rain* and *Foreign Gods, Inc.* Ndibe teaches African and African Diaspora literatures at Brown University in Providence, Rhode Island. He is a co-editor (with Chenjerai Hove) of a book titled *Writers, Writing on Conflicts and Wars in Africa.* He earned MFA and PhD degrees from the University of Massachusetts at Amherst, and has taught at Connecticut College (New London, CT), Bard College at Simon's Rock (Great Barrington, MA), Trinity College (Hartford, CT), and the University of Lagos (as a Fulbright scholar). The founding editor of *African Commentary*, a magazine published in the US by the late Nigerian novelist Chinua Achebe, he also served on the editorial board of *Hartford Courant* where his essays won national and state awards. He is currently working on a book of essays titled *Going Dutch and other American Misadventures* and another novel *Return Flights.* He lives in West Hartford, CT with his wife, Sheri and their three children.

**Alastair Niven** After an academic career at the Universities of Ghana, Leeds, and Stirling, Alastair Niven became Director General of the Africa Centre in London for six years, 1978-84. He then served for a decade as Director of Literature at the Arts Council of Great Britain, later Arts Council England. In 1997 he moved from this post to be Director of Literature for the British Council, a unique doubling of these positions. He was President of English PEN 2003-7 and has also served twice as a judge of the Booker Prize for Fiction, in 1994 and again in 2014 when it had become the Man Booker Prize. He has published widely on African and Indian literature, as well as two books on D.H. Lawrence. For thirteen years he was Editor of The Journal of Commonwealth Literature. He is now a Fellow of Harris Manchester College, University of Oxford and Associate Director of the Iraq Britain Business Council.

**Odia Ofeimun** was born in March 1950. He has worked as a factory labourer, teacher, journalist and private political secretary to Nigeria's leader of opposition in the Second Republic. A former General Secretary and President of the Association of Nigerian Authors, he writes poetry and produces dance dramas. His published poetry includes *The Poet Lied, A Handle for the Flutist* and *I Will Ask Questions with Stones If They Take My Voice.* His latest collections of essays; *A House of Many Mansions* and *When Does a Civil War Come to an End* are published by Hornbill House.

**Kole Omotoso** (Bankole Ajibabi Omotoso) was born in Akure, South West Nigeria in 1943 and educated at Oyemekun Grammar School and Kings College Lagos. He went on to do an honours degree in Arabic and Islamic

Studies at the University of Ibadan and a PhD at the University of Edinburgh Department of Arabic and Islamic Studies. He taught contemporary Arabic literature at the Department of Arabic and Islamic Studies, dramatic arts at the then University of Ife (later Obafemi Awolowo University) English Literature at the Universities of Stirling in Scotland, National University of Lesotho in Roma Lesotho and the University of the Western Cape in Cape Town. Omotoso also taught dramatic writing and criticism at the Department of Drama at the University of Stellenbosch and published his first two novels with the African Writers Series. He was the first General Secretary of the Association of Nigerian Authors while Chinua Achebe was president and became president of the association after Achebe. His other publications include: *Just Before Dawn, Achebe or Soyinka?: A Study in Contrasts* and *Season of Migration to the South.*

**Femi Osofisan** is a Nigerian writer, *aka* Okinba Launko, wears many caps as journalist, social activist, poet, novelist, essayist, scholar and most especially playwright, actor, song writer and theatre director. Widely produced and widely studied in and outside the continent and winner of many awards, he retired recently from the University of Ibadan after 38 years in service.

**Niyi Osundare** a Nigerian poet, playwright and essayist who has authored 18 books of poetry, two books of selected poems, four plays, two books of essays and numerous scholarly articles and reviews. His prizes include the Association of Nigerian Authors Poetry Prize, the Cadbury/ANA Poetry Prize (on two occasions), the Commonwealth Poetry Prize, the NOMA Award, the Tchicaya U Tam'si Award for African Poetry and the Fonlon/Nichols Award for *"excellence in literary creativity combined with significant contributions to Human Rights in Africa". In 2004, his* book, *The Eye of the Earth,* was selected as One of Nigeria's Best 25 Books in the Past 25 Years by Spectrum Books. In 2012 one of his poems was selected as Nigeria's contribution to the cultural events that complemented the London Olympics. He holds honorary doctorates from l'Universite de Toulouse-Le Mirail in France and Franklin Pierce University, Rindge, USA. He also writes a weekly poetry column in Nigeria's *Sunday Tribune* and is a frequent contributor to the media on cultural and social matters. A fervent campaigner for Human Rights, social justice and the environment, he was professor and former Chair of English at the University of Ibadan in Nigeria. He is currently Distinguished Professor of English at the University of New Orleans, USA and constantly in touch with Nigeria.

**Eustace Palmer** is a Sierra Leonean who was Professor of English and Chair of the English Department at Fourah Bay College, the University of Sierra Leone and Dean of the School of Arts and Dean of Graduate Studies, before relocating to the United States and becoming a naturalized American citizen. He has extensive teaching experience from both Africa and the United States and has served as African Scholar in Residence at Randolph Macon Women's College in Virginia and as Visiting Fulbright Professor of English at the University of Texas at Austin. His current position is Professor of English at GCSU. Palmer's main areas of specialization are eighteenth-century English Literature and African Literature. His publications include over sixty articles and reviews on African and English Literatures and is the author of nine books: *Studies on the English Novel*; *An Introduction to the African Novel*; *The Growth of the African Novel*; *Knowledge Is More Than Mere Words: A Critical Introduction to Sierra Leonean Literature* (jointly edited with Professor Michael Porter); Or War and Women, Oppression and Optimism: *New Essays on the African Novel*; *A Hanging Is Announced* (fiction); *Canfira's Travels* (fiction); *A Tale of There Women* (fiction); and *A Pillar of the community* (fiction). He was Editor of *African Literature Today*, one of the leading journals on African literature and a past President of the African Literature Association. He received the African Literature Association's "Distinguished Member" award in 2012 for his commitment to teaching and scholarship in African Literature and was named Georgia College and State University's "Distinguished Professor" for 2010/2011.

**Ato Quayson** is Professor of English and inaugural Director of the Centre for Diaspora and Transnational Studies at the University of Toronto. He has published widely on African literature and postcolonial studies. He is General Editor of the Cambridge Journal of Postcolonial Literary Inquiry and his latest book is *Oxford Street, Accra; Urban Evolution, Street Life and the Itineraries of Transnationalism* (Duke University Press, 2014).

**Tijan M. Sallah** is the Gambia's most renowned poet, short story writer and ethnographer after the late Lenrie Peters. Widely anthologized, his recent books include a biography, *Chinua Achebe: Teacher of Light*, which he co-authored with Ngozi Okonjo-Iweala, Nigeria's current Finance Minister and *Dream Kingdom, a collection of selected poems.* A PhD trained economist who has taught at several American universities, he currently works at the World Bank as Sector Manager for Agriculture and Irrigation responsible for East African countries.

**Véronique Tadjo** is a writer, painter and scholar from Côte d'Ivoire. Born in Paris, of an Ivorian father and a French mother, she was brought up in Abidjan. She has a doctorate in African American Studies from the Sorbonne Paris IV.

Her work has been translated in several languages including English, German, Italian and Swedish. She has written several books, among which *L'ombre d'Imana* (*The Shadow of Imana*, 2000) on the genocide in Rwanda and *The Blind Kingdom* (2008) a poetical yet political allegory on Côte d'Ivoire. Her novel *Reine Pokou* (*Queen Pokou*, 2009) which is based on a myth from oral tradition received the prestigious literary prize "Le Grand Prix Littéraire d'Afrique Noire" in 2005. *As the Crow Flies*, her groundbreaking novel was republished by Penguin South Africa in 2009. Her latest novel, *Loin de mon Père* (*Far from my Father*) came out in Paris in 2010. She is also the author of books for young people that she usually illustrates. She has travelled extensively in West Africa, Europe and America and is currently based in Johannesburg where she is Professor of French at the University of the Witwatersrand in Johannesburg.

**Patrick Wilmot** is a graduate of Yale and Vanderbilt Universities.He taught at Ahmadu Bello University in Zaria, Nigeria, from 1970–88.He is now a novelist, columnist and commentator on African affairs and lives in London. His last novel was *Seeing Double* (Jonathan Cape) and his next, *Glass,* is due this year.

**Binyavanga Wainaina** is an author, cultural commentator and satirist who won the Caine Prize for African Writing in 2002 for his short story "Discovering Home" and used his prize money to set up *Kwani?* – the literary journal. He has written for the *Mail and Guardian* in South Africa and his writing has also appeared in *The New York Times, The Guardian*, Granta (which published his most popular satirical essay "How to Write About Africa" and his memoir "One Day I Will Write About This Place" and *National Geographic.* He was the Director of the Chinua Achebe Centre for African Literature and Languages at Bard College, New York, before returning to settle in Nairobi, Kenya.

# Notes, References and Works Cited

### Chapter Eight: Achebe As Publisher – James Currey

Achebe, Chinua. 'My Daughters' and 'Politics and Politicians of Language' in *The Education of British-Protected Child* Allen Lane/Penguin 2009.

Achebe, Chinua. 'The Citadel Press' 176–7 in *There Was a Country: A Personal History of Biafra.* London: Allen Lane/Penguin 2012.

Currey, James. *Africa Writes Back: The African Writers Series and the Launch of African Literature.* Oxford: James Currey; Johannesburg: Wits University Press; Nairobi: EAEP; Dar es Salaam; Mkuki na Nyota; Ibadan: HEBN; Harare: Weaver and Athens: Ohio University Press, 2008.

Currey, James. 'Literary Publishing after Nigerian Independence; Mbari as Celebration' in *Research in African Literatures* Vol 44/2, September 2013.

Hill, Alan. *In Pursuit of Publishing.* London: John Murray, 1988.

Killam, Douglas & Rowe, Ruth (Editors). *The Companion to African Literatures.* Oxford: James Currey, 2000.

Ngũgĩ wa Thiong'o. 'Heinemann, African Writers Series and I': *In the Name of the Mother* Oxford: James Currey 2013.

Nwakanma, Obi. *Christopher Okigbo; Thirsting for Sunlight.* Oxford: James Currey, 2010.

### Chapter Twelve: 'A' is for Achebe – Margaret Busby

1. In Kirsten Holst Peterson and Anna Rutherford (eds), *Chinua Achebe – A Celebration,* Heinemann/Dangaroo Press, 1990, p. 7.
2. Ibid., "Three Poems for Chinua Achebe", p. 72.

### Chapter Fifteen: The Assault on Culture: Achebe on the Crisis of Identity in Colonial Africa – Emmanuel Akyeampong

1. Chinua Achebe, *Things Fall Apart* (London: Heinemann, 1958); Chinua Achebe, *Arrow of God* (London: Heinemann, 1964).
2. Martin A. Klein, "Chinua Achebe's *Things Fall Apart,*" in Margaret Jean Hay, (ed.)

*African Novels in the Classroom* (Boulder and London: Lynne Rienner Publishers, 2000), 25–35.

3. Ngũgĩ wa Thiong'o, *Decolonising the Mind: The Politics of Language in African Literature* (London: James Currey, 1986).
4. Kwasi Wiredu, "Problems in Africa's Self-Definition in the Contemporary World," in Kwasi Wiredu and Kwame Gyekye, ed., *Person and Community: Ghanaian Philosophical Studies, I* (Washington, DC: Council for Research in Values and Philosophy, 1992), 59.
5. Ibid., 63.
6. Emmanuel Akyeampong, "Christianity, Modernity, and the Weight of Tradition in the Life of Asantehene Agyeman Prempeh I, c.1888-1931," *Africa*, 69, 2 (1999): 279–311.
7. Nicholas I. Omenka, "Blaming the Gods: Christian Religious Propaganda in the Nigeria-Biafra War," *Journal of African History*, 51, 3 (2010): 367–89; Dmitri van den Bersselaar, *In Search of Igbo Identity: Language, Culture and Politics in Nigeria, 1900–1966* (Leiden: Leiden University, 1998).
8. Egodi Uchendu, "Being Igbo and Muslim: The Igbo of Southeastern Nigeria and Conversions to Islam, 1930s to Recent Times," *Journal of African History*, 50, 1 (2009): 63–87.
9. Kofi Asimpi, *European Christian Missions and Race Relations in Ghana, 1828–1970* (Baltimore: Publish America, 2010), 79–83.
10. David Kimble, *A Political History of Ghana 1850–1928* (Oxford Clarendon Press, 1963),
11. Benjamin N. Lawrance, Emily Lynn Osborn, and Richard L. Roberts, eds., *Intermediaries, Interpreters, and Clerks: African Employees in the Making of Colonial Africa* (Madison: University of Wisconsin Press, 2006).
12. Asimpi, *European Christian Missions*, 164.
13. Ibid., 164–5.
14. Ibid., 223.
15. Ibid., 224–5.
16. Ibid., 227–30.
17. Kwame Nkrumah, *Consciencism* (New York and London: Modern Reader Paperbacks, 1970 [1964]), 68.
18. David Brokensha, *Social Change at Larteh, Ghana* (Oxford: Clarendon, 1966), 174 & 186.
19. On the "Philosophical Club," that President Nkrumah initiated with the assistance of W. E. Abraham of the Department of Philosophy, University of Ghana, see PRAAD, Accra, SC/BAA/103.
20. Birgit Meyer, "'Make a Complete Break with the Past': Memory and Post-Colonial Modernity in Ghanaian Pentecostalist Discourse," *Journal of Religion in Africa*, 28: 3 (1998), 318.
21. Kwasi Wiredu and Kwame Gyekye, ed., *Person and Community: Ghanaian Philosophical Studies*, (Washington, DC: Council for Research in Values and Philosophy, 1992); Kwame Gyekye, *An Essay on African Philosophical Thought: The Akan Conceptual Scheme*, Revised Edition (Philadelphia: Temple University Press, 1995); Kwasi Wiredu, *Cultural Universals and Particulars: An African Perspective* (Bloomington: Indiana University Press, 1996).
22. Ogbu U. Kalu, "Sankofa: Pentecostalism and African Cultural Heritage," in Veli-Matti Kärkkäinen, ed., *The Spirit in the World: Emerging Pentecostal Theologies*

*in Global Contexts* (Grand Rapids, MI: William B. Eerdmans Publishing Company, 2009), 135–52.

23. Wiredu, "Problems in Africa's Contemporary Self-definition," 60.

**Chapter Sixteen: I Haven't Seen You In 400 Years!": Chinua Achebe and African American Writing – Anne V. Adams**

Achebe, Chinua. "An Image of Africa." *Massachusetts Review*, Vol. 18, No. 4 (Winter 1977), pp. 782–94. *Hopes and Impediments.* (New York: Doubleday, 1989) pp. 1–20.

Achebe, Chinua. "Africa's Tarnished Name." *Multiculturality and Hybridity in African Literatures.* Hal Wylie and Bernth Lindfors, ed. (Trenton: Africa World Press, 2000) pp. 24. (Orig. published in Chinua Achebe and Robert Lyons *Another Africa.* (New York: Anchor Books, Doubleday, 1998).

Achebe, Chinua. "The Day I Finally Met Baldwin." *Callaloo* 25.2 (2002) 502–4.

Baldwin, James. "Fifth Avenue, Uptown." *The Price of the Ticket: Collected Nonfiction 1948–1985.* (New York: St. Martin's, 1985) pp. 205–13.

Baldwin, James. "*The Fire Next Time.*" *The Price of the Ticket: Collected Nonfiction 1948-1985.* (New York: St. Martin's, 1985) pp. 333–79.

Chametzky, Jules, ed. *A Tribute to James Baldwin: Black Writers Redefine the Struggle* (Amherst: University of Massachusetts Institute for Advanced Study in the Humanities, 1989).

Fleming, Bruce. "Brothers under the Skin: Achebe on *Heart of Darkness.*"

*College Literature,* Vol. 19/20, No. 3/1. Teaching Postcolonial and Commonwealth Literatures (Oct. 1991 – Feb. 1993), pp. 90–99.

Hall, Catherine. "*Playing in the Dark* ...and racing Englishness." *European Journal of Women's Studies* 2011, 18: 87–90.

Mongia, Padmini. "The Rescue: Conrad, Achebe, and the Critics." *Conrad in Africa: New Essays on "Heart of Darkness."* (New York: Columbia U P, 2002).

**Chapter Twenty-Two: From Achebe to Adichie – Carole Boyce Davies**

1. TEDx Euston, London, April, 2013.
2. A panel discussion on Africa's Literary Identity was dedicated to this question of identifying the new generation of writers, Moderated by Uzodinma Iweala, award-winning author of *Beasts of No Nation,* it featured this writer, TMS Ruge, Hannah Pool and Tope Folarin and was held at Pace University on September 27, 2013. Podcast available: http://bit.ly/16CWGBN
3. See for example, 'Molara Ogundipe's "African Women, Culture and another Development" *The Journal of African Marxists* 5(February, 1984): 77–92. "Women on the March"i in the *Journal of African Marxists* which proposed an economic/class based feminist approach to the democratization of African women's rights in the following terms: ... Our vision of feminism has at its very core a process of economic and social development geared to human needs through wider access to economic and political power. Equality, peace and development by and for the poor and oppressed are inextricably interlinked with equality, peace and development by and for women (3).
4. www.caineprize.com/pdf/2013_Folarin.pdf ·
5. At a panel discussion organized by Africare at Pace University on Africa's Literary

Identity, September 27, 2013, New York City, Tope Folarin indicated that his father sold ice cream and cleaned buildings and his mother worked as a nursing assistant in the Midwest US where he was one of only a few black children in the school he attended.

6. *Essays in Honour of Ama Ata Aidoo at 70: A Reader in African Cultural Studies*, ed. Anne Adams (Banbury: Ayebia, 2012).
7. Chimamanda Adiche in an interview on CNN "African Voices," 2010, described the themes that preoccupy her in her then most recent collection of short stories, *The Thing Around Your Neck.*
8. *The Times of India*, 1/25/11.
9. *Journal of African Marxists*, 8:1986, p. 3.
10. www.latimes.com/books/jacketcopy/la-et-jc-beyonce-flawless-chimamanda-ngozi-adichie-20131213,0,3338347.story#ixzz2peTdpJeV
11. *The Atlantic*, December 23, 2013.

**Chapter Twenty-Three: A Poet Daughter's Farewell: Still Morning Yet – Abena P. A. Busia**

* This is an edited and corrected version of the words I spoke at the African Literature Association Conference Tribute to Chinua Achebe on March 22, 2013 in Charleston, South Carolina. On that occasion, I also read the poem as originally written which can be found in my collection *Traces of a Life: A Collection of Elegies and Praise Poems*, (Ayebia Clarke Publishing Limited: Oxford, 2008).

**Chapter Twenty-Four: Chinua Achebe and the Matrix of Womanhood – Helen Chukwuma**

Amadiume, Ifi., *Afrikan Matriarchal Foundations: The Igbo Case.* London: Karnak House, 1987.

Amadiume, Ifi., *Reinventing Africa.* London: Zed Books Ltd. 1997.

Egejuru Phanuel and Ketu Katrak eds. *Nwnyibu, Womanbeing and African Literature.* Africa World Press, 1997.

Mbonu, Caroline, "The Power of Naming: A Case of Beatrice, Nwanyibuife in Anthills of the Savannah," in *Achebe's Women: Imagism and Power.* (ed.) Helen Chukwuma. Africa World Press, 2012. pp. 223–55

Nwodo, Christopher S. *Philosophical Perspectives on Chinua Achebe.* University of Port Harcourt Press, 2004.

**Chapter Twenty-Six: Chinua Achebe: Some Reflections – Anani Dzidzienyo**

1. Achebe's discussions of the issues facing new post-independence African nations and the gap between the new "elites" with access to power and material resources, their venality is well captured in the person of Chief Nanga in *A Man of the People.* (London: Heinemann, 1966).
2. Bringing together Sam (*Anthills*) and Nanga is a form of showing the continuities over a generation in the course of which nothing much changed for the "people." Sam and his "friends" in *Anthills of the Savannah* (1987) represent the personalization of the state and the freezing out of the general population whose citizens' rights are trampled upon.

3. *The Trouble with Nigeria* (1985) is an uncompromising text against corruption and indiscipline. The indictment is not just specific to Nigeria.
4. Kwame Nkrumah's famous dictum, "Seek Ye First the Political Kingdom and All other Things Shall be Added unto You" has been the subject of both approbation and disputation. There are some who aver that by its very nature, the dictum made short thrift of the inescapable economic exigencies, the harbinger of neocolonialism. Parenthetically, Nkrumah's 1965 book was titled, *Neocolonialism: The Last Stage of Imperialism*, New York: International Publishers.
5. Coups, their makers, conspiratorial connections based on historical or recent "friendships", the unravelling of ties, the casualties in loyalties are all well-captured in *Anthills of the Savannah.*
6. Kolanuts were an important part of certain aspects of life and culture which were of certain regional and religious provenance. *Things Fall Apart* revealed the centrality of kolanuts elsewhere.
7. Chinua Achebe, *Morning Yet on Creation Day*, New York: Anchor Press, 1975, Ngũgĩ wa Thiong'o, *Decolonizing the Mind: The Politics of Language in African Literature*, 2005, Oxford: James Currey. Also, Susan VanZanten, "Linguistic Power: Encounter with Chinua Achebe," The Christian Century, 1997.
8. Eduardo Galeano, "The Dictatorship and Its Aftermath: The Hidden Wounds," in, Saul Sosnowski and Louise B. Popkin, editors, *Repression, Exile, and Democracy*, Durham and London: Duke University Press, 1993 (103–7).
9. The Achebe Colloquium on Africa at Brown University, 2009, 2010, 2011, 2012. Themes ranged from Prospects for the 2010 Nigerian Elections, Focus on Nigeria, Rwanda and Congo, to the Arab Spring and Crisis in Darfur, to security matters in northern, central, eastern Africa and peace-building initiatives in southern Africa.
10. Achebe in Brazil. He had visited Brazil in the early 1960s and had read the well-known writer, Jorge Amado's Gabriela, *Clove and Cinnamon. Arrow of God* was published as *Flecha de Deus* in 2011 and *The Education of a British-Protected Child* as, *A Educaçacão de uma criança sob o Protetorado Britanico* in 2012. They were both published in São Paulo by Companhia das Letras.
11. At the Brown University Commencement in 1998, he was awarded an Honorary Doctorate in Humane Letters. The Saturday before Commencement had featured Ray Charles at the Pops Concert on Campus. Having a ticket to see Ray Charles, he said with a smile, was a condition of agreeing to come for the degree ceremony.
12. Cyprian Ekwensi, *Jagua Nana*, 1961, *People of the City*, 1963, both published by Heinemann.
13. The concept of Road Makers and ancestors' path clearing is borrowed from Efua Sutherland, *The Road Makers: A Picture Book of Ghana.* Photographs by Willis E. Bell. Planned and written by Efua Sutherland.
14. Dennis Abrams, "Was Chinua Achebe the "Father of African Literature"?, Frankfurt Academy Publishing Perspectives, 2013/05, May 21, 2013.
15. Portal Geledes, 3/24/13 www.geledes.org.br/em-debate/Cidinha-da-Siva/17723-chinua-achebe-por cidinha-da-silva

**Chapter Twenty-Seven: *In Memoriam*: Morning, March 22, 2013 Charleston, South Carolina – Maureen Ngozi Eke**

Achebe, Chinua. *Hopes and Impediments: Selected Essays.* New York & London: Doubleday, 1989. Print.

Achebe, Chinua. "Named for Victoria, Queen of England." Ashcroft, Griffiths and Tiffin (143-145). Print.

Achebe, Chinua. *There Was a Country: a Personal History of Biafra.* New York: Penguin Press, 2012. Print.

Achebe, Chinua. *Things Fall Apart.* London: Heinemann, 1958. Print.

Achebe, Chinua. *The Trouble with Nigeria.* London & Nairobi: Heinemann, 1988. Print.

Ashcroft, Bill, Gareth Griffiths and Helen Tiffin, eds. *The Postcolonial Studies Reader.* 2e. London & New York: Routledge, 2066, 2007. Print.

Conrad, Joseph. *Heart of Darkness.* 1899. Ed. Ross C. Murfin. Boston & New York: Bedford Books of St, Martin's Press, 1996. Print.

Kingsolver, Barbara. *The Poisonwood Bible.* New York: HarperCollins Publishers, 1998. Print.

Murfin, Ross C. "A Critical History of *Heart of Darkness*." Murfin (99–114). Print.

**Chapter Twenty-Eight: Chinua Achebe: The Passing of a Comet – Ernest N. Emenyonu**

Achebe, Chinua. *Things Fall Apart.* London: Heinemann,1958.

Achebe, Chinua. *A Man of the People.* London: Heinemann, 1966.

Achebe, Chinua. "The Role of a Writer in a New Nation." *Nigeria Magazine,* 81, June 1964, pp. 157–60.

Achebe, Chinua. "The Novelist as Teacher." *New Statesman,*29 January, 1965.

Achebe, Chinua. "English and the African Writer." *Transition,* IV, 18, 1965.

Achebe, Chinua. "The African Writer and the Biafran Cause." *The Conch,* 1, 1, March 1969.

Achebe, Chinua. *There Was a Country.* London/New York: Penguin, 2012.

Achebe, Chinua. *The Trouble With Nigeria.* Enugu: Fourth Dimension, 1983.

**Chapter Thirty-Four: Achebe in Texas – Bernth Lindfors**

1. "Interview with Chinua Achebe," in *Palaver: Interviews with Five African Writers in Texas,* eds. Bernth Lindfors, Ian Munro, Richard Priebe and Reinhard Sander (Austin: African and Afro-American Research Institute, The University of Texas at Austin, 1972), 7.
2. Chinua Achebe, "The Writer and the African Revolution," in Bernth Lindfors, *Early Achebe* (Trenton, NJ: Africa World Press, 2009), 241.
3. "Panel on Literature and Commitment in South Africa," in *Contemporary Black South African Literature: A Symposium,* (ed.) Bernth Lindfors (Washington, DC: Three Continents Press, 1985), 86.
4. Ibid., 86–7.
5. Ibid., 87–9.
6. "Chinua Achebe, "An Image of Africa," *Research in African Literatures* 9. 1 (1978): 1–15.
7. Chinua Achebe, "Africa's Tarnished Name," in *Multiculturalism and Hybridity in*

*African Literatures*, (ed.) Hal Wylie and Bernth Lindfors (Trenton, NJ: Africa World Press, 2000), 24.

**Chapter Thirty-Six: Celebrating Achebe's *Utu* and Creative Genius in Oracy, Orature and Literature – Mĩcere Gĩthae Mũgo**

1. Pio Zirimu and Austin Bukenya, "Oracy as a Skill and as a Tool for African Development," in Okpaku, Opubor & Oloruntimehia, Eds. *The Arts and Civilization of Black and African Peoples, Vol 10, Chapter 9.*
2. In many *zamani* African oratures, stories were often told around the hearth, usually in the evening, either as families waited for dinner, or as they relaxed after the meal.
3. I successfully defended my dissertation and received my Ph.D. in 1973, but somebody, somewhere decided that I graduated from the University of Toronto in 1978 and that erroneous internet information seems to have stuck.
4. *Visions of Africa*...Nairobi: East African Literature Bureau, 1978.
5. A G k y proverb roughly meaning that persistent efforts are the same as possibilities.
6. Ngũgĩ had just taken over as the chair of the new department, after a prolonged struggle to do away with the traditional English Department of the colonial era.
7. Known as the "African Writers of English Expression" Conference, this historical gathering brought together established and emerging African writers, including Chinua Achebe, Ama Ata Aidoo, Wole Soyinka, Jonathan Kariara, Rebeka Nja , Peter Nazareth, Ngũgĩ wa Thiong'o (then James Ngugi), Ezekiel Mphahlele, Nuruddin Farah, David Rubadiri, Lewis Nkosi and others.
8. *Op.cit, 1978.*
9. Op.cit, 1976.

**Chapter Thirty-Seven: Reading Chinua Achebe: Footholds in the Flood of History – Njabulo S. Ndebele**

1. Peter Thuynsma. Es'kia Mphahlele Remembered. www.letterkunde.up.ac.za/argief/46_1/17%20Tuynsma%2003.pdf
2. Njabulo S. Ndebele. *Fine Lines from the Box: further thoughts about our country. South Africa*: Umuzi 2007. pp. 9–10.
3. Chinua Achebe. *No Longer at Ease.* London: Heinemann, 1963. p. 36.
4. Ibid, pp. 38–9.

**Chapter Forty-Four: A Tribute to Chinua Achebe: The Father of Modern African Literature – Eustace Palmer**

*A Man of the People.* London: Heinemann, 1965.

*Anthills of the Savannah.* New York: Grove Press, 1988. (First published London: Heinemann, 1987).

*Arrow of God of God.* London: Heinemann, 1964.

*No Longer at Ease.* London: Heinemann, 1962.

*The Trouble With Nigeria.* London : Heinemann, 1984.

*Things Fall Apart.* London: Heinemann, 1958. (Quotations are from the anchor books edition, New York: Anchor Books Doubleday, 1994).

Boyce Davies, Carole. "Motherhood in the Works of Male and Female Igbo Writers." In

*Ngambika: Studies of Women in African Literature*, eds. Carole Boyce Davies and Anne Adams Graves. Trenton, NJ: Africa World Press, 1986, 241–56.

Cary, Joyce. *Mister Johnson*. London: Penguin, 1939.

Conrad, Joseph. *Heart of Darkness*. In *Youth: a Narrative, and Two Other Stories*. London: William Blackwood, 1902.

Holst Petersen, Kirsten. "First Things First: Problems of a Feminist Approach to African Literature." *Kunapipi* 6. 3(1984): 30–9.

Iyasere, Solomon. "Narrative Techniques in *Things Fall Apart*." In *Critical Perspectives on Chinua Achebe,* eds. C.L. Innes and Bernth Lindfors. Washington, DC: Three Continents Press, 1978, 92–110.

Nasser, Merun. "Achebe and His Women: A Social Science Perspective." *Africa Today* 27.3 (1980): 221–28.

Soyinka, Wole. *The Interpreters*. London: Andre Deutsch, 1965.

Stratton, Florence. *Contemporary African Literature and the Politics of Gender*. London: Routledge, 1994.

**Chapter Forty-Five : Chinua Achebe and the Literary Compass – Ato Quayson**

1. "Criticism, Realism and the Disguises of Both: an analysis of Chinua Achebe's *Things Fall Apart* with an evaluation of the criticism relating to it," *Research in African Literatures* 25.4 (1994): 117–36.
2. That dissertation was published as *Strategic Transformations in Nigerian Writing* (Oxford and Bloomington: James Currey and Indiana University Press, 1997).
3. I provide a fuller account of the chi concept in "Modernism and Postmodernism in African Literature," for the *Cambridge Companion to African Literature*, edited by Abiola Irele and Simon Gikandi, (Cambridge: Cambridge University Press, 2004).
4. See also, "Self-Writing and Existential Alienation in African Literature: Chinua Achebe's *Arrow of God*", *Research in African Literatures* 42.2 (March, 2011): 30–45.

**Chapter Forty-Seven : Chinua Achebe's Legacy – Véronique Tadjo**

* In its original form this essay was delivered at the "Fall for the Book" festival in George Mason University, Fairfax (USA) on 21 September 2008 and subsequently published in Recherche Littéraire/Literary Research, Volume 25 – Summer 2009.

Achebe, Chinua. *Hopes and Impediments*. New York: Doubleday, 1988.

Achebe, Chinua. Interview with Carol Cooper. 19 Feb 2008. Bard College, Annandale-on-Hudson, NY.

Achebe, Chinua. Interview,

Les liens de l'exil. In *Le Courrier de l'Unesco*, june 2001, no 18, p. 47–50. *My translation.*

Achebe, Chinua. *The Education of a British-Protected Child,* London: Penguin Books, *2009.*

Achebe, Chinua. *Things Fall Apart*. 1958; rpt. New York: Knopf-Everyman's Library, 1992.

Anohu, V.A. *Eagle on Iroko: International Symposium for Chinua Achebe's 60th Birthday, Book of Abstracts*. Nsukka: Faculty of Arts, University of Nigeria, 1990.

Biondi, Jean-Pierre. *Senghor ou la tentation de l'universel.* Paris: Denöel, 1993. *My translation.*

Cooper, Carol. Interview with Chinua Achebe. 19 Feb 2008.
Kourouma, Ahmadou. *Les soleils des indépendences.* Paris: Editions du Seuil, 1992.
Resources for Achebe's *Things Fall Apart*: Thoughts on Okonkwo, His Flaws and His Society. www.lawrence.edu/dept/freshman_studies/resource/fsachebe.html.
Strong-Leek, Linda. "Reading as a Woman: Chinua Achebe's *Things Fall Apart* and Feminist Criticism." *African Studies Quarterly* 5(2): 2 (2001). http://web.africa.ufl.edu/asq/v5/v5i2a2.htm.
Tadjo, Véronique. *Queen Pokou: Concerto for a sacrifice.* Trans. Amy Baram Reid, Oxford, Ayebia Clarke, 2009.

# Index

Beti, Mongo 26, 56, 60, 213